International and Development Education

The International and Development Education Series focuses on the complementary areas of comparative, international, and development education. Books emphasize a number of topics ranging from key higher education issues, trends, and reforms to examinations of national education systems, social theories, and development education initiatives. Local, national, regional, and global volumes (single authored and edited collections) constitute the breadth of the series and offer potential contributors a great deal of latitude based on interests and cutting-edge research. The series is supported by a strong network of international scholars and development professionals who serve on the International and Development Education Advisory Board and participate in the selection and review process for manuscript development.

Series Editors
W. James Jacob, *FamilySearch International*
Rebecca Clothey, *Drexel University*
Gustavo Gregorutti, *Andrews University*

International Editorial Advisory Board
Clementina Acedo, *Webster University, Switzerland*
Philip G. Altbach, *Boston University, USA*
N'Dri Thérèse Assié-Lumumba, *Cornell University, USA*
Carlos E. Blanco, *Universidad Central de Venezuela*
Sheng Yao Cheng, *National Chung Cheng University, Taiwan*
Evelyn Coxon, *University of Auckland, New Zealand*
Wendy Griswold, *University of Memphis, USA*
Ruth Hayhoe, *University of Toronto, Canada*
Yuto Kitamura, *University of Tokyo, Japan*
Jing Liu, *Tohoku University, Japan*
Wanhua Ma, *Peking University, China*
Ka Ho Mok, *Lingnan University, China*
Christine Musselin, *Sciences Po, France*
Yusuf K. Nsubuga, *Ministry of Education and Sports, Uganda*
Namgi Park, *Gwangju National University of Education, Republic of Korea*
Val D. Rust, *University of California, Los Angeles, USA*
Suparno, *State University of Malang, Indonesia*
Xi Wang, *University of Pittsburgh, USA*
John C. Weidman, *University of Pittsburgh, USA*
Weiyan Xiong, *Education University of Hong Kong, China*
Sung-Sang Yoo, *Seoul NationalUniversity, Republic of Korea*
Husam Zaman, *UNESCO/Regional Center for Quality and Excellence in Education, Saudi Arabia*

Takeshi Sekiya • Keiichi Ogawa
Yuto Kitamura • Akemi Ashida
Editors

Towards Ensuring Inclusive and Equitable Quality Education for All

Analyzing School Enrolment Patterns

Editors
Takeshi Sekiya
School of International Studies
Kwansei Gakuin University
Nishinomiya, Japan

Keiichi Ogawa
Graduate School of International
Cooperation Studies
Kobe University
Kobe, Japan

Yuto Kitamura
Graduate School of Education
The University of Tokyo
Tokyo, Japan

Akemi Ashida
Graduate School of International
Development
Nagoya University
Nagoya, Japan

ISSN 2731-6424   ISSN 2731-6432   (electronic)
International and Development Education
ISBN 978-3-031-70265-5   ISBN 978-3-031-70266-2   (eBook)
https://doi.org/10.1007/978-3-031-70266-2

This Palgrave Macmillan imprint is published by the registered company Springer Nature
Switzerland AG.
The registered company address is: Gewerbestrasse 11, 6330 Cham, Switzerland

If disposing of this product, please recycle the paper.

ACKNOWLEDGMENTS

This work was supported by JSPS KAKENHI Grant Numbers JP 22402054 and JP 26257114.

Praise for *Towards Ensuring Inclusive and Equitable Quality Education for All*

"This excellent research book provides a global, comprehensive yet in-depth understanding of 'school enrolment,' the most fundamental and core issue in education development research. Readers will be struck by the complexity and diversity of school enrolment in developing countries. This publication is an important intellectual contribution to the achievement of SDG 4, and a must-read for educational development professionals."

—Kazuo Kuroda, *Professor, Waseda University, Japan and Vice President of the Comparative and International Education Society*

CONTENTS

NOTES ON CONTRIBUTORS

Akemi Ashida is an Associate Professor at the Graduate School of International Development, Nagoya University. Currently, she also serves as a Research Associate at the University of Tokyo. She received a PhD from Kobe University. Her research areas are comparative education and the sociology of education, and she has worked on empirical studies targeting Latin America and Southeast Asia, particularly Honduras and Cambodia. She has worked as a Programme Officer at the UNESCO Asia-Pacific Regional Bureau for Education (UNESCO Bangkok), as a Postdoctoral Fellow at the University of Tokyo, and as an Assistant Professor at Waseda University. Her notable publications include The Role of Higher Education in Achieving the Sustainable Development Goals, In *Sustainable Development Disciplines for Humanity: Breaking Down the 5Ps—People, Planet, Prosperity, Peace, and Partnerships* (Contributor, Springer Singapore, 2023) and *The Actual Effect on Enrollment of "Education for All": Analysis Using Longitudinal Individual Data* (Union Press, 2018). This book was selected for Japan Society for International Development 2018 Incentive Award.

Khishigbuyan Dayan-Ochir is an Education Consultant at the World Bank Mongolia Country Office. She graduated from the University of Minnesota, USA, with an MA in Comparative and International Education. Her research interests include sector analysis, education policy review, education project design and management, and research methodology. She managed two World Bank investments in Mongolian education: the Rural Education and Development (READ) project and the Education

Quality Reform Project. She has also worked on international development programs and activities with agencies such as ADB, World Vision, UNDP, UNESCO, and UNICEF. She is the author of the book, Eyes on Past and Present of Mongolia (Nepko Publisher), which provides a comparative perspective of the Mongolian education system before and after the democratic transition.

Naruho Ezaki is an Associate Professor at the Faculty of Global Culture and Communication, Aichi Shukutoku University. She received a PhD from Kwansei Gakuin University and has worked there as an Assistant Professor. During her doctoral studies, she did research work under the Research Fellowship for Young Scientists of the Japan Society for the Promotion of Science. From then until now, she has been engaged in academic field research targeting South Asia and Sub-Saharan Africa, particularly Nepal and Zambia. She has been contributing to international cooperation in the field of education by conducting relevant projects. Her notable publications include *Impact of the 2015 Nepal Earthquakes on Individual Children's Enrolment Situation: Seeking "High-quality Education,"* (Union Prress, 2021) and 'Relation between Educational Qualifications and Occupations/Incomes in a Globalised World: Focusing on Nepalese Youth' (*International Journal of Comparative Education and Development*, 2021).

Sheikh Rashid Bin Islam is an aspiring education economist, currently pursuing his postgraduate studies as a Japanese Government Scholarship recipient at Kobe University's Graduate School of International Cooperation Studies (GSICS), under the supervision of Professor Dr. Keiichi Ogawa. His research delves into the economics of education, education policy analysis, and comparative international education. He has lent his expertise to numerous impactful projects funded by organizations like the GPE's "Education Out Loud" fund, Lego Foundation, FHI360, and the Annual Status of Education Report (ASER). Additionally, he has provided valuable insights to consultation projects for ADB, UNDP, the Ministry of Communications and Information Technology of Bangladesh, the Japan External Trade Organization (JETRO), and the Japan Foundation. His contributions extend beyond academia, with published research articles in esteemed international peer-reviewed journals and book chapters from reputable international publishers, underscoring his commitment to advancing the discourse and practice of education economics.

Jun Kawaguchi is an Associate Professor at the Department of Education, Faculty of Letters, Keio University. His research focus lies in comparative education and international educational cooperation, and he has worked on empirical studies in Africa and South Asia, particularly Malawi and Sri Lanka. He has also worked as an International Education Specialist for JICA, UNICEF, and UNESCO education projects in more than seven developing countries, especially in the area of inclusive education development and in-service teacher education. He has many book and journal publications, and one of his major publications is a book entitled, *Inclusive Education in the Era of SDGs: Challenges of the Global South* (Akashishoten) published in 2024. He received a PhD from Waseda University.

Yuto Kitamura is a Professor at the Graduate School of Education at the University of Tokyo. He received his PhD in Education from University of California, Los Angeles (UCLA). He had worked at UNESCO in Paris as an Assistant Education Specialist and taught as an Associate Professor at Nagoya University and Sophia University. He has served as a Fulbright Scholar at the George Washington University, a Visiting Professor at the University of Dhaka, and a Special Advisor to the Rector of the Royal University of Phnom Penh. He specializes in comparative education and has been conducting extensive research on education policies of developing countries in Asia, particularly Cambodia. His notable publications include *Memory in the Mekong Regional Identity, Schools, and Politics in Southeast Asia* (co-editor, Teachers College Press 2022) and *The Political Economy of Schooling in Cambodia* (co-editor, Palgrave Macmillan, 2015).

Keiichi Ogawa is a Professor/Department Chair at the Graduate School of International Cooperation Studies (GSICS), Kobe University. He is also a Governing Board Member of the UNESCO International Institute for Educational Planning (IIEP) and an Honorary Professor at Kyrgyz National University, National University of Laos, and the University of Dhaka. He has served at various universities as an Affiliate Professor (University of Hawaii at Manoa), Adjunct Professor (Fudan University, George Washington University, Airlangga University), and Visiting Professor (Columbia University, University of Tokyo). He is a former Education Economist at the World Bank and has rich development experiences at various organizations including ADB, JBIC, JICA, UNICEF, and UNESCO. He has worked on development assistance activities in over 30 countries and has authored or co-edited 10 books and over 150 journal articles/book chapters. He holds his PhD in Comparative International Education and Economics of Education from Columbia University.

Chea Phal is currently a Senior Research Fellow at the Cambodia Development Resource Institute (CDRI). He served as a Director of the Centre for Educational Research and Innovation from 2023 to 2024. He holds a PhD in Economics from Kobe University, Japan. He has a rich background in both academic and applied research, having worked as a Consultant for the World Bank and held affiliated positions as an Adjunct Researcher at Kobe University, a Visiting Scholar at the University of Melbourne, and currently as a Designated Associate Professor at Nagoya University. His work primarily focuses on the economics of education, education policy, equity in education, and post-secondary education and training, contributing valuable insights to the field and influencing educational development policies in Cambodia and beyond.

Takeshi Sekiya is Professor of International Studies at Kwansei Gakuin University, Japan. He was engaged in international cooperation for over 15 years as an Education Specialist of the Japan International Cooperation Agency (JICA). He led Project for Improvement of Teaching Method in Mathematics (PROMETAM), funded by the Japanese Official Development Assistance (ODA). Starting with Honduras, he successfully expanded the project into a regional technical cooperation project, further covering El Salvador, Nicaragua, Guatemala, and the Dominican Republic. He has also been appointed as an Evaluator for several Japanese ODA technical cooperation projects. His research focuses on analyzing children's school records at the individual level with longitudinal data obtained from schools. His key publications include "Individual Patterns of Enrolment in Primary Schools in the Republic of Honduras" (*Education 3-13*, 2014) and "An Analysis of Primary School Dropout Patterns in Honduras" (Co-author, *Journal of Latinos and Education*, 2017).

James Wokadala is an Associate Professor/Dean at the School of Statistics and Planning at Makerere University in Uganda. He is a member of the Makerere University Senate and the Central Technical Advisory Committee in charge of the National Housing and Population Census 2024. He was a Visiting Professor at Kabale University and Kampala International University in Uganda. He also served as a Visiting Associate Professor at the Graduate School of International Cooperation Studies (GSICS), Kobe University in Japan. He has served as a Consultant at the

World Bank on the Adoptable Program Lending (APL) Project. He is the Technical Advisor on the Gender for Development Uganda (G4DU) project under UNICEF – Uganda. He has had experiences working with AfDB, UN-Women, UNDP, 3ie, CLEAR AA, and Twende Bele, among others. He has authored and/or co-authored about 30 journal articles/book chapters. He holds a PhD in Economics of Education from Kobe University in Japan.

Natsuho Yoshida is a Lecturer in the Graduate School of Education, Hyogo University of Teacher Education. She received a PhD from Kwansei Gakuin University. Prior to joining Hyogo University of Teacher Education, she served as a JSPS Research Fellowship (DC) and as an Assistant Professor at Takasaki City University of Economics. She also had the experience of engaging academic field research as an international graduate student at Yangon University of Teacher Education in Myanmar. She has been working in academic research and studies on educational development, primarily in Asian countries such as Myanmar, Laos, Nepal, and Japan. Her key publications include "Socio-economic Status and the Impact of the 'Continuous Assessment and Progression System' in Primary Education in Myanmar" (*Education* 3-13, 2020) and "Enrolment Status Disparity: Evidence from Secondary Education in Myanmar" (*International Journal of Comparative Education and Development*, 2020).

LIST OF FIGURES

LIST OF TABLES

CHAPTER 1

Introduction

Takeshi Sekiya and Akemi Ashida

1   How to Observe Educational Dissemination in the World

It is often commented that the natural sciences underwent accelerated development during the twentieth and twenty-first centuries. However, what about the humanities? Over two millennia have transpired since the time of the Greeks; however, some believe that it is already difficult to discover new truths. If we were to boldly refute the criticism we are prepared to receive, it could be said that the accumulation of sociological knowledge, aided by advances in the methods and techniques of scientific research, is progressing rapidly, even within the humanities, and is contributing to the complex development of human society. If one were to be

T. Sekiya
School of International Studies, Kwansei Gakuin University, Nishinomiya, Japan
e-mail: tsekiya@kwansei.ac.jp

A. Ashida (✉)
Graduate School of International Development, Nagoya University, Nagoya, Japan
e-mail: ashida@gsid.nagoya-u.ac.jp

© The Author(s), under exclusive license to Springer Nature Switzerland AG 2024
T. Sekiya et al. (eds.), *Towards Ensuring Inclusive and Equitable Quality Education for All*, International and Development Education, https://doi.org/10.1007/978-3-031-70266-2_1

1

charitable, it could be said that the recent achievements of the newly established discipline of educational development are one of the accumulation of sociological knowledge. Although social issues such as regional conflict and poverty continue to challenge humanity, it is reasonable to assert that after nearly 80 years free of world wars, as well as the changing political and diplomatic environment, considerable progress has been made in terms of the explication of the state of education in countries around the world. Moreover, these advancements have been aided by advances in science and technology.

The recent development and spread of Internet communication networks have made it easier to obtain information regarding the state of education, and anyone can access education statistics about any country in the world. Access to the statistical information in the databases of the United Nations Educational, Scientific and Cultural Organization (UNESCO) and other international organisations enables anyone to reference a variety of different types of education statistics, from basic education statistics to statistics related to the target indicators of the Sustainable Development Goals (SDGs), which have a deadline of 2030.

One catalyst that contributed to this improved access to data was a survey carried out between 1969 and 1970 by the UNESCO International Bureau of Education. Since before the 1960s, UNESCO has played a major role in collecting school enrolment data. Based on the country reports, education statistics at that time only recorded the number of students enrolled in school. Data indicates that the number of students decreased as the school year progressed; however, no further statistical processing was done, and therefore, it is not possible to determine the extent of grade repetition and dropout, which are seen as a waste of educational input. In 1969, the UNESCO International Bureau of Statistics conducted a survey of countries to determine the number of students enrolled in primary and secondary schools and those who repeated a grade. Subsequently, UNESCO researchers applied the reconstructed cohort method to reveal the alarming nature of grade repetition and dropout in Africa and Latin America (Berstecher, 1970; UNESCO Office of Statistics, 1970; UNESCO, 1972). The results of this study are now almost 50 years old.

Since then, such a macro-sectional data approach to monitoring the state of education has become commonplace and is still used today. The *Global Education Monitoring Report* (formerly the *Global Monitoring Report*), which has been published regularly by UNESCO since 2002, records the progress made towards achieving common global development goals.

Although there has been some delay between the reporting of the findings and their incorporation into national education policies and the aid policies of international donors, various approaches to promoting education on a global scale—including Education for All (EFA), the Millennium Development Goals (MDGs) and the SDGs—have been adopted. These efforts are the result of a shift in perception that recognises education as a fundamental human right. As a result, access to basic education has increased dramatically around the world. Indeed, the adjusted net enrolment rate and lower secondary total net enrolment rate in the world reached 91% and 85%, respectively (UNESCO, 2023). Sustainable Development Goal 4.1 seeks to 'ensure that all girls and boys complete free, equitable and quality primary and secondary education leading to relevant and effective learning outcomes' by 2023. This SDG is measured using thematic indicators related to access to education (participation), such as gross intake ratio to the last grade, completion rate, out-of-school rate and percentage of children overage for grade.

These cross-sectional data are based on enrolment information reported by schools and aggregated by district, provincial and state education offices; subsequently, they are presented to the Ministry of Education. The cross-sectional data are an amalgamation of different individual cases, and therefore, the repetition rates, dropout rates, completion rates and more are simply calculated averages. Thus, while it is possible to identify macro-level trends related to education, such as the high rate of dropout in the first year of primary school in Latin American and South Asian countries (McGinn et al., 1992; Eisemon, 1997; UNESCO, 2011), it is not possible to retrospectively identify the enrolment statuses of individual children from cross-sectional aggregated data, and the realities of the population they form are not mentioned in the macro-data. The failure to achieve 100% enrolment may be due to the existence of children whose enrolment status differs from that of the population considered to be the majority. That is, achieving universal primary education across the globe requires a focus on the individual children who encounter obstacles to continuing their education yet are not captured by the macro-data.

2   OBJECTIVES AND CONTRIBUTIONS OF THIS BOOK

Cross-sectional data are convenient and useful for identifying broad trends; however, longitudinal studies such as investigations utilising panel data are often considered more appropriate for detecting causal relationships between events (Ma, 2010). Longitudinal studies allow researchers to continuously follow up with the same subjects and are thus apt for analysing changes in a single experimental group over a long term. Therefore, longitudinal data are widely used in studies conducted in developed countries (Temple & Polk, 1986; Wilson, 2001; Ou & Reynolds, 2008; Robertson & Reynolds, 2010; Albrecht & Albrecht, 2010).

However, in many developing countries with inadequate education systems, it has been difficult to collect robust longitudinal data commensurate with that of developed countries. Therefore, few studies conducted in developing countries have employed longitudinal data: a study that tracked the factors determining secondary education enrolment in one Indian district over four years (Siddhu, 2011) and another investigation tracked the relationship between early childhood nutrition and schooling in the Philippines (Glewwe et al., 2001). However, these studies used longitudinal data collected over a relatively short period or employed data from the healthcare sector. Moreover, because collecting and analysing longitudinal data requires considerable time and effort (Gropello, 2003), longitudinal studies are not widely available, even in developed countries with robust data collection infrastructure. Consequently, there is a limited body of studies that have traced and clarified the processes leading to grade repetition and dropout, especially in developing countries (Hunt, 2008). Therefore, to the best of our knowledge, no existing study has comprehensively tracked the schooling of children from enrolment until they leave school.

In addition to the aforementioned academic context, we would like to present the rationale informing our focus on longitudinal data and the actual circumstances of students. Sekiya, one of the editors of this book, worked in Honduras in Central America as a Japan International Cooperation Agency (JICA) expert in 2000, participating in international cooperation projects at the embassy. The Honduran government was then engaged in developing a Poverty Reduction Strategy Paper (PRSP) while international donors were collaborating to discuss and support the country's education policy. He was responsible for the education sector at the working-level meeting organised under the purview of the Ambassadors' Meeting. He was also involved in the formulation of the PRSP and spent a significant amount of time discussing the education policy at the macro-level. When the aforementioned discussions were concluded, the Japanese embassy in Honduras and JICA assigned him the task of devising an education project. He was also tasked with establishing a project to improve mathematics instruction skills for teachers at the primary education level. Moreover, as project chief adviser, he was responsible for developing mathematics textbooks for students and instruction manuals for teachers at the national level. This technical cooperation project was classified as a grassroots-level international collaboration.

As the project chief adviser, he experienced a certain degree of discomfort during his visits to project sites in Honduras as the discussions between policymakers and international donors vis-à-vis the PRSP formulation process and their ideas about the necessary actions did not match the ground reality. What policymakers and donors envisioned in the policy-making process and what they witnessed firsthand during field visits differed substantively. This discrepancy caused him to contemplate whether the instituted policy could become meaningless if it was not appropriately scrutinised. While working on the project, he inspected the records maintained by each school and confirmed the authenticity of the events that came to light, cross-checking each individual fact with children, parents, teachers and other influential people in the community. In this manner, he discovered surprising facts that no one had noticed. For example, Honduras exhibited a high-grade repetition rate of more than 10% in the 1980s and 1990s. Thus, in 2000, educators generally assumed that the average enrolment period for primary school students was approximately 4.5 years. However, his sequential scrutiny of the actual schooling of children revealed that the most common enrolment pattern was to graduate without repeating a grade. The second most common pattern showed that children who registered in the first grade left immediately (i.e. dropped out) without completing the first grade and never returned to school. These two decisively contrasting enrolment patterns are the most common. Evidently, this reality differs from the assumptions made during discussions on macro-level education policy.

These experiences enabled him to construct a longitudinal database comprising primarily data obtained from school records and interviews conducted with school principals, teachers and communities in the Central American Republic of Honduras. Sekiya (2014) analysed the enrolment patterns of individual children from entry to graduation or dropout. He indicated that the average is no longer valid when the population is polarised between these two patterns such as graduation without repeating a grade and dropping out immediately. Therefore, average values cannot be employed as the basis of policy decisions. A group of scholars built on Sekiya's (2014) work and formed a research team to study myriad countries in Latin America, Asia and Africa. This team of researchers collected and analysed longitudinal data on school records in the targeted countries. The team conducted a micro-analysis of the actual state of schooling by focusing on individual children encompassed in the averages and successfully elucidated previously unreported details about the state of schooling for individual learners. Thus, this team of researchers delivered policy recommendations that could contribute to the resolution of related problems.

3   OUTLINE OF THIS BOOK

We employ the macro-perspective in Part 1 of this book to examine changes in child enrolment rates by region using cross-sectional data and referencing international education development initiatives, such as EFA, the UN MDGs and the SDGs. Specifically, we examine trends in cross-sectional datasets from monitoring reports from Central America, South and Southeast Asia and Sub-Saharan Africa. Our macro-review of the findings reveals the extent of the contributions and limitations of cross-sectional data. We also highlight the need to study the educational realities confronting children from a micro-perspective using longitudinal data.

In Part 2 of the book, we explore from a micro-perspective the factors that prevent continued schooling. To this end, we carefully examine the schooling environments of individual children at the primary and secondary levels in ten developing countries in Central America, South and Southeast Asia and Sub-Saharan Africa. We conduct a detailed examination of school records and corroborating studies that include interviews and present the findings of our case-based analyses of individual children to provide new insights that can facilitate the achievement of SDG 4. The chapters in Part 2 outline our findings and offer clues on how nations can achieve inclusive and equitable quality education.

Part 3 presents the results of a comparative analysis of schooling in the three countries covered in Part 2. We analyse the data generated from the school records obtained from the three countries and account for the cultural and historical contexts of each examined country to present new and interesting findings, focusing on the impact of grade repetitions, dropouts and school transfers. In addition, we draw on Japan's experiences with educational development to consider the challenges faced by specific countries. The following two historical events were important for shaping the contemporary state of education in Japan: (1) the introduction of a modern education system at the end of the nineteenth century and (2) Japan's defeat in World War II and subsequent occupation by the United States. Japan's unique educational development has also attracted attention in the field of international development cooperation. We are confident that the Japanese experience can offer useful lessons to address the obstacles that countries discussed in this publication experience in their attempts to construct inclusive and participatory education systems.

The final chapter comprehensively reviews the implications of the findings. It also discusses the key challenges to achieving SDG 4 by 2030 and provides recommendations for future research that could serve as a valuable resource of information for policymakers, practitioners, researchers and research students specialising in comparative education, international education development and international cooperation.

References

Albrecht, C. M., & Albrecht, D. E. (2010). Social status, adolescent behavior, and educational attainment. *Sociological Spectrum, 31*(1), 114–137. https://doi.org/10.1080/02732173.2011.525698

Berstecher, D. (1970). *Costing educational wastage: A pilot simulation study.* UNESCO.

Eisemon, T. O. (1997). *Reducing repetition: Issues and strategies.* UNESCO.

Glewwe, P., Jacoby, H. G., & King, E. M. (2001). Early childhood nutrition and academic achievement: A longitudinal analysis. *Journal of Public Economics, 81*(3), 345–368. https://doi.org/10.1016/S0047-2727(00)00118-3

Gropello, D. E. (2003). *Monitoring educational performance in the Caribbean.* World Bank Working Papers, no. 6. The International Bank for Reconstruction and Development/The World Bank.

Hunt, F. (2008). Dropping out from school: A cross country review of literature, Create Pathways to Access. *Research Monograph, 16,* CREATE: Centre for International Education, Sussex School of Education, University of Sussex.

Ma, X. (2010). Longitudinal evaluation designs. In P. Peterson, E. Baker, & B. Mcgaw (Eds.), *International encyclopedia of education* (pp. 754–764). Elsevier Science.

McGinn, N., Reimers, F., Loera, A., Soto, M. del C., & S. Lo'pez. (1992). *Why do children repeat grades? A study of rural primary schools in Honduras.* Bridges Research Report Series No. 13. Harvard Institute for International Development.

Ou, S.-R., & Reynolds, A. J. (2008). Predictors of educational attainment in the Chicago longitudinal study. *School Psychology Quarterly, 23*(2), 199–229. https://doi.org/10.1037/1045-3830.23.2.199

Robertson, D. L., & Reynolds, A. J. (2010). Family profiles and educational attainment. *Children and Youth Services Review, 32*(8), 1077–1085. https://doi.org/10.1016/j.childyouth.2009.10.021

Sekiya, T. (2014). Individual patterns of enrolment in primary schools in the Republic of Honduras. *Education 3–31: International Journal of Primary, Elementary and Early Years Education, 42*(5), 460–474. https://doi.org/1 0.1080/03004279.2012.715665

Siddhu, G. (2011). Who makes it to secondary school? Determinants of transition to secondary schools in rural India. *International Journal of Educational Development, 31*(4), 394–401. https://doi.org/10.1016/j.ijedudev.2011.01.008

Temple, M., & Polk, K. (1986). A dynamic analysis of educational attainment. *Sociology of Education, 59*(2), 79–84. https://doi.org/10.2307/2112433

United Nations Educational, Scientific and Cultural Organization (UNESCO). (1970). The statistical measurement of educational wastage (drop-out, repetition and school retardation). Paper presented at the international conference on education XXXIInd session, July 1–9, in Geneva, Switzerland.

United Nations Educational, Scientific and Cultural Organization (UNESCO). (2011). *EFA global monitoring report 2011 – The hidden crisis: Armed conflict and education.* UNESCO.

United Nations Educational, Scientific and Cultural Organization (UNESCO). (2023). *Global education monitoring report summary 2023: Technology in education: A tool on whose terms?* UNESCO.

United Nations Educational, Scientific and Cultural Organization (UNESCO) Office of Statistics. (1972). *A statistical study of wastage at school.* UNESCO.

Wilson, K. (2001). The determinants of educational attainment: Modeling and estimating the human capital model and education production functions. *Southern Economic Journal, 67*(3), 518–551. https://doi.org/10.1002/j.2325-8012.2001.tb00355.x

Traditional Approaches to Children's School Enrolment Analyses: The Overview of the Regional Cross-sectional Approach

Challenges for Providing Quality Education in Central America: Lessons from the Achievements of the Past Four Decades

Akemi Ashida ⓘ *and Takeshi Sekiya*

1   INTRODUCTION: OVERVIEW OF CHANGING TRENDS IN EDUCATIONAL DEVELOPMENTS UNTIL THE PRESENT

Education is now widely recognised as an important topic across the globe, and it has become linked to the achievement of several of the Sustainable Development Goals (SDGs). A key catalyst of this shift in perception was

A. Ashida (✉)
Graduate School of International Development, Nagoya University, Nagoya, Japan
e-mail: ashida@gsid.nagoya-u.ac.jp

T. Sekiya
School of International Studies, Kwansei Gakuin University, Nishinomiya, Japan
e-mail: tsekiya@kwansei.ac.jp

© The Author(s), under exclusive license to Springer Nature Switzerland AG 2024
T. Sekiya et al. (eds.), *Towards Ensuring Inclusive and Equitable Quality Education for All*, International and Development Education, https://doi.org/10.1007/978-3-031-70266-2_2

the 1990 Education for All (EFA) World Conference in Jomtien, Thailand. This conference recognised education as a fundamental human right and brought the concept of basic education into focus. The conference placed significant emphasis on the promotion and expansion of basic education, with the objective of ensuring that all children, adolescents, and adults were given equal opportunity to acquire the knowledge and skills necessary to live equally within society. This conference produced significant outcomes, such as the international recognition that the goal of ensuring access to basic education is a shared global responsibility. Furthermore, donors and agencies that attended the conference agreed to implement or support a range of education policies and measures intended to achieve this goal.

In 2000, the World Education Forum was held in Dakar, Senegal, as a follow-up to the EFA World Conference. At this international conference, attendees recognised that, despite the efforts of countries throughout the 1990s, key targets remained unmet, presenting a significant challenge for future progress. Participants demonstrated a shared recognition that further efforts, backed by strong political will, would be necessary to achieve the targets. Consequently, the Dakar Framework for Action, which was composed of 6 goals and 12 strategies, was developed. This framework calls for the expansion and improvement of pre-primary education, increased access to free and quality compulsory education, the fulfilment of the learning needs of adolescents and adults, the improvement of literacy among adults (particularly women), the narrowing of the gender gap in primary and secondary education, and the enhancement of the quality of education for the acquisition of basic life skills.

In September of the same year, the UN Millennium Summit was held. This summit led to the adoption of the eight Millennium Development Goals (MDG 8), which were scheduled to be achieved by 2015. The MDG 8 included two education-related goals: achieving full primary education coverage and closing the gender gap in primary and secondary education by 2005 and at all levels by 2015. The *EFA Global Monitoring Report 2013/4*, which was issued by UNESCO ahead of the 2015 deadline for achieving the MDG 8, states that disparities in access to education have risen as a result of the inadequate provision of educational opportunities for marginalised groups.

Furthermore, efforts to enhance the quality of education have also been inadequate. This prompted the adoption of Education 2030 as part of the Incheon Declaration in May 2015. Education 2030 is a shared global education objective with a target achievement year of 2030. Furthermore, the focus of the SDGs, the successor common international community goals adopted at UN Headquarters in New York in September 2015, has shifted from 'access' to 'quality', particularly in the field of education. Likewise, participating countries have agreed to the global objective of 'providing inclusive, equitable and quality education for all and promoting lifelong learning opportunities'. The international community is currently engaged in a range of activities with the objective of achieving these education-related goals by 2030. In addition, 167 targets related to 18 goals of SDGs have been established to facilitate the monitoring of progress.

UNESCO and other international organisations have employed cross-sectional data to provide an overview of the state of education worldwide. In the 1990s, the international community did not conduct regular monitoring, and therefore, it lacked a clear understanding of the state of education. This situation prompted calls for the implementation of a monitoring system. In 2002, UNESCO began to regularly publish the *Global Education Monitoring Report* (GEMR; formerly called the *Global Monitoring Report*). This report is still published, and in recent years, it has begun to feature specifically themed reports regarding certain SDG 4 Quality Education target indicators.

This chapter focuses on Latin America and the Caribbean and surveys the changes in the schooling situations of children from the 1980s to the present by using data provided by UNESCO and the World Bank.

2   A Review of the Diffusion and Universalisation of Primary and Lower Secondary Education over the Past 40 Years

Improved Access to Education

This section presents a historical overview of the improvements made to education access for children in Latin America and the Caribbean over the last 40 years. Figure 2.1 illustrates trends in gross and net enrolment rates at primary schools in Latin America and the Caribbean from 1980 to 2022. In 1980, the gross and net enrolment rates were 116.6% and 89.9%, respectively, which is relatively high compared to rates in other regions of the world. The gross enrolment rate is defined as the ratio of total enrolment, regardless of age, to the population of the age group that corresponds to the relevant education level.

A high gross enrolment rate indicates that there are students enrolled who are above the appropriate age for enrolment. The total enrolment

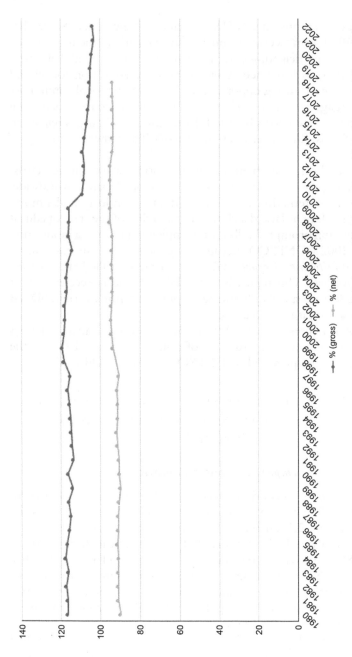

Fig. 2.1 Primary education enrolment rates in Latin America and the Caribbean (1980–2022). (Source: The authors developed this figure based on the data retrieved from the World Bank (2024). World Development Indicators. Retrieved May 26, 2024, from https://databank.worldbank.org/source/world-development-indicators)

rate remained relatively stable throughout the 1980s at 116.5% in 1980 and 116.3% in 1990. However, since 2000, access to primary education has expanded markedly in Latin America and the Caribbean, and consequently, more students with appropriate age are now enrolled in primary education. The gross enrolment rate began to decline, dropping to 108.9% in 2010. The rate continued to gradually decline, reaching 104.6% in 2022, which is close to an optimal level. Nevertheless, it is theorised that the gross enrolment rate has not fallen to 100% because there are still some overage students, such as those who have had to repeat a grade. Meanwhile, the net enrolment rate reached about 90% in 1990 from 89.7% in 1980. In 2018, the net enrolment rate reached 93.7%; therefore, more students are now enrolled in primary education that is appropriate for their age.

Next, this chapter compares gross and net enrolment rates for secondary education level (Fig. 2.2). In 1980, the gross enrolment rate for secondary education was 50.1% (boys 49.7%, girls 50.4%). Data for both the net and gross enrolment rates are only available from 1986, when the gross enrolment rate was 55.3% (boys 54.3%, girls 56.3%), and the net enrolment rate was 59.2%. An analysis of subsequent years reveals an increase in both gross and net enrolment rates. The gross enrolment rate reached 96.9% (boys 94.1%, girls 99.7%) in 2022. The net enrolment rate reached 77.5% (boys 75.9%, girls 79.0%) in 2018. Although it is still challenging to ascertain whether students enrolled in secondary education are of the appropriate age compared to those in primary education, it is evident that the situation has improved significantly over the past 40 years.

Eliminating Gender Disparities

The Gender Parity Index (GPI) is an assessment of parity in access to education between men and women. The GPI, in terms of the gross enrolment ratio, is defined as the ratio of girls to boys enrolled at a specific level of public or private schools. A value close to 0 indicates more unequal access to education between men and women, whereas a value close to 1 indicates more equal access. In short, a GPI between 0.97 and 1.03 indicates parity between the genders (UNESCO-UNEVOC, n.d.; IIEP-UNESCO, n.d.). Likewise, a value above 1.03 indicates a higher enrolment rate for girls, while a value below 0.97 signifies a higher enrolment rate for boys. When we look at GPI in Latin America and the Caribbean, the GPI scores for primary education were almost same such as 0.97 in 1980,

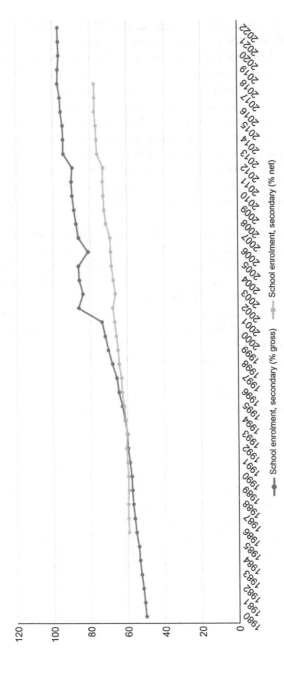

Fig. 2.2 Secondary education enrolment rates in Latin America and the Caribbean (1980–2022). (Source: The authors developed this figure based on the data retrieved from the World Bank (2024). World Development Indicators. Retrieved May 26, 2024, from https://databank.worldbank.org/source/world-development-indicators)

0.97 in 2000, and 0.98 in 2020. As the GPI indicates, there is little disparity between the sexes (Fig. 2.3).

For secondary education, the GPI was 1.03 in 1980, 1.06 in 2000, and 1.05 in 2020 (Fig. 2.3). Whereas the GPI for primary education was consistently below 1, it is consistently above 1 for lower secondary education, demonstrating higher secondary education enrolment rates for girls. Existing studies, particularly those targeting the Latin American region, have shown that boys are more likely to leave school and engage in work when they reach the age at which they are expected to do so, which is approximately ten years of age (McGinn et al., 1992). This phenomenon, where women experienced better access to education compared to men, has been described in higher education research as the 'reverse gender gap'. In Latin America and the Caribbean, the 'reverse gender gap' has been consistently observed at the secondary education level.

Improving the Internal Efficiency of Education

The grade repetition rate, which represents the internal efficiency of an education system, is another indicator that has been highlighted as a challenge that must be addressed in the region. The grade repetition rate is defined as the percentage of students who remain in the same grade without advancing to the next year, and it is expressed as a proportion of the total number of students in a grade in a single school year. In Latin America and the Caribbean, the grade repetition rate for primary education reached 14.1% in 1980 (boys 15.7%, girls 12.5%). When the EFA was proposed in 1990, the rate was still 12.4% (boys 13.8%, girls 10.9%), revealing that Latin America and the Caribbean had higher repetition and dropout rates than other regions. Indeed, the low internal efficiency in education in Latin America and the Caribbean remained a concern in the 1990s.

Figure 2.4 illustrates the change in grade repetition rates between 1980 and 2018. Although the repetition rate was remaining at a relatively high level for some years, it began to decline in the 2000s. The rate fell from 12.1% (boys 12.8%, girls 11.3% for girls) in 2000 to 9.5% (boys 10.2%, girls 8.7%) in 2005. The downward trend continued unabated, with the rate falling to 4.3% (boys 4.7%, girls 3.9%) by 2015, the deadline for achieving the MDGs. Nevertheless, the figures have remained elevated compared to those of other regions, such as 1.7% (boys 1.7%, girls 1.6%) in South Asia, with a considerable number of children still repeating grades as of 2015 (UNESCO, 2014; World Bank, 2024). Considering that

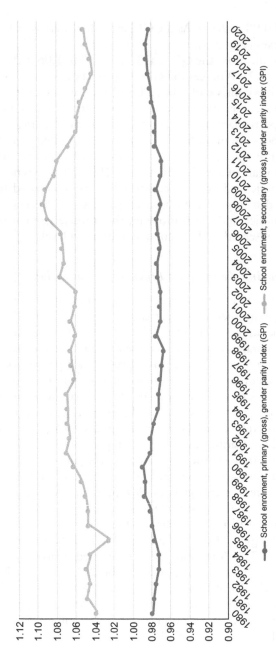

Fig. 2.3 The Gender Parity Index in Latin America and the Caribbean region (1980–2020). (Source: The authors developed this figure based on the data retrieved from the World Bank (2024). World Development Indicators. Retrieved May 26, 2024, from https://databank.worldbank.org/source/world-development-indicators)

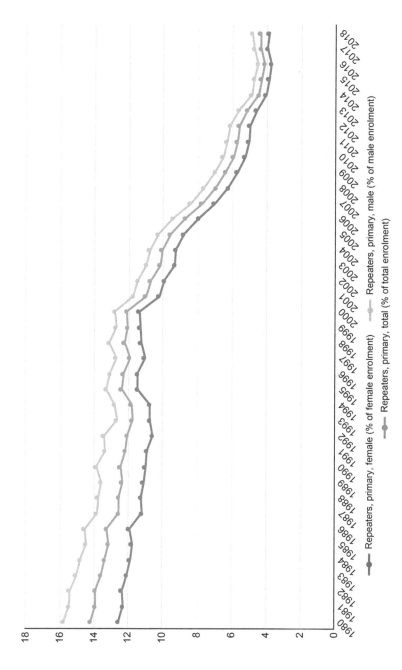

Fig. 2.4 Changes in grade repetition rates in primary education in Latin America and the Caribbean region (1980–2018). (Source: The authors developed the figure based on the data retrieved from the World Bank (2024). World Development Indicators. Retrieved May 26, 2024, from https://databank.worldbank.org/source/world-development-indicators)

sufficient understanding of learning contents and quality assurances of education, the effectiveness of grade repetition should be discussed. However, it is preferable to keep repetition to a minimum, because one potential consequence of repeating a grade is the phenomenon of 'dropping out', which signifies a complete departure from the school.

A study conducted in Latin America and the Caribbean found that children who experienced repetition were less likely to make it to the final grade of schooling. The survival rate is defined as the proportion of a cohort of children who entered primary school in the same school year who successfully complete the final grade. Studies show that children who repeat a grade are more likely to drop out of school. Various studies have been conducted to investigate the causes of this phenomenon and to identify effective strategies for addressing it. Because of various measures, the dropout rate in the region decreased from 21.5% to 11.8% between 2000 and 2012 (UNESCO, 2014). Furthermore, the percentage of students who successfully progressed to the final year of primary school (Grade 6) reached 77% in 2011. Furthermore, while almost all children in Chile, Cuba, and Mexico reached the final grade of primary school, in seven countries, including Brazil and Honduras, the percentage of those who progressed to the final grade was below 80%. In these countries, one-fifth of children leave school early (UNESCO, 2015). Estimates by UNESCO Statistics for 2017 indicate a primary school completion rate of 86% in the region (UNESCO, 2020), demonstrating that not all children enrolled in school are able to complete their primary education.

Nevertheless, although students at the primary level continue to face obstacles to completing primary school in certain countries across Latin America and the Caribbean, universal access to primary education has been almost achieved, and internal efficiency issues, such as grade repetition, are improving. Nevertheless, the region still tends to lag behind other regions according to certain indicators of educational outcomes, including survival rates, considering the size of the population and economic growth (Adelman & Székely, 2017).

Completion of Primary and Lower Secondary Education

In some countries in the region, such as Costa Rica, advancement to the next grade is partly automatic (Rodriguez-Segura, 2020). This principle is also sometimes employed as a provisional measure in Honduras, such as in the event of a natural disaster or coups d'état (Ashida, 2018). However, a significant number of countries in Latin America and the Caribbean do not follow an automatic grade promotion system. Instead, advancement to the next grade is contingent upon grades and other conditions. Consequently, it is possible for students in these countries to repeat a grade, and therefore, relevant data, such as grade repetition rates, have been collected on an ongoing basis. What trends can be identified in the completion rate data for primary and lower secondary education?

First, the completion rate for primary education was 74.6% (boys 73.6%, girls 75.5%) in 1980 (Fig. 2.5). Thereafter, the rate demonstrated a consistent upward trend, reaching 84.4% (boys 82.3%, girls 86.6%) in 1990, 90.6% (boys 89.2%, girls 92.0%) in 2000, and 97.3% (boys 96.2%, girls 98.4%) in 2014.The completion rate displayed a downward trend from 97.3% in 2014 to 93.5% in 2019. However, the upward trend returned, and the rate recovered to 94.9% (boys 93.5%, girls 96.4%) in 2022. In recent years, the completion rate for primary education has consistently remained above 90%. Completion rates for lower secondary education, meanwhile, display an upward trend, with rates increasing from 41.9% in 1980 to 51.0% (boys 49.0%, girls 53.1%) in 1990, 59.8% (boys 57.6%, girls 62.0%) in 2000, 71.4% (boys 69.0%, girls 73.9%) and 74.1% (boys 72.2%, girls 76.0%) by 2022 (Fig. 2.6). Indeed, the data clearly indicates that completion rates have been improving for both primary and lower secondary education despite some differences between the two.

Challenges Facing Latin America and the Caribbean

This section examines several of the pressing challenges that Latin America and the Caribbean must address in the future in order to realise SDG 4, which has an achievement deadline of 2030. The first challenge is reducing the number of out-of-school children in the region. According to UNESCO, there were approximately 4 million out-of-school children at the primary level in 1999. This number has decreased through 3.7 million in 2012 to 2.26 million in 2018 (UNESCO, 2015, 2020; UNESCO UIS, 2018). However, there are also differences in the percentage of improvement between Latin America and the Caribbean; for example, there was an 8.9% decrease in out-of-school children in Latin America at the time of 2012, while in the Caribbean, there was an 11.4% increase (UNESCO, 2015). In the region as a whole, access to education has improved, and net enrolment rates are approaching reasonable values. However, the issue of out-of-school students who have no overall access to education remains a

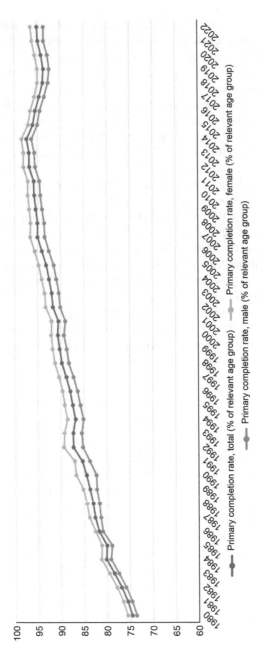

Fig. 2.5 Changes in primary completion rates in Latin America and the Caribbean region (1980–2022). (Source: The authors developed this figure based on the data retrieved from the World Bank (2024). World Development Indicators. Retrieved May 26, 2024, from https://databank.worldbank.org/source/world-development-indicators)

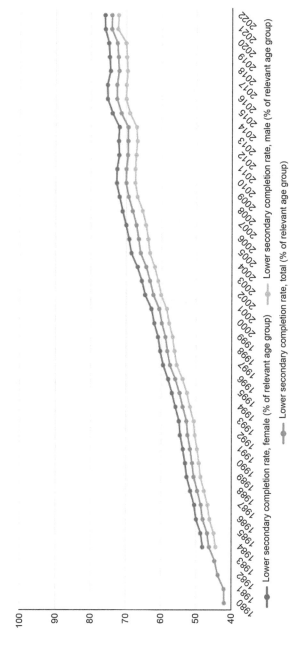

Fig. 2.6 Changes in lower secondary completion rates in Latin America and the Caribbean region (1980–2022). (Source: The authors developed this figure based on the data retrieved from the World Bank (2024). World Development Indicators. Retrieved May 26, 2024, from https://databank.worldbank.org/source/world-development-indicators)

significant challenge. Furthermore, as will be discussed below, it is important to also acknowledge the children who have left school and become unschooled children newly due to the loss of learning opportunities caused by the COVID-19 pandemic.

Second, this region also faces the problem of dropout, which refers to a student enrolling in school but then leaving in the middle of a course. In many countries in the region, universal access to primary education has been achieved, and completion rates are improving. However, in some countries, dropout among primary school students remains a problem. In addition, the dropout phenomenon is most pronounced during the transition from primary to lower secondary education and from lower secondary to upper secondary education. For example, Gibbs and Heaton (2014) analysed the transition from primary to secondary education in Mexico and noted that students are most likely to leave school during this transition period. Likewise, several studies have analysed the factors that contribute to dropout during this transition and during secondary education and have considered various preventative measures (Adelman & Székely, 2017; Adelman et al., 2018).

The third challenge is poor learning outcomes. Children in countries of this region have achieved low scores on international achievement tests despite the prevalence of schooling in the region (Breton & Canavire-Bacarreza, 2018). Target 4.1 of SDG 4, which deals with the quality of education, incorporates monitoring initiatives to measure minimum proficiency in reading and maths. Therefore, low academic achievement is an issue that must be addressed in the region.

The fourth challenge, which is related to the above three points, is the disparity in access to education between different regions of Latin America and the Caribbean. When discussing education on an international scale, Latin America and the Caribbean are often grouped together; however, there are acute disparities between the countries in this region. In particular, levels of school enrolment rates, dropout rates, and academic performance in Caribbean countries are poorer than in Latin America. Thus, out-of-school children, dropout, low academic achievement, and intra-regional disparities constitute urgent challenges in the region that must be addressed. Finally, it is necessary to consider the impacts of the COVID-19 pandemic, which are likely to be related to the four challenges mentioned above.

The Impact of the COVID-19 Pandemic

The COVID-19 pandemic, which began in early 2020, has resulted in lost learning opportunities at all levels of education. Following the outbreak of the pandemic, educational institutions around the world were forced to suspend their educational activities and close their doors. These school closures created new disparities in access to educational opportunities between those who have access to distance education, including online education, and those who do not. Such disparities, which continue to widen, are often due to place of residence, with urban residents enjoying improved access to education than rural residents. This gap is also due to differences in SES. The negative impacts of school closures were more pronounced in low- and middle-income countries, as online learning opportunities were not as readily available in such areas. Nevertheless, many also questioned the quality of the education that was available through distance learning. Full and partial disruptions to face-to-face schooling lasted for an average of five months worldwide. In Latin America, however, these disruptions lasted much longer, for approximately 16 months. Scholars have noted that this loss of learning opportunities may have long-term effects on students, further exacerbating existing inequalities in educational opportunities (ECLAC, 2022; UNESCO, 2024).

Various international organisations and related stakeholders have conducted a survey measuring children's academic achievement levels to estimate the impacts of school closures and the associated loss of learning opportunities due to the COVID-19 crisis (World Bank et al., 2022). It indicates that there has been a significant decline in basic academic skills, with younger age groups, lower-income pupils and girls, in particular, being impacted the most. In addition, this failure to achieve minimum proficiency in basic academic skills is not simply a temporary problem. Rather, these academic shortcomings may affect children's performance as they progress into higher education. They may even impact whether they are able to continue on to higher education at all. Insufficient academic proficiency skill might also lead to barrier to access to better employment opportunities in the labour market after leaving schooling. The impact of this loss of learning opportunities on children, therefore, needs to be observed and analysed over the long term and not just temporarily through macro cross-sectional data.

3   Conclusion

In recent years, the Global Education Monitoring Report (GEMR) has introduced new GEM reporting tools, such as PEER and SCOPE. We hope that this will improve access more for anyone to data and monitoring indicators regarding the effects of national and global education legislation and policies (UNESCO, 2020).

The 2023 report also describes the development of a new cohort model (new estimates for out-of-school students and completion rates). Until now, experts have had to make estimates regarding out-of-school children and completion rates due to a lack of data; they have also supplemented existing data with household data and other metrics. Therefore, in order to calculate more accurate values, the GEM report team and the UNESCO Institute for Statistics engaged in a joint estimation project using household data (UNESCO, 2021; UNESCO, 2023). Although we question the extent to which the use of alternative data to compensate for missing data and the method of layering estimates on top of each other will be effective, it is hoped that these new cohort models will provide new insights into the schooling situation of children that have not been seen in previous data. It is important to consider the challenges for achieving SDG 4 from a comprehensive perspective that includes both a macro perspective that considers cross-sectional data and a micro perspective that focuses on individual issues. We would like to conclude by asserting that, in addition to closely monitoring the trend of this new cohort model, scholars should not limit themselves to either quantitative or qualitative methods of analysis; rather, they should attempt to understand education issues from a comprehensive perspective that incorporates macro and micro perspectives.

References

Adelman, M., Haimovich, F., Ham, A., & Vazquez, E. (2018). Predicting school dropout with administrative data: New evidence from Guatemala and Honduras. *Education Economics, 26*(4), 356–372. https://doi.org/10.108 0/09645292.2018.1433127

Adelman, M. A., & Székely, M. (2017). An overview of school dropout in Central America: Unresolved issues and new challenges for education progress. *European Journal of Educational Research, 6*(3), 235–259. https://doi. org/10.12973/eu-jer.6.3.235

Ashida, A. (2018). *The actual effect on enrollment of 'Education for All': Analysis using longitudinal individual data.* Union Press.

Breton, T. R., & Canavire-Bacarreza, G. (2018). Low test scores in Latin America: Poor schools, poor families or something else? *Compare: A Journal of Comparative and International Education, 48*(5), 733–748. https://doi.org/10.1080/03057925.2017.1342530

Economic Commission for Latin America and the Caribbean (ECLAC). (2022). *Social Panorama of Latin €i0America and the Caribbean 2022: Transforming €i0education as a Basis for Sustainable Development.* Santiago. https://on.unesco.org/3u0d9Bj

Gibbs, B. G., & Heaton, T. B. (2014). Drop out from primary to secondary school in Mexico: A life course perspective. *International Journal of Educational Development, 36*, 63–71. https://doi.org/10.1016/j.ijedudev.2013.11.005

IIEP-UNESCO. (n.d.). Gender Parity Index (GPI). In *IIEP Learning Portal.* International Institute for Educational Planning. https://learningportal.iiep.unesco.org/en/glossary/gender-parity-index-gpi

McGinn, N., Reimers, F., Loera, A. d. C., Soto, M., & López, S. (1992). *Why do children repeat grades? A Study of Rural Primary Schools in Honduras* (Bridges Research Report Series no. 13). Bridges Publications.

Rodriguez-Segura, D. (2020). Strengthening early literacy skills through social promotion policies? Intended and unintended consequences in Costa Rica. *International Journal of Educational Development, 77*, 102243. https://doi.org/10.1016/j.ijedudev.2020.102243

UNESCO. (2014). *Latin America and the Caribbean education for all 2015 regional review.* UNESCO.

UNESCO. (2015). *Education for All 2000–2015: Achievements and challenges. Education for all global monitoring report 2015. Regional overview: Latin America and the Caribbean.* UNESCO.

UNESCO. (2020). *Global Education Monitoring Report 2020. Inclusion and education: All means all.* UNESCO.

UNESCO. (2021). *Global Education Monitoring Report 2021/2: Non-state actors in education: Who chooses? Who loses?* UNESCO.

UNESCO. (2023). *Global Education Monitoring Report 2023: Technology in education-A tool on whose terms?* UNESCO.

UNESCO. (2024). *The urgency of educational recovery in Latin America and the Caribbean.* UNESCO. https://unesdoc.unesco.org/ark:/48223/pf0000388399_eng

UNESCO-UIS. (2018). One in five children, adolescents and youth is out of school. *Fact Sheet*, No. 48. Retrieved March 14, 2018, from http://uis.unesco.org/sites/default/files/documents/fs48-one-five-children-adolescents-youth-out-school-2018-en.pdf

UNESCO-UNEVOC International Centre for Technical and Vocational Education and Training. (n.d.). Gender Parity Index (GPI). In TVETipedia Glossary. https://unevoc.unesco.org/home/TVETipedia+Glossary/lang=en/show=term/term=Gender+parity+index

World Bank. (2024). *World Development Indicators.* Retrieved May 26, 2024, from https://databank.worldbank.org/source/world-development-indicators

World Bank, United Nations Educational, Scientific and Cultural Organization, United Nations Children's Fund, & United States Agency for International Development. (2022). *FCDO.* Bill & Melinda Gates Foundation. The State of Global Learning Poverty: 2022 Update.

CHAPTER 3

Notable Progress and Prospective Challenges in Diverse Regions of South and Southeast Asia

Natsuho Yoshida

1   PROGRESS TOWARDS THE UNIVERSAL PRIMARY EDUCATION

Asia includes a range of countries that feature a wide range of political systems, economic situations and socio-cultural environments. In spite of this, the region as a whole has made steady progress in universal primary and basic education. In 1959 and 1960, UNESCO hosted the Regional Meeting of Representatives of Asian Member States on Primary and Compulsory Education in Karachi, Pakistan. There, the Karachi Plan was formulated, with the ambitious goal of doubling the rate of development of that of the previous decade to achieve a minimum of seven years of universal free and compulsory education for every inhabitant. However,

N. Yoshida (✉)
Graduate School of Education, Hyogo University of Teacher Education, Kato, Japan
e-mail: nyoshida@hyogo-u.ac.jp

© The Author(s), under exclusive license to Springer Nature Switzerland AG 2024
T. Sekiya et al. (eds.), *Towards Ensuring Inclusive and Equitable Quality Education for All*, International and Development Education, https://doi.org/10.1007/978-3-031-70266-2_3

few countries in Asia were able to achieve this goal. Following this, the Asia-Pacific Programme of Education for All (APPEAL) was proposed at the Fifth Conference of Ministers of Education and Those Responsible for Economic Planning in 1985 (UNESCO, 1997). APPEAL is an advanced programme in three key areas: universal primary education, the eradication of illiteracy and continuing education for development, seeking to achieve each of these areas through collaboration in Asia.

In 1990, the World Conference on Education for All (EFA), jointly organised by the World Bank, UNESCO, UNICEF and the United Nations Development Programme, was held in Jomtien, Thailand. From that time, APPEAL has been developed in a global EFA framework.[1] In addition, the World Education Forum, held in Dakar, Senegal, in 2000, set up 'The Dakar Framework for Action, EFA' (The World Conference on EFA, 1990). There, six goals were set for the achievement of EFA (UNESCO, 2000). In addition, likewise in 2000, the UN Millennium Summit was held in New York, where the Millennium Development Goals (MDGs) were adopted as common goals for the international community in the field of development, including education. The education sector goals common to the EFA and the MDGs are the achievement of universal primary (compulsory) education and gender equality in education. What progress have countries in Asia made towards achieving education goals? This section focuses on the diversity of Asia, particularly in the regions of South and Southeast Asia, to which the case study countries covered in this publication belong, and it identifies the progress that has been made so far towards achieving the EFA/MDGs.

Trends in Enrolment in Primary Education

To identify the progress that has been made towards achieving the goals of education in the EFA/MDG in Southeast Asia and South Asia, we first review the gross enrolment rates in primary education in both regions (Fig. 3.1). For Southeast Asia, between 1990, when the EFA was proposed, and 2020, the gross enrolment rate in primary education is above

---

[1] Although APPEAL had a strong presence in Asia when it was first proposed, its significance and the extent of its role declined in relative terms as large-scale EFA projects, such as the World Bank's First Track Initiative and its successor, the Global Partnership for Education, were implemented by bilateral donors, including international organisations and the Japan International Cooperation Agency (JICA).

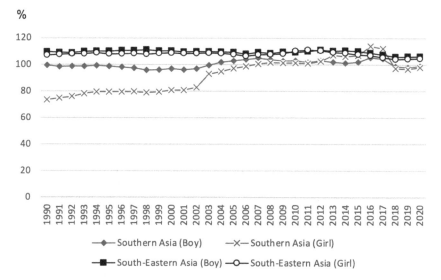

Fig. 3.1 Trends in gross enrolment rates in primary education by gender in Southeast and South Asia. (Source: UNESCO Institute for Statistics [2024])

100%, showing a very small gender gap. In South Asia, the gross enrolment rate in primary education for boys remained almost 100% from 1990 to 2020, in line with the global average. However, the gross enrolment rate for girls in primary education was low, at 70%–80% from 1990 to 2002, with a large gender gap. In recent years, however, this gender gap has largely disappeared, as the gross enrolment rate for girls in primary education exceeded 90% in 2003 and has been above 100% since 2007. The Gender Parity Index (GPI) was 96% for the education sector in South Asia, as high as the GPI for East Asia and the Pacific region, which includes Southeast Asia (95.5%) (World Economic Forum, 2022). Thus, the targets for access to primary education and gender equality have largely been achieved in both Southeast and South Asia.

Next, we review the gross and net primary enrolment rates by country in recent years in Southeast and South Asia (Fig. 3.2). Net enrolment rate is above 94% in all countries in Southeast Asia, a rate that is close to universal primary education. On the other hand, there is a large gap of 15%–20% between gross and net enrolment rates in Cambodia, Myanmar, Timor-Leste and Vietnam. This implies that these countries have

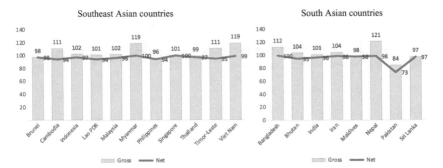

Fig. 3.2 Gross and net primary enrolment rates by country in Southeast and South Asia. (Note: For Myanmar, data from 2018 are used. For Bangladesh and Pakistan, data from 2018 and 2021 are used, respectively. For all other countries, data from 2020 are used. No data for Afghanistan on net enrolment rate could be found. Source: UNESCO Institute for Statistics [2024])

problems with overage children entering primary education and with frequent grade repetition. In South Asia, net enrolment rates are above 95% in most countries, but in some, such as Pakistan, there has been little improvement in access to primary education. Pakistan's gross enrolment rate remained flat from 2007 (74.2%) to 2015 (74.8%), which was the deadline for achieving the EFA/MDGs, with little improvement. UNESCO (2015) reported that 'more than a third of the world's out-of-school children are from conflict areas'. A number of other studies have identified the negative impact of conflict and civil war on children's educational performance (e.g. Poirier, 2012). This suggests that Pakistan's lack of improvement in school enrolment is due to long-standing insecurity resulting from frequent terrorist attacks and related factors. Pakistan had 22,286,829 out-of-school youth in 2021 (UNESCO Institute for Statistics, 2024), the highest number in Southeast and South Asia after India. The rate of out-of-school youth relative to population is clearly higher in Pakistan than in India. In Bangladesh and Nepal, the gap between gross and net enrolment rates is large, around 20%. It can thus be inferred that these countries have the same problems of overage and grade repetition as the Southeast Asian countries of Cambodia, Myanmar, Timor-Leste and Vietnam. An analysis of primary education enrolment in Southeast and South Asian countries at the national level indicates that the targets for access to primary education are being met in general, but the particularities of this vary from country to country.

Trends in Completion of Primary Education

The EFA/MDGs for universal primary education include not only children who are simply entering school, but also who are reaching graduation. In the following section, therefore, we review the progress made in the completion of primary education in Southeast and South Asia, verifying trends in the percentages of children completing the final year of primary education (Figs. 3.3 and Fig. 3.4). The rate of graduating the final year of primary education in Southeast Asia steadily increased for both sexes, from 70% to 95% between 1990, when the EFA was proposed, and 2019 (Fig. 3.3). The gross enrolment rate in primary education remained slightly lower for girls than boys, but the opposite was true for the survival rate, with girls performing better throughout all years. Furthermore, looking at the survival rates up through the final year of primary education by country in Southeast Asia (Fig. 3.4), Thailand has almost fully achieved

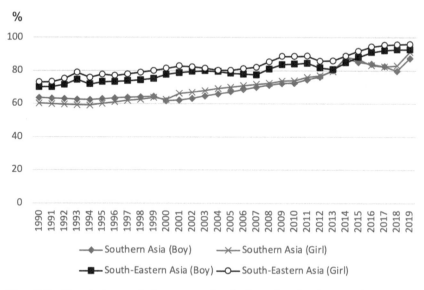

Fig. 3.3 Trends in survival rates to the final grade of primary education in Southeast and South Asia. (Source: UNESCO Institute for Statistics [2024])

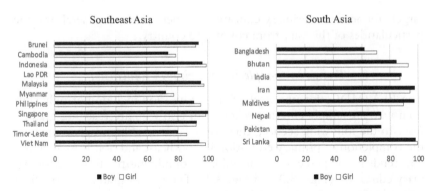

Fig. 3.4 Survival rates to the final grade of primary education by country and by gender in Southeast and South Asia. (Source: UNESCO Institute for Statistics [2024])

gender equality, while only Brunei and Singapore show a slightly higher performance for boys. By contrast, the remaining Southeast Asian countries show higher performance for girls. This suggests that in many Southeast Asian countries, girls are slightly less likely than boys to be enrolled in school, but once they are enrolled, girls are more likely to graduate.

The survival rate to the final year of primary education in South Asia has steadily increased between 1990 and 2019, from 60% to 91%, approaching the rate of the Southeast Asia (Fig. 3.3). There were no large gender differences in the survival rate or the total enrolment rate; in fact, in some years, the survival rate was slightly higher for girls than for boys. The gender survival rates by country (Fig. 3.4) show that only three countries (Bangladesh, Bhutan and Sri Lanka) have a higher rate for girls than boys, while all others have higher rates for boys. This suggests that in South Asia, gender differences in performance for the completion of primary education vary widely from country to country. While countries with large gender differences can be identified, overall, the survival rate for children until the final year of primary education steadily increased in both the Southeast and South Asia.

2   Current Status of Repetition and Dropouts with Regard to the Quality of Education

The achievement of the EFA/MDGs for universal primary education naturally involves the question of the quality of education. This section identifies internal efficiency with respect to quality of education, i.e. the rate at which children repeat grades and or drop out of school in Southeast and South Asia.

Status of Grade Repetition in Primary Education

To identify trends in primary school repetition in Southeast Asia and South Asia, we review trends in primary school repetition rates by country. In Table 3.1, it can be seen that between 2000 and 2016/2017, primary school repetition rates have decreased in each country in Southeast and South Asia. However, the high repetition rates in Timor-Leste (12.8%), Cambodia (6.5%), Laos (4.0%) and Nepal (7.4%) still show room for improvement.

Table 3.1 Trends in primary school repetition rates by country in Southeast and South Asia

Southeast Asia				South Asia			
Countries	Repetition rates			Countries	Repetition rates		
	2000	2017	Progress		2000	2016	Progress
Brunei	7.9	0.1	-7.8	India	3.7	0.6	-3.1
Cambodia	17.8	6.5	-11.3	Iran	4.6	1.4	-3.2
Indonesia	6.2	1.3	-4.9	Maldive	11.1	0.1	-11.0
Lao PDR	19.7	4.0	-15.7	Nepal	23.0	7.4	-15.6
Myanmar	0.7	0.5	-0.2	Pakistan	3.3	2.3	-1.0
Philippines	2.0	1.3	-0.6	Sri Lanka	6.9	0.9	-5.9
Singapore	0.3	0.2	-0.2				
Thailand	3.8	1.4	-2.4				
Timor-Leste	19.5	12.8	-6.7				
Vietnam	2.8	0.8	-1.9				

Note: Instead of 2000 data, data from 1994 for Brunei, 2007 for Singapore and 2008 for East Timor in Southeast Asia and from 1996 for Maldives, 2004 for Pakistan and 1991 for Sri Lanka in South Asia are used. Note that data for Malaysia, Afghanistan, Bangladesh and Bhutan are not included because no data could be found
Source: UNESCO Institute for Statistics (2024)

Of these, for Laos, significant differences in repetition rates were found between urban and rural areas and between northern and southern areas (Lao Statistics Bureau, 2023). For example, when the author visited and surveyed primary schools in a coffee plantation area in southern Laos in 2017, she encountered the shocking reality that approximately one in two enrolled children were repeating a grade in school. While in India, the repetition rate was very low, at 0.6% as of 2016, and there appear to be no major problems with regard to repetition, this by no means guarantees the quality of education: according to Dréze and Sen (2013), in India, the Free and Compulsory Education Act 2010 entails that children are automatically promoted to the next grade regardless of what they have learned and mastered, and qualifying examinations for promotion are prohibited until grade 8. In place of the qualification examinations, a system of comprehensive and continuous assessment has been established, but the details of this system are not clear, and in practice, it seems to be understood in schools as to be functionally no assessment. Therefore, it is difficult to say that quality of education is guaranteed under these circumstances, and there is the risk in practice that children in India may complete their primary education without having learned enough. One reason for this may relate to the school management problems that are frequently identified in South Asia. Furthermore, Myanmar also appears to have no particular problems with grade repetition, with a very low repetition rate of 0.5%, as of 2017. However, household surveys indicate that the actual repetition rate in primary education in the country is much higher than education statistics gathered by international organisations show (Spohr, 2015).

These examples indicate that the actual status of student repetition in relation to the quality of education cannot be accurately grasped from macro education statistics alone. Therefore, even in countries that feature low rates of repetition in terms of education statistics, the quality of education is not necessarily guaranteed, and it is possible that the actual repetition rate is higher than that reported. Therefore, to obtain more reliable data on the reality of grade repetition in Southeast and South Asia, supplementary micro longitudinal studies are necessary that will focus on individuals and will not rely solely on cross-sectional macro data.

School Dropout Status in Primary Education

To clarify the status of primary school dropout in Southeast and South Asia, we again focus on the survival rate to the final year of primary education by country (Fig. 3.4). Countries with a survival rate below 90% to the final year of primary education include Cambodia, Laos, Myanmar and East Timor in Southeast Asia and Bangladesh, Bhutan, India, Nepal and Pakistan in South Asia. The dropout rate in these countries has been poor in recent years. Why do so many children still drop out of school in these countries?

A literature review by Fernández-Suárez et al. (2016) suggests that school dropouts can be explained by multiple factors operating at different levels (individual, family, school and neighbourhood). For example, No et al. (2016), who analysed school dropout factors in Cambodia, found that important factors in dropping out were, for grades 1–4, parents' divorce, relationships with friends and late schooling beyond the official school age, while for grads 4–9, factors were grade repetition and relative academic achievement. Sabates et al. (2013), who analysed the relative strength of different factors associated with school dropout in Bangladesh, found that in addition to age and gender, economic constraints such as inadequate income and school fees expenditure were the top predictors of children dropping out of school. Furthermore, child labour due to poverty leads to school dropout in Myanmar (ILO, 2015). According to Yoshida (2020a), overaged children from poor families are more likely to drop out of school and go to work in urban areas, as work becomes easier to obtain as age increases. In addition, in Myanmar, boys are more likely to get jobs than girls, as it is believed that boys are better suited for heavy work, taking solo trips to distant places that involve driving and working late into the night. This may be why Yoshida's (2020a) analysis of secondary school enrolment status by SES showed a dropout rate for boys that was almost twice that of girls.

This discussion suggests that when examining the achievement of the EFA/MDGs (universal primary education) in Southeast and South Asia improvement remains to be archived regarding grade repetition and dropping out.

3 Remaining Challenges and Towards Achieving SDG 4

The Sustainable Development Goals (SDGs), the successor to the EFA/MDGs, are set as an education goal to 'ensure inclusive and equitable quality education and promote lifelong learning opportunities for all'

(SDG 4). Targets subordinate to SDG 4 include the following: 'By 2030, ensure that all girls and boys complete free, equitable and quality primary and secondary education leading to relevant and effective learning outcomes' (SDG 4.1) and 'By 2030, eliminate gender disparities in education and ensure equal access to all levels of education and vocational training for the vulnerable, including persons with disabilities, indigenous peoples and children in vulnerable situations' (SDG 4.5). Countries in Southeast and South Asia have made their own effort to achieve universal primary education and gender equality. This has led to some countries achieving their targets, while others have fallen behind. However, the problem with respect to educational disparities between regions and countries, as well as within countries, is becoming more apparent (UNESCO, 2015). Here, therefore, we focus on this educational gap, discussing the challenges in schooling for children in Southeast and South Asia to find clues that can contribute to the achievement of SDG 4.

Educational Challenges Related to Ethnic Minorities

In multi-ethnic states, such as the countries of Southeast and South Asia, educational policies are implemented that emphasise the culture, values and language of the majority ethnic group to promote national integration in education and to ensure stable state management. However, as a result, approximately 40% of the world's population is unable to receive education in a language that they speak or understand (Walter & Benson, 2012). This is particularly true in countries that have high linguistic diversity, where language barriers can contribute to educational disparities between members of majority and minority ethnic groups (UNDP, 2004; UNESCO, 2016).

For example, although Vietnam has indicated that it will allow ethnic minority languages to be studied in schools (Socialist Republic of Vietnam, 2005), classes in primary education in Vietnam are conducted in Vietnamese, the language of the Kinh ethnic majority, and the textbooks are also written in Vietnamese. Previous studies have found that, compared to the Kinh, minority ethnic groups' primary education outcomes, participation in secondary education and completion of it are poor, and an enrolment gap persists between the majority and minority ethnic groups (Dang & Glewwe, 2018; DeJaeghere et al., 2021). For Laos, Inui (2020), citing MOES and RIES (2014), noted that the Assessment of Student Learning Outcome in 2012, conducted with third-year primary school students, found that ethnic minority children scored significantly worse in Lao language and mathematics outcomes than their majority ethnic counterparts. Furthermore, in Myanmar, there are 135 ethnic groups, and the Burmese, the majority ethnic group, account for about 70% of the population in total. Burmese is used in schools as the medium of instruction. Members of ethnic minorities have expressed dissatisfaction with this, and there have been moves in many places to provide education in the language of different ethnic groups (Bertrand, 2022).

Thus, in spite of recent attempts by countries to make a shift towards multiculturalism, educational disparities for ethnic minority children persist (UNESCO, 2016). Thus, to achieve true educational equality for ethnic minorities and reach SDG 4.5, countries must seriously promote initiatives to address ethnic minorities rather than maintaining the status quo (Skutnabb-Kangas, 2016).

Education Challenges Related to the Socio-economic Situation

Previous studies from around the world have consistently found that children's SES can influence their educational performance (Buchmann & Hannum, 2001; Hannum & Buchmann, 2005). A comparison of completion rates by socio-economic level in Myanmar (UIS, 2022) showed that for primary education, the richest group had a completion rate of 92.6%, with a rate of 64.7% for the poorest group. Lower secondary education was completed by 74.7% of the richest group and 13.3% of the poorest group. Finally, upper secondary education was completed by 44.7% of the richest group and only 1.7% of the poorest group. This comparison indicates the magnitude of the problem of educational disparities according to SES. A household survey conducted in Bangladesh in the South Asia found that 'lack of money' was the most important reason why children did not enrol in or dropped out of school (Ahmed et al., 2007). Elsewhere in South Asia, socio-economic factors have also been found to significantly influence children's educational outcomes in India and Sri Lanka (Ranasinghe & Hartog, 2002; Filmer & Pritchett, 1999; Arunatilake, 2006).

Furthermore, as the focus has shifted from the quantitative expansion (access) of education to improvements in the quality of education in the transition from EFA/MDGs to SDGs, the number of children who are enrolled in private schools is on the rise globally (UNESCO, 2015). In particular, a rapid increase has been seen in the number of children in South Asian, such as India, Nepal and Pakistan, who are opting for private schools in pursuit of what they perceive as a higher-quality education (Dahal & Nguyen, 2014). Naturally, unlike public schools, private schools are not free. So it is conceivable that socio-economic factors could further widen educational inequalities as a result of their growth.

Current Status and Remaining Challenges in the Universal Secondary Education

The SDG 4 now includes universal secondary education and primary education. Hence, to understand the current state of achievement of SDG 4.1 in Southeast and South Asia, the following section first provides an overview of the total enrolment rate in secondary education in the two regions (Fig. 3.5). It then identifies the remaining challenges to achieving SDG 4. For Southeast Asia, the gross enrolment rate in secondary education steadily increased between 1990 and 2020, and it is improving at a rate that will soon bring it to reach 90%. In terms of the gross enrolment rate, the advantage held by boys in 1990 reversed in 2003, and since then, girls have had a slight advantage. In general, girls are more disadvantaged

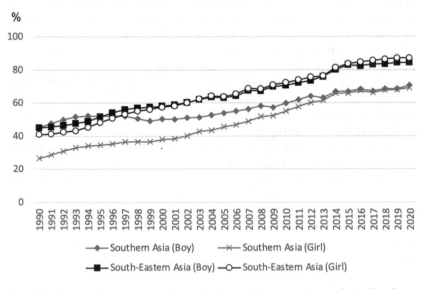

Fig. 3.5 Trends in gross secondary school enrolment rates by gender in Southeast and South Asia. (Source: UNESCO Institute for Statistics [2024])

in terms of schooling, but in Southeast Asia, girls are more dominant at higher levels of education, contrary to the prevailing theory. In South Asia, the gross enrolment rate in secondary education has increased steadily between 1990 and 2020, but it remains around 70%, a slower improvement than in the Southeast Asia region. On the other hand, as in the primary education phase, the gross secondary education enrolment rate for girls has also improved significantly, and the gender gap has almost been eliminated since 2014.

We next review the gross and net enrolment rates in lower secondary education in recent years by country (Fig. 3.6). Cambodia, Laos, Myanmar, Bangladesh and Pakistan appear to have particularly large gaps with respect to SDG 4.1. Cambodia, Laos and Myanmar are all identified as being Least Developed Countries, while Pakistan, as noted, has long suffered from instability due to terrorism and other related factors. Yoshida (2020b) notes that efforts in the education sector alone have had limited effects in improving children's schooling and achieving the equitable and universal primary and secondary education. Therefore, to reach SDG 4, in addition to traditional efforts in the education sector, it is also necessary to work simultaneously on boosting the national economy and stabilising society.

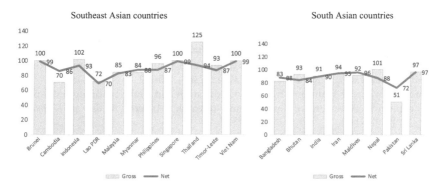

Fig. 3.6 Gross and net enrolment rates in lower secondary education by country in Southeast and South Asia. (Note: Myanmar uses 2018 data; all other Southeast Asian countries use 2020 data. Only Iran and the Maldives in South Asia use data from 2020, while the other South Asian countries use data from 2021. Note that no data could be found for Afghanistan. Source: UNESCO Institute for Statistics [2024])

4   CONCLUSION

Based on the case study of countries in Southeast and South Asia, this chapter investigates trends, current situations and challenges of the educational situation in relation to macro cross-sectional data, with a particular focus on Southeast and South Asia. However, macro cross-sectional data alone have limitations in accurately understanding the actual situation of grade repetition and school dropouts in Southeast and South Asia, and problems with schooling occur with respect to ethnic minority groups and disparate socio-economic conditions. Therefore, it is necessary to utilise micro longitudinal data, which focuses on and values the individual, together with macro cross-sectional data. From this point onwards, each of the chapters in the case studies of the Southeast and South Asian countries dealt with in this publication presents findings from research results based on micro longitudinal data that can contribute to addressing the educational challenges referred to in this section. We hope that these will provide hints for the full achievement of SDG 4.

REFERENCES

Ahmed, M., Ahmed, K. S., Khan, N. I., & Ahmed, R. (2007). *Access to education in Bangladesh: Country analytic review of primary and secondary schools.* Consortium for Research on Educational Acess, Transitions & Equity (CREATE).

Arunatilake, N. (2006). Education participation in Sri Lanka—Why all are not in school. *International Journal of Educational Research, 45*(3), 137–152.

Bertrand, J. (2022). Education, language, and conflict in Myanmar's ethnic minority states. *Asian Politics and Policy, 14*(1), 25–42.

Buchmann, C., & Hannum, E. (2001). Education and stratification in developing countries: A review of theories and research. *Annual Review of Sociology, 27*(1), 77–102.

Dahal, M., & Nguyen, Q. (2014). *Private non-state sector engagement in the provision of educational services at the primary and secondary levels in South Asia: An analytical review of its role in school enrolment and student achievement (Policy Research Working Paper No. 6899).* World Bank South Asia Region Education Unit.

Dang, H. A., & Glewwe, P. W. (2018). Well begun, but aiming higher: A review of Vietnam's education trends in the past 20 years and emerging challenges. In Dang, H. A. (2012). Vietnam: a widening poverty gap for ethnic minorities. *The Journal of Development Studies, 54*(7), 1171–1195.

DeJaeghere, J., Dao, V., Duong, B. H., & Luong, P. (2021). Inequalities in learning in Vietnam: Teachers' beliefs about and classroom practices for ethnic minorities RISE working paper. Series, 21/061.

Dréze, J., & Sen, A. (2013). *An uncertain glory: India and its contradictions.* Penguin Books Ltd..

Fernández-Suárez, A., Herrero, J., Pérez, B., Juarros-Basterretxea, J., & Rodríguez-Díaz, F. J. (2016). Risk factors for school dropout in a sample of juvenile offenders. *Frontiers in Psychology, 7,* 1993.

Filmer, D., & Pritchett, L. (1999). Educational enrollment and attainment in India: Household wealth, gender, village, and state effects. *Administration, 13*(2), 135–164.

Hannum, E., & Buchmann, C. (2005). Global educational expansion and socioeconomic development: An assessment of findings from the social sciences. *World Development, 33*(3), 333–354.

International Labour Organization. (2015). *Rapid assessment on child labour in the Hlaing Thar Yar industrial zone in Yangon, Myanmar, 2015.* International Labour Organization.

Inui, M. (2020). Impact of the 'Grade Zero' system on minority children in Laos: A qualitative study of pre- primary schools in a rural province. *Education 3–13, 48*(1), 118–130.

Lao Statistics Bureau. (2023). Statistical yearbook 2022. Ministry of Planning and Investment.

Moes & RIES. (2014) [Report]. *National assessment of student learning outcome (ASLO III) Grade 3* (Ministry of Education and Sports & Research Institute for Educational Science).

No, F., Taniguchi, K., & Hirakawa, Y. (2016). School dropout at the basic education level in rural Cambodia: Identifying its causes through longitudinal survival analysis. *International Journal of Educational Development, 49*(C), 215–224.

Poirier, T. (2012). The effects of armed conflict on schooling in sub-Saharan Africa. *International Journal of Educational Development, 32*(2), 341–351.

Ranasinghe, A., & Hartog, J. (2002). Free-education in Sri Lanka. Does it eliminate the family effect? Does it eliminate the family effect? *Economics of Education Review, 21*(6), 623–633.

Sabates, R., Hossain, A., & Lewin, K. M. (2013). School drop out in Bangladesh: Insights using panel data. *International Journal of Educational Development, 33*(3), 225–232.

Skutnabb-Kangas, T. (2016). Language rights and bilingual education. In O. Garcia, A. Lin, & S. May (Eds.), *In bilingual and multilingual education* (pp. 1–13). Springer.

Socialist Republic of Viet Nam. (2005). *National assembly of the socialist republic of Vietnam, 11th legislature, seventh session, education law.*

Spohr, C. (2015). *Republic of the Union of Myanmar: Support for postprimary education development (project number: 47177)*. Asian Development Bank.

The World Conference on Education for All. (1990). World declaration on Education for All: Meeting basic learning needs, UNESDOC, Jomtien.

United Nations Development Program. (2004). *Human development report 2004: Cultural liberty in today's diverse world*. United Nations Development Programme.

United Nations Educational, Scientific and Cultural Organization. (1997). *Challenges of education for all in Asia and the pacific and the APPEAL response*, p. 26. UNESCO.

United Nations Educational, Scientific and Cultural Organization. (2000a). *World Education Forum final report*. UNESCO.

United Nations Educational, Scientific and Cultural Organization. (2015). *EFA global monitoring report 2015—Education for all 2000–2015: Achievements and challenges*. UNESCO.

United Nations Educational, Scientific and Cultural Organization. (2016). *Global Education Monitoring Report Policy Paper 24: If you don't understand, how can you learn?* UNESCO.

United Nations Educational, Scientific and Cultural Organization Institute for Statistics. (2022). *UIS. Stat*. Retrieved March 31, 2022, from http://data.uis.unesco.org/

United Nations Educational, Scientific and Cultural Organization institute for Statistics. (2024). *UIS. Stat*. Retrieved May 23, 2024, from http://data.uis.unesco.org/

Walter, S. L., & Benson, C. (2012). Language policy and the medium of instruction in formal education. In B. Spolsky (Ed.), *In the Cambridge handbook of language policy* (pp. 278–300). Cambridge University Press.

World Economic Forum. (2022). *Global gender gap report 2023*.

Yoshida, N. (2020a). Enrolment status disparity: Evidence from secondary education in Myanmar. *International Journal of Comparative Education and Development, 22*(2), 101–114.

Yoshida, N. (2020b). Socio-economic status and the impact of the 'continuous assessment and progression system' in primary education in Myanmar. *Education 3–13, 48*(6), 674–689.

CHAPTER 4

Access or Quality? New Challenges in Sub-Saharan Africa

Naruho Ezaki ⓘ *and Keiichi Ogawa* ⓘ

1   REMARKABLE DIFFUSION OF BASIC EDUCATION

Progress Since Independence by African Countries in the 1960s

Since the end of the nineteenth century, descendants of Africans brought to the Americas by the slave trade have sought their own identity and advocated Pan-Africanism. Pan-Africanism calls for the emancipation and solidarity of people of African descent and became the catalyst and spiritual prop for the African independence movement. This movement led to the independence in the 1960s of many colonial African countries from their colonising nations. Subsequently, African leaders aiming to embody

N. Ezaki (✉)
Faculty of Global Culture and Communication, Aichi Shukutoku University, Nagoya, Japan
e-mail: nezaki@asu.aasa.ac.jp

K. Ogawa
Graduate School of International Cooperation Studies, Kobe University, Kobe, Japan
e-mail: ogawa35@kobe-u.ac.jp

© The Author(s), under exclusive license to Springer Nature Switzerland AG 2024
T. Sekiya et al. (eds.), *Towards Ensuring Inclusive and Equitable Quality Education for All*, International and Development Education, https://doi.org/10.1007/978-3-031-70266-2_4

Pan-Africanism established the Organisation of African Unity in 1963, and each independent nation began its nation-building process. In building a country 'by Africans for Africans', securing human resources was imperative; thus, all African countries prioritised education and its dissemination. As a result, the gross enrolment rate in primary and secondary education in Sub-Saharan Africa has been increasing for 50 years, from 1970 to 2020 (Fig. 4.1). In particular, the growth from the 1970s to the 1980s and from the 2000s to the 2010s has been phenomenal.

Two oil crises and declines in international prices of primary commodities occurred in the 1970s, which negatively affected the economies of African countries. Thus, rather than shrinking, the economic disparity

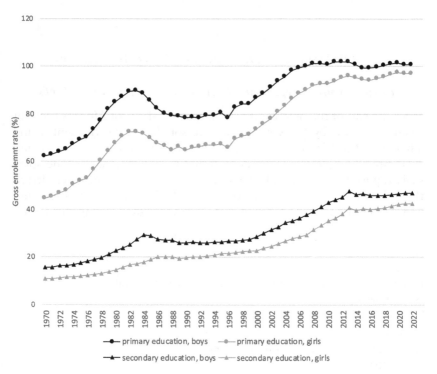

Fig. 4.1 Trends in gross enrolment rates for primary and secondary education in Sub-Saharan Africa. (Source: Created by the authors based on the data from the World Development Indicator (WDI), World Bank (1970–2022))

within each country continued to widen and the severity of poverty increased. These circumstances led these countries to focus on issues of inequality, specifically poverty and unemployment. Subsequently, the concept of Basic Human Needs (BHN) was proposed, which places the development goal on human well-being. BHN includes food, clothing, shelter and living conditions such as access to safe drinking water and sanitation, medical care, education and employment. Regarding education, basic education was considered an element to ensure basic human rights, and education was considered an investment objective. Additionally, because of the importance of acquiring the basic knowledge and skills necessary for life, primary education was emphasised in African countries, and access increased for boys and girls.

The 1980s are referred to as the 'lost decade' of development. Many developing countries experienced economic and debt crises, and the International Monetary Fund and the World Bank implemented structural adjustment policies in response to this crisis. In each country, fiscal austerity measures such as decentralisation, reduction of various subsidies, and privatisation of state-owned enterprises were implemented. In the social sector and education, there were substantial spending cuts. Moreover, once eliminated in many African countries, tuition fees were reintroduced and their prices increased. As a result, enrolment in primary education declined for boys and girls. For example, Tanzania began free primary education in 1974, earlier than other African countries. According to the WDI of the World Bank (1970–2022), the gross enrolment rate increased rapidly from 44.8% in 1974 to 96.1% in 1981. Thereafter, it declined slightly and then, starting in 1985, declined sharply in response to primary education becoming fee based. Since then, the gross enrolment rate has been stagnant, hovering at approximately 60%. However, in 2001, primary education became free again, and the rate increased, exceeding 100% in 2004. This example of Tanzania shows the magnitude of the tuition burden and that, for approximately 15 years, structural adjustment policies deprived many children of the opportunity to receive an education.

In March 1990, the World Conference on Education for All was held in Jomtien, Thailand. At this conference, the slogan 'Education for All' (EFA) was adopted, and there was international agreement that the universal goal should be to provide basic education for all. Additionally, the concept of basic education, which until then was understood mainly as primary education, was expanded to include preschool education, lower secondary education and non-formal education (e.g. adult education and literacy education). This comprehensive international goal with a time frame was the world's first and thus considered ground-breaking. Since the mid-1990s, many African countries have strengthened their commitment to primary education and eliminated tuition, making it free. For instance, Malawi, Uganda and Zambia, the countries covered in this book, implemented free primary education in 1994, 1997 and 2002, respectively. However, many African countries did not achieve sufficient results in the 1990s.

In April 2000, the World Education Forum was held in Dakar, Senegal. At this forum, there was recognition that achieving EFA by 2015 would be challenging, and the EFA Dakar Framework for Action was adopted. In September of the same year, the United Nations Millennium Summit was held in New York, where the Millennium Development Goals (MDGs) were set as common goals for the international community in the development field. The MDGs advocated poverty reduction as a top priority, and subsequently, in Africa, policies related to poverty reduction have been emphasised. As a result, according to the WDI of the World Bank (2024), the poverty headcount ratio at $2.15 a day in Sub-Saharan Africa decreased significantly from 56% in 2000 to 38.2% in 2015. In education, various initiatives have led to a marked increase in the gross enrolment rate for primary education.[1] For example, the net enrolment rate of children of formal school age increased from 52% in 1990 to 80% in 2015 (United Nations, 2015), and per the World Bank data (1970–2018), the repetition rate for children (Fig. 4.2), 12–13% in the 1970s, decreased to 7% in 2018. Moreover, since the 2000s, some countries have extended their free education policies to lower secondary education, and access to secondary education has increased.

In 2015, the deadline for achieving the MDGs, the United Nations Summit was held in New York, and the 2030 Agenda for Sustainable Development was adopted. The Sustainable Development Goals (SDGs) were then announced to address the remaining concerns in the MDGs and the new concerns. The achievement deadline of the SDGs, comprising 17 goals and 169 targets, is 2030. The goal of the education sector (i.e. SDG 4)

---

[1] The gross enrolment ratio is the ratio of the total number of students enrolled in a grade to the population that should be enrolled in that grade (regular school age). The net enrolment rate represents the ratio of the number of students of the age at which they should be enrolled in a given grade to the population of the age at which they should be enrolled in that grade (regular school age).

Fig. 4.2 Trends in repetition rates for primary education in Sub-Saharan Africa. (Source: Created by the authors based on the data from the WDI, World Bank (1970–2018))

was to 'ensure inclusive and equitable quality education and promote lifelong learning opportunities for all', and various efforts are underway in each country to reach the target.

New Goals for 2063 and Educational Positioning

In the midst of this global trend, a unique movement was observed in Africa; in 2013, the African Union (AU) celebrated its 50th anniversary, which includes the years of its predecessor, the Organisation of African

Unity.[2] In commemoration of the event, Agenda 2063 was developed as a long-term vision for the socioeconomic transformation of Africa over the next 50 years. In 2015, when the international community adopted the 2030 Agenda for Sustainable Development, the AU adopted Agenda 2063. The subtitle of Agenda 2063, 'Africa We Want', expresses the desire for a vision of Africa's future that Africans want. Agenda 2063 has 20 goals based on seven aspirations and 15 flagship projects to achieve these goals (Table 4.1). The mid-term goals are to be achieved during the first ten years. In 2020, a progress report on Agenda 2063 was presented by President Ouattara of Côte d'Ivoire. Since then, it is required every two years.

For the education sector, the goal, 'well-educated citizens and skills revolution underpinned by science, technology and innovation', was the second of the 20 goals. The goal entails achieving seven specific targets: increase early childhood education enrolment to at least 300% of the 2013 rate; attain a 100% enrolment rate in basic education; increase the number of qualified STEM teachers by at least 30%; ensure universal access to secondary education to attain a 100% enrolment rate; facilitate tertiary education for at least 30% of secondary school leavers, with a focus on ensuring at least 40% of these are female; provide further skills development options to at least 70% of secondary school graduates not entering tertiary education; and enhance public perception of education quality by at least 70% at all levels (UNECA, 2024). These targets demonstrated that Agenda 2063 emphasises disseminating basic education and developing human resources in science and technology. In 2019, the overall performance of Goal 2 was 24% (AU Development Agency, NEPAD, 2020), and in 2021, it increased to 44% (AU Development Agency, NEPAD, 2022).

The Continental Education Strategy for Africa (CESA) 2016–2025 has also been developed. This strategy is consistent with the 2016–2025 Framework of the AU 2063 Agenda. The mission of CESA 2016–2025 is 'reorienting Africa's education and training systems to meet the knowledge, competencies, skills, innovation, and creativity required to nurture African core values and promote sustainable development at the national, sub-regional and continental levels' (AU, 2017, p. 21). Such a strategy is consistent with the direction of the SDGs, which are common goals of the international community.

---

[2] The AU is one of the largest regional organisations in the world, with 55 African countries and regions as members.

Table 4.1   Seven aspirations, 20 goals, and 15 flagship projects for the 'Africa We Want' set out by Agenda 2063

Seven aspirations

1. A prosperous Africa based on inclusive growth and sustainable development
2. An integrated continent, politically united based on the ideals of Pan-Africanism and the vision of Africa's Renaissance
3. An Africa of good governance, democracy, respect for human rights, justice and the rule of law
4. A peaceful and secure Africa
5. An Africa with a strong cultural identity, common heritage, values and ethics
6. An Africa whose development is people-driven, relying on the potential of African people, especially its women and youth, and caring for children
7. Africa as a strong, united, resilient, and influential global player and partner

Agenda 2063 Goals

Goal 1: A high standard of living, quality of life and well-being for all
Goal 2: Well-educated citizens and skills revolution underpinned by science, technology and innovation
Goal 3: Healthy and well-nourished citizens
Goal 4: Transformed economies and job creation
Goal 5: Modern agriculture for increased productivity and production
Goal 6: Blue/ocean economy for accelerated economic growth
Goal 7: Environmentally sustainable climate resilient economies and communities
Goal 8: United Africa (federal or confederate)
Goal 9: Key continental financial and monetary institutions established and functional
Goal 10: World-class infrastructure criss-crosses Africa
Goal 11: Democratic values, practices, universal principles of human rights, justice, and the rule of law entrenched
Goal 12: Capable institutions and transformed leadership in place at all levels
Goal 13: Peace, security and stability are preserved
Goal 14: A stable and peaceful Africa
Goal 15: A fully functional and operational African peace and security architecture
Goal 16: African cultural renaissance is pre-eminent
Goal 17: Full gender equality in all spheres of life
Goal 18: Engaged and empowered youth and children
Goal 19: Africa as a major partner in global affairs and peaceful co-existence
Goal 20: Africa takes full responsibility for financing her development

Fifteen flagship projects

1. Integrated High-Speed Train Network
2. Formulation of an African Commodities Strategy
3. Establishment of the African Continental Free Trade Area (AfCFTA)
4. The African Passport and Free Movement of People
5. Silencing the Guns by 2020
6. Implementation of the Grand Inga Dam Project
7. Establishment of a Single African Air-Transport Market (SAATM)
8. Establishment of an Annual African Economic Forum
9. Establishment of the African Financial Institutions
10. The Pan-African E-Network
11. Africa Outer Space Strategy
12. An African Virtual and E-University
13. Cyber Security
14. Great African Museum
15. Encyclopedia Africana

Source: Created by the authors based on information from the African Union (2015, 2024); African Union Development Agency, NEPAD (2022)

In this manner, since independence in the 1960s, African countries have focused on educational development for their nation-building. Despite the influence of international socioeconomic conditions, the spread of primary education has increased significantly, enabling many children to attend school. However, some original issues remain, and new issues have emerged; thus, the next section explores both.

2   REMAINING AND NEW CHALLENGES

Children Not Enrolled in School and Low Completion Rates

Although the expansion of primary education has been achieved through the EFA and MDGs, many challenges remain. For example, African countries set specific goals to reduce the proportion of children not enrolled in school by approximately two-thirds and increase the primary education level completion rate from 70% to 85% by 2030 to fulfil the CESA and SDGs (UNESCO, 2022). In other words, the goal is to guarantee educational opportunities for children who still do not have access to education and to increase the percentage of children who not only enrol in school but also complete school. However, in the last school year before the COVID-19 pandemic, 64 million children in primary-age schools worldwide were still not enrolled in school (UNESCO, 2021).[3] Many of these children live in Africa, and one in five children in primary-age school remains not enrolled in school (UNESCO, 2022).

There is wide variation among countries regarding changes in the number of children not enrolled in school. By region, between 2012 and 2020, the number of children not enrolled in school remained flat in Eastern and Southern Africa, increasing by 0.9 million in Central Africa and 1.8 million in Western Africa (UNESCO, 2022). Reducing the number of children not enrolled in school in Africa, which is experiencing rapid population growth, is a major challenge.[4] In many cases, the remaining children not enrolled in school experience complex and difficult challenges such as poverty, malnutrition, disabilities and conflict. Children

---

[3] For secondary school-age adolescents and youth, 63 million adolescents of lower secondary age and 132 million youths of upper secondary age were out of school (UNESCO, 2021).

[4] However, it is important to note that the outcomes differ even among countries experiencing the same population growth. For example, between 2000 and 2020, the number of out-of-school children decreased by 68% in Burundi, stagnated in the Democratic Republic of the Congo, and increased by 38% in Chad (UNESCO, 2022).

with disabilities are at especially high risk of being excluded from education. Until recently, there was no consensus on the definition of disability or its measurement, and its relationship to school attendance and learning achievement was vague (UNESCO, 2020), which is also a problem. Moreover, many children in poor countries under the influence of conflict do not have access to education (Lewin, 2009; Moyi, 2012; UNESCO, 2011). During times of conflict, school facilities and buildings are targeted for destruction, sometimes turned into military bases and the fear of abduction, sexual assault and gunfire dramatically reduces children's motivation to attend school (Sommers, 2002). Notably, girls are the most negatively affected (Moyi, 2012; Sommers, 2002; Shemyakina, 2011). For children experiencing these challenges, the need to improve their surrounding environment is urgent, for example, creating stable livelihoods, avoiding detrimental practices such as child labour, promoting health, building an inclusive and equal society and peacebuilding. Interventions in the education sector alone will have difficulty opening educational opportunities for children in these difficult circumstances; thus, cooperation with other sectors is essential.

Even with the provision of educational opportunities, completing primary education is challenging for children in Sub-Saharan Africa. For example, although the completion rate of primary education from 1970 to 2020 increased from approximately 50% to 70% (Fig. 4.3), only two of three children completed primary education.[5] The low completion rate in Sub-Saharan Africa is readily apparent because, in 2019, completion rates in other regions were approaching or above 90% (UNESCO, 2021). Moreover, in Sub-Saharan Africa, only one in two children in rural areas and one in three children in poor household complete primary education (UNESCO, 2022), a rate substantially lower than that of urban areas and wealthy households. In other words, disparities between regions and between rich and poor remain a serious issue. The SDGs include the elimination of various disparities, such as regional disparities and disparities between rich and poor, and the improvement of completion rates in primary and secondary education. As the 2030 deadline for achieving this goal looms, policies to increase the rate of improvement must be considered.

---

[5] This information is based on the data from the WDI, World Bank (1970–2020).

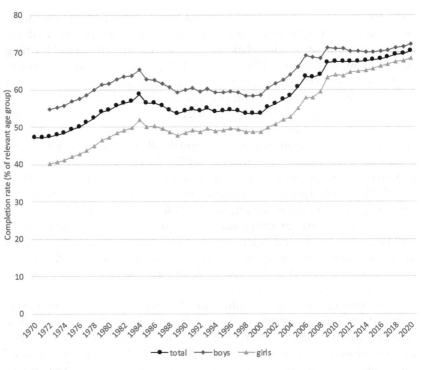

Fig. 4.3 Changes in completion rates for primary education in Sub-Saharan Africa. (Source: Created by the authors based on the data from the WDI, World Bank (1970–2020))

Learning Crisis of Concern

Enrolling in and completing school and the knowledge and skills acquired during schooling are important. However, UNESCO (2017a) estimated that more than 387 million children of primary school age (approximately 6–11 years old) and 230 million adolescents of lower secondary school age (approximately 12–14 years old) worldwide have not mastered the basics of reading and mathematics. Notably, the situation in Sub-Saharan Africa is particularly serious, where 202 million children and adolescents will not be able to master the basics of reading and mathematics (UNESCO, 2017a). The World Bank used the term 'learning crisis' to describe this situation in its 2018 World Development Report, 'Learning to realise education's promise' (World Bank Group, 2018).[6] It also asserted the need to improve learning as an urgent issue for the international community.[7]

What exactly is a learning crisis? For example, Uwenzo Ease Africa (2014), which summarised findings from Kenya, Mainland Tanzania and Uganda, reported that less than one-third of children enrolled in third grade have basic literacy and numeracy skills, and two in ten children enrolled in seventh grade do not have second-grade level literacy and numeracy skills. Additionally, the Programme d'Analyse des Systèmes Éducatifs de la CONFEMEN (PASEC, 2020), a commonly administered achievement test in French-speaking Africa, reported that more than half (52.1%) of all participating countries were below the standard at the end of primary school in reading and more than 60% in mathematics were below the standard. For reading, results were particularly poor in Madagascar, Chad, the Democratic Republic of Congo, Burundi and Niger. For mathematics, results were particularly poor in Chad, Niger, Ivory Coast, the Democratic Republic of Congo and Madagascar.

Essentially, education, at the individual level, develops an individual's potential and subsequently promotes employment, income and health. At the societal level, education is expected to break the cycle of poverty and correct social disparities. Education also contributes to maintaining local communities and promoting a sense of social cohesion and economic growth. However, these benefits can only be achieved if children acquire sufficient knowledge and skills through their studies at school. As such, the World Bank (2018) argued that many of those benefits depend on learning and that schooling without learning is a 'waste of opportunity' and an even greater 'injustice'.

Barriers to Children's Learning

Difficulties for children who enter primary school but cannot acquire academic skills or complete primary education occur mainly due to three

---

[6] Since 1978, the World Bank has published the World Development Report, an annual report that discusses timely themes, analyses issues and makes policy recommendations.

[7] Moreover, in October 2019, to accurately identify the current state of the learning crisis and monitor improvement, the World Bank developed a new indicator: the learning poverty rate, which shows the percentage of children who have not acquired adequate reading skills by age ten. The World Bank then proposed a global goal of 'at least halving the learning poverty rate by 2030'.

factors: a decline in the quality of public schools due to the quantitative expansion of education, the medium of instruction and overage students. The first factor is the decline in the quality of public schools due to the quantitative expansion of education. That is, although various countries' policies have increased the number of children attending school, the construction of schools, development of classrooms and facilities, training of teachers and preparation of teaching materials have not kept pace. Hence, problems such as too few classrooms and facilities, an increased number of students per teacher, overcrowded classes and a shortage of teaching materials have occurred (e.g. Hartwig, 2013). Moreover, the number of unqualified teachers has increased, negatively affecting teaching and learning activities. This shortage of qualified teachers stems from insufficient recruitment practices and inadequate training procedures, particularly in specific areas (Tanaka, 2012). Additionally and unfortunately, many teachers have not acquired the minimum subject knowledge required to teach language and math (Bold et al., 2017); many learning hours are lost due to teacher absenteeism (Bold et al., 2017; Tooley et al., 2011); and problems have been observed regarding principles, including with the selection process and their leadership. These problems often stem from inadequate qualifications, limited management training opportunities and various other barriers hindering effective leadership within educational institutions (Taole, 2013).

The second factor is the medium of instruction. Due to the influence of colonial rule, many African countries continue to use the language of the former colonising nation as their medium of instruction. In Zambia, for example, more than 70 tribes coexist, including Tongan, Nyanja, Bemba and Lunda, each with its own language. However, the official language is English, the language of the former sovereign nation of Great Britain. Specifically, seven local languages, including Bemba, Nyanja and Tongan, are used from first through fourth grade, and starting in fifth grade, the medium of instruction switches to English. Thus, due to the difference between the ethnic language used at home and the language used at school, some children are unable to keep up with their schoolwork and repeat a grade; additionally, some children are anxious to start English classes in the fifth grade and relearn from one grade down instead of staying in the regular grade (Ezaki & Sekiya, 2017). When the author of this chapter observed fifth-grade classes at primary schools in 2019, several times, after providing explanations in English, teachers provided explanations in the local language when they perceived their students did not understand the content. Additionally, the teachers have commented on the negative effects of changing the teaching language in the middle of the primary curriculum.

Uganda has more than 60 ethnic groups, and English, Swahili and Ludanga are the main languages spoken. In schools, the medium of instruction changes from ethnic languages (i.e. local languages) to English in the fourth year. Kabay (2016) surveyed children in 136 primary schools across Uganda and found the highest repetition rates in the fourth grade. She stated that this finding suggested the need to adapt to the increased use of English in the classroom. Additionally, she suggested that the repetition of the third grade may represent the teachers' concern that their students have not mastered the English level required to achieve the forthcoming learning objectives.

Kenya has more than 70 ethnic languages and uses English and Swahili as its official languages. Starting in fourth grade, the medium of instruction is English, as in Uganda. Because English is a global language, many parents in Kenya believe that learning English will expand their children's opportunities for higher education and employment. Parents in Sub-Saharan Africa and other regions have similar sentiments (e.g. James & Woodhead, 2014; Subedi et al., 2013). However, Sheikh et al. (2023) demonstrated that using English as the medium of instruction not only results in the loss of a unique linguistic and cultural identity but also leads to learning delays because children cannot master English as well as their native language and cannot understand concepts related to their subjects.

In many African countries, national standardised exams are administered during the final year of each educational level. Only the students who pass the exam are allowed to advance to the next level of education. Research has shown that the longer the delay in learning due to the medium of instruction, the longer the duration before passing the exam. For example, focusing on students in Zambia who failed the test to progress to secondary education, Ezaki and Sekiya (2017) investigated the cause and found that more than half of those who did not advance to secondary education in seventh grade dropped out of school after failing the national standardised examinations administered at the end of the school year. Although there are economic reasons for children dropping out of school, the researchers discussed 'failing exams' as the direct trigger (see Chap. 14 for details). These problems with teaching language and national standardised exams have been identified in Zambia and other African countries.

The third factor is overage students. As in Zambia, if students have failing scores or grades and repeat a grade level or do not enter school at the official school entrance age and become late entrants, they will enter primary school as overage students. Reasons for late entry vary but include poverty, child labour, health issues and parents' undervaluing education. Studies (UNESCO Institute for Statistics [UIS] & UNICEF, 2005; UNESCO, 2009; Wils, 2004) have shown that children who enter school as overage students are more likely to drop out than children who enter at the official age. UNESCO (2021) data showed that although the percentage of overage students per grade in most regions was ≤9%, the estimated percentage of overage students per grade in Sub-Saharan Africa was 23%.[8] Among these countries, South Sudan and Liberia have by far the highest values, followed by Madagascar, Eswatini, Equator Guinea, Mauritania and Mozambique. Uganda, at 34%, also has a high percentage in Sub-Saharan Africa (UNESCO, 2021), and a study demonstrated that the overage phenomenon is a hidden factor in the country's low primary education completion rate (Weatherholt et al., 2019). Kabay (2016) also found that student age was a strong, statistically significant predictor of dropout, highlighting the importance of school entrance age.

3   RISE OF LOW-FEE PRIVATE SCHOOLS

As the era of EFA and MDGs shifted to the era of SDGs, the focus on education shifted from 'quantity' to 'quality'. Various policies in various countries, including the introduction of free primary education, have achieved substantial results in the quantitative expansion of education. However, with the rapid increase in the number of children in public schools, school management has become extremely difficult (Sect. 2.3). Additionally, many challenges must be overcome to achieve SDG 4, such as the new and existing learning crises.

Under these circumstances, a new type of school emerged: private school. According to UNESCO (2021), the share of private institutions at the primary education level increased from 10% in 2002 to 17% in 2013, and at the secondary education level, from 19% in 2004 to 26% in 2014. The percentage of children enrolled in such private schools is also increasing. Particularly notable is the sharp increase in Sub-Saharan Africa, for

[8] Oceania was the only region outside Sub-Saharan Africa with a double-digit percentage: 16% (UNESCO, 2021).

example, Congo, Gambia and Guinea (UNESCO, 2015), and South Asia, for example, India, Pakistan and Nepal (Dahal & Nguyen, 2014). Among the types of private schools, low-fee private schools (LFPs) have been attracting attention. LFPs are considered affordable even for poor and marginalised individuals. In achieving the goal of EFA, expanding LFPs is expected to decrease the cost and increase the efficiency of the provision of free education in public schools, which are heavily subsidised (Tooley & Dixon, 2007; Tooley et al., 2007).

Another problem is educational disparity between public and private schools. As aforementioned, many African countries have succeeded in quantitatively expanding education, but the quality of public schools is declining owing to the many challenges of the rapidly increasing enrolment. Private schools use English as the medium of instruction, owing to it being an international language, and have low pupil-teacher ratios and students with high performance on the national standardised examinations. For example, Day et al. (2014) conducted a literature review and found moderately strong evidence that private school learners tended to perform better than public school learners. In an individual case study, Kabay (2021), who studied primary education in Uganda, found that private school learners performed better than public school learners. Moreover, Hartwig (2013) surveyed secondary schools in Tanzania and found that the average pass rate in government and private schools was 36% and 82%, respectively. She also found that the average pupil-teacher ratio in government and public schools was 61:1 and 23.5:1, respectively.

Many parents are willing to send their children to private schools to ensure exposure to education conditions superior to those of public schools. For example, Nishimura and Yamano (2013) used panel data and school information from 1712 children aged 6–15 years in rural areas of central and western Kenya to examine issues related to school choice, progression and transfer under the Free Primary Education policy. They reported that the higher the average pupil-teacher ratio in public schools (i.e. the lower the quality of education tended to be), the more likely the parents were to enrol their children in private schools or transfer them to other schools.[9] Zuilkowski et al. (2018) studied primary education in Nairobi and noted that parents choose LFP schools because of the quality

---

[9] The study measures the quality of education by the average pupil-teacher ratio, which is taken to mean that the higher the average pupil-teacher ratio, the lower the quality of education (Nishimura & Yamano, 2013).

of education. Moreover, a strong demand for LFP preschool was identified in urban informal settlements in Zambia. Thus, parents in urban poor households are increasingly viewing their investment in LFP preschools as an important household strategy to transform their children into 'modern' citizens and ultimately out of their stigmatised lifestyles and marginalised social status (Okitsu et al., 2023).

However, despite the emergence of LFPs, studies in countries within and outside the African region have reported that socially vulnerable groups such as girls and poor children tend to be less likely to have access to private schools than groups that are not socially vulnerable (Härmä, 2009, 2011; Nishimura & Yamano, 2013; Woodhead et al., 2013).[10] In areas where public schools are dysfunctional, limited access to the functional conditions in private schools means that children must learn in the current educational conditions and will likely not reach their potential in education. However, private schools built owing to inadequate public education services can exacerbate disparities (UNESCO, 2016). Thus, to improve equity, some arguments support firm measures to regulate private schools (UNESCO, 2017b).

4   RECENT TRENDS AND NEGATIVE IMPACTS OF COVID-19 ON EDUCATION

From 2015 (when the SDGs were adopted) to 2019, various initiatives were undertaken in each country, but no fundamental SDG reforms were issued. Therefore, in 2020, a decade before the targeted achievement of the SDGs, the United Nations launched a 'Decade of Action' involving governments, civil society, businesses and individuals. The Decade of Action calls for the accelerated implementation of sustainable solutions to all of the world's most critical issues, including poverty, gender inequality, climate change and lack of finance, broadening its prior scope. The specific goals are threefold: involve everyone, everywhere, to ensure that no one is left behind; take immediate and bold action by holding leaders accountable and showcasing achievable outcomes; and promote new ideas and solutions by promoting innovation, investment and technology while empowering youth leadership in our communities and cities (Biggeri, 2021). However, just as the international community was reaffirming its

---

[10] For gender, however, the results are debatable, with some reports indicating that girls are not less likely than boys to have access to private schools (e.g. Srivastava, 2006).

commitment to accelerate its efforts to achieve the SDGs on the basis of the declaration of the Decade of Action, the outbreak of COVID-19 and the war in Ukraine occurred.

The COVID-19 pandemic has threatened individuals' lives, livelihoods and dignity of people worldwide, especially those in vulnerable situations, such as those earning low incomes. These effects also set back progress on the SDGs, which had been advancing. The impact of this change was observed in the education sector as well. According to UNESCO (2022), in Africa, from March 2020 to October 2021, on average, schools were completely closed and partially closed for 25% and 18% of the scheduled school days. For example, for 95% and 94% of the scheduled school days in Uganda (68% completely closed) and Ghana (15% completely closed), schools were closed, severely disrupting children's access to education. Comoros, Eswatini, Mozambique, Rwanda, South Sudan and Zimbabwe had the second longest complete school closures after Uganda, at approximately 40% (UNESCO, 2022). The inability to attend school leads to poor academic performance, psychological distress and reduced development of social skills.

In this difficult situation, AU member states enacted policies and implemented programmes to increase enrolment at various levels of education, for instance, universal primary and secondary school education programmes, increased budget allocations to the education sector, the establishment of teacher councils, the recruitment of qualified educators, the implementation of strategic activities and the introduction of affirmative action programmes (AU Development Agency, NEPAD, 2022). These efforts are insufficient to realise the goals in Agenda 2063, but some countries have shown improving trends. Notably, unforeseen setbacks have occurred due to phenomena such as climate change and natural disasters. Thus, for the guarantee of education, implementing the necessary social security systems and policies is crucial to protect the rights of vulnerable children and empower them to break the cycle of poverty.

5 CONCLUSION

This chapter offers a comprehensive exploration of the educational development history in Africa, focusing on the period after the independence of many countries in the 1960s. Drawing primarily from cross-sectional data, it delves into the manifold challenges experienced and strides made. The narrative spans the rise of low-fee private schools, which have been garnering increasing attention, and discusses the profound impact of the COVID-19 pandemic on educational landscapes. The findings underscore a notable improvement in children's access to education over the past five decades. However, entrenched challenges persist, including a decline in the quality of public education, manifesting in a learning crisis. Additionally, problems such as language barriers, overage enrolment and persistent inequalities persistently impede progress. The emergence of the COVID-19 pandemic in 2020 exacerbated these challenges, particularly in nations where access to education was severely disrupted, necessitating swift and adaptive responses from educators and policymakers.

The Executive Secretary of the United Nations Economic Commission for Africa (UNECA) highlighted that despite the negative impact of COVID-19, it has also presented significant opportunities, particularly in the realms of innovation and tourism. Moreover, Africa stands poised for substantial growth and job creation, with its youth population playing a pivotal role (UNECA, 2021). With Africa boasting the youngest median age globally, at 20 years (He et al., 2020), there is a pressing imperative to enhance the educational landscape and deliver quality education. This investment is essential to empower Africa's youth, who represent the future leaders of the continent, equipping them with the requisite knowledge and skills to contribute meaningfully to society. Addressing the challenges of the SDG era and transitioning effectively to the post-SDG landscape hinge upon this critical foundation of education.

REFERENCES

African Union. (2015). *Agenda 2063: The Africa we want.* The African Union Commission.

African Union. (2017). *Continental Education Strategy for Africa 2016–2025.* African Union.

African Union. (2024). *Flagship project of agenda 2063.* African Union. Retrieved April 30, 2024, from https://au.int/en/agenda2063/flagship-projects

African Union Development Agency, NEPAD. (2020). *Agenda 2063: First Continental Report on the Implementation of Agenda 2063.* African Union Development Agency, NEPAD.

African Union Development Agency, NEPAD. (2022). *Agenda 2063: Second Continental Report on the Implementation of Agenda 2063.* African Union Development Agency, NEPAD.

Biggeri, M. (2021). Editorial: A "Decade for Action" on SDG localisation. *Journal of Human Development and Capabilities, 22*(4), 706–712.

Bold, T., Filmer, D., Martin, G., Molina, E., Stacy, B., Rockmore, C., Svensson, J., & Wane, W. (2017). Enrollment without learning: Teacher effort, knowledge, and skill in primary schools in Africa. *Journal of Economic Perspectives, 31*(4), 185–204.

Dahal, M., & Nguyen, Q. (2014). *Private non-state sector engagement in the provision of educational services at the primary and secondary levels in South Asia: An analytical review of its role in school enrollment and student achievement* (Policy Research Working Paper No. 6899). World Bank South Asia Region Education Unit.

Day-Ashley, L., Mcloughlin, C., Aslam, M., Engel, J., Wales, J., Rawal, S., Batley, R., Kingdon, G., Nicolai, S., & Rose, P. (2014) *The role and impact of private schools in developing countries: a rigorous review of the evidence.* Final report. Education Rigorous Literature Review. Department for International Development.

Ezaki, N., & Sekiya, T. (2017). Study on individual children's enrollment patterns in the Republic of Zambia: Focusing on children who cannot move on to secondary education. *Kwansei Gakuin University Social Science Review, 22*, 19–31.

Härmä, J. (2009). Can choice promote education for all? Evidence from growth in private primary schooling in India. *Compare: A Journal of Comparative and International Education, 39*(2), 151–165.

Härmä, J. (2011). Low cost private schooling in India: Is it pro poor and equitable? *International Journal of Education Development, 31*(4), 350–356.

Hartwig, K. A. (2013). Using a social justice framework to assess educational quality in Tanzanian schools. *International Journal of Educational Development, 33*(5), 487–496.

He, W., Aboderin, I., & Adjaye-Gbewonyo, D. (2020). *Africa Aging: 2020,* U.S. Census Bureau, International population reports. Washington, DC: U.S. Census Bureau.

James, Z., & Woodhead, M. (2014). Choosing and changing schools in India's private and government sectors: Young lives evidence from Andhra Pradesh. *Oxford Review of Education, 40*(1), 73–90. https://doi.org/10.1080/03054985.2013.873527

Kabay, S. (2016). Grade repetition and primary school dropout in Uganda. *Harvard Educational Review, 86*(4), 580–606.

Kabay, S. (2021). *Access, quality, and the global learning crisis: Insights from Ugandan primary education.* Oxford University Press.

Lewin, K. M. (2009). Access to education in sub-Saharan Africa: Patterns, problems and possibilities. *Comparative Education, 45*(2), 151–174.

Moyi, P. (2012). Who goes to school? School enrollment patterns in Somalia. *International Journal of Educational Development, 32*(1), 163–171.

Nishimura, M., & Yamano, T. (2013). Emerging private education in Africa: Determinants of school choice in rural Kenya. *World Development, 43*, 266–275.

Okitsu, T., Edwards, D. B., Mwanza, P., & Miller, S. (2023). Low-fee private preschools as the symbol of imagined 'modernity'?: Parental perspectives on early childhood care and education (ECCE) in an urban informal settlement in Zambia. *International Journal of Educational Development, 97.* https://doi.org/10.1016/j.ijedudev.2022.102723

Programme d'analyse des systèmes éducatifs de la Confemen (PASEC). (2020). *PASEC 2019: Quality of education systems in French-speaking Sub-Saharan Africa: Teaching/learning performance and environment in primary education, executive summary.* Programme for the Analysis of Education Systems of CONFEMEN.

Sheikh, F., Rich, M., & Galvão, W. (2023). Language of instruction and education policies in Kenya. *Reconsidering Development, 7*(1) https://pubs.lib.umn.edu/index.php/reconsidering/article/view/4569

Shemyakina, O. (2011). The effect of armed conflict on accumulation of schooling: Results from Tajikistan. *Journal of Development Economics, 95,* 186–200.

Sommers, M. (2002). *Children, education and war: Reaching the Education for All (EFA) objectives in countries effected by war* (World Bank Working Papers No. 24789). : World Bank.

Srivastava, P. (2006). Private schooling and mental models about girls' schooling in India. *Compare, 36*(4), 497–514.

Subedi, G., M. G. Shrestha, R. Maharjan, & M. Suvedi. (2013). *Dimensions and implications of privatization of education in Nepal: The case of primary and secondary schools.* (Education Support Program (ESP) Working Paper Series), 48: 1–78.

Tanaka, C. (2012). Profile and status of untrained teachers: Experiences in basic schools in rural Ghana. *Compare: A Journal of Comparative and International Education, 42*(3), 415–438. https://doi.org/10.1080/03057925.2011.634540

Taole, M. J. (2013). Exploring principals' role in providing instructional leadership in rural high schools in South Africa. *Studies of Tribes and Tribals, 11*(1), 75–82. https://doi.org/10.1080/0972639X.2013.11886668

Tooley, J., Bao, Y., Dixon, P., & Merrifield, J. (2011). School Choice and academic performance: some evidence from developing countries. *Journal of School Choice, 5*(1), 1–39.

Tooley, J., & Dixon, P. (2007). Private schooling for low-income families: A census and comparative study in East Delhi. *International Journal of Educational Development, 27*(2), 205–219.

Tooley, J., Dixon, P., & Gomathi, S. V. (2007). Private school and the millennium development goals of universal primary education: A census and comparative survey in Hyderabad. *India, Oxford Review of Education, 33*(5), 539–560.

UNESCO Institute for Statistics (UIS) & UNICEF. (2005). *Children out of school: Measuring exclusion from primary education.* UNESCO UIS.

United Nations. (2015). *The Millennium Development Goals Report 2015.* United Nations.

United Nations Economic Commission for Africa (UNECA). (2024). *Agenda 2063: Overview.* Integrated planning and reporting toolkit. Retrieved May 30, 2024, from https://iprt.uneca.org/agenda/agenda2063/overview/19

United Nations Economic Commission for Africa (UNECA). (2021, December 23). *Africa's youth renew commitment to the SDGs.* Africa Renewal. Retrieved April 30, 2024, from https://www.un.org/africarenewal/magazine/january-2022/africa%E2%80%99s-youth-renew-commitment-sdgs

United Nations Educational, Scientific and Cultural Organization (UNESCO). (2016). *Global education monitoring report 2016—Place: Inclusive and sustainable cities.* : UNESCO.

United Nations Educational, Scientific and Cultural Organization (UNESCO). (2009). *EFA Monitoring Report 2009—Overcoming inequality: Why governance matters. Regional Overview: Latin America and the Caribbean.* UNESCO.

United Nations Educational, Scientific and Cultural Organization (UNESCO). (2011). *EFA global monitoring report 2011—The hidden crisis: Armed conflict and education.* UNESCO.

United Nations Educational, Scientific and Cultural Organization (UNESCO). (2015). *EFA Global Monitoring Report: EDUCATION FOR ALL 2000–2015.* UNESCO.

United Nations Educational, Scientific and Cultural Organization (UNESCO). (2017a). *More than one-half of children and adolescents are not learning worldwide* (Fact sheet No. 46). UNESCO.

United Nations Educational, Scientific and Cultural Organization (UNESCO). (2017b). *Global education monitoring report 2017—Accountability in education: Meeting our commitments.* UNESCO.

United Nations Educational, Scientific and Cultural Organization (UNESCO). (2020). *Global education monitoring report 2020—Inclusion and education: All means all.* UNESCO.

United Nations Educational, Scientific and Cultural Organization (UNESCO). (2021). *Global Education Monitoring Report 2021/2—Non-state actors in education: Who chooses? Who loses?* UNESCO.

United Nations Educational, Scientific and Cultural Organization (UNESCO). (2022). *Spotlight on basic education completion and foundational learning in Africa: Born to learn.* UNESCO.

Uwenzo Ease Africa. (2014). *Are Our Children Learning?: Literacy and numeracy across East Africa 2013.* Uwenzo East Africa.

Weatherholt, T., Jordan, R., Crouch, L., Barnett, E., & Pressley, J. (2019). Challenge and drivers of over-enrollment in the early years of primary school in Uganda. *International Journal of Early Childhood, 51*(23), 23–40.

Wils, A. (2004). Late entrants leave school earlier: Evidence from Mozambique. *International Review of Education, 50*(4), 17–37. https://doi.org/10.1023/b:revi.0000018201.53675.4b

Woodhead, M., Frost, M., & James, Z. (2013). Does growth in private schooling contribute to education for all? Evidence from a longitude, two cohort study in Andhra Pradesh, India. *International Journal of Educational Development, 33*(1), 65–73.

World Bank. (2024). World development indicators. Retrieved April 30, 2024, from https://databank.worldbank.org/source/world-development-indicators

World Bank Group. (2018). *World development report 2018: Learning to realize education's promise*. World Bank Group.

Zuilkowski, S. S., Piper, B., Ong'ele, S., & Kiminza, O. (2018). Parents, quality, and school choice: why parents in Nairobi choose low-cost private schools over public schools in Kenya's free primary education era. *Oxford Review of Education, 44*(2), 258–274. https://doi.org/10.1080/03054985.2017.1391084

PART II

Country Case Studies: Findings from Enrolment Pattern Analysis

Who Has Still Been Left Behind? A Comparative Analysis of Children's Enrolment Patterns in Different Geographical Areas of Honduras

Akemi Ashida ⓘ *and Takeshi Sekiya*

1   INTRODUCTION[1]

Challenges in the Latin American Region: Regional Disparities within Countries

The Sustainable Development Goals (SDGs) represent a set of common objectives for all nations to achieve by 2030. In the area of education, the focus has shifted from access to the issues of quality, equity and learning. Indeed, the international community has committed to ensuring that all

---

[1] This chapter was prepared with major augmentations and modifications, including updated analytical data of Ashida, A. (2021). Comparative analysis of schooling situations

---

A. Ashida (✉)
Graduate School of International Development, Nagoya University, Nagoya, Japan
e-mail: ashida@gsid.nagoya-u.ac.jp

© The Author(s), under exclusive license to Springer Nature Switzerland AG 2024
T. Sekiya et al. (eds.), *Towards Ensuring Inclusive and Equitable Quality Education for All*, International and Development Education, https://doi.org/10.1007/978-3-031-70266-2_5

69

girls and boys have access to free, equitable and quality education. In pursuit of the promise to 'leave no one behind', various activities to achieve SDG4 ('Quality Education') are being implemented at the global, regional and national levels. In particular, Latin American and Caribbean countries have conspicuously improved access to primary education and completion rates over the past two decades, but inequalities between countries persist (UNESCO, 2020). Inequalities have also been observed among regions within a country. For example, the primary school completion rate for Honduras in 2018 was 91.0% in urban areas but 82.8% in rural areas, compared to 60.2% and 58.6%, respectively, in 2000, indicating significant improvement, especially in rural areas. However, equality between regions has not yet been achieved. In addition, regarding the transition from primary education to secondary education, the gross enrolment rate for 2019 was 66.4% (62.5% of boys and 70.2% of girls) and the net enrolment rate was 45.9% (40.4% of boys and 51.5% of girls) (UNESCO UIS, 2020). This highlights the challenge for Honduras of promoting a transition from primary to secondary school in pursuit of SDG4.

In this context, the COVID-19 pandemic led to school closures and disrupted learning opportunities worldwide. The school closures lasted for more than 16 months in Latin America, particularly in Honduras, where face-to-face lessons were cancelled for 81 weeks (UNESCO, 2022). During that time, teaching in Honduras took the form of virtual classes and workbook distribution, as well as online lectures and videos. However, not all students were able to benefit in a country where the per capita internet usage rate was 31.7% (World Bank, 2021). Children from economically disadvantaged families, particularly in rural areas, have often been deprived of learning opportunities, as they are frequently unable to attend such distance classes.

Much attention has focused on how this worldwide loss of learning opportunities will manifest itself in the future. For example, international organisations have conducted a simulation measuring children's learning

using longitudinal data: Improving enrollment patterns of individual children in Honduras. *International Journal of Comparative Education and Development*, 23(4), 261–279. https://doi.org/10.1108/IJCED-03-2021-0026

T. Sekiya
Graduate School of International Studies, Kwansei Gakuin University, Nishinomiya, Japan
e-mail: tsekiya@kwansei.ac.jp

loss (World Bank et al., 2022). They report a significant decline in basic academic skills. In particular, younger students, students from lower-income groups and girls have been significantly affected by the loss of learning opportunities. In addition, as mentioned above, the availability of access to online and distance learning within Honduras during the COVID-19 pandemic was largely dependent on the region of residence, which raises concerns that regional differences may become increasingly widespread in the future.

The Republic of Honduras: An Overview

This chapter examines the case of Honduras, which is located in Central America and borders Guatemala, El Salvador and Nicaragua. With an area of 112,490 km², it faces both the Caribbean Sea and the Pacific Ocean. Honduras has a population of 10.43 million, 91% of whom are of mixed European and Indigenous descent (*mestizo*), while 6% are of Indigenous descent and 2% are of African and 1% of European descent. The capital is Tegucigalpa; Spanish is the official language; and the main religion is Catholicism, with freedom of religion constitutionally guaranteed. Coffee, bananas and farmed shrimp are the main industries. Honduras had a GDP per capita of USD 3040 in 2022, a GDP growth rate of 4.0% and an unemployment rate of 6.8% in 2023 (Japan's Ministry of Foreign Affairs, 2024; World Bank, 2022). The country has a Human Development Index score of 0.624 and is ranked 138th out of 193 countries, placing it in the medium range (United Nations Development Programme, 2024).

Honduras is one of the major recipient countries of international aid. In particular, in the field of education, one of the technical cooperation projects of the Japanese International Co-operation Organisation (JICA) is the 'Proyecto de Mejoramiento de la Enseñanza Técnica en el Area de Matemática' (PROMETAM), an eight-year project for improving math teaching skills that was launched in 2003 in collaboration with the Honduran Ministry of Education. The project developed national mathematics textbooks and their instructional manuals, a students' workbook and teacher training programmes. Other donors greatly admired the clarity of the research, the logical project-planning process and the high quality of the deliverables. At the time, aid coordination was being actively promoted and with the financial participation of other donors, the impact of the project spread nationwide, as it expanded to four other Central American countries (Kitamura & Ashida, 2023). In addition to JICA, other bilateral development donors have provided assistance to the education sector in Honduras. These include the Spanish Agency for International Development (Agencia Española de Cooperación Internacional para el Desarrollo: AECID) and the United States Agency for International Development (USAID), both in the fields of formal and non-formal education.

Long-standing Educational Issues in Honduras: Grade Repetition and Dropping Out of School

The expansion of primary education in Honduras is underway, with international organisations providing active assistance to the education sector. However, one of the remaining challenges in the early 2000s was the low completion rate as students dropped out of school after enrolment. A report by the Honduran Ministry of Education identified factors such as age of entry, lack of pre-school education, child absenteeism, grade repetition, dropout, incomplete schools and teacher quality and management as impediments to completing primary education (Secretaría de Educación, 2002b).

As part of a USAID-funded research project on the causes of grade repetition and dropout, McGinn et al. (1992) used cross-sectional data to examine factors affecting grade repetition. They concluded that low academic achievement was the main cause of grade repetition, that most children who dropped out of school had experienced at least one repeating year and that dropping out of school was a result of repeating a grade. Similarly, Alexander et al. (1994) found that grade repetition tended to increase dropout rates and Marshall (2003) noted that grade repetition was a predictor of failure. Barnes (1999) conducted a literature review of the causes of dropout in Latin America and concluded that grade repetition was a root cause of school leaving.

Considering the issue of school dropout in Honduras, it is necessary to distinguish between two categories: (1) to stop going to school in the middle of the school year ('temporary dropout') and (2) to leave schooling completely ('total dropout'). The Honduran Ministry of Education explains that abandonment of schooling in the middle of the school year leads to total dropout (Secretaría de Educación, 2002a). Thus, many studies of Latin America have assumed that children drop out of school and fail to graduate because of frequent grade repetition.

Ashida and Sekiya (2016) analysed the actual context of the school dropout phenomenon based on the true cohort method, focusing on the relationship between repeating a grade and dropping out. Their results indicated that although the category of 'dropout children' included many grade repeaters, many children suddenly dropped out without repeating a grade. Furthermore, the most common cases of school dropout by year of completion did not include students who repeated a grade in any year of school. In other words, when one examines the longitudinal data, which is suitable for observing the causal relationship between grade repetition and dropout, cases of school dropout without repeating a grade fall into a number of patterns.

With that said, the following are the results of data analysis for the regional city in Honduras. As mentioned above, primary school completion rates continue to differ between urban and rural areas in Honduras. It is, therefore, desirable, when considering future national education policy, to examine not only examples from the regional city but also those from various regions of the country with different socio-economic characteristics.

The Objective of This Chapter

Sekiya (2014) and Ashida (2018) have conducted studies using school records from the target schools in the regional city, focusing on the actual enrolment situations of children in the target schools. These studies have analysed such phenomena as graduation, grade repetition and dropout by investigating student enrolment patterns and both elucidated the realities and examined the backgrounds of these phenomena. In this study, 'enrolment' refers to a student's involvement with the school system, including the grade at which the student registered, passing or failing at the end of the school year, repetition of a grade level, dropping out, graduation and transfer to another school. Here, 'entrance' means a student's first admission to school. Further, 'enrolment pattern' refers to a student's specific schooling situation and describes the process, including the passing and failing of students, from entrance to graduation or dropout (Ashida, 2021).

For this study, we collected data on the student enrolment situations in three regions of Honduras by examining different socio-economic and geographic characteristics. They conducted analyses of both the regional city (Ashida & Sekiya, 2016; Ashida, 2018) and the insular zone (Ashida, 2017) and a comparative analysis of a regional city and the capital (Ashida,

2021). Based on these studies, this chapter attempts to provide a more comprehensive discussion focusing on the different enrolment situations of children in the three regions. Specifically, in addition to the different socio-economic and geographical characteristics of the capital, regional city and insular zone, the enrolment is classified according to different years of school entrance for comparison purposes. We attempt a further discussion based on the results of this comparison between regions and groups of school entrance years. Honduras has achieved universal primary education, thanks to the UN's Education for All initiative and completion rates have improved in recent years. As priorities have shifted from access to quality in education, this study looks at the process by which children gain access to education and then either graduate or drop out of school. We examine how improvements in enrolment have helped achieve today's universal primary education, considering circumstances specific to regional and school entrance years.

2   RESEARCH METHODOLOGY

Analytical Framework

This study uses longitudinal data, not cross-sectional data, of the kind that is often collected and crunched by governments and international agencies. Longitudinal data are appropriate to observe whether changes have occurred and when. Therefore, educational evaluation research typically employs longitudinal data (Ma, 2010). Statistical techniques for analysing longitudinal data, such as the multilevel growth model, survival model and cross-lagged model, are generally used. However, as Goos et al. (2013) noted, the outlier that does not belong to the majority would be removed from the statistical analysis. It is not a matter of seeing a rough trend of observed variables; however, individual students using the micro perspective this study focuses on might be statistical outliers and we might not be able to observe their situations.

Therefore, this study applies a true cohort analysis that observes the same target and traces it repeatedly over time (UNESCO, 1970). Applying a true cohort analysis based on longitudinal data entails many data collection requirements. A well-reported school record is necessary to trace the progress of students from grade to grade in past years (Gropello, 2003). Sekiya (2014) confirmed the school records at various school levels in the target areas and developed a longitudinal database by tracking each child's progress based on school records. He revealed that the enrolment situation of individual students was not covered by the mean value. Following Sekiya (2014), this study applies a true cohort analysis and clarifies individual student enrolment situations and changes over time in different geographical and socio-economic areas.

Target and Data Collection

To identify gaps in individual children's enrolment situations in different areas, we selected the capital, a regional city and the insular zone of Honduras, each of which is located in a different geographical area with particular socio-economic features. Following Sekiya (2014), we selected a mid-sized regional city in the Department of El Paraíso that is representative of the general population according to social and education indices (United Nations Development Programme, 1998). Applying the true cohort method, we collected longitudinal data on students from year-end academic evaluation results that covered the period from their entrance to their school leaving, as a result of either graduating or dropping out.

We surveyed 4390 students who were enrolled at eight different primary schools in Honduras between 1986[2] and 2004. We developed a database consisting of data from 1658 students from one school (a single-grade classroom) in the capital city, Tegucigalpa; 2358 students from six schools (single-grade classrooms at two schools and multi-grade classrooms at four schools) in a mid-sized regional city, hereinafter referred to as 'regional city A'; and 132 students from one school (multi-grade classroom) in an insular zone. Semi-structured interviews were conducted with schoolteachers to verify the consistency of data and the situations of students after leaving school. Several former students and their families, local residents and other relevant individuals were also deemed necessary and therefore interviewed. According to Sekiya and Ashida (2017), registered students face the possibility of returning to the target schools with a temporary dropout or transferring to another school and advancing to graduation or total dropout from the target schools. Therefore, this study tracked all registered students for at least ten years of school records by confirming their graduation or dropout status from school completely.

[2] Due to the availability of school records, the data in an insular zone will be from the 1987 school entrance.

Analysis Procedure

Instead of comparing the schooling situations of children according to the last grade passed, our analysis involved textually describing the grade-by-grade enrolment situation of each student from their entrance in school up until the last grade attended, including whether students passed, failed, repeated or dropped out. These data were then summarised as a pattern. By tracking students' schooling situations and trajectories in the target school, it was possible to observe how students could reach the final grade, including through passing and failure. This process cannot be observed from cross-sectional data (Ashida, 2021).

We divided students into two groups according to school entrance years. According to the UNESCO Institute for Statistics (2020), the grade repetition rate of students completing their first year of primary school in Honduras has fluctuated in recent decades. It was 23% in 1993 before decreasing to 19% in 1994. By 2008, it had decreased further to 8.7%. Honduras introduced automatic grade promotion in 2009 based on academic achievements by the third quarter as a provisional measure to offset the negative impact of temporary school closures and a shorter academic year due to the military coup (Altschuler, 2010).

Students who entered school in 2004 could reach the sixth grade in 2009 if they passed each grade without grade repetition. In other words, they might receive the effect of automatic promotion in the final evaluation of the last grade; however, the repetition rate of Grade 6 improved to 0.3% in 2008. Consequently, the effect of automatic promotion was small for those students who continued their schooling until Grade 6. Therefore, those students who entered in 2004 were included in the analysis. In addition, a previous analysis that targeted a regional city found that the enrolment performance of students who entered in 1994 was not superior to that of other entrance years. This was due to the influence of school attributes and bad weather (Ashida, 2018).

To control for the effect of political, school and natural environment issues, we set 2004 as the maximum target entrance year and divided students into two cohorts. Group 1 consists of those who entered school between 1986 and 1994 and Group 2 consists of those who entered school between 1995 and 2004. With a focus on grade repetition, students' actual schooling situations were examined as patterns and analysed according to three dimensions: (1) an overview of graduates and dropouts and age of entrance, (2) enrolment patterns and (3) dropout patterns.

3 RESULTS

Overview of Graduates, Dropouts and the Age of Entrance by Geographical Region and Year of Entrance

Table 5.1 shows an overview of the graduates and dropouts (total: 4390 students) in the target schools by geographical region and year of entrance. In regional city A, the percentage of graduates among students who entered primary school from 1995 to 2004 (Group 2) increased by 17.8% compared to the percentage of graduates among students who entered school between 1986 and 1994 (Group 1). A less dramatic improvement of 6.1% was observed in the capital city when the same equivalent two groups were compared. However, the insular zone appears to have deteriorated, with enrolments increasing, while the number of graduates has not increased markedly.

Next, to assess the age of entrance to the target schools, we prepared Figure 5.1 to display the distribution of entrance age by region (χ^2 = 539.314, df = 30, $P < 0.01$). In Group 1, for students in regional city A, initial registration occurred at the ages of 5 (0.4%), 6 (41.8%), 7 (37.7%), 8 (11.1%), 9 (4.2%), 10 (2.5%), 11 (1.2%), 12 (0.5%), 13 (0.4%), 14 (0.1%) or 15 (0.1%). The distribution ranged from 5 to 15 years. In the

Table 5.1 Overview of graduates and dropouts at target schools

	Group 1 (1986–1994)		Group 2 (1995–2004)		Changes
	Number of students	*%*	*Number of students*	*%*	
Regional city A					
Graduation	648	53.9	847	71.7	17.8%
Dropout	555	46.1	335	28.3	
Total	1203		1182		
Capital					
Graduation	527	67.8	651	73.9	6.1%
Dropout	250	32.2	230	26.1	
Total	777		881		
Insular zone					
Graduation	19	47.5	23	25.0	(22.5%)
Dropout	21	52.5	69	75.0	
Total	40		92		

Source: The table for regional city A and capital was revised for this paper based on Ashida (2021)

Note: Due to the availability of school records, the data in an insular zone shall be from the 1987 entrance in Group 1

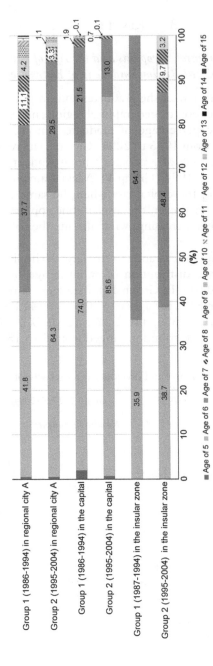

Fig. 5.1 Age of entrance by groups and regions. (Source: The figure was revised and developed for this chapter based on Ashida [2021]. Note: The statistical analysis was applied to the data from the capital and regional city A, except the value from the insular zone)

capital, students initially registered at the ages of 5 (1.9%), 6 (75.0%), 7 (21.5%), 8 (1.9%), 9 (0.1%), 10 (0.3%) or 11 (0.3%). The distribution range from 5 to 11 years was smaller than that of regional city A.

In Group 2, for students in regional city A, initial registration occurred at the ages of 5 (0.4%), 6 (64.3%), 7 (29.5%), 8 (3.3%), 9 (1.1%), 10 (0.8%), 11 (0.3%) or 12 (0.3%). The distribution ranged from 5 to 12 years. In the capital, students first registered at the ages of five (0.6%), six (85.6%), seven (13.0%), eight (0.7%) or nine (0.1%). The distribution from five to nine years was smaller than that of Group 1 in the capital. In Group 2, 98.6% of students in the capital entered the target school at the official entrance age of six or seven (one year late).

In the insular zone, data on the age of entrance are limited due to the availability of school records. Therefore, the same statistical analysis was not conducted as for the data from the capital and regional city A. Entrance ages for those students whom we were able to identify as having entered school between 1986 and 1994 (Group 1, 31 students) were six (38.7%), seven (48.4%), eight (9.7%) and nine (3.2%). Of the students who entered school between 1995 and 2004 (Group 2, 64 students), we observed a convergence around the ages of six (35.9%) and seven (64.1%). In all three regions, most students entered school either at the official school enrolment age of six or one year later, at age seven, indicating that the age of entry was becoming adequate.

Changes of Common Enrolment Patterns in the Three Regions

We formulated enrolment patterns describing students' records of passing or failing from entrance to graduation or dropout based on the students' enrolment situations at the respective target schools. Each pattern consists of numbers indicating grades attended and letters indicating the results of academic evaluation in the grade preceding each letter, with P for passing, R for repetition and D for dropout. All identified patterns were arranged in descending order according to the number of students who fit each pattern (frequency of occurrence). Tables 5.2 and 5.3 show the most common patterns by geographical region and group.

In Group 1, for students in regional city A (Table 5.2), a total of 291 enrolment patterns were identified. For these students, 15 patterns described 10 or more students each and 213 patterns described only one student each. The most frequently occurring enrolment pattern was completing Grade 6 in six years (1P2P3P4P5P6P). The second most frequent

Table 5.2 Frequency of enrolment patterns by region (Group 1)

Group 1 (1986–1994)

	Regional city A					Capital					Insular zone			
Rank	Enrolment patterns	Number of students (%)	Years registered	Last grade passed	Rank	Enrolment patterns	Number of students (%)	Years registered	Last grade passed	Rank	Enrolment patterns	Number of students (%)	Years registered	Last grade passed
1	1P2P3P4P5P6P	352 (29.1)	6	6	1	1P2P3P4P5P6P	359 (46.2)	6	6	1	1P	8 (20.0)	1	1
2	1D	110 (9.1)	1	0	2	1P	63 (8.1)	1	1	2	1P2P	3 (7.5)	2	2
3	**1R**1P2P3P4P5P6P	79 (6.5)	7	6	3	1P2P	35 (4.5)	2	2	2	1P2P3P4P5P6P	3 (7.5)	6	6
4	1P2D	47 (3.9)	2	1	4	**1R**1P2P3P4P5P6P	25 (3.2)	7	6	2	**1R**1P	3 (7.5)	2	1
5	**1R**1D	42 (3.5)	2	0	5	**1R**	22 (2.8)	1	1	5	1P2P3P4P5P6P	2 (5.0)	7	6
6	1P**2R**2P3P4P5P6P	27 (2.2)	7	6	6	1P2P3P	17 (2.2)	3	3	5	1P**2R**2P3P4P5P6P	2 (5.0)	7	6
7	1P2P3D	24 (2.0)	3	2	6	1P2P**3R**3P4P5P6P	17 (2.2)	7	6	5	**1R**	2 (5.0)	1	0
8	1P2P**3R**3P4P5P6P	23 (1.9)	7	6	8	1P2P3P4P	16 (2.1)	4	4	8	1P1P1P2P3P4P5P6P	1 (2.5)	8	6
9	1P2P3P**4R**4P5P6P	20 (1.7)	7	6	9	1P**2R**2P3P4P5P6P	14 (1.8)	7	6	8	1P1P2P3P4P5**R**5P6P	1 (2.5)	8	6
10	1P2P3P4D	16	4	3	10	1S2P3P4P5P6P	13 (1.7)	6	6	8	1P1P**2R**2P3P4P5P6P	1 (2.5)	8	6

No. of patterns with 10 or more students: 15 patterns
No. of patterns with only 1 student: 213 patterns
Total 291 patterns, 1203 students

No. of patterns with 10 or more students: 11 patterns
No. of patterns with only 1 student: 86 patterns
Total 116 patterns, 777 students

No. of patterns with 10 or more students: 0 patterns
No. of patterns with only 1 student: 17 patterns
Total 24 patterns, 40 students

Note: The letter 'P' means that the student passed the grade; the letter 'R' means that the student failed the grade (required to repeat it); and the letter 'D' means that the student dropped out

Source: The table was revised for this paper based on Ashida (2017) and Ashida (2021)

Table 5.3 Frequency of enrolment patterns by region (Group 2)

Group 2 (1995–2004)

Regional city A

Rank	Enrolment patterns	Number of students (%)	Years registered	Last grade passed
1	1P2P3P4P5P6P	526 (44.4)	6	6
2	**1R**1P2P3P4P5P6P	93 (7.8)	7	6
3	1D	37 (3.1)	1	0
4	1P2P**3R**3P4P5P6P	28 (2.4)	7	6
5	1P**2R**2P3P4P5P6P	24 (2.0)	7	6
6	1P2P3P4P5P	14 (1.2)	5	5
7	1P2P3P4P	13 (1.1)	4	4
8	1P2P	12 (1.0)	2	2
8	1P2P3P4P**5R**5P6P	12 (1.0)	7	6
8	**1R**	12 (1.0)	1	0
8	**1R**1D	12 (1.0)	2	1

No. of patterns with 10 or more students: 13 patterns
No. of patterns with only 1 student: 197 patterns
Total 237 patterns, 1182 students

Capital

Rank	Enrolment patterns	Number of students (%)	Years registered	Last grade passed
1	1P2P3P4P5P6P	492 (55.6)	6	6
2	1P	55 (6.2)	1	1
3	1P2P	38 (4.3)	2	2
4	1P2P3P	37 (4.2)	3	3
5	1P2P3P4P	22 (2.5)	4	4
6	1P2P3P4P5P	18 (2.0)	5	5
7	**1R**1P2P3P4P5P6P	15 (1.7)	7	6
8	1P2P**3R**3P4P5P6P	11 (1.2)	7	6
9	**1R**	10 (1.1)	1	1
10	1S2P3P4P5P6P	9 (1.0)	6	6

No. of patterns with 10 or more students: 9 patterns
No. of patterns with only 1 student: 70 patterns
Total 103 patterns, 881 students

Insular zone

Rank	Enrolment patterns	Number of students (%)	Years registered	Last grade passed
1	1P	42 (45.7)	1	1
2	1P2P3P4P5P6P	7 (7.6)	6	6
3	1P2P	6 (6.5)	2	2
3	**1R**	6 (6.5)	1	0
5	**1R**1P2P3P4P5P6P	4 (4.3)	5	6
6	1P2P3P4P5P	3 (3.3)	5	5
7	1P1P	2 (2.2)	2	1
7	1P1P2P3P4P5P6P	2 (2.2)	7	6
9	1P1P1P2P3P4P5P6P	1 (1.1)	8	6
9	1P1P2P	1 (1.1)	3	2

No. of patterns with 10 or more students: 1 pattern
No. of patterns with only 1 student: 20 patterns
Total 28 patterns, 92 students

Source: The table was revised for this paper based on Ashida (2017) and Ashida (2021)

pattern was dropping out by the end of the first year of evaluation (1D). In Group 1, for students in the capital, a total of 116 enrolment patterns were identified. Among this group, 11 patterns described 10 or more students each and 86 patterns described only one student each. The most frequently occurring enrolment pattern was completing Grade 6 in six years (1P2P3P4P5P6P). The second most frequent pattern was dropping out after passing Grade 1 at the end of the first year of enrolment (1P). The third most frequent pattern in regional city A and the fourth most frequent pattern in the capital included grade repetition.

In Group 1, for students in the insular zone, 24 enrolment patterns were identified, with 17 patterns describing only one student each. If we examine the frequency ranking of the patterns, a different pattern was identified in the insular zone than in the two previous regions, the capital and regional city. The most frequent pattern involved dropping out after passing Grade 1 at the end of the first year of enrolment (1P), followed by completing Grade 6 in six years (1P2P3P4P5P6P), dropping out after passing Grade 2 at the end of the second year of enrolment (1P2P) and failing Grade 1 in the first year but passing Grade 1 after re-registering in the second year and then dropping out of school (1R1P). A pattern of graduation without repetition accounted for 20% of all enrolment patterns. Patterns involving grade repetitions ranked second in terms of frequency.

In Group 2, for students in regional city A (Table 5.3), a total of 237 enrolment patterns were identified. Among them, 13 patterns described 10 or more students each and 197 patterns described only one student each. The most frequently occurring enrolment pattern was completing Grade 6 in six years (1P2P3P4P5P6P). The second most frequent pattern was completing Grade 6 after repeating the first grade (1R1P2P3P4P5P6P). In Group 2, for students in the capital, a total of 103 enrolment patterns were identified. Among them, 9 patterns described 10 or more students each and 70 patterns described only one student each. The most frequently occurring enrolment pattern was completing Grade 6 in six years (1P2P3P4P5P6P). The second most frequent pattern was dropping out after passing Grade 1 at the end of the first year of enrolment (1P). In regional city A, patterns that included grade repetition included the second-ranked pattern, as well as other less frequent patterns. In the capital, a pattern including grade repetition ranked as the seventh most frequent.

In both regional city A and the capital, for students in Group 2, the most frequent enrolment pattern was completing Grade 6 in six years; however, regional differences were observed, beginning with the second most frequent pattern. In regional city A, grade repetition was the second most frequent ranking, with immediate dropout during Grade 1 as the third most frequent pattern. In the capital, however, the second to the sixth most frequent patterns involved dropping out without repetition. Additionally, a graduation pattern with grade repetition was the seventh most frequent pattern. In the insular zone, unlike in regional city A and the capital, the most frequent pattern of enrolment was not returning to school the following year after passing the first year (1P), followed by graduation without repetition (1P2P3P4P5P6P). The third and subsequent ranked patterns involved one year of grade repetition.

Regarding the variety of enrolment patterns, in both regional city A and the capital, Group 2 displayed a narrower variety of overall patterns and fewer patterns that described only one student. However, when considered by geographical region, the picture is more complicated. In Group 2, the total number of enrolment patterns remained high (237 patterns) in regional city A; however, only 103 patterns were identified in the capital. On the other hand, the insular zone featured a different enrolment situation from the capital and regional city A: 45.7% of all students in the insular zone did not return to school after passing their first year (1P). The next most common pattern of graduation was graduating without repeating a grade; only 7.6% of all students in the insular zone fell into that category.

3.3 *Changes of Enrolment Patterns Resulting in Dropout in the Three Regions*

We classified the above enrolment patterns according to which patterns most frequently resulted in dropouts (dropout patterns, Tables 5.4 and 5.5). For Group 1 students, the most frequent pattern in regional city A was dropping out before the end of the first year (1D). In the capital, the most frequent pattern was passing Grade 1 and leaving school without registering for Grade 2 (1P). In both regional city A and the capital, dropping out in the early grades of primary school was the most frequent pattern. In the insular zone, dropping out of school after passing the first year (1P) was the most frequent pattern of enrolment, and in all regions, early school dropout was the most frequent pattern of enrolment.

Table 5.4 Frequent dropout patterns (Group 1)

	Group 1 (1986–1994)														
	Regional city A					Capital					Insular zone				
Rank	Enrolment patterns	Number of students (%)	Years registered	Last grade passed	Rank	Enrolment patterns	Number of students (%)	Years registered	Last grade passed	Rank	Enrolment patterns	Number of students (%)	Years registered	Last grade passed
1	1D	110 (19.8)	1	0	1	1P	63 (25.2)	1	1	1	1P	8 (38.1)	1	1
2	1P2D	47 (8.5)	2	1	2	1P2P	35 (14.0)	2	2	2	1P2P	3 (14.3)	2	2
3	1R1D	42 (7.6)	2	0	3	1R	22 (8.8)	1	0	2	1R1P	3 (14.3)	2	1
4	1P2P3D	24 (4.3)	3	2	4	1P2P3P	17 (6.8)	3	3	4	1R	2 (9.5)	1	0
5	1P2P3P4D	16 (2.9)	4	3	5	1P2P3P4P	16 (6.4)	4	4	5	1P1R	1 (4.8)	2	1
6	1R1P2P3D	13 (2.3)	4	2	6	1P2P3P4P5P	10 (4.0)	5	5	5	1P2R	1 (4.8)	2	1
7	1P2P3R3D	10 (1.0)	5	5	7	1P2R	9 (1.0)	3	6	5	1R1P2P3P4R	1 (4.8)	5	3
7	1R1R1D	10 (2.0)	5	5	8	1R1P	5 (1.0)	0	5	5	1R1R1P	1 (4.8)	5	1
										5	1R1R1R	1 (4.8)	3	0

Total 167 patterns, 555 students

Total 61 patterns, 250 students

Total 9 patterns, 21 students

Source: The table was revised for this chapter based on Ashida (2017) and Ashida (2021)

Note: The letter 'P' means that the student passed the grade; the letter 'R' means that the student failed the grade (required to repeat it); and the letter 'D' means that the student dropped out

Table 5.5 Frequent dropout patterns (Group 2)

	Group 2 (1995–2004)														
	Regional city A					Capital					Insular zone				
Rank	Enrolment patterns	Number of students (%)	Years registered	Last grade passed	Rank	Enrolment patterns	Number of students (%)	Years registered	Last grade passed	Rank	Enrolment patterns	Number of students (%)	Years registered	Last grade passed
1	1D	37 (11.0)	1	0	1	1P	55 (23.9)	1	1	1	1P	42 (60.9)	1	1
2	1P2P3P4P5P	14 (4.2)	5	5	2	1P2P	38 (16.5)	2	2	2	1P2P	6 (8.7)	2	2
3	1P2P3P4P	13 (3.9)	4	4	3	1P2P3P	37 (16.1)	3	3	2	**1R**	6 (8.7)	1	0
4	1P2P	12 (3.6)	2	2	4	1P2P3P4P	22 (9.6)	4	4	4	1P2P3P4P5P	3 (4.3)	5	5
4	**1R**	12 (3.6)	1	0	5	1P2P3P4P5P	18 (7.8)	5	5	5	1P1P	2 (2.9)	2	1
4	**1R**1D	12 (3.6)	2	0	6	**1R**	10 (4.3)	1	0	6	1P1P2P	1 (1.4)	3	2
7	1P	10 (3.0)	1	1	7	1P**2R**	5 (2.2)	2	1	6	1P1P2P3P4P5P	1 (1.4)	5	5

Total 143 patterns, 336 students   Total 39 patterns, 230 students   Total 28 patterns, 91 students

Patterns that included grade repetition were neither the most frequent nor the second most frequent pattern for both the capital and regional city A. Instead, such patterns ranked third or lower. On the other hand, they ranked second in the insular zone. Despite differences in the number of students and percentages of enrolment patterns, a similar tendency was observed in the regional city A and the capital. Additionally, Grade 1 was the grade most often repeated by capital and regional city A students.

The most frequent dropout patterns for Group 2 in both regional city A and the capital were not different from those of Group 1, that is, 1D in regional city A and 1P in the capital. However, in Group 2, patterns involving grade repetition ranked no higher than fourth in regional city A and sixth in the capital. In particular, patterns involving grade repetition were not frequently observed in the capital, suggesting that fewer students in Group 2 dropped out following grade repetition than in Group 1. On the other hand, patterns including grade repetition in the insular zone continued to rank high, in second place in frequency of enrolment patterns.

4   DISCUSSION

Changes in Enrolment Situations and Decrease in Grade Repetition as Revealed Through Patterns in the Capital and Regional City A

The overall student enrolment situation improved during the period studied in this chapter, as both the number of graduates who completed primary education in six years and the overall percentage of graduates increased both in regional city A and the capital. If we compare Group 1 and Group 2, the percentage of graduates to total students increased from 53.9% to 71.7% in regional city A. This increase is consistent with the national trends in Honduras observed by cross-sectional data. According to the UNESCO Institute for Statistics (2020), the primary school completion rate increased from 68.1% (80.2% in urban areas and 58.6% in rural areas) in 2001 to 80.8% (89.5% in urban areas and 74.3% in rural areas) in 2010 and 86.9% (91.0% in urban areas and 82.8% in rural areas) in 2018. On the other hand, no significant increase was observed in graduates without repeating a grade on the insular zone.

In the capital, the number of enrolment patterns with grade repetition decreased significantly. In Honduras, repetition rates have been decreasing for decades. The grade repetition rate fell from 12.3% in 1990 to 4.5% in 2010 and 3.5% in 2019. The final evaluation by teachers considers the test results for each semester and students' daily attitudes, among other factors, to determine whether to advance the student to the next grade or have them repeat a year. If a student fails to obtain an evaluation score of 60 or higher in each subject, the student is deemed to have failed. As suggested by the Honduran government and international donors, a make-up test was introduced at primary schools to reduce grade repetition in the 1990s. Therefore, students who failed a grade once could advance to the next grade by passing a make-up test. In addition, in 2002, the Honduran government adopted the educational slogan 'Salvemos primer grado' (meaning 'Let's help first-grade students'). The slogan was aimed at preventing repetition and dropout among first-grade students, but it was not backed up by concrete programmes. Nevertheless, the Board of Education encouraged schools to allow first-graders to advance to the second grade and beyond, and some schools with high repetition rates were even required to explain to the Board of Education why they held back certain students (Ashida, 2018). Considering the final evaluation method by teachers, there is little logical basis for implying that reduced grade repetition led to improved academic achievement. However, the decreasing frequency of dropout patterns among all enrolment patterns as well as the decrease in dropout patterns with grade repetition could be among the benefits of the Honduran government's policies to reduce grade repetition.

Student's Age as a Factor in Dropout

In Group 2 of regional city A, dropout patterns with grade repetition were frequently observed. Dropping out was especially common during the early years of primary school. Although the national dropout rate decreased from 40.0% in 1991 to 25.2% in 2010 and finally to 17.3% in 2016 (UNESCO Institute for Statistics, 2020), this improvement was not sufficient to offset grade repetition and presents a challenge that the Honduran government must overcome. Studies have frequently mentioned age as a factor affecting primary school completion. According to McGinn et al. (1992), some students and their parents in rural areas of Honduras do not find value in school and students and, therefore, stop attending school when their parents no longer feel that their child needs an education. This often occurs around age 10 when students start to work on their parents' farms. In addition, after observing primary education in Honduras in the 1990s, the World Bank (1995) reported that students commonly drop out before acquiring functional literacy when they enter a school at the age of eight or above.

We also observed regional differences in the age at which students leave school ($\chi2$ = 204.591, df = 27, P < 0.01) (Figure 5.2). In Group 1, most students in the capital dropped out at the ages of six (20.6%), seven (26.5%), or eight (19.4%), accounting for 66.5% of all dropouts. In Group 2, most students in the capital dropped out at age six (21.3%), seven (23.3%) or eight (24.0%), accounting for 68.6% of all dropouts, similar to that of Group 1 in the capital. Contrary to the data from the capital, with regard to Group 1 in regional city A, most students dropped out at age 10 (17.6%), followed by age 11 (14.2%) and 7 (12.3%). In Group 2, most students in regional city A dropped out at age 10 (16.8%), followed by age 7 (15.1%) and 8 (15.1%). In the capital, school dropouts were common among both groups, with most students dropping out between ages six and eight, at a relatively young age. In regional city A, school dropouts were evenly distributed among all age groups, rather than being limited to certain age groups. In other words, a wide age range can be observed at the time of withdrawal. As mentioned above, studies have focused on dropout at a particular age and countermeasures have been noted. However, our analysis of the data suggests that measures that are not limited to a specific age are necessary to address school dropouts, especially in regional city A.

On the other hand, in the insular zone, data on the age of dropping out of school are limited because school records are unavailable. Therefore, the statistical analysis was not applied as in the case of the capital and regional city A. A distribution of age at leaving school showed that in the 1986–1994 cohort (Group 1, 45 students), the most common age at leaving school was 7 (40.0%), followed by 6 (26.7%), 10 (8.9%) or 12 (8.9%), 7 (6.7%), 8 (4.4%) or 9 (4.4%). In 1995–2004 (Group 2, 12 students), the most common age at school leaving was 8 (50.0%), followed by 6 (25.0%), 7, 9 or 10 (8.3% each).

Thus, in the insular zone, although the number of dropout students has fallen by a third, from 45 to 12, most dropout students entered Group 1 at age 8, whereas the majority entered Group 2 at age 6. This means that most students enrol but drop out early. In other words, students tended to enrol but leave the target school early. To examine the environment surrounding children in the insular zone separately, interviews were conducted with teachers. Through these interviews, we learned that many of

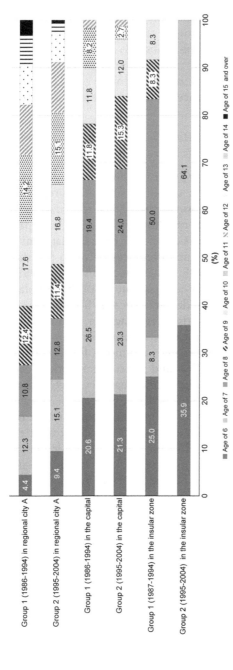

Fig. 5.2 Age of dropout by groups and regions. (Source: The figure was revised and developed for this chapter based on Ashida (2021). Note: The statistical analysis was applied to the data from the capital and regional city A, except the value from the insular zone)

the parents living in this area had engaged in seasonal labour as fishers and that families had frequently changed their places of residence. Therefore, many students moved from the islands to accommodate their parents' work, leading them to leave the target school without returning to school the following school year. This tendency to leave the target school early can be attributed to circumstances specific to the insular zone.

Differences in the Main Socio-economic Activities in the Three Regions

A comparison of the enrolment patterns in the three regions shows a similar trend of improvement in the schooling situation in regional city A and the capital, but only the situation in the insular zone differed. The possibility of children dropping out of school early due to their parents' occupation was given particular consideration for the insular zone. Therefore, we focus on the socio-economic differences between the three regions. Figure 5.3 summarises the 1988 and 2001 census population for ages 10 years and above by occupation[3] as a percentage of the population in each target area (Instituto Nacional de Estadística, 1988, 2001).

In regional city A in 1988, the percentage for each occupation was as follows: 59% for farmers, livestock breeders and forestry workers, followed by 8% for crafts- and tradespersons, accounting for 67% of the total. In 2001, farmers, livestock breeders and agricultural workers accounted for 63%, followed by workers in the textile, masonry, mechanical industries, etc. (7%), for a combined 70% of the total, with the percentage changing as the year progressed. However, the main occupations have remained the same with each new year. In the capital, the percentages for each occupation in 1988 were as follows: 18% for crafts- and tradespersons; 15% for farmers, livestock breeders and forestry workers; 15% for personal services workers; 13% for technical and related professionals; and 10% for vendors and related traders. In 2001, the most common occupations were as follows: workers in the textile, masonry, mechanical industries, etc. (18%); professionals, technicians and persons in related occupations (15%); merchants and vendors (15%); farmers, livestock breeders and agricultural workers (13%); and personal services workers (13%). Slight variations were observed in the percentages for each occupation, but no significant

---

[3] Despite slight differences in the wording of the 1988 and 2001 classifications, we tried to follow the original wording as closely as possible.

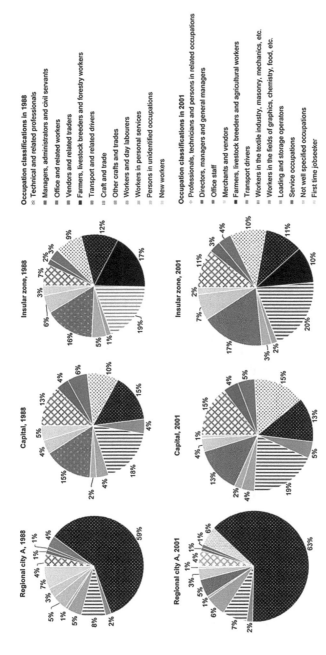

Fig. 5.3 Distributions of the 1988 and 2001 census population aged 10 years and over by occupation. (Source: The author created it by using data from the national census (INE, 1988, 2001))

changes occurred as the year progressed. In the insular zone, the main occupations were as follows: crafts- and tradespersons (19%); transport and related drivers (17%); personal services workers (16%); farmers, live-stock breeders and forestry workers (12%); merchants and vendors (9%); and technical and related professionals (7%). In 2001, the main occupa-tions were as follows: workers in the textile, masonry, mechanical indus-tries, etc. (20%); service occupations (17%); transport drivers (10%); farmers, livestock breeders and agricultural workers (11%); professionals, technicians and persons in related occupations (11%); and merchants and vendors (10%). As in the capital, slight variations occur in the proportions between the different occupations, but no significant changes were observed as the year progressed.

A comparison of the three regions shows a diversity of occupations in the capital. In contrast, in regional city A, farmers, livestock breeders and agricultural workers accounted for approximately 60% of the total, fol-lowed by crafts- and tradespersons (1988)/workers in the textile, masonry, mechanical industries, etc. (2001) and occupational categories showed a lack of diversity. In addition, the share of professionals, technicians and persons in related occupations is only 4%, much lower than for the capital. This shows that in regional city A, occupations that require a high level of educational background have not become major local industries. The insular zone is characterised by a diversity of occupations, as is the capital. However, these data for the insular zone pertain to the whole province and are not specific to the area where the target schools are located. Therefore, we specified the area where the target school is located and observed the details of the proportion of the occupations (Figure 5.4). In 2001, the occupational categories were as follows: service occupations (37%); farmers, livestock breeders and agricultural workers (36%); trans-port drivers (10%); and workers in the textile industry, masonry, mechan-ics, etc. (10%). In sharp contrast to what was observed for the province as a whole, the service sector, including the tourism industry and the primary industry, agriculture, accounted for 73% of the occupations in the area. This indicates that in the target school's locations, occupations that require a particularly high educational background are not the primary industries and the occupational categories are characterised by less diversity.

These results suggest that individual measures and recommendations based on each region's characteristics and circumstances will need to be considered when further improving the enrolment situation. In addition, where local occupations suffer from a lack of diversity, particularly where

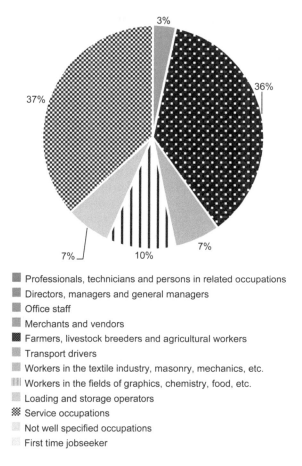

Professionals, technicians and persons in related occupations
Directors, managers and general managers
Office staff
Merchants and vendors
Farmers, livestock breeders and agricultural workers
Transport drivers
Workers in the textile industry, masonry, mechanics, etc.
Workers in the fields of graphics, chemistry, food, etc.
Loading and storage operators
Service occupations
Not well specified occupations
First time jobseeker

Fig. 5.4 Distributions of the 2001 census population by occupation in the area of target school. (Source: The author created it by using data from the national census [INE, 2001])

occupations that require a high educational background are not the main economic activity in the area, approaches such as comprehensive community development that target the whole area, rather than simply the education sector, would be effective.

Possibility of Introducing an Automatic Progression System to Further Improve the Actual State of Study

One of the strategies to improve internal education efficiency is automatic promotion practice. UNESCO UIS defines this as 'a policy whereby all children are systematically promoted to the next grade except in exceptional circumstances (e.g. extended absenteeism due to illness)' (UNESCO, 2012). This is also referred to as 'social promotion' and studies have discussed various aspects of social promotion such as its economic, pedagogical and psychological effects (N'tchougan-Sonou, 2001).

Regarding the effectiveness of automatic promotion practice, both positive and negative results are reported. Okurut (2018) examined Uganda's primary education level, notably the effect of the automatic promotion policy on the dropout rate, by applying a difference-in-difference approach. Okurut (2018) reported that the dropout rate among third-grade students improved with automatic promotion practice; however, the dropout rate did not improve among sixth-grade students. A positive effect was observed on third-grade students' dropout rate in urban areas; however, dropout rates did not improve among sixth-grade students in urban areas and among both third-grade students and sixth-grade students in rural areas. Automatic promotion practice was also observed to have a different effect in terms of geographical differences.

In 2014, the Central American country of Costa Rica introduced social promotion policies (SPPs) that allowed first-grade students to advance to the next grade automatically. Rodriguez-Segura (2020) analysed the policy effect of SPPs using a difference-in-difference approach and reported that the rate of grade repetitions in the second and third grades increased by 77% and 24%, respectively. This implied that first-grade students advanced to the next grade without acquiring sufficient literacy skills. In addition, the negative effect on students from low SES school communities was evident.

In Honduras, an automatic promotion system was introduced temporarily as an emergency measure in the aftermath of Hurricane Mitch in 1998 and again after the military coup in 2009. Since the automatic promotion of 1998 was an emergency remedial measure included in the coverage of this study, we observed this temporary automatic promotion effect at the individual student level. However, the measure had no discernible influence on each student observed. The interviews with the target school principals in regional city A revealed that the number of grade repeaters increased after temporary automatic grade promotion because students advanced to the next grade without meeting the academic requirements to pass the grade (Ashida, 2018). In addition, after the automatic promotion practice in 2009, the repetition rate in primary education in 2010 increased to 4.5% from 3.2% in 2008 according to the UNESCO Institute for Statistics (2020).

In 1998, the Southeast Asian country of Myanmar introduced the Continuous Assessment and Progression System (CAPS), which is similar to automatic promotion. Grade repetition at the primary education level was reduced with the introduction of CAPS; however, school dropouts did not improve, especially for students of low SES (Yoshida, 2019). Furthermore, Yoshida (2021) observed the effect of CAPS across lower-secondary education levels and reported no improvement in dropout rates of students who were of low SES.

Ahmed and Mihiretie (2015) focused on primary schools in Ethiopia and examined the impact of the automatic promotion policy based on interviews and questionnaire surveys to teachers and parents. They concluded that the automatic promotion enabled students with poor academic performance to graduate without adequate learning support and it would reduce their learning and attendance incentives, eventually leading them to drop out. Considering these results, it would be difficult to reduce grade repetition and dropout rates only by introducing an automatic promotion policy. When adopting the policy, a remedial opportunity must be provided to support students experiencing difficulty in achieving a minimum proficiency level within the national curriculum.

5   Conclusion

In this chapter, we tried to clarify the actual state of school enrolment patterns in each of the three regions with different socio-economic characteristics—the capital, regional city and insular zone—of different years of entrance groups, using longitudinal data, in order to conduct a comprehensive examination.

The results indicate that the enrolment situation has improved both in the capital and in the regional cities. Both the number of direct graduates and the overall proportion of graduates have increased. In terms of enrolment year groups, the increase in the proportion of graduates in regional city A is particularly striking, at 17.8%. On the other hand, while enrolment increased in the insular zone, the number of graduates did not increase significantly. Although the schooling situation in the islands differs from that in the capital and provincial cities, all three regions have experienced a significant increase in the proportion of children enrolled at the official school age of six years. This suggests the formation over the past 20 years of a school-age group suitable for study.

Enrolment patterns involving grade repetition declined significantly in the capital, a trend that reflects the decline in repetition rates across the country. In the capital, both Groups 1 and 2 had better enrolment situations than in regional city A. The superior enrolment situation of students in urban areas was also observed in research on Guatemala comparing dropout and grade repetition rates of urban and rural students (Porta & Laguna, 2007). In contrast, enrolment patterns with grade repetition were often observed in regional city A and in the insular zone.

Many students in the capital and the insular zone dropped out at a relatively young age—mostly between six and eight years of age. In regional city A, dropouts were evenly distributed among all age groups, not limited to certain age groups. On the islands, some children did not return to the target school the year after passing the first grade but left the target school early and were expelled from the school on record. This can be attributed to the fact that many children move from one family unit to another in connection with family business, which is a phenomenon peculiar to the island regions. Although some studies have addressed dropping out at specific ages, the results of the present analysis from regional city A suggest that measures that are not limited to specific age groups may be necessary in this context. Additionally, in regional city A, cases were observed of students who left the target school and moved to a new location after leaving the school (Ashida, 2021), suggesting that cross-regional migration of students within the country was becoming more common, not only in the insular zone.

This study, which focused on the socio-economic differences between the three regions, found that those target schools located in rural cities and on islands were characterised by a lack of occupational diversity, especially in those regions where the occupations do not require a high educational background. This is not the main economic activity in the area. Therefore, approaches such as comprehensive community development that target the whole area, rather than simply the education sector, may be more effective. In conclusion, these results indicate that further improvements in the educational system will require the consideration of individual measures and recommendations based on the specific characteristics and circumstances of each region. In implementing an automatic promotion system, it is essential not only to introduce the system itself but also to provide supplementary support for students who may experience academic difficulties.

Finally, it should be noted that the data analysed in this study do not include those students affected by the school closure measures implemented in response to the COVID-19 pandemic. The return of children to the classroom, who were previously unable to attend due to the disruption to learning opportunities, has become a significant factor that cannot be overlooked. Future monitoring of the education situation will require further continuous observation and scrutiny, with a particular focus on the impact of such pandemics.

Acknowledgements The authors would like to express their gratitude to Lic. Zoila Herrera. We would like to express our gratitude to Lic. Donaldo Cárcamo and Lic. Sury Valladares for their invaluable assistance in data collection and analysis. This study was financially supported by the Japan Society for the Promotion of Science KAKENHI under Grant Numbers 26257114, 19K14119 and 24K05761.

References

Ahmed, A. Y., & Mihiretie, D. M. (2015). Primary school teachers and parents' views on automatic promotion practices and its implications for education quality. *International Journal of Educational Development, 43*, 90–99. https://doi.org/10.1016/j.ijedudev.2015.05.003

Alexander, K. L., Entwisle, D. R., & Dauber, S. L. (1994). *On the success of failure: A reassessment of the effects of retention in the primary grades.* Cambridge University Press.

Altschuler, D. (2010, March 8). Between resistance and co-optation: The politics of education in the Honduran crisis. *NACLA Report on the Americas, 43*(2), 23–19. https://nacla.org/article/between-resistance-and-co-optation-politics-education-honduran-crisis. https://doi.org/10.1080/10714839.2010.11725490

Ashida, A. (2017). Actual enrollment situation in Bay Islands of Honduras: Analysis using the data of primary school children in Caribbean resort area. *Journal of Global Tourism Research, 2*(2), 87–92. https://doi.org/10.37020/jgtr.2.2_87

Ashida, A. (2018). *The actual effect on enrollment of 'Education for All': Analysis using longitudinal individual data.* Union Press.

Ashida, A. (2021). Comparative analysis of schooling situations using longitudinal data: Improving enrollment patterns of individual children in Honduras.

International Journal of Comparative Education and Development, 23(4), 261–279. https://doi.org/10.1108/IJCED-03-2021-0026

Ashida, A., & Sekiya, T. (2016). Changes in the repetition and dropout situation in Honduran primary education since the late 1980s. Education 3–13. *International Journal of Primary, Elementary and Early Years Education, 44*(4), 458–477.

Barnes, D. (1999). Causes of dropping out from the perspective of education theory. In L. Randall & J. B. Anderson (Eds.), *Schooling for success: Preventing repetition and dropout in Latin American primary schools* (pp. 14–22). M. E. Sharpe.

Goos, M., Damme, J. V., Onghena, P., Petry, K., & Bilde, J. (2013). First-grade retention in the Flemish educational context: Effects on children's academic growth, psychosocial growth, and school career throughout primary education. *Journal of School Psychology, 5*(3), 323–347.

Gropello, D. E. (2003). *Monitoring educational performance in the Caribbean.* World Bank Working Papers, no. 6. Washington, DC: International Bank for Reconstruction and Development/the World Bank.

Instituto Nacional de Estadística (INE) (National Institute of Statistics). (1988). Censo nacional de población y vivienda 1988 [National population and housing census 1988]. *Republica de Honduras.*

Instituto Nacional de Estadística (INE) (National Institute of Statistics). (2001). Censo nacional de población y vivienda 2001 [National population and housing census 2001]. *Republica de Honduras.*

Kitamura, Y., & Ashida, A. (2023). International cooperation in education through multifaceted partnerships. In G. A. Postiglione, C. J. Johnstone, & W. R. Teter (Eds.), *Handbook of education policy.* Edward Elgar Publishing.

Ma, X. (2010). Longitudinal evaluation designs. In P. Peterson, E. Baker, & B. McGaw (Eds.), *International encyclopedia of education* (3rd ed., pp. 754–764). Elsevier Science.

Marshall, J. H. (2003). Grade repetition in Honduran primary schools. *International Journal of Educational Development, 23,* 591–605. https://doi.org/10.1016/S0738-0593(03)00060-9

McGinn, N., Reimers, F., Loera, A., Soto, M. d. C., & López, S. (1992). *Why do children repeat grades? A Study of Rural Primary Schools in Honduras.* Bridges Research Report Series no. 13. Cambridge, MA: Bridges Publications.

Ministry of Foreign Affairs of Japan. (2024). Honjurasu Kyowakoku. (Republic of Honduras). https://www.mofa.go.jp/mofaj/area/honduras/index.html (in Japanese).

N'tchougan-Sonou, C. H. (2001). Automatic promotion or large-scale repetition—Which path to quality? *International Journal of Educational Development, 21*(2), 149–162. https://doi.org/10.1016/S0738-0593(00)00016-X

Okurut, J. M. (2018). Automatic promotion and student dropout: Evidence from Uganda, using propensity score in difference in differences model. *Journal of Education and Learning, 7*(2), 191–209. https://doi.org/10.5539/jel.v7n2p191

Porta, E., & Laguna, J. R. (2007). Equidad de la Educación en Guatemala [Education equity in Guatemala]. *USAID Guatemala and Academy for Educational Development, 4* (in Spanish).

Rodriguez-Segura, D. (2020). Strengthening early literacy skills through social promotion policies? Intended and unintended consequences in Costa Rica. *International Journal of Educational Development, 77*, 102243. https://doi.org/10.1016/j.ijedudev.2020.102243

Secretaría de educación. (2002a). Mientras dure la emergencia Educandos revivirán sus clases en el canal hondureño Telebásica, [Education services will be re-delivered through channels of Telebásica during the emergency]. Ministry of Education. Retrieved from https://www.se.gob.hn/detalle-articulo/1412/

Secretaría de Educación [Ministry of Education]. (2002b). *Fast track initiative, education for all Honduras 2003–2015*. Submitted to World Bank. Proposal approved. Tegucigalpa.

Sekiya, T. (2014). Individual patterns of enrolment in primary schools in the Republic of Honduras, *Education 3–13*. *International Journal of Primary, Elementary and Early Years Education, 42*(5), 460–474.

Sekiya, T., & Ashida, A. (2017). An analysis of primary school dropout patterns in Honduras. *Journal of Latinos and Education, 16*(1), 65–73. https://doi.org/10.1080/15348431.2016.1179185

UNESCO Institute for Statistics (UIS). (2012). *Global education digest 2012: Opportunities lost: The impact of grade repetition and early school leaving*. UNESCO-UIS.

UNESCO-UIS. (2020). *UIS Stat*. http://data.uis.unesco.org

United Nations Development Programme. (2024). *Human Development Report 2023–24: Breaking the gridlock: Reimagining cooperation in a polarised world*.

United Nations Development Programme (UNDP). (1998). *Informe sobre desarrollo humano Honduras 1998*. Honduras: Information on Human Development. Tegucigalpa: United Nations Development Programme.

United Nations Educational, Scientific and Cultural Organization. (2020). *Global Education Monitoring Report 2020—Latin America and the Caribbean—Inclusion and education: All means all*. UNESCO.

United Nations Educational, Scientific and Cultural Organization. (2022). Global monitoring of school closures, COVID-19 impact on Education. https://webarchive.unesco.org/web/20220629024039/https://en.unesco.org/covid19/educationresponse/

United Nations Educational, Scientific and Cultural Organization (UNESCO). (1970, July 1–9). The statistical measurement of educational wastage (dropout, repetition and school retardation) Proceeding of International Conference on Education XXXII nd Session. Geneva, Switzerland.

World Bank. (1995). *Staff appraisal report: Honduras basic education project.* Tegucigalpa.

World Bank. (2021). Individuals using the Internet (% of population). Honduras. https://data.worldbank.org/indicator/IT.NET.USER.ZS?locations=HN

World Bank. (2022). *Open data.* World Bank. https://data.worldbank.org/country/honduras?view=chart

World Bank, UNESCO, UNICEF, USAID, FCDO, Bill & Melinda Gates Foundation. (2022). *The State of Global Learning Poverty: 2022 Update.* Conference edition, June 23. https://www.unicef.org/media/122921/file/StateofLearningPoverty2022.pdf

Yoshida, N. (2019). Socio-economic status and the impact of the 'Continuous Assessment and Progression System' in primary education in Myanmar. *Education 3–13. International Journal of Primary, Elementary and Early Years Education, 48*(6), 674–689.

Yoshida, N. (2021). Socioeconomic status (SES) and the benefits of the 'continuous assessment and progression system (CAPS)' in lower secondary education in Myanmar. *International Journal of Comparative Education and Development, 23*(4), 335–352. https://doi.org/10.1108/IJCED-11-2020-0084

Changes in Female Primary and Secondary School Enrolment in El Salvador since the Early 1980s

Akemi Ashida ⓘ

1 INTRODUCTION[1]

Female School Enrolment in the Latin America Region

Gender inequality has been a significant global problem, especially in education. After the World Conference on Education for All (EFA) in 1990, a resolution to resolve educational gender inequality was incorporated to the United Nations' Millennium Development Goals and Sustainable

[1] This chapter was prepared with translation, major augmentations and modifications, including updated analytical data of parts of pp. 59–78 of Ashida, A (2018) Erusarubadoru chihou toshi no syoujyotachi no ashiato (Girls' footsteps in a regional city in El Salvador) in Sekiya, T. (ed.) Kaihatsutojyokoku de manabu kodomotachi (Children learning in developing countries). Nishinomiya: Kwansei Gakuin University Press.

A. Ashida (✉)
Graduate School of International Development, Nagoya University,
Nagoya, Japan
e-mail: ashida@gsid.nagoya-u.ac.jp

© The Author(s), under exclusive license to Springer Nature
Switzerland AG 2024
T. Sekiya et al. (eds.), *Towards Ensuring Inclusive and Equitable Quality Education for All*, International and Development Education, https://doi.org/10.1007/978-3-031-70266-2_6

Development Goals (SDGs). However, an EFA Global Monitoring Report that examined the progress made up to 2015 identified that gender inequality in many parts of the world was still in a parlous state, especially access to basic education; hence, further efforts were needed to achieve the SDGs (UNESCO, 2015).

Global educational gender inequality varies. Compared to other regions, educational gender equality in Latin America and the Caribbean has been improving, especially in academic performance. While it is more often females that do not attend school in these regions, once enrolled, they tend to perform better than their male peers (UNESCO, 2015). However, regional comparative studies and international academic assessment results from Latin America/Caribbean, such as the Trends in International Mathematics and Science Study, revealed that female scores are lower than males, especially for STEM subjects (UNESCO Santiago, 2014). Household surveys from Brazil, Columbia and Mexico determine that due to household chores, female students are more likely to encounter greater learning obstacles than males (Guarcello et al., 2015).

Following the global trend towards resolving gender equality and because the number of females not enrolled in school was significantly higher than males, during the first half of the 1990s in the Republic of El Salvador, which is this study's target country, national policies were adopted for the first time to address gender inequality. One such policy was the First National Women's Policy in which a strategy was outlined to expand female access to formal and informal education (Edwards et al., 2015).

El Salvador and its neighbouring countries underwent the Central American crisis in the late 1970s. The EFA Global Monitoring Report 2011 cited armed conflict as being a major obstacle to achieving its 'Education for All' goals (UNESCO, 2011). Several studies have examined the effects of armed conflict on education (León, 2012; Chamarbagwala & Morán, 2011; Justino, 2016, Gómez Soler, 2016). Chamarbagwala and Morán (2011) focused on the number of years of schooling[2] during the Guatemalan civil war in the provincial areas of Guatemala, finding that females were attending school for shorter periods than males, with the average years of schooling for boys being 4.66 and for girls being 3.83.

---

[2] The term 'years of schooling' is used here and is interchangeable with 'years of (school) education'.

Overview of the Republic of El Salvador

El Salvador is situated in Central America and borders Guatemala, Honduras and the Pacific Ocean. The country is 21,040 square kilometres and has a population of 6.33 million; therefore, El Salvador is a highly densely populated country. The national capital is San Salvador and the official language is Spanish. The population, which is primarily Roman Catholic, comprises mixed European (Spanish) (84%), indigenous ancestry (5.6%) and European ancestry (10%). El Salvador's main industries are light manufacturing, such as textiles for export, and agriculture, with coffee and sugar being its principal products. In 2001, the currency integration law replaced El Salvador's old currency with the US dollar. Thus, when the country's economy became dollar based, interest rates dropped and inflation stabilised. Since the end of the civil war in 1992, Central and South America have frequently been devastated by natural disasters, including two major earthquakes and hurricanes, all of which caused severe damage. Nevertheless, El Salvador has continued to have positive economic growth, although it has been among the lowest in Central America (2.38% in 2019). The country's unemployment rate is approximately 6.3% (Ministry of Foreign Affairs of Japan 2024; World Bank, 2022).

Notably, El Salvador's economy relies on remittances from Salvadorans living in the United States. In 2016, total remittances were approximately USD 5.91 billion, up by 7.2% from the previous year and accounting for 23% of the country's GDP (Ministry of Foreign Affairs of Japan, 2024). The 2023/2024 United Nations Development Programme Human Development Report stated that El Salvador's human development index was 0.674 in 2022, which was 127th of the 193 countries listed and slightly higher than neighbouring Honduras (0.624; UNDP, 2024).

El Salvador and Japan have traditionally maintained friendly ties. Due to the many characteristics shared by the two countries, such as high population density, poor natural resources and the frequent occurrence of natural disasters (e.g. hurricanes, earthquakes and volcanic eruptions), Japan has offered diverse assistance to El Salvador such as post-conflict and post-disaster reconstruction. El Salvador was the first country in Central America to receive Japan Overseas Cooperation Volunteers (JOCV) from the Japanese International Cooperation Agency (JICA). The first JOCV project involved improving school mathematics instruction, which is discussed in Chap. 5. Various other Japanese technical cooperation projects have been conducted in El Salvador, such as a nursing education project, Chagas disease control project, seismic housing project for low-income families and community disaster risk reduction project.

Education in El Salvador

Since education develops human resources, especially in countries poor in natural resources, to rebuild its economy after the 12-year conflict, El Salvador has prioritised basic education since the end of the civil war, during which 641 schools were destroyed. In the 1990s, the Japanese government helped El Salvador construct new schools. Rural areas were severely damaged by the civil war; however, these communities always had poor educational facilities as no public schools had ever been built. Furthermore, in agricultural and low-income areas, children who did enrol in school would often drop out to assist their families on the farms. As the government's education budget had been inadequate, developing educational infrastructure and improving educational systems, teaching skills and educational materials were pressing issues (Japanese International Cooperation Agency, 1994).

In such a great difficult education environment, El Salvador developed a unique approach to school administration. During the civil war, the central government refused to send teachers or allocate funds to guerrilla-controlled areas. Consequently, community residents gathered resources to prevent the suspension of school education, such as serving as substitute teachers, repairing school facilities and engaging in other grass-roots acts of solidarity. This movement continued after the war, primarily in mountainous regions, and has become a resident-participatory school administration system known as EDUCO (*Programa de Educación para Adoministrado por la Cuminidad en las Zonas Rurales*).

This resident-participatory system for community-based education improvement offers teachers and classrooms in rural areas, promotes resident involvement and community participation in school administration, registers the teachers to be dispatched to the rural areas, provides salary supplements and focuses on nutritional improvements for children. The EFA Global Monitoring Report 2009 cites EDUCO as an example of autonomous school administration (or school-based management) that has succeeded in popularising and expanding school education (UNESCO, 2008).

Education statistics in El Salvador in recent years reveal, for example, that in 2022, the expected years of learning was 11.9 and the mean years of schooling was 7.2. Compared to neighbouring Honduras, where the expected years of learning was 10 years and mean years of schooling was 7.3 years, El Salvador's education provision had recovered from the war.

Chapter Objective

This chapter employed longitudinal data to examine female schooling during and immediately after the civil war, from a micro-scale perspective, allowing us to trace individual situations. By comparing cohorts from school entrance years, we were able to observe and clarify the actual state of schooling for female students since 1980.

2   RESEARCH METHODOLOGY

During the long-drawn-out civil war in El Salvador from 1980 to 1992, school facilities, records and documents were destroyed in areas in which there were intense battles. Because of these conditions, we needed to investigate female schooling over time in areas in which there were sufficient records. Therefore, we chose a school in a regional city that had not been directly affected by the civil war military hostilities. This school was a girls-only school until 1998, after which it was merged with a nearby boys' school and became co-educational.

True cohort analysis (Sekiya, 2014) was adopted for this study, which involved the collection and analysis of longitudinal academic performance records for individual girls from the time they entered school until they dropped out or graduated. We also interviewed teachers at the school to collect information about the target schools and educational situations in the target area, as necessary.

In this study, 'enrolment' refers to when a student attended school, including their grade, their end-of-year results and whether they repeated the grade level, dropped out, graduated or transferred to another school, 'entrance' refers to when the student first attended school and 'enrolment pattern' refers to the student's specific school situation from entrance to graduation or dropout and their results (Sekiya, 2014)

We focused on 1758 girls who entered the target school from 1980 to 1997. To elucidate the student situations and compare them with Honduras, we sorted the data into three cohorts based on entrance year: early 1980s, that is, those who had entered the target school between 1980 and 1985; late 1980s, that is, those that entered the target school between 1986 and 1990; and the 1990s, that is, those who entered the target school between 1991 and 1997. This categorisation was similar to the categorisation used in Ashida and Sekiya's (2016) analysis of Honduran education.

3   RESULTS

Enrolment Status and Patterns in the Target School

Table 6.1 demonstrates the enrolment status for the 1758 females examined in this study. As the database was only established from academic performance information retained by the school, our analysis did not include students who entered the school at the beginning but dropped out before the end of the school year and did not receive the year-end academic evaluation.

Entrance by the Early 1980s' Cohort

The data for analysis were from 724 female students who entered school between 1980 and 1985. During this period, the entrance was set at 100%. By the end of the first year, 30.1% (218 students) had dropped out. In the second year, 12.2% repeated the grade and were re-registered as first graders and 57.5% advanced to the second grade and were registered as second graders. In the third year, 43.0% advanced to the next grade and were registered as third graders and 1.7% were registered in the first grade for the third time. The highest number of years for continually being registered as a first grader was five years. Thus, the overall percentage of children who graduated primary school was 24.4% (177 students), including one student who had taken nine years to graduate. The overall percentage of girls who graduated from lower secondary education was 4.8% (35 students), including three students who took ten years to graduate.

Of the students, 17.3% (125 students) graduated from the six years of primary education without repeating a grade and 4.4% (32 students) graduated from the nine years of lower secondary education without repeating a grade.

Table 6.1 Cohort student enrolment

	First grade	Second grade	Third grade	Fourth grade	Fifth grade	Sixth grade	Seventh grade	Eighth grade	Ninth grade	Completion of sixth grade	Completion of ninth grade
Early 1980s cohort											
Year 1	100.0										
Year 2	12.2	57.7									
Year 3	1.7	14.0	42.0								
Year 4	0.1	4.1	12.0	32.6							
Year 5	0.1	0.3	5.4	9.0	25.4						
Year 6		0.1	1.0	4.1	7.7	19.2				17.3	
Year 7			0.1	1.2	3.3	6.1	5.7			5.1	
Year 8				0.1	0.8	2.2	1.1	4.4		1.9	
Year 9					0.1	0.4	0.6	0.4	4.4	0.1	4.4
Year 10							0.1		0.4		0.4
Year 11											
Subtotal										24.4	4.8
Late 1980s cohort											
Year 1	100.0										
Year 2	13.2	60.5									
Year 3	1.4	17.9	39.1								
Year 4	0.4	2.5	15.6	32.7							
Year 5	0.2	0.2	2.9	12.8	27.2						
Year 6		0.2	0.8	2.5	10.9	21.4				20.6	
Year 7			0.2	0.8	1.9	8.8	6.4			8.6	
Year 8				0.2	0.6	1.6	2.1	4.3		1.6	

(continued)

Table 6.1 (continued)

	First grade	Second grade	Third grade	Fourth grade	Fifth grade	Sixth grade	Seventh grade	Eighth grade	Ninth grade	Completion of sixth grade	Completion of ninth grade
Year 9					0.2	0.4	0.2	1.8	4.3	0.4	4.3
Year 10								0.2	1.8		1.8
Year 11											
Subtotal										31.3	6.2
1990s cohort											
Year 1	100.0										
Year 2	12.7	61.4									
Year 3	1.0	13.1	47.6								
Year 4	0.2	1.7	11.9	38.0							
Year 5		0.2	1.2	10.2	32.8						
Year 6			0.2	1.5	8.6	28.8				28.4	
Year 7				0.2	1.0	7.7	13.6			7.7	
Year 8					0.2	0.8	1.7	9.8		0.6	
Year 9							0.2	1.7	9.8	0.0	9.8
Year 10								0.2	1.0		1.0
Year 11											
Subtotal										36.7	10.7

Source: The author created it based on collected data

Entrance for the late 1980s' Cohort

The data for analysis were from 514 female students who entered the school between 1986 and 1990 with the time of entrance set at 100%. By the end of the first year, 26.3% (135 students) had dropped out of school. In the second year, 13.2% repeated their grade and were re-registered as first graders and 60.5% advanced to the next grade and were registered as second graders. In the third year, 39.1% advanced to the next grade and were registered as third graders and 1.4% re-registered in the first grade for the third time. The highest number of years for continually being registered as a first grader was five years. The overall percentage of children who graduated primary education was 31.3% (161 students), which included one student who had taken ten years to graduate. The overall percentage of girls who graduated lower secondary education was 6.2% (32 students), which included three students who had taken 11 years to graduate.

Of the students, 20.6% (106 students) in this cohort graduated primary education in six years without repeating a grade and 4.3% (22 students) graduated lower secondary education in nine years without repeating a grade.

Entrance in the 1990s' Cohort

The data for analysis were from 521 students who entered school between 1991 and 1997, with 100% set at the time of entrance. By the end of the first year, 25.9% (135 students) had dropped out of school. In the second year, 12.7% repeated their grade and were re-registered as first graders. Furthermore, 61.4% had advanced to the next grade and registered as second graders. In the third year, 47.6% of the children advanced to the next grade and were registered as third graders and 1% were registered in the first grade for the third time. The highest number of years for continually being registered as a first grader was four years. The overall percentage of children who graduated primary education was 36.7% (191 students), including one student who had taken eight years to graduate. Moreover, the overall percentage of children who had graduated lower secondary education was 10.7% (56 students), including five students who took 10 years to graduate.

Of the students, 28.4% (148 students) graduated primary education in six years without repeating a grade and 9.8% (51 students) graduated lower secondary education in nine years without repeating a grade.

Frequent Enrolment Patterns

We further examined the actual enrolment patterns, as shown in Table 6.2. The numbers in Table 6.2 denote the grades, and the letters after each number indicate the academic assessment results, indicating whether the student passed the grade (P) or failed and was required to repeat (R). In the early 1980s' cohort, 142 patterns were identified. Of these, 14 were followed by at least 10 girls, and 98 patterns were followed by only one girl. The most frequent pattern was dropping out of school after passing Grade 1 in the first year (1P), followed by completing Grade 6 in six years without repeating a grade (1P2P3P4P5P6P). Overall, four patterns, including the two most frequently followed ones, comprised 44.8% of the total. The other two patterns were dropping out of school after passing Grade 2 (1P2P) and after failing Grade 1 (1R). Completing Grade 9 in nine years without repeating a year (1P2P3P4P5P6P7P8P9P) was the fifth most frequently occurring pattern; however, this only accounted for 4.4% of the total.

Similar to the early 1980s' cohort, the most common pattern in the late 1980s' cohort and the 1990s' cohort was dropping out of school after passing Grade 1 in the first year (1P), followed by completing Grade 6 in six years without repeating a year (1P2P3P4P5P6P). In only the 1990s' cohort, completing Grade 9 in nine years without repeating a year (1P2P3P4P5P6P7P8P9P) was the third most frequent pattern. Therefore, in all three cohorts, we were able to confirm the opposing situations of girls giving up school after only a few years of attendance and girls continuing until course completion.

The enrolment pattern comparison by cohort indicated that these enrolment patterns reduced over time—from 142 in the early 1980s' cohort to 96 in the late 1980s' cohort and to 76 in the 1990s' cohort. This indicated female student enrolment improved from the early 1980s to the 1990s. However, the pattern of dropping out of school after passing Grade 1 in the first year (1P), which was the most common in all three cohorts, increased to 1.3% in the 1990s' cohort compared to the late 1980s' cohort.

Table 6.2 Enrolment pattern frequencies by cohort

Early 1980s cohort

Rank	Enrolment patterns	Number of students (%)	Years registered	Last grade passed
1	1P	127 (17.5)	1	1
2	1P2P3P4P5P6P	82 (11.3)	6	6
3	1R	61 (8.4)	1	1
4	1P2P	54 (7.5)	2	2
5	1P2P3P4P5P6P7P8P9P	32 (4.4)	9	9
6	1P2P3P	26 (3.6)	3	3
7	1P2P3P4P	25 (3.5)	4	4
8	1P2P3R	21 (2.9)	3	2
9	1P2R	20 (2.8)	2	1
10	1P2P3P4P5P	17 (2.3)	5	5

No. of patterns with 10 or more students: 14 patterns
No. of patterns with only 1 student: 98 patterns
Total 142 patterns, 724 students

Late 1980s cohort

Rank	Enrolment patterns	Number of students (%)	Years registered	Last grade passed
1	1P	78 (15.2)	1	1
2	1P2P3P4P5P6P	72 (14.0)	6	6
3	1P2P	51 (9.9)	2	2
4	1R	39 (7.6)	1	0
5	1P2P3P4P5P6P7P8P9P	22 (4.3)	9	9
6	1P2P3P4P	17 (3.3)	4	4
7	1P2P3P4P5P	17 (3.3)	5	5
8	1P2R	16 (3.1)	2	1
9	1P2P3P	14 (2.7)	3	3
10	1R1P2P3P4P5P6P7P	14 (2.7)	7	6

No. of patterns with 10 or more students: 11 patterns
No. of patterns with only 1 student: 53 patterns
Total 96 patterns, 513 students

1990s cohort

Rank	Enrolment patterns	Number of students (%)	Years registered	Last grade passed
1	1P	86 (16.5)	1	1
2	1P2P3P4P5P6P	74 (14.2)	6	6
3	1P2P	49 (9.4)	2	2
4	1P2P3P4P5P6P7P8P9P	49 (9.4)	9	9
5	1R	38 (7.3)	1	0
6	1P2P3P	36 (6.9)	3	3
7	1P2P3P4P5P	21 (4.0)	5	5
8	1R1P2P3P4P5P6P	21 (4.0)	7	6
9	1P2P3P4P	20 (3.8)	4	4
10	1P2P3P4P5P6P7P	10 (1.9)	7	7

No. of patterns with 10 or more students: 10 patterns
No. of patterns with only 1 student: 44 patterns
Total 76 patterns, 521 students

Source: The author created it based on collected data

NB: The letter 'P' means the student passed the grade; the letter 'R' means the student failed the grade (required to repeat it); the letter 'D' means the student dropped out; the symbol '/' means no registration and skip the year

Graduation Patterns: How Did the Girls Reach Graduation?

We further examined the graduation patterns for the students who completed their primary or lower secondary education. Table 6.3 presents the primary and lower secondary graduation patterns in the order of frequency. In the early 1980s' cohort, the most frequently occurring pattern was completing primary education in six years without repeating a year (1P2P3P4P5P6P; 52.2%), followed by completing lower secondary education in nine years without repeating a year (1P2P3P4P5P6P7P8P9P; 20.4%). The third most frequently occurring graduation pattern was repeating Grade 1 once and advancing to each subsequent grade until completing Grade 6 without repeating another year (1R1P2P3P4P5P6P; 52.2%). These three enrolment patterns were common for 75.2% of the early 1980s' cohort graduates.

In the late 1980s' and the 1990s' cohorts, completing Grade 6 in six years without repeating a year (1P2P3P4P5P6P) was the most common pattern, followed by completing Grade 9 in nine years without repeating a year (1P2P3P4P5P6P7P8P9P) and repeating Grade 1 once and completing Grade 6 without repeating another year (1R1P2P3P4P5P6P9). Moreover, patterns involving repetition were the third most frequent in all three cohorts. The percentage of students repeating a year increased from 5.7% in the early 1980s' cohort to 9.4% in the late 1980s' cohort and to 12.6% in the 1990s' cohort. This may have been due to the increase in the number of students who continued their studies to completion after repeating a grade once. The percentage completing Grade 6 in six years fell over time from 52.2% in the early 1980s' cohort to 48.3% in the late 1980s' cohort and to 44.3% in the 1990s' cohort. However, the percentage completing Grade 9 in nine years increased from 20.4% in the early 1980s' cohort to 24.8% in the late 1980s' cohort and to 29.3% in the 1990s' cohort. Since the number of students who completed both primary and lower secondary education increased, it was evident that the overall enrolment situation improved over time.

4   DISCUSSION

Enrolment Changes over Time

A comparison of the three cohorts reveals that the percentage of graduates increased. Of the students, 177 (24.4%), 161 (31.3%) and 191 (36.7%) graduated Grade 6 from the early 1980s', late 1980s' and 1990s' cohorts, respectively. Moreover, the percentage of girls who completed

Table 6.3 Graduation patterns by cohort

Early 1980s cohort

Rank	Enrolment patterns	Number of students (%)	Years registered	Last grade passed
1	1P2P3P4P5P6P	82(52.2)	6	6
2	1P2P3P4P5P6P7P8P9P	32 (20.4)	9	9
3	1R1P2P3P4P5P6P	9 (5.7)	7	6
4	1P2P3P4R4P5P6P	5 (3.2)	7	6
5	1P2R2P3P4P5P6P	4 (2.5)	7	6
6	1P2P3P4P5P6R6P	3 (1.9)	7	6
7	1P2P3R3P4P5P6P	2 (1.3)	7	6
7	1R1P2P3P4P5P6R6P	2 (1.3)	8	6

No. of patterns with 10 or more students: 2 patterns
No. of patterns with only 1 student: 17 patterns
Total 26 patterns, 157 students

Late 1980s cohort

Rank	Enrolment patterns	Number of students (%)	Years registered	Last grade passed
1	1P2P3P4P5P6P	72 (48.3)	6	6
2	1P2P3P4P5P6P7P8P9P	22 (14.8)	9	9
3	1R1P2P3P4P5P6P	14 (9.4)	6	6
4	1P2P3P4P5P6P	8 (5.4)	6	6
5	1P2R2P3P4P5P6P	3 (2.0)	6	6
5	1P2P3P4P5P6P7P8P9P	3 (2.0)	10	9
5	1P2P3P4R4P5P6P	3 (2.0)	7	6
5	1R1P2P3P4P5P6P7P8P9P	3 (2.0)	10	9
9	1P//2P3P4P5P6P	3 (2.0)	7	6
9	1P2P3P4P5R5P6P	3 (2.0)	7	6

No. of patterns with 10 or more students: 3 patterns
No. of patterns with only 1 student: 16 patterns
Total 26 patterns, 149 students

1990s cohort

Rank	Enrolment patterns	Number of students (%)	Years registered	Last grade passed
1	1P2P3P4P5P6P	75 (44.9)	1	6
2	1P2P3P4P5P6P7P8P9P	49 (29.3)	6	9
3	1R1P2P3P4P5P6P	21 (12.6)	2	6
4	1P2P3P4P5P6P	3 (1.8)	9	6
4	1R1P2P3P4P5P6P7P8P9P	3 (1.8)	1	9
5	1P2P3R3P4P5P6P	2 (1.2)	3	6

No. of patterns with 10 or more students: 3 patterns
No. of patterns with only 1 student: 14 patterns
Total 20 patterns, 167 students

Source: The author created it based on collected data

NB: The letter 'P' means the student passed the grade; the letter 'R' means the student failed the grade (required to repeat it); the letter 'D' means the student dropped out; and the symbol '/' means no registration and skip the year

each education level without repeating a grade improved over time. The required years to complete their education reduced slightly to the maximum of 8 years in primary education and a maximum of 10 years in lower secondary education in the 1990s' cohort from the maximum of 9 years in primary education and a maximum of 11 years in lower secondary education in the early 1980s' cohort. Therefore, the female enrolment situation improved over time. In a similar regional city 1986–1994 cohort in Honduras, 51.1% of girls completed Grade 6 and 31% of girls graduated without repeating a year. Therefore, the percentage of girls completing Grade 6 in this target school in El Salvador was lower than in the Honduran study.

Over time, fewer girls dropped out after only a few years and more girls continued until course completion. As the educational environment was polarised, as in Sekiya's (2014) study on Honduran female education, it was not possible to evaluate the internal efficiency of the education based on the average grade repetition and dropout rates or the number of years of schooling.

Repetition and Dropping Out?

Many studies that have examined repetition and dropout in Latin American schools (Randall & Anderson, 1999; Marshall, 2003; Cardoso & Verner, 2007) concluded that children often drop out of school after they have repeated a grade several times (McGinn et al., 1992; Alexander et al., 1994). Sekiya and Ashida (2017) analysed the dropout patterns in a regional city in Honduras, finding that although many dropouts had repeated a grade, many other students who had not repeated a year dropped out for other reasons. Therefore, it was speculated that this may also have been the case in the three cohorts in this study in El Salvador. To this end, we investigated the dropout and enrolment patterns based on the last grade the students passed.

Dropout Patterns

Table 6.4 presents the dropout pattern for the girls who failed to complete their primary education. In the early 1980s' cohort, the most frequently occurring patterns for 42.7% of those failing to graduate were dropping out after passing Grade 1 (1P) and Grade 2 (1P2P) and dropping out after repeating a grade (1R). A 10.8% of the primary school dropouts dropped out after repeating a grade (1R). Other dropout patterns after repeating a grade were ranked in sixth (3.7%), seventh (3.5%), ninth (3.0%) and tenth places (2.8%). These patterns indicated that grade repetition mostly occurred in Grades 1, 2, 3 and 5.

Table 6.4 further presents the dropout patterns for the late 1980s' and the 1990s' cohorts. The most frequently occurring pattern was dropping out after passing Grade 1 (1P), followed by dropping out after passing Grade 2 (1P2P) and failing Grade 1 (1R). The second and third ranks, therefore, were different from the early 1980s' cohort. However, in all three cohorts, of all dropouts, 42.7%, 46.1% and 48.8% dropped out after passing Grade 1 (1P), passing Grade 2 (1P2P) and failing Grade 1 (1R), respectively. The percentage of the first most frequent dropout pattern (1P) fell from 22.4% in the early 1980s' cohort to 21.4% in the late 1980s' cohort but rose again to 24.3% in the 1990s' cohort.

These figures suggest that dropout for girls in El Salvador was not adequately addressed. At both primary and lower secondary levels, few dropouts were triggered by failure in the previous grade attended, as evidenced in the two most frequent dropout patterns. We did not follow up on these cohorts to assess the individual situations after the students left the school, but we speculated that those who dropped out after passing Grade 1 or 2 (1P or 2P) may have transferred to another school. However, interviews with the school teachers established that there were no other schools within a commutable distance the girls could have attended, making it highly unlikely that they would have continued their education elsewhere unless their families had moved. Further, the academic performance records we consulted did not mention any school transfers for these girls.[3]

Enrolment Patterns Classified by the Last Grade Passed
We examined the most frequently occurring enrolment patterns classified by the last passed grade to more closely assess the grade repetition in the different grades (Table 6.5). When the last grade passed was zero, that is, failure in Grade 1, the most frequently occurring enrolment pattern in all three cohorts was dropping out after failing Grade 1 in the first year of enrolment (1R). Furthermore, when Grade 1 was the last grade passed, the most frequently occurring enrolment pattern was dropping out after passing Grade 1 in the first year of enrolment (1P). For all other

---

[3] School transfer during a school year is mentioned in academic records.

Table 6.4 Dropout patterns by cohort

	Early 1980s cohort				Late 1980s cohort				1990s cohort			
Rank	Enrolment patterns	Number of students (%)	Years registered	Last grade passed	Enrolment patterns	Number of students (%)	Years registered	Last grade passed	Enrolment patterns	Number of students (%)	Years registered	Last grade passed
1	1P	127 (22.4)	1	1	1P	78 (21.4)	1	6	1P	86 (24.3)	1	1
2	1R	61 (10.8)	1	0	1P2P	51 (14.0)	6	9	1P2P	49 (13.8)	2	2
3	1P2P	54 (9.5)	2	2	1R	39 (10.7)	2	6	1R	38 (10.7)	1	0
4	1P2P3P	26 (4.6)	3	3	1P2P3P4P	17 (4.7)	1	6	1P2P3P	36 (10.2)	3	3
5	1P2P3P4P	25 (4.4)	4	4	1P2P3P4P5P	16 (4.4)	9	6	1P2P3P4P5P	21 (5.9)	5	5
6	1P2P3R	21 (3.7)	3	2	1P2R	16 (4.4)	4	9	1P2P3P4P	20 (5.6)	4	4
7	1P2R	20 (3.5)	2	1	1P2P3P	14 (3.8)	5	9	1P2P3P4P5P6P7P	10 (2.8)	2	7
8	1P2P3P4P5P	17 (3.0)	5	5	1P2P3R	10 (2.7)	2	9	1P2R	9 (2.5)	8	2
9	1P2P3P4P5R	17 (3.0)	5	4	1R1R	9 (2.5)	3	6	1P2P3P4P5P6P7P8P	6 (1.7)	2	8
10	1R1P	16 (2.8)	2	1	1R1P	8 (2.2)	6	6	1R1P	6 (1.7)	7	1

No. of patterns with 10 or more students: 12 patterns
No. of patterns with only 1 student: 81 patterns
Total 117 patterns, 567 students

No. of patterns with 10 or more students: 8 patterns
No. of patterns with only 1 student: 35 patterns
Total 69 patterns, 364 students

No. of patterns with 10 or more students: 7 patterns
No. of patterns with only 1 student: 29 patterns
Total 55 patterns, 354 students

Source: The author created it based on collected data

NB: The letter 'P' means the student passed the grade, the letter 'R' means the student failed the grade (required to repeat it), and the letter 'D' means the student dropped out

Table 6.5 Enrolment patterns classified by the last grade passed

Entrance-in-early-1980s group				Entrance-in-late-1980s group				Entrance-in-1990s group			
Last grade passed	Enrolment patterns	No. of students	No. of repetitions	Last grade passed	Enrolment patterns	No. of students	No. of repetitions	Last grade passed	Enrolment patterns	No. of students	No. of repetitions
0	1R	61	1	0	1R	39	1	0	1R	38	1
	1R1R	8	2		1R1R	9	2		1R1R	5	1
					1R1R1R	2	3				
1	1P	127	0	1	1P	78	0	1	1P	86	0
	1P2R	20	1		1P2R	16	1		1P2R	9	1
	1R1P	16	1		1R1P	8	1		1R1P	6	1
	1R1P2R	5	2		1R1P2R	5	2		1P//2P	2	0
	1P//2R	3	1		1P//2R	2	1		1P1R	2	1
	1P2R2R	2	2		1P2R2R	2	2				
	1R1R1P2R	2	3								
2	1P2P	54	0	2	1P2P	51	0	2	1P2P	49	0
	1P2P3R	21	1		1P2P3R	10	1		1R1P2P	4	1
	1R1P2P	6	1		1P2R2P	4	1		1P2P3R	4	1
	1P2P3R3R	5	1		1P//2P	2	0		1P2P2P	2	0
	1P2R2P	5	1		1P2P3N	2	0		1P2R2P	2	1
	1R1P2P3R	5	2		1P2R2P3R	2	2				
	1P2P//3R	3	1		1R1P//2P	2	1				
	1P//2P	2	0		1R1P2P3R	2	2				
3	1P2P3P	26	0	3	1P2P3P	14	0	3	1P2P3P	36	0
	1P2P3P4R	12	1		1P2P3P4R	7	1		1P//2P3P	3	0
	1P2P3P4R4R	2	2		1P2P//3P	4	0		1P2P3P4R	2	1
	1P2P3R3P4R	2	2		1P2R2P3P4R	2	2		1P2P3R3P	2	1
	1P2N3P	2	3		1R1P2R2P3P4R	2	3		1R1P2P3P	2	1
4	1P2P3P4P	25	0	4	1P2P3P4P	17	0	4	1P2P3P4P	20	0
	1P2P3P4P5R	17	1		1P2P3P4P5R	7	1		1R1P2P3P4P	4	1

(continued)

Table 6.5 (continued)

Entrance-in-early-1980s group

Last grade passed	Enrolment patterns	No. of students	No. of repetitions
	1R1P2P3P4R	4	2
	1P2P3P4P5R	3	2
	1P2P3P4R5R	2	2
	1P2P3R3R4P5R	2	3
5	1P2P3P4P5P	17	0
	1P2P3P4P5P6R	10	1
	1P2P3P4P5R5P	3	1
	1P2R2P3P4P5P	2	1
6	1P2P3P4P5P6P	82	0
	1R1P2P3P4P5P6P	9	1
	1P2P3P4R4P5P6P	5	1
	1P2R2P3P4P5P6P	4	1
	1P2P3P4P5P6R6P	3	1
	1P2R3P3P4P5P	2	2
	1R1P2P3P4P5R	2	2
	1R1P2P3P4P5P6R6P	2	2
7	1P2P3P4P5P6P7P	6	0
	1P2P3R3P4P5P6P	2	1
	1P//2P3P4P5P6P7P	1	0
	1P2P3R3P4P5P6P7P	1	1
	1P2R2P3P4P5P6P7P	1	1
	1R1P2P3P4P5P6P7P	1	1
	1P2R2R2P3P4P5P6P7P	1	1
	1R1P2R2P3P4P5P6P7P	1	1
8	1P2P3P4P5P6P7P8P	3	0
	1R1P2P3P4P5P6P7P8P	1	1
	1P2R2R2P3P4P5P6P7P8P	1	2
	1P////2P3P4P5P6P7P8P	1	0

Entrance-in-late-1980s group

Last grade passed	Enrolment patterns	No. of students	No. of repetitions
	1P//2P3P4P	2	0
	1P2R2P3P4P	2	1
5	1P2P3P4P5P	17	0
	1P2P3P4P5P6R	3	1
	1P2P3P4P5R5P	2	1
	1P2P3R3P4P5P	2	1
	1P2P3P4P5P	2	1
6	1P2P3P4P5P6P	72	0
	1R1P2P3P4P5P6P	14	1
	1P2P3P4P5P6P	8	1
	1P2P3R3P4P5P6P	3	1
	1P//2P3P4P5P6P	2	0
	1P2P3P4P5R5P6P	2	1
	1P2R2P3P4R4P5P6P	3	2
7	1P2P3P4P5P6P7P	4	0
	1P2P3P4P5P6P7P7P	1	0
	1P2P3P4P5P6P7P8R	1	1
	1P2R2P3P4P5P6P7P	1	1
8	1P2P3P4P5P6P7P8P	5	0

Entrance-in-1990s group

Last grade passed	Enrolment patterns	No. of students	No. of repetitions
5	1P2P3P4P5P	21	0
	1R1P2P3P4P5P	4	1
	1P2P3P4P5P6R	2	1
6	1P2P3P4P5P6P	74	0
	1R1P2P3P4P5P6P	21	1
	1P2R2P3P4P5P6P	3	1
	1P2P3P4P5P6P7R	2	1
	1P2P3R3P4P5P6P	2	1
7	1P2P3P4P5P6P7P	10	0
	1P2P3P5P5P6P7P	1	0
	1P//2P3P4P5P6P7P	1	0
	1R1P2P3P4P5P6P7P8R	1	2
8	1P2P3P4P5P6P7P8P	6	0
	1P2P3P4P5P6P7P8R	1	1
	1P2P3R3P4P5P6P7P8P	1	1

9			9			9		
1P2P3P4P5P6P7P8P9P	32	0	1P2P3P4P5P6P7P8P9P	22	0	1P2P3P4P5P6P7P8P9P	49	0
1R2P3P4P5P6P7P8P9P	1	1	1P2R2P3P4P5P6P7P8P9P	3	1	1R1P2P3P4P5P6P7P8P9P	3	1
1P2P3R3P4P5P6P7P8P9P	1	1	1R1P2P3P4P5P6P7P8P9P	3	1	1P2P3P4R5P6P7P8P9P	1	1
1P2R2P3P4P5P6P7P8P9P	1	1	1P//2P3P4P5P6P7P8P9P	1	0	1P2P3P4S5P6P7P8P9P	1	0
			1P2P3R3P4P5P6P7P8P9P	1	1	1P//2P3P4P5P6P7P8P9P	1	0
			1R1P2P3P4P5R6P7P8P9P	1	2	1P2P3P//4P5P6P7P8P9P	1	0
			1R1P2R2P3P4P5P6P7P8P9P	1	2			

Notes: For primary education, the pattern is described where two or more people fall into this category

For lower secondary education, all patterns are described

Source: The author created it based on collected data

Wenrolment patterns from Grade 2 to Grade 9, the most frequently occurring pattern was advancing to the next grade each year until the last grade without repeating a year. For each last grade passed, except for Grade 0, the most frequently occurring enrolment patterns included no repetition. Likewise, except for Grade 0, enrolment patterns with grade repetition were ranked second or lower for each last grade passed, and there was only one grade repetition. Therefore, similar to the enrolment situation analysis in the Honduran regional city study, most students dropped out abruptly without any repetition.

Based on the findings from our analysis, the overall enrolment situation for the El Salvadoran girls was less favourable than their Honduran peers, which was contrary to previous reports that compared the female enrolment situations in Honduras and El Salvador and generally put El Salvador in a better position. In the EFA Development Index,[4] indicating the degree of achievement of the EFA goals (UNESCO, 2015), El Salvador scored 0.909 compared to 0.870 in Honduras. In the following section, we examine El Salvador's situation based on the data characteristics from the Salvadoran school and the country's social background.

Salvadoran School Data Characteristics and El Salvador's Social Background During the Study Period

Unlike Sekiya's (2014) analysis of schools in the Honduran regional city, we constructed the database using data collected from the year-end academic performance records that had been retained by the school. As in Honduras, at the beginning of each school year in El Salvador, parents register their children at the schools that they are to attend, and this information is entered into the schools' registers. Because Salvadoran schools were not required by law to retain their registers, it was up to each school to retain these documents. Academic performance records were similarly treated, that is, there was no law requiring schools to retain these records. Therefore, when we collected the data for this study in 2014, without

[4] EFA (Education for All) Development Index (EDI) indicates the degree of achievement by a country of the EFA goals, calculated on the basis of four indicators (primary adjusted net enrolment ratio, adult literacy rate, gender-specific EFA index and survival rate to Grade 5). Since the EDI can only be obtained when data on the four indicators are available, it is not easy to calculate it for developing countries, where educational systems are often not fully established and necessary data are not readily available. The 2012 data used in the EFA Monitoring Report 2015 are of 113 countries only.

these school registers, it was impossible to track the least desirable enrolment pattern: students who registered as first graders and dropped out mid-year (1D); therefore, our analysis of the Salvadoran school did not include the 1D pattern. Nonetheless, the results revealed that the enrolment situation was less favourable than in Ashida and Sekiya's (2016) study of Honduran schools. From this, we surmised that the school we chose for this study had some serious enrolment problems.

The girls analysed in this study entered school between 1980 and 1997. The civil war (1980–1992) in El Salvador was in progress during this period. Lai and Thyne (2007) studied governmental spending for education and schooling situations during and after civil wars using data from countries that suffered from domestic armed conflicts between 1980 and 1997. They determined that due to increased civil war military spending, there was reduced government education funding, thereby leading to a decrease in school enrolments and attendance. Moreover, the negative impact of reduced education funding affected the post-conflict years, which, in some cases, destroyed education systems. For example, Gómez (2016) analysed the impacts of the Columbian civil war on the academic achievements of higher secondary school students, identifying that the conflict may have led to lower scores in Mathematics and Spanish. León (2012) examined the impact of civil war on the number of years of children's schooling in Peru and found that there was on average a noticeable decrease of 0.31 years of schooling until adulthood. Chamarbagwala and Morán's (2011) study in Guatemala determined the average years of schooling during the civil war were 4.66 years for boys and 3.83 years for girls, pointing out the particularly negative consequence for girls.

The interviews with teachers at the school in this study confirmed that the school had not been physically impacted by the civil war as there had not been any demolition of school facilities. Furthermore, the school was not operated by the community-participatory system, EDUCO. Still, the studies cited above and the EFA Global Monitoring Report refer to actual situations wherein, education, in particular, secondary education for girls, is hindered by armed conflict (UNESCO, 2011). Therefore, one cannot deny the possibility that the studied school, although not directly affected by the civil war, could have been indirectly influenced by the social situation at the time, school education being disrupted especially for girls.

5   Conclusion

Based on the academic performance records from a school offering basic education in a regional city in El Salvador, this chapter discussed the individual education situation for female students during and immediately after El Salvador's civil war. The enrolment status and pattern analyses allowed us to confirm two opposing situations of students dropping out during the first years of school and the number of students who continued until graduation in three cohorts, namely early 1980s, late 1980s and from 1990 to 1997. The primary school dropout pattern analysis identified that enrolment patterns with repetition were not ranked at the first place in terms of frequency of occurrence. In the early 1980s' cohort, repetition was identified as the second place common enrolment pattern; however, this was only 10% of dropouts. Meanwhile, in the late 1980s' and the 1990s' cohorts, patterns including repetition were identified from the third most common pattern; however, this represented only 10.7% of the total dropouts.

In the analysis of the frequent enrolment patterns, which were classified by the last grade passed and excluded Grade 0, the most common enrolment patterns did not include grade repetition; that is, most girl students who abruptly quit school had not repeated a grade. These findings were similar to those obtained in a similar Honduran study (Ashida & Sekiya, 2016).

Due to the challenges, the girls who entered school experienced during and immediately after the civil war, our analysis identified the dropouts after they had passed first grade and the grade repetition in the early primary grades, namely Grades 1 and 2. At the end of the civil war, El Salvador adopted a national policy, emphasising basic education. Furthermore, the country began accepting international assistance. Consequently, El Salvador has seen a marked improvement in education, with the primary education completion rate reaching 88.4% in 2014 (90.3% when only girls are considered) and the lower secondary completion rate reaching 72.5% (73.2% for girls only; UNESCO-Institute for Statistics [UIS], 2018). Due to these improvements, analysing how this desired enrolment was achieved in a country that had been severely disrupted by civil war could be instructive for countries that have had similar experiences.

Finally, a limitation of this study is that the school records used for the data analysis had to be constructed using only the evaluation book as the school registration book was unavailable. Therefore, we were unable to include any analyses of the girls who had enrolled in the school but left before the end-of-year assessment. As data such as the age at school entrance could also not be collected, we were unable to determine whether the girls were of the appropriate age for schooling.

Acknowledgements The author would like to express her gratitude to Ms Mayra Valle Torres and Ms Sury Valladares for their invaluable assistance in data collection and database development. This study was financially supported by the Japan Society for the Promotion of Science KAKENHI under Grant Numbers 26257114, 16J03171 and 19K14119.

REFERENCES

Alexander, K. L., Entwisle, D. R., & Dauber, S. L. (1994). *On the success of failure: A reassessment of the effects of retention in the primary grades.* Cambridge University Press.

Ashida, A., & Sekiya, T. (2016). Changes in the repetition and dropout situation in Honduran primary education since the late 1980s. *Education 3–13, 44*(4), 458–477. https://doi.org/10.1080/03004279.2014.991414

Cardoso, A. R., & Verner, D. (2007). School drop-out and push-out factors in Brazil: The role of early parenthood, child labor, and poverty. *Policy Research Working Paper*, no. 4178. *SSRN Electronic Journal.* World Bank. https://doi. org/10.2139/ssrn.955862

Chamarbagwala, R., & Morán, H. E. (2011). The human capital consequences of civil war: Evidence from Guatemala. *Journal of Development Economics, 94*(1), 41–61. https://doi.org/10.1016/j.jdeveco.2010.01.005

Edwards, D. B., Jr., Victoria Libreros, J. A., & Martin, P. (2015). The geometry of policy implementation: Lessons from the political economy of three education reforms in el Salvador during 1990–2005. *International Journal of Educational Development, 44*, 28–41. https://doi.org/10.1016/j.ijedudev. 2015.05.001

Gómez Soler, S. C. (2016). Educational achievement at schools: Assessing the effect of the civil conflict using a pseudo-panel of schools. *International Journal of Educational Development, 49*, 91–106. https://doi.org/10.1016/j. ijedudev.2016.02.004

Guarcello, L., Lyon, S., & Valdivia, C. (2015). Evolution of the relationship between child labour and education since 2000: Evidence from 19 developing countries, *Background paper prepared for the Education for All Global Monitoring Report 2015.*

Japan International Cooperation Agency (JICA). (1994). *Erusarubadoru Kyowakoku Shoto/chuto gakko kensetsu keikaku jizen chosa hokokusho* [*Preliminary survey report for the primary and lower secondary school building construction project in el Salvador*]. JICA. (in Japanese)

Justino, P. (2016). Supply and demand restrictions to education in conflict-affected countries: New research and future agendas. *International Journal of Educational Development, 47,* 76–85. https://doi.org/10.1016/j.ijedudev.2016.01.002

Lai, B., & Thyne, C. (2007). The effect of civil war on education, 1980–97. *Journal of Peace Research, 44*(3), 277–292. https://doi.org/10.1177/002234 3307076631

León, G. (2012). Civil conflict and human capital accumulation: The long-term effects of political violence in Perú. *Journal of Human Resources, 47*(4), 991–1023. https://doi.org/10.1353/jhr.2012.0036

Marshall, J. H. (2003). Grade repetition in Honduran primary schools. *International Journal of Educational Development, 23*(6), 591–605. https://doi.org/10.1016/S0738-0593(03)00060-9

McGinn, N., Reimers, F., Loera, A., Soto, M., & López, S. (1992). *Why do children repeat grades? A study of rural primary schools in Honduras.* Bridges Research Report Series no. 13. Harvard Institute for International Development.

Ministry of Foreign Affairs of Japan. (2024). Erusarubadoru Kyowakoku. (Republic of El Salvador). https://www.mofa.go.jp/mofaj/area/elsalvador/index.html (in Japanese).

Randall, L., & Anderson, J. B. (1999). *Schooling for Success: Preventing repetition and dropout in Latin American primary schools.* M.E. Sharpe.

Sekiya, T. (2014). Individual patterns of enrolment in primary schools in the republic of Honduras. *Education 3–13, 42*(5), 460–474. https://doi.org/10.1080/03004279.2012.715665

Sekiya, T., & Ashida, A. (2017). An analysis of primary school dropout patterns in Honduras. *Journal of Latinos and Education, 16*(1), 65–73. https://doi.org/10.1080/15348431.2016.1179185

UNESCO. (2008). *Overcoming inequality: Why governance matters. Education for all global monitoring report 2009.* UNESCO.

UNESCO. (2011). *The hidden crisis: Armed conflict and education. Education for all global monitoring report 2011.* UNESCO.

UNESCO. (2015). *Education for All 2000–2015: Achievements and challenges. Education for all global monitoring report 2015. Regional overview: Latin America and the Caribbean.* UNESCO.

UNESCO Institute for Statistics (UIS). (2018). *UIS.Stat,* completion rate, primary and lower secondary, both sexes and female. Retrieved March 15, 2018, from http://data.uis.unesco.org

UNESCO Santiago. (2014). *Latin America and the Caribbean education for all 2015 regional review*. UNESCO.

United Nations Development Programme. (2024). *Human Development Report 2023–24: Breaking the gridlock: Reimagining cooperation in a polarized world*.

World Bank. (2022). Open data. El Salvador: World Bank. https://data.world-bank.org/country/el-salvador

Barriers to Completion of Basic Education: Individual Children's Actual Enrolment Status in Nepal

Naruho Ezaki

1 ENVIRONMENT SURROUNDING BASIC EDUCATION IN NEPAL

Current Trends in Educational Development Since 1990 and the Present

Education for All (EFA) and Millennium Development Goals (MDGs) were agreed upon as common goals for the international community in 1990 and 2000, respectively, and international efforts were undertaken to fully disseminate primary and basic education. As a result, primary education enrolment has improved significantly in South and West Asia (United Nations Educational, Scientific and Cultural Organization [UNESCO],

N. Ezaki (✉)
Faculty of Global Culture and Communication, Aichi Shukutoku University, Nagoya, Japan
e-mail: nezaki@asu.aasa.ac.jp

© The Author(s), under exclusive license to Springer Nature Switzerland AG 2024
T. Sekiya et al. (eds.), *Towards Ensuring Inclusive and Equitable Quality Education for All*, International and Development Education, https://doi.org/10.1007/978-3-031-70266-2_7

127

2015). The net enrolment rate for primary education in the region rose from 78% in 1999 to 94% in 2012 (UNESCO, 2015)[1] and has remained in the 90% range since then (UNESCO, 2020, 2021). In the Federal Democratic Republic of Nepal (hereinafter Nepal), one of the least developed countries (LDCs) in South Asia, the net enrolment rate exceeded 90% in 2008/2009 (Ministry of Education, 2009), and the quantitative expansion of primary education is close to being achieved. Moreover, for basic education, the net enrolment rate in 2021/22 reached 94.7% (Centre for Education and Human Resource Development [CEHRD], 2021). Enrolment in primary and basic education is relatively satisfactory. However, it faces challenges in terms of internal efficiency, including a high repetition rate in the lower grades, and the completion rate for basic education is only 75.3% (CEHRD, 2021). In other words, many children in Nepal, once entered in school, drop out without ever graduating, a situation that needs significant improvement to achieve SDG 4.

Basic Information and School Education in Nepal

Nepal, the country treated in this chapter, is a landlocked country located in South Asia, sandwiched between the two major powers of China and India. The population was about 29.16 million as of 2021 (National Statistics Office, 2021), with 126 ethnic groups living together (Central Bureau of Statistics [CBS], 2012). The official language is Nepali, but 123 languages are spoken (CBS, 2012), making it a multi-ethnic and multilingual nation in South Asia. The main industries are agriculture and forestry, trade and wholesale trade and transportation and communication, with one in five of the population engaged in agriculture, forestry and fishing (CBS, 2019). The country ranks 143rd out of 191 countries in the 2020 human development index ranking (United Nations Development Programme [UNDP], 2022).

The education system in Nepal is an 8–4 system: eight years of basic education (Grades 1–8) and four years of secondary education (Grades 9–12). Basic education is considered free and compulsory and is divided into lower basic education for Grades 1–5 and upper basic education for Grades 6–8. Moreover, one year of pre-school education was also positioned as basic education, making nine years of basic education to be

---

[1] As in South and West Asia, there has been a marked improvement in sub-Saharan Africa, with the net enrolment rate rising from 59% in 1999 to 79% in 2012 (UNESCO, 2015).

exact. One of the major challenges in the education sector is the educational gap between public and private schools. The dysfunction of public schools has been noted in various previous studies; examples include absenteeism by teachers, strong political colouration of teachers and poor quality of education (Bhandari, 2016; Joshi, 2014; Subedi et al., 2013). Conversely, private schools have higher pass rates in examinations that are important for higher education and employment than public schools (Bhatta, 2004; Thapa, 2015). Moreover, in general, Nepali is the language of instruction in public schools,[2] while in private schools the language of instruction is either English, an international language, or Nepali and English. Therefore, people prefer to send their children to private schools because they believe that private schools offer a better education than public schools (Ezaki, 2021a).

Against this backdrop, the number of children entered in private schools has increased. Today, even the middle class makes economic sacrifices and sends their children to private schools when they have the chance. As a result, some are concerned about the 'impoverishment' of public schools, such that public schools may become places where poor children go (Bhatta, 2009; Bhatta & Budathoki, 2013). What is the actual enrolment status for children who are left behind in the trend away from public schools to private schools in pursuit of 'high-quality education'?

Why Do So Many Children in Nepal Fail to Complete Basic Education?

Thanks to the efforts of the Nepalese government and international aid agencies, the quantitative expansion of education in basic education is nearing completion. However, there is the issue of entering school but not completion, and completion rate remains at 75.3% (CEHRD, 2021). A report issued by the Ministry of Education, Science and Technology of Nepal lists physical distance, household economic difficulties, discrimination, social and household pressure, to join the labour force, early marriage, etc. as factors that may cause students to drop out of school and thus hinder completion of basic education (CEHRD, 2021). Moreover, according to the National Living Standards Survey of Household, 25% of respondents cited poor academic progress as a reason for leaving school

[2] With the trend towards an emphasis on English in Nepal, some public schools have introduced English medium instruction in recent years (Joshi, 2016).

(CBS, 2011). Thus, children who fail academically and must repeat a grade are more likely to drop out (Ministry of Education, United Nations Children's Fund [UNICEF] & UNESCO, 2016). In response to this situation, the country introduced the continuous assessment system (CAS) to support the quality of education. However, the dysfunction of CAS has been pointed out for some time, and issues such as repetition and dropout have not been resolved. With less than six years remaining before the deadline for achieving SDG 4, where should we focus our efforts to prevent children from dropping out of school and increase completion rates?

It is common to overview children's enrolment status using a cross-sectional data approach, and cross-sectional data have been used in many studies. However, cross-sectional data are an amalgamation of various different individual cases and are only visible in the aggregate. In order to achieve the SDGs under the slogan 'No one will be left behind', it is necessary to shed light on individual children, which can never be seen simply by tracking changes in cross-sectional statistical data such as school attendance, repetition and dropout rates announced annually. One way to do this is through studies using longitudinal data. Because longitudinal studies require a great deal of effort and time, there are few examples of reports in developing countries where the research environment is not conducive to such studies. However, a longitudinal study from a micro perspective would be essential.

Based on this awareness of these issues, the author has been conducting research in Nepal by tracing the enrolment trajectories of individual children longitudinally using school records in target schools and studying their actual enrolment conditions. This study analyses each of the phenomena related to enrolment in schools, such as graduation, repetition and dropout, by considering enrolment as a pattern and examines the actual situation and background of these phenomena. This chapter attempts to present concrete measures that could lead to the completion of basic education through the cases that have been identified so far from the analysis conducted using longitudinal data.

Target Area, School and Data of Study

The target area for this study was selected as (1) areas where the establishment of private schools has increased rapidly in recent years, (2) somewhat isolated areas where the enrolment of children can be tracked and (3) areas where cooperation can be obtained from local people. The study then determined that Town X, a suburb in Bhaktapur District, Bagmati Province, was appropriate for these conditions. Bhaktapur District is an area where children's attendance in private schools has increased in recent years (Department of Education, 2011). Town X is located on a small hill and has an isolated position with only one access road to the city. The target schools for this study are all five public schools located in this Town X. Four of these five schools receive children in pre-primary through Grade 5, the last grade of lower basic education, while the remaining school receives children in pre-primary through Grade 12, the last grade of secondary education. Hence, many children entered in the four schools that only offer up to Grade 5 tend to transfer to the one remaining school that offers up to Grade 12 before or after the completion of fifth grade. The subjects of this study are children who entered in the target schools between 2003 and 2007 and graduated or dropped out by 2017. The longitudinal data were constructed from the school records of the target schools and the results of a home-visit survey and interviews.

2 INDIVIDUAL CHILDREN'S ACTUAL ENROLMENT STATUS

Frequent Enrolment Patterns

As noted above, there have been many observations regarding the dysfunction of public schools in Nepal. Improving the quality of education in public schools is also explicit in government-issued reports (see, e.g., Ministry of Education, Science and Technology, 2021). However, to the best of my knowledge, there are no research reports that focus on individual children and reveal how they follow their enrolment trajectories.

Ezaki (2019) therefore analysed the enrolment patterns of each of the 84 children in lower basic education. Table 7.1 lists the enrolment patterns in descending order of frequency, which shows patterns that apply to two or more children. The numbers in the enrolment pattern refer to grades, and the letters in the alphabet refer to end-of-year evaluations. 'P' is for pass, 'F' is for fail and 'D' is for dropout. '//' indicates that the children have not been in school for one year. The most common pattern was '1P2P3P4P5P', in which children entered the first grade and advanced to the fifth grade without experiencing a single grade repetition or temporary dropout. Such a pattern is called 'straight graduation'. This straight graduation is the most ideal pattern in terms of enrolment pattern, but its percentage is only 31.0% (Ezaki, 2019). The next most common patterns

Table 7.1 The frequently observed enrolment patterns

Rank	Enrolment pattern	No. of children	Ratio
1	1P2P3P4P5P	26	31.0
2	1D	6	7.1
2	1P//2P3P4P5P	6	7.1
4	1F1P2P3P4P5P	4	4.8
4	1F1F1P2P3P4P5P	4	4.8
6	1P2P3P4P5D	3	3.6
7	1P2P3P4D	2	2.4
7	1P2F2D	2	2.4
7	1P2D	2	2.4
	Total	84	

Note: P = pass, F = fail, D = dropout, // = one-year dropout

Source: Reproduced by the author based on Ezaki (2019)

are two examples. One is the '1D' pattern, in which children enter the first grade and drop out within less than a year. The other pattern was '1P//2P3P4P5P', in which the children dropped out for one year after passing the first-year class but returned the following year, successfully advanced and graduated (7.1% each; Ezaki, 2019). Thus, the most ideal straight graduation or graduation pattern and the worst pattern of leaving school after a short period of study are located in the top two positions. In other words, the reality of the enrolment is at both extremes. With the population so close to polarisation, it is difficult to believe that repetition rates, dropout rates and years of completion, which are simply viewed as averages, accurately represent the picture of the population.

Enrolment Status by Gender

In many developing countries, not only in Nepal, when gender is discussed, girls are the target of support. Because Nepal is a male-dominated society, girls have been subjected to various forms of discrimination. For example, there was a tendency in society as a whole to place more importance on education for sons who would look after the parents at their old age than for daughters who would marry into other families in the future.[3]

---

[3] This trend is also seen in neighboring India, where, according to James and Woodhead (2014), one parent believes that 'it is better to give our eldest son an education because he will be taking care of us in the future.'

Thus, the enrolment rate of girls was lower than that of boys for a long time. Due to government efforts, the gender gap in enrolment in lower basic education has now been eliminated (CEHRD, 2021). However, are girls, who study hard under these circumstances, performing worse than boys in terms of enrolment patterns?

Ezaki (2019) analysed gender differences by classifying the 84 children's previous enrolment patterns into five groups by gender: straight graduation, pattern of repeating the first year but graduating, other graduation patterns, other dropout patterns and 1D (Fig. 7.1). The results showed that the overall graduation rate is higher for girls than for boys. Girls were also more likely to have the most ideal pattern of 'straight graduation', while girls were less likely to have the opposite pattern, '1D'. Although there was no statistically significant difference in their distribution, it was clear that girls were slightly better off in their enrolment status than boys (Ezaki, 2019). However, disparities as to which types of schools one can study at still exist. Until now, the main issue for girls has been whether they can go to school, but that issue has now shifted to whether they can go to private schools (Ezaki, 2020).

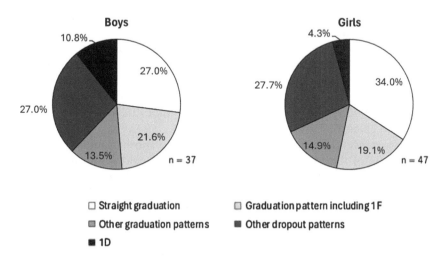

Fig. 7.1 Enrolment status by gender. (Source: Reproduced by the author based on Ezaki, 2019)

Extraordinary Enrolment Patterns

In studies of other countries using longitudinal data, surprising enrolment realities that cannot be captured by cross-sectional data were revealed. For example, although the regions differ, several patterns were identified in Malawi, Africa, where children were failing one grade level, temporarily dropped out, and when they returned to school, they were registered in the next grade level, a pattern that is difficult to understand (Kawaguchi, 2018). In Zambia, also in Africa, a pattern was observed of children restudying from one grade level below due to the medium of instruction[4] and lack of school facilities, which is worse than the normal repetition (Ezaki & Nakamura, 2018).

These extraordinary enrolment patterns were also observed in the target schools in Nepal. In this country, there are no school district regulations like in Japan; therefore, children are free to choose their school and change schools.[5] Hence, many children change schools, both in and out of semesters, to suit their own and their families' circumstances (Ezaki, 2018). In this section, the study focuses on the unique patterns resulting from school transfers.

Figure 7.2 (Nos. 2–8) shows extraordinary enrolment patterns due to school transfers (Ezaki, 2019). The vertical axis of the figure represents the grade, the horizontal axis represents the number of years that children registered, and 'T' in the figure indicates the time of transfer. The lower right-hand corner of each figure shows (1) enrolment pattern, (2) grade-level change and (3) school type before and after the transfer. As a comparison, the No. 1 figure shows the 'straight graduation' pattern. These transfer patterns can be divided into three groups: (A) a pattern in which grades are lowered (Nos. 2, 3 and 4), (B) a pattern in which grades are increased (No. 5) and (C) a pattern in which grades are lowered and then increased (Nos. 6, 7 and 8) (Ezaki, 2019).

For instance, the child in No. 2 transferred to another public school in the middle of the fourth grade year. Since he was already in the fourth grade, he would normally be registered in the fourth grade at his new school, but he was actually registered in the second grade. The reason for grade lowering is that the children's academic ability was not at the level required by the new school, and in a sense, this can be seen as a rational

---

[4] In Zambia, the medium of instruction changes from the local language to English in Grade 5.

[5] However, rules for transfer are established.

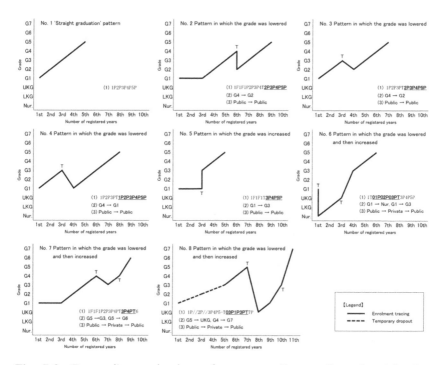

Fig. 7.2 Extraordinary school transfer patterns. (Source: Reproduced by the author based on Ezaki, 2019)

decision (Ezaki, 2019). The child in No. 5 transferred to another public school in the middle of the first-grade year and would normally be registered in the first grade at the new school. However, she was actually registered in the third grade. For this pattern of grade levels being moved up two or more grades, the continuity of learning may be lost.

Even more serious is Group (C). In this group, the school grade is lowered when the child transfers from a public school to a private school, while the grade is increased when the child transfers from a private school to a public school (Ezaki, 2019). For instance, No. 6 child was registered in the first grade of a public school but was transferred to a private school in the middle of the school year. He would normally be registered in the first grade, but he was registered in the nursery class at his new school. He then completed upper kindergarten and was transferred to a public school. He was supposed to be transferred to the first grade; however, he was registered in the third grade. Although private schools are generally considered to be at a higher level than public schools, the content of study at each grade level in public and private schools is the same. It is therefore highly likely that the continuity of learning has been disrupted by the placement of children in grades whose legitimacy is questionable due to school transfers, especially in subject education where systematics is important, such as mathematics and science (Ezaki, 2019). Under these conditions, children cannot keep up with classes and have difficulty acquiring academic skills.

The national assessment of student achievement in mathematics, conducted with fifth graders in 2018, revealed that 72% of children did not have sufficient knowledge and skills and were underachieving[6] (Education Review Office [ERO], 2019). There are many possible factors behind this, but the loss of continuity in learning as described above may be one of them. Without a steady acquisition of basic academic skills at each grade level, it will be difficult for children to advance to the next step of upper basic education (Grades 6–8) and continue their studies thereafter.

3   Until the Children Dropped Out of School

Relationship Between Grade Repetition and School Dropout

This chapter has so far analysed the enrolment patterns of individual children in the lower basic education level. In this section, the study expands the educational level to upper basic education and examines how children actually drop out of school, focusing on the relationship between grade repetition and school dropout.

Repeating a grade has been a problematic factor for a long time, and previous studies (Agarwal, 2020; Brophy, 2006; Jimerson et al., 2002; Rose & AI-Samarrai, 2001) have pointed to the strong association between grade repetition and school dropout, such that the higher the repetition rates, the higher the dropout rates. Concerns about grade repetition continue to this day, and discussions on automatic grade promotion as a possible countermeasure are ongoing (UNESCO, 2020).

However, recent studies have reported that repetition and dropout are considered to be two different things. For example, Sekiya and Ashida (2017) used longitudinal data to analyse the dropout patterns of

---

[6] In Nepali, 55% of children were found to be underachieving (ERO, 2019).

individual children in primary schools in Honduras, Central America. The results revealed that (1) although many of the dropouts included those who had repeated a grade, there were many children who dropped out suddenly without experiencing repetitions and (2) the most frequent dropout pattern for each completed grade did not include those who had repeated a grade in any of the grades. This argues that repetition and dropout should not be viewed as being in the same family, but rather as separate entities. Moreover, Kabay (2016), who conducted a study of 136 primary schools in Uganda, also found that repeating a grade did not increase the likelihood of dropping out; rather, age at school entry, which indicates at what age children entered school, was important.

Turning to Nepal, the high repetition rate in the lower grades is a challenge, especially for first-year children, which is extremely high at 14.4% (CEHRD, 2021). In response to these challenges, the country introduced the CAS to support the quality of education.[7] However, various challenges have long been identified, including the cumbersomeness of CAS (Poyck et al., 2016), class sizes that are incompatible with CAS (Dahal et al., 2019) and lack of faculty capacity (British Council, 2020; Dahal et al., 2019), among other issues. Furthermore, negative effects on children due to lack of proper CAS have also been reported. According to Dahal et al. (2019), a female student who was advanced by CAS despite falling behind in her studies was unable to cope with the standards of the next grade's curriculum and was expelled from school. Thus, although CAS was introduced with the aim of supporting the quality of education, it faces various challenges, and the problem of repetition and dropout in the country remains. Then, how is the relationship between repetition and dropout?

Dropout Patterns by Grade Completed

Against the above background, Ezaki (2024) compared the experience of repetitions and the number of repetitions for graduates and dropouts by using the data of 78 children. The results did not show a statistically significant difference; nevertheless, the tendency for dropouts to repeat a grade was readily apparent. Therefore, to directly examine the relationship between repetition and dropout, Ezaki (2024) analysed the dropout

---

[7] CAS was originally initiated for lower grades, but since 2009 has been introduced for Grades 1–7.

patterns of 44 individual children. Table 7.2 shows all dropout patterns by the grades the children were able to complete.

The frequent patterns that apply to more than one person were identified in the completed grades 0, 1, 3, 4, 6 and 7. First, looking at these frequent patterns, two out of seven cases (5 out of 23 children) included repetitions, which were the completed grades 1 and 6. Moreover, only one case (two children) was noted in which children repeated a grade

Table 7.2 Dropout patterns by grade completed

Grade completed	Enrolment pattern	No. of children	No. of repetitions
Grade 0	1D	6	0
	1-1D	1	0
	1-////1D	1	0
	1-1F**1F**1D	1	2
	1F1F//**1F**1D	1	3
Grade 1	1P2D	2	0
	1P2**F**2D	2	1
	1F1P2-**2F**2D	1	2
	1F1-////1P2D	1	1
	1F1P//2F**2F**2D	1	3
Grade 2	1P2P3D	1	0
	1F1P2P3D	1	1
	1-2P3-////3D	1	0
Grade 3	1P2P3P4D	2	0
	1P2F2P3P4D	1	1
	1P2P3F3P**4F**4D	1	2
Grade 4	1P2P3P4P5D	3	0
	1P//2P3P4P5D	1	0
	1F1F1P2P3P4P5D	1	2
Grade 5	1P2P3P4P5P6D	1	0
	1F1P2P3P4P5P6D	1	1
	1F1P2P3P4P5F5P6D	1	2
	1F1P2P3F3P4P5P6D	1	1
Grade 6	1F1F1P2P3P4P5P6P7D	3	2
	1F1F1-3P4P5P6P7D	1	2
	1P//2P3P4P5P6P7D	1	0
Grade 7	1P2P3P4P5P6P7P8D	4	0
	1F1P2P3-3P4P5P6P7P8D	1	1
	1F//1P//2P3P4P5P6P7P8D	1	1
	Total	44	

Note: P = pass, F = fail, D = dropout, -= no end-of-year evaluation, // = one-year dropout

Source: Reproduced by the author based on Ezaki (2024)

immediately prior to leaving, which may have triggered the children to drop out ('1P2F2D': passed the first grade, failed the second grade and re-registered in the second grade the following year but dropped out). Thus, the study found that patterns of children suddenly dropping out of school for one reason or another without experiencing any repetition is more common such as '1D' (dropped out of school less than a year after registration), '1P2D' (passed the first grade and advanced to the second grade but dropped out) and '1P2P3P4D' (passed first to third grades without any repetitions, advanced to the fourth grade but dropped out; Ezaki, 2024). The result of the frequent patterns of not including repetition in the pattern is similar to the result of Sekiya and Ashida (2017).[8]

Second, overall, the pattern including repetitions was 17 out of 28 cases. Of these, only six cases were found to have been repeated a grade immediately prior to dropping out of school, which could have triggered their dropout (Ezaki, 2024), which is a mere 15.9% of the total. Hence, Ezaki (2024) states that although repetition is one of the triggers for dropping out, it is not the main cause. This result is consistent with Sekiya and Ashida (2017) and Kabay (2016). If repeating a grade is not the main cause of dropping out, then what is the problem?

4 ENROLMENT STATUS AND AGE

Age at School Entry of Graduates and Dropouts

When discussing the causes of dropping out of school, age at school entry is often pointed out, similar to grade repetition (Sabates et al., 2013; Sekiya, 2014; UNESCO Institute for Statistics [UIS] & UNICEF, 2005; UNESCO, 2009; Wils, 2004). Among them, Sekiya (2014), who conducted a study in Honduras, reported that the graduation rate decreases as an age at school entry increases. While 68.5% of the children in the five- to six-year-old group graduated, which includes the official age at school entry of 5, only 49.6% of the children in the overage seven- to eight-year-old group graduated. Furthermore, as for the nine-year-old or older group, even fewer (10.5%) of the children graduated.

In Nepal, the country covered in this chapter, there is an underage problem and an overage problem. Therefore, Ezaki (2024) classified the

---

[8] In Sekiya and Ashida (2017)'s study, the most frequent patterns for all grades (completed grades 0–5) did not include any repetitions.

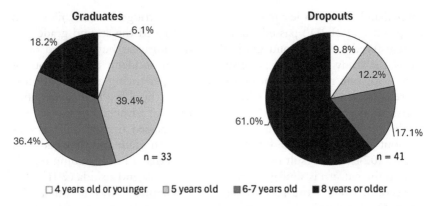

Fig. 7.3 Comparison of age at school entry of graduates and dropouts. (Source: Reproduced by the author based on Ezaki, 2024)

age at school entry of graduates and dropouts in the previous section into four groups and analysed the differences between them, that is, (1) underage: four years old or younger, (2) official age at school entry: five years old, (3) overage: six–seven years old and (4) overage: eight years old or older. The results confirmed that the largest percentage of graduates was at the age of five years (39.4%), which aligns with the official school entry age (Fig. 7.3). This was followed by those aged six–seven years (36.4%). In contrast, the majority of dropouts were older, with eight years or older accounting for over half of the total (61.0%). A significant variance in school entry age was evident between the two groups. Thus, Ezaki (2024) states that these results indicate a strong correlation between age at school entry and school dropout, and children are more likely to leave school if their age at school entry is more than three years older than the official school entry age.

Dropout Pattern by Age at School Entry

In the analysis of the previous section, it was found that the turning point is whether the child is three years older than the official age at school entry, that is, whether the child is younger than eight years old or eight years old or older at the time of school entry. Thereafter, what differences can be observed in the enrolment patterns of the groups whose age at school entry is (1) younger than eight years old and (2) eight years old or older? Ezaki (2024) classified the dropouts into the two aforementioned groups and analysed their enrolment status thoroughly (Table 7.3). The results affirmed that for the group of younger than eight years old, most

Table 7.3 Enrolment patterns of children whose age at school entry were under than eight years old and eight years old or older

No.	Enrolment pattern	No. of children	Grade completed	Ratio
Under eight years old				
1	1D	3	0	18.8
2	1P2F2P3P4D	1	3	6.3
3	1P2P3P4P5D	1	4	18.8
4	1P//2P3P4P5D	1	4	
5	1F1F1P2P3P4P5D	1	4	
6	1F1P2P3P4P5P6D	1	5	18.8
7	1F1P2P3F3P4P5P6D	1	5	
8	1F1P2P3P4P5F5P6D	1	5	
9	1F1F1-3P4P5P6P7D	1	6	18.8
10	1F1F1P2P3P4P5P6P7D	2	6	
11	1P2P3P4P5P6P7P8D	1	7	18.8
12	1F1P2P3-3P4P5P6P7P8D	1	7	
13	1F//1P//2P3P4P5P6P7P8D	1	7	
	Total	16		
Eight years old or older				
1	1D	3	0	28.0
2	1-1D	1	0	
3	1-1F1F1D	1	0	
4	1-////1D	1	0	
5	1F1F//1F1D	1	0	
6	1F1-////1P2D	1	1	24.0
7	1F1P//2F2F2D	1	1	
8	1P2D	1	1	
9	1P2F2D	2	1	
10	1F1P2-2F2D	1	1	
11	1P2P3D	1	2	8.0
12	1F1P2P3D	1	2	
13	1P2P3P4D	2	3	12.0
14	1P2P3F3P4F4D	1	3	
15	1P2P3P4P5D	2	4	8.0
16	1P2P3P4P5P6D	1	5	4.0
17	1P//2P3P4P5P6P7D	1	6	4.0
18	1P2P3P4P5P6P7P8D	3	7	12.0
	Total	25		

Source: Reproduced by the author based on Ezaki (2024)

children were able to advance to the fourth grade, which is in the middle of the basic education level (81.2%). Conversely, for the eight years or older group, the percentage was only 40%, almost half of the total. Hence, children whose age at school entry was eight years or older had a relatively brief period of attendance and might not have fully grasped the curriculum from the lower grade levels.

Furthermore, children in the eight years or older group have unique and complex schooling trajectories, including repeating the same grade without obtaining an end-of-year evaluation and experiencing multiple repetitions and temporary dropouts (Ezaki, 2024). For instance, child No. 5 experienced a disruption in her schooling. She repeated the first grade twice and took a year off from school. She returned in the fourth year again but again repeated the first grade. Finally, she registered for the first grade again in the fifth year but ultimately dropped out in the following year (enrolment pattern: 1F1F//1F1D). Child No. 6 also faced academic challenges. He initially failed the first grade in the first year and then registered for the first grade again in the second year. However, he subsequently dropped out for two years without completing his final evaluation. He returned to school in the fifth year, passed the first grade and progressed to the second grade in the sixth year. Unfortunately, he left school in the following year (enrolment pattern: 1F1-////1P2D).

Causes Leading to Dropouts

A report issued by the Nepalese Ministry of Education, Science and Technology lists physical distance, household economic difficulties, discrimination, social and household pressure to join the labour force, early marriage, etc., as causes of school dropouts (CEHRD, 2021). However, are there any differences in the causes of school dropouts by age at school entry? Ezaki (2024) used the results of the interview surveys to analyse the causes leading to school dropouts for children who were eight years old or older when they started school and for those who were younger than eight years old. The results revealed that for children whose age at school entry was eight years or older, the reasons were due to issues beyond their control, such as economic reasons, illness or death of a parent or guardian, their own health condition, disability or marriage. Meanwhile, the reasons for dropping out of school for children under the age of eight at the time of school entry were due to (1) the child's low motivation to learn, friendships and other factors, which were often the result of the child's own will and (2) parents' low incentives for their children to receive education for a long time (Ezaki, 2024).

In the target area of this study, there is a problem of labour market limitation, and there is a mismatch between educational attainment and occupation/income. For instance, Ezaki (2021b) analysed the occupations and monthly income of the subjects by educational attainment and identified that there was little difference in the percentage of brainwork and high income from the lower basic education (Grades 1–5) to first two years of secondary education (Grades 9–10). Contrarily, these percentages increased in the higher education level, showing a different trend from the other education levels (Ezaki, 2021b). Thus, if they do not continue their education to the higher education level, they will not have a wide range of vocational options and will be less likely to find a better job. Chen (2018), who conducted a study in other regions of Nepal, also stated that higher education is a determining factor in the transition to stable and long-term employment in Nepal. These results are consistent with the findings of previous studies not only in Nepal but also in Ghana, Africa (Fasih, 2008), and other developing countries (Sparreboom & Staneva, 2014).

In such an environment, parents must decide how long their children, who can be a valuable workforce, will be educated. As noted in the previous section, most children under the age of eight at the time of school entry were able to advance to the fourth grade but dropped out of school after that. Most of the children were ten years old or older at the time of dropping out of school (Ezaki, 2024). According to No et al. (2016), who conducted a study in India, a neighbouring country of Nepal, parents believe that it is better to drop out of school if they are not performing well after Grade 4 or work if they cannot go on to secondary education. Although the target area is different, Sekiya and Ashida (2017) also found frequent school dropouts around age 10, and according to McGinn et al. (1992), the age at which parents decide that education is no longer necessary is nearly ten years, after which they leave school and become engaged in work. Ezaki (2024) states that in the target area, children under the age of eight may have advanced to the fourth grade and beyond and then dropped out of school because of the parents' thinking as described above.

5   To Eliminate Barriers to Completing Basic Education

This chapter examined the enrolment status of individual children through cases that have been revealed by the analysis of longitudinal data constructed from school records kept at schools, the results of the home-visit survey and the results of the interview surveys thus far. The results revealed the following causes as obstacles to children's completion of basic education, namely, fragile family environment, parents' lack of understanding of and incentives for education, overage and harsh enrolment situation. Thus, the following four points are considered essential for improving children's enrolment status and achieving completion of basic education.

The first is support for vulnerable children. For children who were eight years old or older when they started school, the reasons for dropouts were economic reasons, illness or death of a parent or guardian, their own health, disability, marriage or other issues beyond their control. To support children in these vulnerable positions, Ezaki (2019, 2021a) presented the case of Zambia, located in sub-Saharan Africa. The country has a support system for vulnerable children as many are orphans due to HIV/ AIDS and other diseases. Teachers pay close attention to these children on a daily basis and submit a monthly list of orphan and vulnerable children to the District Education Office. This list makes it easier for the government and other organisations to support these children. If a similar system were developed in Nepal, vulnerable children with challenging family backgrounds would receive more attention and support. Moreover, communication between schools and parents is also crucial. It is important for public schools to organise some events to interact with parents and enlighten parents directly through the schools. Furthermore, the use of existing programmes, which were initiated to address poverty, such as the conditional cash transfer programme, scholarship programme and school feeding programme, could be considered as one way to address the issue (Ezaki, 2024).

The second are measures against overage. Laos, also located in Asia, launched an 'age 6 entry into grade 1' policy to address overage issues and emphasised pre-school access for five-year-old children to ensure school readiness (Somsanith & Noonan, 2020). Consequently, participation in pre-primary increased, and the percentage of overage dropped significantly. In light of this, Ezaki (2024) insists that Nepal should probably focus more on pre-school education using this case as a guide.

The third are measures to address the problem of school transfers that disrupt the continuity of learning. Although there are rules regarding school transfers in Nepal, these rules are not strictly followed in the target area, and we observed extraordinary enrolment patterns due to school transfers. Hence, Ezaki (2019, 2021a) states that there may be a need to review the rules regarding transfers and tighten the rules, such as prohibiting placement in a grade whose validity is questionable at the time of transfer.

Fourth, a mismatch in educational attainment and occupation/income exists as a limitation of the target area. Children tend not to have a wide range of options in occupations and are less likely to find better conditions for jobs if they do not continue their schooling through the higher education level (Ezaki, 2021b). In such an environment, it is difficult to create incentives for parents and children to continue their schooling; thus, it is important to create jobs in the area that are attractive to parents and children and put incentives to work (Ezaki, 2021a).

This study is a case study of the actual enrolment status in the target schools located in Bhaktapur, and the results cannot be applied to Nepal as a whole. It is desirable to conduct similar surveys in other areas with different characteristics and to compare the trends in each area.

REFERENCES

Agarwal, M. (2020). *Retain, promote or support: How to reduce inequality in elementary education*. Global Education Monitoring Report Fellowship Paper. Paris: UNESCO.

Bhandari, B. M. (2016). *Educational challenge in Nepal: Gender, caste and ethnicity based discrimination*. Makalu Publication House.

Bhatta, D. S. (2004). *A Descriptive Analysis of the Disparities in School Performance in the SLC Exams*. SLC Study Report #1 Kathmandu, Nepal: The Education Sector Advisory Team, Ministry of Education and Sports. http://pustakalaya.org/eserv.php?pid=Pustakalaya:1261&dsID=SDBhatta2004_DescriptiveAnalysisOfSLC.pdf

Bhatta, P. (2009). *Education in Nepal: Problems, Reforms and Social Change*. Martin Chautari.

Bhatta, P., & Budathoki, B. S. (2013). Understanding private educationscape(s) in Nepal. *Education Support Program (ESP) Working Paper Series, 57*, 1–34. http://www.periglobal.org/sites/periglobal.org/files/WP-No57-01-24-2014-FINAL.pdf

British Council. (2020). *Nepal's school sector development plan: TA facility*. Capacity and institutional assessment (CIA) for implementation of the SSDP, Final Report. Kathmandu: British Council.

Brophy, J. (2006). *Grade repetition*. The International Institute for Educational Planning & The International Academy of Education.

Center for Education and Human Resource Development (CEHRD), Ministry of Education, Science and Technology, Government of Nepal. (2021). *Flash 1 report 2077 (2020-021)*. Center for Education and Human Resource Development.

Central Bureau of Statistics (CBS), National Planning Commission Secretariat, Government of Nepal. (2011). *Nepal Living Standards Survey 2010/11*. Central Bureau of Statistics.

Central Bureau of Statistics (CBS), National Planning Commission Secretariat, Government of Nepal. (2012). *National population and housing census 2011*. CBS.

Central Bureau of Statistics (CBS), National Planning Commission Secretariat, Government of Nepal. (2019). *Report on Nepal labour force survey 2017/18*. CBS.

Chen, S. (2018). Education and transition to work: Evidence from Vietnam, Cambodia and Nepal. *International Journal of Educational Development, 61*, 92–105.

Dahal, T., Topping, K., & Levy, S. (2019). Educational factors influencing female students' dropout from high schools in Nepal. *International Journal of Educational Research, 98*, 67–76.

Department of Education, Ministry of Education, Government of Nepal. (2011). *School level educational statistics of Nepal: consolidated report 2010 (2067)*. Department of Education.

Education Review Office (ERO), Ministry of Education, Science and Technology, Government of Nepal. (2019). *National assessment of student achievement 2018: Main report: Report on the national assessment of student achievement in Mathematics and Nepali for grade 5*. ERO.

Ezaki, N. (2018). Nepal ni okeru 'shitsu no takai kyōiku' wo motomeru dainamizumu to sono haigo ni hisomu kage [Dynamism seeking 'high-quality education' and lurking shadows in Nepal]. In T. Sekiya (Ed.), *Kaihatsu tojōkoku de manabu kodomotachi: Makuroseisaku ni shisuru mikurona shūgakujittaibunseki [Children who are Learning in Developing Countries: Micro analysis of state of enrolment that contributes to macro policies]* (pp. 215–237). Kwansei Gakuin University Press.

Ezaki, N. (2019). Enrolment patterns of individual children left behind in the trend towards 'quality education': A case study of primary education in Nepal. *Education 3-13, International Journal of Primary, Elementary and Early Years Education, 47*(5), 520–533.

Ezaki, N. (2020). A study of equality of educational opportunity in Nepal using logistic regression analysis. *International Journal of Comparative Education and Development, 22*(4), 249–262.

Ezaki, N. (2021a). *Impact of the 2015 Nepal earthquakes on individual children's enrolment situation: Seeking 'high-quality education'*. Union Press.

Ezaki, N. (2021b). Relation between educational qualifications and occupations/ incomes in a globalised world: focusing on Nepalese youth. *International Journal of Comparative Education and Development, 23*(1), 23–43. https:// doi.org/10.1108/IJCED-12-2020-0088

Ezaki, N. (2024). Analysing the dropout patterns of individual children in Nepal: relationship between school dropout and grade repetition/entrance age. *International Journal of Comparative Education and Development,* https:// doi.org/10.1108/IJCED-04-2023-0028

Ezaki, N., & Nakamura, S. (2018). Sutorēto ni shinkyū dekinai Zambia chūtō kyōiku no seitotachi [Secondary education students who cannot advance to the next grade smoothly in Zambia]. In T. Sekiya (Ed.), *Kaihatsu tojōkoku de manabu kodomotachi: Makuroseisaku ni shisuru mikurona shūgakujittaibunseki [Children who are Learning in Developing Countries: Micro analysis of state of enrolment that contributes to macro policies]* (pp. 119–138). Kwansei Gakuin University Press.

Fasih, T. (2008). *Linking education policy to labor market outcomes.* The World Bank.

James, Z., & Woodhead, M. (2014). Choosing and changing schools in India's private and government sectors: Young lives evidence from Andhra Pradesh. *Oxford Review of Education, 40*(1), 73–90. https://doi.org/10.1080/ 03054985.2013.873527

Jimerson, R. S., Anderson, E. G., & Whipple, D. N. (2002). Winning the battle and losing the war: Examining the relation between grade retention and dropping out of high school. *Psychology in the Schools, 39*(4), 441–457.

Joshi, P. (2014). Parent decision-making when selecting schools: The case of Nepal. *Prospects, 44*(3), 411–428.

Joshi, P. (2016). Experiencing and responding to private competition: The importance of subjectivity and intermediate outcomes. *Comparative Education Review, 60*(3), 571–600.

Kabay, S. (2016). Grade repetition and primary school dropout in Uganda. *Harvard Education Review, 86*(4), 580–606.

Kawaguchi, J. (2018). 'Kyūgaku' wo katsuyou suru Malawi no zyoshi seitotachi: Malawi no chūtō gakkou no zyūdanteki shūgaku kiroku kara [Female students who take advantage of leave on absence in Malawi: From the longitudinal enrolment record of secondary education school in Malawi]. In T. Sekiya (Ed.), *Kaihatsu tojōkoku de manabu kodomotachi: Makuroseisaku ni shisuru mikurona shūgakujittaibunseki [Children who are Learning in Developing Countries:*

Micro analysis of state of enrolment that contributes to macro policies] (pp. 119–138). Kwansei Gakuin University Press.

McGinn, N., Reimers, F., Loera, A., Soto, M., & López, S. (1992). *Why do children repeat grades? A study of rural primary schools in Honduras.* Bridges Research Report Series No. 13. Cambridge, MA: Harvard Institute for International Development.

Ministry of Education, Government of Nepal. (2009). *School sector reform plan 2009–2015.* Ministry of Education.

Ministry of Education, Science and Technology, Government of Nepal. (2021). *Nepal: Education sector analysis 2021 (2078 BS).* Ministry of Education, Science and Technology.

Ministry of Education, United Nations Children's Fund (UNICEF), & United Nations Educational, Scientific and Cultural Organization (UNESCO). (2016). *Global initiative on out of school children: Nepal country study.* UNICEF.

National Statistics Office, Office of the Prime Minister and Council of Ministers, Government of Nepal. (2021). *National population and housing census 2021: National report.* National Statistics Office.

No, F., Taniguchi, K., & Hirakawa, Y. (2016). School dropout at the basic education level in rural Cambodia: Identifying its causes through longitudinal survival analysis. *International Journal of Education Development, 49,* 215–224.

Poyck, C. M., Koirala, N. B., Aryal, N. P., & Sharma, K. N. (2016). *Joint evaluation of Nepal's school sector reform plan programme 2009–16.* GFA Consulting Group GmbH.

Rose, P., & Al Samarrai, S. (2001). Household constraints on schooling by gender: Empirical evidence from Ethiopia. *Comparative Education Review, 45*(1), 36–63.

Sabates, R., Hossain, A., & Lewin, K. M. (2013). School Drop Out in Bangladesh: Insights Using Panel Data. *International Journal of Educational Development, 33,* 225–232. https://doi.org/10.1016/j.ijedudev.2012.09.007

Sekiya, T. (2014). Individual patterns of enrolment in primary schools in the Republic of Honduras. *Education 3–31: International Journal of Primary, Elementary and Early Years Education, 42*(5), 460–474.

Sekiya, T., & Ashida, A. (2017). An analysis of primary school dropout patterns in Honduras. *Journal of Latinos and Education, 16*(1), 65–73.

Somsanith, P., & Noonan, R. (2020). Preschool and primary education. In R. Noonan (Ed.), *Education in the Lao People's Democratic Republic on track for the twenty-first century. Education in the Asia-Pacific region: Issues, concerns and prospects 51* (pp. 63–86). Springier. https://doi.org/10.1007/978-981-15-3319-8_3

Sparreboom, T., & Staneva, A. (2014). Is education the solution to decent work for youth in developing economies?: Identifying qualifying mismatch from 28 school-to-work transition surveys. Work4Youth Publication Series No.23.

Youth Employment Programme, Employment Policy Department, Geneva: International Labour Office.

Subedi, G., Shrestha, M. G., Maharjan, R., & Suvedi, M. (2013). Dimensions and implications of privatization of education in Nepal: The case of primary and secondary schools. *Education Support Program (ESP) Working Paper Series, 48,* 1–78. http://www.periglobal.org/sites/periglobal.org/files/WP-No48-01-21-2014-FINAL.pdf

Thapa, A. (2015). Public and private school performance in Nepal: An analysis using the SLC examination. *Education Economics, 23*(1), 47–62. https://doi.org/10.1080/09645292.2012.738809

UNESCO Institute for Statistics (UIS), & UNICEF. (2005). *Children out of school: Measuring exclusion from primary education.* UNESCO UIS.

United Nations Development Programme (UNDP). (2022). *Human development report 2021/2022: Uncertain times, unsettled lives: Shaping our future in a transforming world.* UNDP.

United Nations Educational, Scientific and Cultural Organization (UNESCO). (2009). *EFA Monitoring Report 2009 – Overcoming inequality: Why governance matters. Regional Overview: Latin America and the Caribbean.* : UNESCO.

United Nations Educational, Scientific and Cultural Organization (UNESCO). (2015). *EFA global monitoring report 2015 –Education for all 2000-2015: Achievements and challenges.* UNESCO.

United Nations Educational, Scientific and Cultural Organization (UNESCO). (2020). *Global education monitoring report 2020 –Inclusion and education: All means all.* UNESCO.

United Nations Educational, Scientific and Cultural Organization (UNESCO). (2021). *Global education monitoring report 2021/2 –Non-state actors in education: Who choose? Who loses?* UNESCO.

Wils, A. (2004). Late entrants leave school earlier: Evidence from Mozambique. *International Review of Education, 50*(4), 17–37. https://doi.org/10.1023/b:revi.0000018201.53675.4b

Analysis of Enrolment Patterns in Myanmar's Primary Education by Socioeconomic Status

Natsuho Yoshida

1   INTRODUCTION

Trends and Current Situation of Primary Education in Myanmar

The Republic of the Union of Myanmar (hereafter "Myanmar"), the subject of this chapter, has long been managed by the military government and has been called "the last research target country in Southeast Asia" in the field of international affairs research. Although the country was once transferred to civilian government in 2011, it is currently back under military government due to a coup d'état that occurred in February 2021. Due to such unique political conditions of Myanmar, overseas donors and researchers had difficulty conducting assistance and research. Notably, foreign assistance in the education sector has been severely restricted. Since

N. Yoshida (✉)
Graduate School of Education, Hyogo University of Teacher Education, Kato, Japan
e-mail: nyoshida@hyogo-u.ac.jp

© The Author(s), under exclusive license to Springer Nature Switzerland AG 2024
T. Sekiya et al. (eds.), *Towards Ensuring Inclusive and Equitable Quality Education for All*, International and Development Education, https://doi.org/10.1007/978-3-031-70266-2_8

1990, following the Education for All (EFA) trend, Myanmar has also promoted initiatives aimed at the universal primary and basic education. In particular, in 1998, the Continuous Assessment and Progression System (CAPS) was introduced to continuously assess student learning outcomes (Ministry of Education, 2012) based on chapter-end tests and semester-end tests for each subject. As a result, the CAPS is nearly equivalent to the automatic promotion system in primary education in the whole country.

Perhaps due to the aforementioned results of such national educational initiatives, according to the latest educational statistical data, Myanmar's net enrolment rate of primary education has improved from 64.3% in 1978 to 98.1% in 2018 (UNESCO Institute for Statistics, 2022), and full enrolment seems possible. The completion rate of primary education has also increased significantly from 45.8% in 1990 to 83.2% in 2020 (UNESCO Institute for Statistics, 2022). The repetition rate of primary education was 17.7% in 1990, before introducing CAPS (Union of Myanmar, 1999), and decreased to 0.5% in 2017, after introducing CAPS (UNESCO Institute for Statistics, 2022). Therefore, CAPS, introduced during the military government and continued by the new civilian government, appeared to have decreased students' grade repetition.

On the other hand, trends in Myanmar's primary education completion rate by the socioeconomic situation, the poorest group completion rate improved from 20.9% in 2000 to 64.7% in 2016, and the richest group completion rate improved from 78.1% in 2000 to 92.6% in 2016, but there is still a big disparity between the two. It has been also indicated that a Myanmar household survey estimated that the repetition rate is much higher than that found in educational statistics of international organisations (Spohr, 2015). In addition, it has been reported that children from families with lower socioeconomic status (SES) are more likely to repeat grades (Yoshida, 2020a). From these facts, it can be inferred that the poorer the children, the more difficult their educational situations are.

Research Purpose

Cross-sectional data, including educational statistics published by international organisations, is suitable for overviewing the macro educational situation, such as at the national level. However, because cross-sectional data present only the average value of the whole, accurately reflecting the actual individual educational situation might not be possible. Therefore, even in Myanmar, it would be difficult to accurately grasp the actual educational situations of children from families with lower socioeconomic status who are in a more severe environment from cross-sectional data. On the other hand, a research method that tracks individuals longitudinally based on school records can clarify the actual enrolment status (i.e. individual enrolment status from school entrance through grade promotion/ repetition until leaving school due to completion or dropout, etc.) of a certain number of children (Sekiya, 2014). The Sustainable Development Goals (SDGs) in 2015, which are the successor goals of EFA in 1990, have set the goal of "leaving no one behind" by 2030. In order to achieve this goal, it is necessary to use a longitudinal research method to clarify the actual enrolment status of children that cannot be picked up by cross-sectional data and to consider measures to approach children who are left behind.

Against this background, this study tracked individual enrolment patterns[1] in children of different socioeconomic backgrounds, using longitudinal data to understand the microscopic situation. Next, based on socioeconomic background, this study analysed the current enrolment status; the results demonstrated the challenges that must be understood and resolved. Subsequently, by trying to extract knowledge that contributes to the improvement of children's educational situation in each SES group and the elimination of educational disparities between each SES group, this study proposed recommendations to achieve universal primary education in Myanmar.

2   Methodology

Target Area and Schools

This study was conducted in the Yangon Region, the principal area of habitation for the Burmese (who are the majority of the Myanmar population), to eliminate the additional effect of ethnic characteristics. Townships from the Yangon Region with different socioeconomic conditions were selected to assess the variation in individual enrolment status on that basis. Selection was based on the latest Myanmar Population and

---

[1] In this study, according to Sekiya (2014), "enrolment" refers to the status of individual's involvement in the school system (e.g. a registered grade, a pass or failure in the end-of-year evaluation, grade repetition, completion, dropout). "Entrance" refers to a student's first entrance into school.

Housing Census for the target region (Department of Population, 2015). With permission from the Myanmar Ministry of Education, this study used basic education schools[2] from each of these townships as the target schools.

Data and Target Children

The data sources were academic enrolment registries that listed basic information related to children and their enrolment statuses. These registries were used to create a database that longitudinally tracked the enrolment trajectory of children at target schools, from school entrance to departure (i.e. completion of primary education, dropping out of school, or transferring schools). Children who entered each academic year were analysed as cohorts. The cohort-based analysis confirmed the number of children who entered and left their target school each year, either by completion or by dropout.[3]

Furthermore, to restrict the analysis to target schools, data for children who transferred into or out of schools were excluded from the analysis. In Myanmar's basic education schools, due to the strictness with which the education system is operated, in principle, transferring between basic education schools without presenting a transfer certificate is impossible. Notably, children who transfer within the first year of entrance are not obliged to obtain a transfer certificate, and first-grade students can transfer among basic education schools and re-enter by providing only a birth certificate. Accordingly, for children who left a target school within the first year of enrolment without obtaining a transfer certificate, determining from the academic enrolment registry whether a child had transferred to another school or dropped out of school was difficult.[4] Therefore, to

---

[2] Basic education school is a school under the Myanmar Ministry of Education, and there are 45,387 schools nationwide. The number is larger than that of monastery schools (1538 schools) and private schools (438 schools) in Myanmar (Ministry of Education, 2016). The private schools mentioned in this chapter are schools approved by the Ministry of Education based on The Private School Registration Law. Therefore, they are distinguished from international schools and religious schools, which are not under the Ministry of Education.

[3] This cohort-based analysis also confirmed that some of the target children were still studying in target schools in AY2017 when the survey was conducted. More information on that group is provided in the results section.

[4] Teachers interviewed at the target schools stated that for children in a city such as Yangon, not attending school at all was unusual. Therefore, this study presumed that few children in the target schools had not completed one year of primary education.

increase data reliability, such children were excluded from analyses. After applying these exclusions, the final study sample was 4509 children who entered primary education at one of five target schools from academic year (AY) 2008 to AY2012.

Grouping by Socioeconomic Status (SES)

SES is a measure of the socioeconomic background of individuals or groups by, for example, occupation, income, or education (Scott & Marshall, 2009). According to the preliminary survey interview of the education staff at several schools in the Yangon Region, children are generally enrolled in primary schools in the township in which they reside. On this basis, this study assessed the characteristics of two groups, children enrolled in a target school and the residents of the township in which that target school is located. First, the teachers and staff of each target school were interviewed to confirm the number of children enrolled in the school who resided in the same township. Next, from the latest Myanmar Population and Housing Census (Department of Population, 2015), the author collected information related to the SES for each township. Thus, the SES level for the children's households of each target school was estimated by linking to the SES of the township in which each school was located. Each target school was classified as belonging to one of three groups: high SES, middle SES, or low SES.[5]

According to the result of the survey interviews with teachers and staff at each target school, almost all students enrolled in S2, S3, S4, and S5 resided in the same township (T) as their respective target school (S2 = T2, S3 = T3, S4 and S5 = T4). Regarding S1, the majority of children were residents of T1, and the rest were residents of several other surrounding townships. Table 8.1 presents information related to the SES indicators for the townships in which each target school was located (T1, T2, T3, and T4). All indices consistently rank T1 as the highest SES and T4 as the lowest SES, with T2 and T3 in the middle. Thus, townships in which target schools were located were ranked by SES from high to low: T1 (the location of S1) > T2 (S2) and T3 (S3) > T4 (S4 and S5).

---

[5] This method was applied to survey the SES level of children and classify SES into three groups for analysis because author did not have permission from the Myanmar government to conduct home visit surveys.

Table 8.1 SES indices for the townships in which each target school is located

Township (School)		T1 (S1)	T2 (S2)	T3 (S3)	T4 (S4 & S5)
Highest level of education completed (population 25 years and over) (%)	Primary school	10.2	16.5	22.6	30.7
	University/college/post-graduate and above	49.0	34.9	22.2	12.0
Material and facility in conventional households (%)	Wall Tile/brick/concrete	88.8	71.3	36.8	19.6
	Wood	7.4	21.1	29.5	27.8
	Bamboo	2.8	4.4	28.3	43.7
	Floor Tile/brick/concrete	80.5	64.8	36.2	21.3
	Wood	17.0	32.4	54.6	58.3
	Bamboo	0.7	1.0	7.5	18.5
	Type of toilet Flush	31.2	14.6	5.4	1.9
Main source of lighting in conventional households (%)	Electricity	99.7	98.9	89.8	73.4
Availability of communication and related amenities in conventional households (%) (radio/TV/landline phone/mobile phone/computer/Internet at home)	Households with all of the items	8.3	7.7	2.3	0.6
	Household with none of the items	1.2	3.3	10.3	21.3
Availability of transportation item in conventional households (%)	Car/truck/van	25.9	18.0	9.0	3.8

Note: The figure of Yoshida (2020a) created based on Myanmar Population and Housing Census (Department of Population 2015) is quoted with some modifications to suit the present study.

Two points corroborate the high SES of children attending S1 who reside in other townships surrounding T1. First, many basic education schools in each surrounding township offer primary education to which children can walk. Because these children's guardians enrol them in S1 (one of the best schools with the highest university acceptance rate in the target region) despite the proximity of other schools, education is probably prioritised. Second, the main means of transportation to attend S1 from surrounding townships are a fee-charging school bus or privately

Table 8.2 Analysis target by SES

SES group	Target school	Township of school	Characteristic of township	No. of target children
High	S1	T1	Up-market and academic area	1746
Middle	S2	T2	Suburban town	1798
	S3	T3		
Low	S4	T4	Satellite town including an industrial zone	965
	S5			

Note: Created by the author on the basis of the collected data

owned car. Thus, household finances are probably spent on such transportation costs. These points demonstrated that many children from high-SES homes attended S1. Therefore, the target schools can be ordered by SES at the school level: S1 (T1 + α) > S2 (T2) and S3 (T3) > S4 and S5 (both T4). Accordingly, the target schools were classified into SES groups: S1 (T1 + α) = high-SES group, S2 (T2) and S3 (T3) = middle-SES group, and S4 and S5 (both T4) = low-SES group (Table 8.2).

Procedure for Analysis

In this study, in order to clarify the enrolment status of each different SES group, which cannot be picked up from the cross-sectional data, the analysis proceeds with the following procedure. First, the individual enrolment patterns from the entrance to the departure (i.e. completion of primary education or school dropout without a transfer certificate) were traced longitudinally, and the actual detailed educational situation for each SES group was reviewed. Second, the individual enrolment patterns of each SES group were compared to clarify their respective challenges. Finally, based on the findings from these analyses, further implications were extracted that apply to the elimination of educational disparities between different SES groups and the achievement of universal primary education in Myanmar.

3   Results: Enrolment Patterns of the SES Groups

The enrolment patterns for each SES group are presented in order of frequency in Table 8.3. The enrolment pattern numbers and symbols refer to the following: numbers = academic grades, P = pass, F = fail, and C =

Table 8.3 All enrolment patterns in each SES group

Rank	Enrolment pattern	N	%
High-SES group			
1	1P2P3P4P5P	1,732	99.2
2	1P2P	4	0.2
3	1P2P3P4P	3	0.2
3	1P2P3P	3	0.2
3	1P	3	0.2
4	1P2P3P4F4P5P	1	0.1
Total	6 patterns	1746	100.0
Middle-SES group			
1	1P2P3P4P5P	1760	97.9
2	1P	10	0.6
3	1F1P2P3P4P5P	6	0.3
4	1P2P3F3P4P5P	5	0.3
5	1P2P3P	4	0.2
5	1P2F2P3P4P5P	4	0.2
6	1P2P3P4P5F5P	1	0.1
6	1P2P3P4P	1	0.1
6	1P2P3P4F4P5P	1	0.1
6	1P2P3P4F4P5C	1	0.1
6	1P2P3F3P4P5C	1	0.1
6	1P2P	1	0.1
6	1P2F2P3P4P5C	1	0.1
6	1P2F2F2P3P4C	1	0.1
6	1F1P2P3P	1	0.1
Total	15 patterns	1798	100
Low-SES group			
1	1P2P3P4P5P	849	88.0
2	1P2F2P3P4P5P	21	2.2
3	1F1P2P3P4P5P	20	2.1
4	1P	17	1.8
5	1P2P	10	1.0
6	1P2P3P	8	0.8
7	1P2P3P4P	5	0.5
7	1F1P2P3P4P5C	5	0.5
8	1P2P3F3P4P5P	3	0.3
9	1P2P3P4P5F5C	2	0.2
9	1P2P3P4F4P5P	2	0.2
9	1F1P2P3P4F4P5C	2	0.2
9	1F1P2P	2	0.2
9	1F1P2F2P3P4P5P	2	0.2
10	1P2P3P4F4P5C	1	0.1

(*continued*)

Table 8.3 (continued)

Rank	Enrolment pattern	N	%
10	1P2P3F3P4P	1	0.1
10	1P2F2P3P4P5F5P	1	0.1
10	1P2F2P3P4F4P5P	1	0.1
10	1P2F2P3P4F4P5C	1	0.1
10	1P2F2P3P4F4P	1	0.1
10	1P2F2P3P4F	1	0.1
10	1P2F2P3P	1	0.1
10	1P2F2P3F3P4P5F5P	1	0.1
10	1P2F2F2P3P4C	1	0.1
10	1F1P2P3P4P5F5P	1	0.1
10	1F1P2P3P4P5F5F5P	1	0.1
10	1F1P2P3P4P	1	0.1
10	1F1P2P3P	1	0.1
10	1F1P2P3F3P4C	1	0.1
10	1F1P2F2P3P4P5F5F	1	0.1
10	1F1P	1	0.1
Total	31 patterns	965	100

Note 1: Numbers = academic grades, P = pass, F = fail, C = continue to attend target school even at the time of the survey

Note 2: Created by the author on the basis of the analysis result

continue to attend target school even at the time of the survey. The analysis results[6] of the enrolment patterns of each SES group are as follows.

Enrolment Patterns of the High-SES Group

The number of target children in the high-SES group was 1746, of which 945 were boys and 801 were girls. The number of children who completed primary education was 1733 (99.3%), and the number of children who dropped out of school without obtaining a transfer certificate was 13 (0.7%). Six enrolment patterns were confirmed.

Of the enrolment patterns that corresponded to three or more children, the most frequent pattern was to complete primary education

---

[6] An overview of the analysis results of high- and low-SES groups from this section onwards has been highlighted in Yoshida (2023), Column 4: Myanmar toshibu no OOSCY no tokucho [Column 4: Characteristics of OOSCY in urban Myanmar]. In Inui, M. (Ed.), ASEAN shokoku no gakkou ni ikenai kodomotachi [Children out of school in ASEAN countries], 68–72. Toshindo. However, it is only a very brief and partial one. Therefore, this chapter discusses and shows the results in more detail based on Yoshida (2023).

without repeating a grade (1P2P3P4P5P: 1732 children, 99.2% of the total). The second most frequent pattern was to leave the target school after completing the second grade without repeating a grade (1P2P: 4 children, 0.2% of the total). The third most frequent patterns were (1) leaving the target school after completing the fourth grade without repeating a grade, (2) leaving the target school after completing the third grade without repeating a grade, and (3) leaving the target school after completing the first grade without repeating a grade (1P2P3P4P, 1P2P3P, and 1P; 3 children, 0.2% of the total, respectively).

Enrolment Patterns of the Middle-SES Group

The number of target children in the middle-SES group was 1798, of which 924 were boys and 874 were girls. The number of children who completed primary education was 1777 (98.8%), and the number of children who dropped out of school without obtaining a transfer certificate was 17 (0.9%). At the time of the survey, four children (0.2%) were still studying at target schools. Fifteen enrolment patterns were confirmed.

Of the enrolment patterns that corresponded to three or more children, the most frequent pattern was to complete primary education without repeating a grade (1P2P3P4P5P: 1760 children, 97.9% of the total). The second most frequent pattern was to leave the target school after completing the first grade without repeating a grade (1P: 10 children, 0.6% of the total). The third most frequent pattern was not passing the first grade and repeating a grade but subsequently completing primary education without repetition (1F1P2P3P4P5P: 6 children, 0.3%). The fourth most frequent pattern was completing second grade and then not passing third grade and repeating a grade and subsequently completing primary education without repeating a grade (1P2P3F3P4P5P: 5 children, 0.3%). The fifth most frequent patterns were (1) leaving the target school after completing third grade without repeating a grade and (2) after completing first grade, not passing second grade and repeating a grade, but subsequently completing primary education without repeating a grade (1P2P3P and 1P2F2P3P4P5P; 4 children, 0.2% of the total, respectively).

Enrolment Patterns of the Low-SES Group

The number of target children in the low-SES group was 965, of which 507 were boys and 458 were girls. The number of children who completed primary education was 902 (93.5%), and the number of children who dropped out of school without obtaining a transfer certificate was 50 (5.2%). At the time of the survey, 13 children (1.3%) were still studying at target schools. Thirty-one enrolment patterns were confirmed.

Of the enrolment patterns that corresponded to three or more children, the most frequent pattern was to complete primary education without repeating a grade (1P2P3P4P5P: 849 children, 88.0% of the total). The second most frequent pattern was completing first grade, not passing second grade and repeating a grade but subsequently completing primary education without repeating a grade (1P2F2P3P4P5P: 21 people applicable, 2.2% of the total). The third most frequent pattern was not passing first grade and repeating a grade but subsequently completing primary education without repetition (1F1P2P3P4P5P: 20 children, 2.1%). The fourth most frequent pattern was leaving the target school after completing first grade without repeating a grade (1P: 17 children, 1.8% of the total). The fifth most frequent pattern was leaving the target school after completing second grade without repeating a grade (1P2P: 10 children, 1.0% of the total). The remaining enrolment patterns were as follows: (1) leaving the target school after completing up to third grade without repeating a grade (1P2P3P: 8 children, 0.8% of the total); (2) leaving the target school after completing up to the fourth grade without repeating a grade and (3) not passing first grade and repeating a grade but subsequently completing up to fourth grade without repetition and still in fifth grade at the time of survey (1P2P3P4P and 1F1P2P3P4P5C: 5 children, 0.5% of the total, respectively); and (4) completing first and second grade, not passing third grade and repeating a grade, and subsequently completing primary education without repeating a grade (1P2P3F3P4P5P: 3 children, 0.3%).

4   DISCUSSIONS: COMPARISON OF THE ENROLMENT PATTERNS OF SES GROUPS

Comparison of Completion Status and Variety of Enrolment Patterns

For all SES groups, the most frequent pattern was completing primary education without repeating a grade, the total completion rate of primary education exceeded 90%, and the difference between the high-SES group and the middle- and low-SES groups was approximately 0.5% and 5.8%, respectively. Of the SES groups, the number of enrolment patterns is remarkably higher in the lower SES groups than in the other groups. The number of enrolment patterns of the middle-SES group was 2.5 times that of the high-SES group, and that of the low-SES group was five times that of the high-SES group.

Why does the number of enrolment patterns differ despite the similar completion rate of primary education among SES groups? What does this difference in the variation of enrolment patterns mean? The enrolment pattern is comprised of a combination of the timing of promotion and repetition, the frequency of repetition, and the timing of completion and school dropout. Therefore, the more children follow a complicated enrolment trajectory (e.g. repeating grades and dropping out of school at various times, and repeating grades many times), the more diverse the enrolment patterns. As a result, the number of enrolment patterns increases proportionally to its diversity. By contrast, for example, when almost all children graduate without repeating a grade because of automatic promotion, as in primary education in Japan, the variation and number of enrolment patterns would approach "1" infinitely.

Thus, in the high-SES group, the number of enrolment patterns is considered small because the patterns are likely to trend towards a pattern of completing primary education without repeating a grade. In the lower the SES groups, the more children who followed the complicated enrolment trajectory in which repetitions and school dropouts occurred at various times; thus, the variations and numbers of enrolment patterns diversified accordingly. Therefore, by focusing on the variation and numbers of enrolment patterns, it would be possible to infer the more detailed individual enrolment status that cannot be understood only from the cross-sectional data such as the educational statistics.

Comparison of Repetition Patterns

This section presents a detailed analysis of the repetition patterns—the enrolment patterns containing repetition. Repetition patterns were extracted and presented in order of frequency by SES group in Table 8.4. The number of repetition patterns was one for the high-SES group, 10 for the middle-SES group, and 26 for the low-SES group. The number of children who corresponded to each of the repetition patterns and its ratio are one child (0.1%) in the high-SES group, 22 children (1.2%) in the middle-SES group, and 76 children (7.9%) in the low-SES group. Thus, the higher the SES, the smaller the number of repetition patterns and the proportion of those who corresponded to it. By contrast, the lower the

Table 8.4 Repetition patterns in each SES group

Rank	Repetition pattern	N	%	Frequency of repetition
High-SES group				
1	1P2P3P**4F**4P5P	1	0.1	1
Total	1 pattern	1	0.1	
Middle-SES group				
1	**1F**1P2P3P4P5P	6	0.3	1
2	1P2P**3F**3P4P5P	5	0.3	1
3	1P**2F**2P3P4P5P	4	0.2	1
4	1P2P3P4P**5F**5P	1	0.1	1
4	1P2P3P**4F**4P5P	1	0.1	1
4	1P2P3P**4F**4P5C	1	0.1	1
4	1P2P**3F**3P4P5C	1	0.1	1
4	1P**2F**2P3P4P5C	1	0.1	1
4	**1F**1P2P3P	1	0.1	1
4	1P**2F2F**2P3P4C	1	0.1	2
Total	10 patterns	22	1.2	
Low-SES group				
1	1P**2F**2P3P4P5P	21	2.2	1
2	**1F**1P2P3P4P5P	20	2.1	1
3	**1F**1P2P3P4P5C	5	0.5	1
4	1P2P**3F**3P4P5P	3	0.3	1
5	1P2P3P4P**5F**5C	2	0.2	1
5	1P2P3P**4F**4P5P	2	0.2	1
5	**1F**1P2P	2	0.2	1
5	**1F**1P2P3P**4F**4P5C	2	0.2	2
5	**1F**1P**2F**2P3P4P5P	2	0.2	2
6	1P2P3P**4F**4P5C	1	0.1	1
6	1P2P**3F**3P4P	1	0.1	1
6	1P**2F**2P3P	1	0.1	1
6	**1F**1P2P3P4P	1	0.1	1
6	**1F**1P2P3P	1	0.1	1
6	**1F**1P	1	0.1	1
6	1P**2F**2P3P4P**5F**5P	1	0.1	2
6	1P**2F**2P3P**4F**4P5P	1	0.1	2
6	1P**2F**2P3P**4F**4P5C	1	0.1	2
6	1P**2F**2P3P**4F**4P	1	0.1	2
6	1P**2F**2P3P**4F**	1	0.1	2
6	1P**2F2F**2P3P4C	1	0.1	2
6	**1F**1P2P3P4P**5F**5P	1	0.1	2
6	**1F**1P2P**3F**3P4C	1	0.1	2
6	1P**2F**2P**3F**3P4P**5F**5P	1	0.1	3
6	**1F**1P2P3P4P**5F5F**5P	1	0.1	3

(continued)

Table 8.4   (continued)

Rank	Repetition pattern	N	%	Frequency of repetition
6	1F1P2F2P3P4P5F5F	1	0.1	4
Total	26 patterns	76	7.9	

Note 1: Numbers = academic grades, P = pass, F = fail, C = continue to attend target school even at the time of the survey

Note 2: Patterns containing "1F" are shaded; patterns containing "2F" are underlined

SES, the larger the number of repetition patterns and the proportion of those who corresponded to it. Furthermore, regarding the frequency of repetition of individual children, in the high- and middle-SES groups, almost all the children repeated a grade only once. In the low-SES group, approximately 20% of all repeaters repeated grades twice or more; among them, several patterns containing three to four repetitions were also confirmed (i.e. 1P2F2P3F3P4P5F5P, 1F1P2P3P4P5F5F5P, and 1F1P2F2P3P4P5F5F). Thus, the higher the SES, the lower the repetition frequency of children, and conversely, the lower the SES, the higher the repetition frequency.

By contrast, as mentioned in the introduction of this chapter, since the CAPS was introduced in AY1998, remedial classes and make-up examinations have been conducted for children not fulfilling the passing criteria at each target school. As a result, the primary education assessment system has become equivalent to automatic promotion in Myanmar. Therefore, grade repetition among children was unlikely to be observed. Thus, why were repetition patterns observed, especially in the low-SES group? To answer this question, we analysed the repetition patterns by focusing on the low-SES group in which a certain number of repeaters was observed. The results demonstrated that 21 patterns that correspond to 80% of all repetition patterns contained repetition of the lower grades (i.e. 1F or 2F). In addition, 67 children corresponded to the patterns with "1F" or "2F," accounting for nearly 90% of all repeaters. Approximately 10% of all repeaters corresponded to the pattern containing repetitions of other grades such as third to fifth grade. Thus, in the low-SES group, repetition in the lower grades is a problem that must be solved, especially when the goal is equity. Why are children in the lower grades (i.e. the first and second grades) repeating grades? To confirm the reasons why, a semistructured interview survey was conducted with the teachers and staff of the target schools that the children in the low-SES group attended. The following three main reasons were confirmed for repeating grades in the lower grades of the low-SES group:

- Children studied at the target school for several months after school entrance but took a leave of absence from school because they were unwilling to go to school.
- Because of frequent daily illness, children were absent from school frequently.
- Because of medical treatment for illness or injury, children took a leave of long absence from school.

Regarding these reasons, teachers reported that children at the low-SES target schools were not receiving sufficient educational support at home because their guardians often worked all day or had less interest in their children's formal education than the parents of the other groups did. In addition, based on a report that the health of young children with a low SES was worse than that of their counterparts with a higher SES (Cameron & Williams, 2009), the long absences due to poor health (particularly in younger children, e.g. those in the lower grades) might have disproportionately affected the low-SES target children. Additionally, the prescribed age for entering primary education in Myanmar (five years)[7] is one year earlier than in many other countries. Undoubtedly, continuing education at such a young age is difficult when left home alone by guardians who are working. Furthermore, because of the expense, access to preschool education in Myanmar is available only to children from economically privileged households.[8] Thus, children from low-SES households will probably be less prepared for school entrance than their high-SES counterparts. Nevertheless, in Myanmar, full-fledged subject-based education commenced immediately upon entrance into primary education.[9] Therefore, insufficient readiness partly explains the frequent repetition of the lower grades by children in the low-SES group. These points are also indicated

[7] As mentioned in the introduction of this chapter, in the new curriculum, the prescribed age to attend first grade, in which full-fledged subject-based education commences, has changed to six years old.

[8] Enrolment rate in pre-primary education for children aged three to five years has remained stable in Myanmar and was 8.2% in 2018 (UNESCO Institute for Statistics, 2020).

[9] For detailed information on the weekly lesson timetable in Myanmar's primary education prior to the transfer to new curriculum, please refer to UNESCO-IBE (2012).

in Yoshida's (Yoshida, 2020a) analysis of the effects of CAPS on primary education in Myanmar.

The minimum conditions for CAPS are that for children to pass a grade, they should attend school daily and take all exams. However, in the low-SES group, some children could not fulfil the minimum conditions for CAPS because of long-term absence due to the poor SES of their family, as aforementioned. Therefore, we presumed that in the low-SES group, a certain number of repetition patterns would be observed even after the introduction of CAPS.

Furthermore, to examine the differences in the reasons for repeating grades among SES groups, a similar semistructured interview survey was also conducted with the teachers and staff of the middle-SES target schools and some repetition patterns were confirmed. The main reason for repeating a grade in the lower grades of the middle-SES group was that guardians worried that their children could not fully master the lesson content and decided that it would be better for them to study a lot even if they reattempted the same grade.[10] Therefore, it would be suggested that even the same grade repetition in the lower grades could be divided into "repetition for positive reasons" and "repetition for negative reasons," depending on the SES of children.

Comparison of School Dropout Patterns

This section analyses the school dropout patterns—the enrolment pattern of leaving the target schools without obtaining a transfer certificate. Table 8.5 presents in order of frequency the dropout patterns for each SES group. In Table 8.5, the higher the SES group, the lower the percentage of children who dropped out of school; conversely, the lower the SES, the higher the percentage of children who dropped out of school. In addition, the higher the SES, the higher the pattern ranking for the pattern of continuing study until the third and fourth grades and then dropping out. By contrast, the lower the SES, the higher the pattern ranking of the patterns leading to dropout in the lower grades. Thus, even with the same school dropout, the higher the SES, the longer the years of schooling, and conversely, the lower the SES, the shorter the years of schooling.

---

[10] On the other hand, whether or not grade repetition leads to better learning outcomes is still an ongoing debate, with many studies indicating the negative impact of grade repetition on children's learning outcomes (Brophy, 2006; Ikeda & García, 2014; Sunny et al., 2017).

Table 8.5 School dropout patterns in each SES group

Rank	Dropout pattern	N	%	Frequency of repetition
High-SES group				
1	1P2P	4	0.2	0
2	1P2P3P4P	3	0.2	0
2	1P2P3P	3	0.2	0
2	1P	3	0.2	0
Total	4 patterns	13	0.7	
Middle-SES group				
1	1P	10	0.6	0
2	1P2P3P	4	0.2	0
3	1P2P3P4P	1	0.1	0
3	1P2P	1	0.1	0
3	1F1P2P3P	1	0.1	1
Total	5 patterns	17	0.9	
Low-SES group				
1	1P	17	1.8	0
2	1P2P	10	1.0	0
3	1P2P3P	8	0.8	0
4	1P2P3P4P	5	0.5	0
5	1F1P2P	2	0.2	1
6	1P2P3F3P4P	1	0.1	1
6	1P2F2P3P	1	0.1	1
6	1F1P2P3P4P	1	0.1	1
6	1F1P2P3P	1	0.1	1
6	1F1P	1	0.1	1
6	1P2F2P3P4P4F	1	0.1	2
6	1P2F2P3P4F	1	0.1	2
6	1F1P2F2P3P4P5P5F5F	1	0.1	4
Total	13 patterns	50	5.2	

Note 1: Numbers = academic grades, P = pass, F = fail, C = continue to attend target school even at the time of the survey

Note 2: Percentage corresponding to each pattern indicates the percentage within the total number of children in each SES group

Note 3: Created by the author on the basis of the analysis result

Why do children drop out of school, especially in the low-SES group? A previous study targeted developing countries reported that repetition and dropout have been directly correlated (Levy, 1971). However, on the basis of the individual dropout patterns in each SES group, the patterns that do not include grade repetition occupy higher positions even in the low-SES group (Table 8.5). In addition, in the repetition patterns in each

SES group mentioned in the prior section (Table 8.4), more than 70% of all repeaters have completed primary education even after repeating grades.[11] Thus, if the relationship between repetition and dropout was examined in detail by focusing on individual enrolment patterns, rather than lumping them together by using an average value, repetition is not necessarily the direct cause of school dropout. Similarly, Sekiya and Ashida (2017) analysed the relationship between repetition and dropout by focusing on individual enrolment patterns and obtained results with the same tendency as the results of this analysis.

The next step was confirming why children dropped out of the target school without obtaining a transfer certificate; thus, a semistructured interview survey was conducted with the teachers and staff of the target schools that the children in each SES group attended. The number of children with confirmed reasons for school dropout was as follows: 4 in the high-SES group (30.8% of all dropouts), 12 in the middle-SES group (70.6% of all dropouts), and 12 in the low-SES group (24.0% of all dropouts) (see Table 8.6). Regarding the reasons for school dropout in the high-SES group, three children transferred to an international school or an overseas school after leaving the target school, and one died while in fourth grade. Thus, even after dropping out of the target school, it is highly possible that children in the high-SES group continued to study at an international school or overseas school where transfer is possible without submitting a transfer certificate. Regarding the reasons for school dropout in the middle-SES group, five children went abroad (the United States, China, and Malaysia) because of family circumstances and parents' job conditions, and two children transferred to private schools and religious schools that did not require submitting a transfer certificate. The other five children left the target school because of family economic difficulties, disagreements between their parents, and family problems such as their parents' death. Thus, in the middle-SES group, there was a mixture of positive dropouts that led to continued study at private or religious schools, and negative dropouts due to family problems that prevented continued schooling. Finally, regarding the reasons for school dropout in the low-SES group, two children transferred to a private school, one child transferred to a monastery school that does not require school expenses, and one child transferred to non-formal education after receiving an offer

---

[11] All repeaters in the high-SES group, 17 of 22 repeaters in the middle-SES group, and 53 of 76 repeaters in the low-SES group have completed primary education.

Table 8.6 Each SES group's reason for school dropout

No.	Entrance year	Sex	Dropout pattern	Reason for school dropout
High-SES group				
H1	2010	M	1P2P	Dropped out due to a transfer to an international school
H2	2012	F	1P2P	Dropped out due to a transfer to an international school
H3	2012	M	1P	Dropped out due to a transfer to a school in Singapore because his father works in Singapore
H4	2012	M	1P2P3P	Removed from school register due to death
Middle-SES group				
M1	2008	F	1P	Dropped out due to family financial problems
M2	2008	M	1P	Dropped out due to emigration to the USA due to family circumstances. He is the older brother of M3
M3	2008	F	1P	Dropped out due to emigration to the USA due to family circumstances. She is the younger sister of M2
M4	2009	F	1P2P3P4P	Dropped out due to emigration to Malaysia due to parents' jobs
M5	2009	M	1P2P3P	Dropped out due to transferring to a school in China because his ethnicity is Wa and he resides near the border with China
M6	2009	M	1P	Dropped out due to a family problem such as a disagreement between parents
M7	2009	F	1F1P2P3P	Dropped out due to work outside due to a family problem such as guardians' death and illness
M8	2010	F	1P	Dropped out due to returning to a hometown (her hometown is in the countryside)
M9	2010	M	1P2P3P	Dropped out due to a transfer to a school in Malaysia due to family's job
M10	2011	M	1P2P3P	Dropped out due to the disappearance of all family members due to father's illegal gambling
M11	2011	F	1P2P	Dropped out due to transfer to a religious school because her religion is Islam
M12	2012	F	1P	Dropped out due to a transfer to a private school

(continued)

Table 8.6   (continued)

No.	Entrance year	Sex	Dropout pattern	Reason for school dropout
Low-SES group				
L1	2009	F	1P2P3P	Dropped out due to work outside to support the family
L2	2009	M	1F1P2F2P3P4P5F5F	Dropped out due to work outside to support the family
L3	2010	F	1P2P3P4P	Dropped out due to work outside to make money
L4	2010	F	1P2P	Dropped out due to a transfer to a monastery school
L5	2010	F	1P2P3P	Dropped out because she opted for non-formal education due to an offer of educational support from an overseas assistance agency
L6	2011	M	1P2P3P4P	Dropped out due to work outside due to a family problem such as a guardian's death
L7	2012	M	1P2P3P	Dropped out due to transferring to a private school
L8	2012	M	1F1P2P3P4P	Dropped out due to family financial problems
L9	2012	F	1P2P3P4P	Dropped out due to a transfer to a private school
L10	2012	M	1P2P3P	Dropped out due to poor performance at school
L11	2012	M	1P2P3F3P4P	Dropped out due to work outside due to a family problem such as guardian's death
L12	2012	F	1P2P3P4P	Dropped out because she became too overweight to fit in her wheelchair; she could not use it and come to school despite her legs being lame

Note: Created by the author based on the collected data through semistructured interview survey

of educational support from an overseas assistance agency. The remaining most students left the target schools mainly because of the poverty of their household. Thus, children in the low-SES group were unlikely to continue to study at private schools even after leaving the target schools, and by contrast, they will probably drop out of school and give up continuing schooling because of the plight of their household's economic situation. Thus, what is highly possible is that the higher the SES, the higher the educational attainment by continuing to study at international schools or overseas schools that do not require a transfer certificate even after leaving target school. By contrast, the lower the SES, the more likely the children are to have left the target schools because of family financial problems and subsequently not continued schooling. Therefore, the actual number of dropouts and its ratio are smaller in the higher SES groups than the value presented in Table 8.5, and conversely, the number in the lower SES group is not much different from the value in Table 8.5.

Relationship Between SES Groups' School Entrance Age and Enrolment Patterns

Starting schooling at an age beyond the regular school entrance age (hereafter "overaged") has been demonstrated to negatively affect the subsequent enrolment status in developing countries (Wils, 2004; Education Policy and Data Center, 2009; UNESCO, 2011). In addition, longitudinal studies have investigated the relationship between individual children's enrolment patterns and the age of starting schooling and reported that after the recommended school entrance age, the older the children are when they start school, the more likely they are to drop out of school (Sekiya, 2014; Ezaki, 2019).

Thus, this section investigated the relationship between school entrance age and individual enrolment pattern. In Table 8.7, the enrolment patterns of each SES group are presented according to children's school entrance age. Table 8.7 presents only the patterns that apply to more than 1% of children in order of frequency. Of the enrolment patterns of the groups that entered school as four and five years old, the pattern of completing primary education occupies the higher ranking of enrolment patterns in all SES groups. Almost all the children of the high- and middle-SES groups completed primary education, and approximately 95% of the low-SES group did the same. Regarding the SES groups that entered school at six years old that is one year older than the regular entrance age, almost all the children of the high-SES group completed primary education. Conversely, dropout patterns also emerged in the higher ranking of enrolment patterns in the middle- and low-SES groups, with less than 90% of children completing primary education. Furthermore, of the SES groups that entered school at seven years old and older, the completion rates of primary education in the middle- and low-SES groups further declined significantly.

Table 8.7 Enrolment patterns for each SES group by school entrance age

High-SES group

Rank	Enrolment pattern	N	%
School entrance at the age of four			
1	1P2P3P4P5P	344	98.9
	Completion patterns	344	98.9
Total	3 patterns	348	100
School entrance at the age of five			
1	1P2P3P4P5P	1370	99.3
	Completion patterns	1371	99.3
Total	6 patterns	1380	100
School entrance at the age of six			
1	1P2P3P4P5P	18	100

Middle-SES group

Rank	Enrolment pattern	N	%
School entrance at the age of four			
1	1P2P3P4P5P	374	98.4
	Completion patterns	376	98.9
Total	7 patterns	380	100
School entrance at the age of five			
1	1P2P3P4P5P	1358	98.2
	Completion patterns	1371	99.1
Total	11 patterns	1383	100
School entrance at the age of six			
1	1P2P3P4P5P	28	82.4
2	1P2P3P	2	5.9
2	1P	2	5.9
3	1P2P3F3P4P5P	1	2.9
3	1P2F2P3P4P5P	1	2.9

Low-SES group

Rank	Enrolment pattern	N	%
School entrance at the age of four			
1	1P2P3P4P5P	155	87.1
2	1P2F2P3P4P5P	5	2.8
2	1F1P2P3P4P5P	5	2.8
3	1P2P3P	3	1.7
4	1P	2	1.1
	Completion patterns	168	94.4
Total	13 patterns	178	100
School entrance at the age of five			
1	1P2P3P4P5P	643	89.8
2	1P2F2P3P4P5P	14	2.0
3	1F1P2P3P4P5P	13	1.8
4	1P	12	1.7
	Completion patterns	677	94.6
Total	26 patterns	716	100
School entrance at the age of six			
1	1P2P3P4P5P	46	78.0
2	1P2P	2	3.4
2	1P2F2P3P4P5P	2	3.4
2	1P	2	3.4
2	1F1P2P3P4P5P	2	3.4
3	1P2P3P	1	1.7
3	1P2F2P3P4P5F5P	1	1.7
3	1P2F2P3P	1	1.7
3	1F1P2P3P	1	1.7

3	1F1P2P	1	1.7
Completion patterns		51	86.4
Total	10 patterns	59	100
1	1P2P3P4P5P	5	41.7
2	1P2P	2	16.7
3	1P	1	8.3
3	1P2P3F3P4P5P	1	8.3
3	1P2P3P	1	8.3
3	1P2P3P4P	1	8.3
3	1P2P3P4P5F5C	1	8.3
Completion patterns		6	50.0
Total	7 patterns	12	100

Completion patterns		30	88.2
Total		34	100
1		1	100

Completion patterns	18	100	
Total	1 patterns	18	100

School entrance at the age of seven and older

No applicable child	1	1P	1	100
Completion patterns		0	0	
Total	1 patterns	1	100	

Note 1: Numbers = academic grades, P = pass, F = fail, C = continue to attend target school even at the time of the survey

Note 2: Only the patterns that apply to more than 1% of children in each SES group are displayed

Note 3: Created by the author on the basis of the analysis result

In the lower SES groups, the older children's entrance age, the worse their primary education completion status. Why did that phenomenon occur? An additional interview survey of the teachers and staff at the target schools demonstrated that children in families with lower SES are more likely to have problems at home. In addition, some interviewees opined that children in families with low SES have less support than those with high SES do for continuing their studies at home. Notably, in Table 8.6, which presents the reasons for children's school dropout used in the analysis, the lower the SES, the more the children who have problems at home, for example, parents' disagreement and death. Additionally, some children resided in a disadvantaged environment where they could not concentrate on their schooling because of their families' financial problems. Moreover, in a city such as Yangon, older children are able to get jobs more easily in the informal sector than younger children; thus, the children of poor families who are overaged enrollees are more likely to leave school and enter the labour market than their counterparts enrolled at the appropriate starting age (Yoshida, 2020b). Notably, a child labour survey of individuals in an industrial area of the Yangon Region where the poor gathered also reported that the main reason for children starting work was living in poverty (International Labour Organization 2015).

Additionally, in general, the higher the family's SES, the more enthusiastic the parents are regarding their children's education, the more expensive the support they purchase to promote their children's schooling, and the higher the price for these goods and services they can afford. Therefore, these children do not have to work to earn money for their families and reside in an environment where they can concentrate on their schooling. Thus, the same overaged enrollees can complete primary education in the high-SES group because they have a favourable environment for continuing their schooling. The lower SES groups were more susceptible than the high-SES groups to the negative effects of overaged school entrance (as aforementioned), and the completion status of primary education was worse. Therefore, to eliminate the negative aspects of overage, it is necessary not only to promote school entrance at the appropriate age but also to ameliorate inequity in the continuation of schooling of children of poor families.

5   CONCLUSION AND IMPLICATIONS FOR UNIVERSAL PRIMARY EDUCATION IN MYANMAR

In this study, to achieve the research purpose, we first analysed individual enrolment patterns by SES group: high, middle, and low. Next, we observed the variety and number of enrolment patterns and individual children's completion, repetition, and school dropout patterns and analysed the differences among the SES groups. Finally, the actual enrolment statuses of individual children of each SES group were clarified. Based on the analysis results presented, our conclusion is that the children, especially those in the low-SES group, are experiencing two main difficulties:

- Repetition due to not satisfying CAPS minimum conditions by long absences, insufficient school readiness, or poor physical condition.
- School dropout due to family problems such as financial difficulties.

Are education policies and reforms planned and implemented to solve the aforementioned problems in primary education in Myanmar? We answered this question by referring to the National Education Strategic Plan 2016–2021 (Ministry of Education, 2016; Yoshida, 2020a), which summarised the recent educational goals and strategies led by the civilian administration. First, regarding measures for improving school readiness, the primary education curriculum has been completely revised since AY2016. Notably, preschool education had never been fully expanded in Myanmar. Nonetheless, children had to immediately receive full-fledged subject-based education after entering primary education. In the new curriculum, the first year of primary education (i.e. kindergarten) is a preparatory period for entering full-fledged subject-based education, and learning through play is emphasised. After the second year (i.e. the first grade), full-fledged subject-based education begins. This reform is expected to improve children's readiness and reduce repetition of lower grades.[12] In addition, the introduction of the preschool grants programme aimed at expanding preschool education in socioeconomically disadvantaged areas

---

[12] In fact, according to a cross-sectional data analysis, it has been reported that the number of grade repetitions immediately after entering the primary school decreased significantly after the introduction of the new kindergarten curriculum (Muta, 2020). Regarding the effect of introducing this new curriculum, we would like to verify whether the same findings as the analysis results using cross-sectional data (Muta, 2020) can be confirmed using longitudinal research methods in the future.

is also planned. This expansion is expected to improve children's readiness, especially those in the low-SES family. Next, as a measure against children's poor physical condition, the introduction of a school meal programme in primary education is projected. The problem of malnutrition in children has been reported in Myanmar (Khaing et al., 2019), and school meal programmes in primary education may improve the situation. Therefore, meal provision can reduce absenteeism due to poor health because the children's nutritional status is improved.

Furthermore, to solve the financial problem on children's continued schooling, measures such as free primary education, school grant programmes, and student stipend programmes have been implemented since the transition to the civilian administration. If these measures effectively decrease education costs for poor families, school dropouts due to family financial problems might decrease. Notably, the literature has reported cases in which the educational situation of the poor deteriorated, especially during severe social and economic crises and in response to natural disasters and economic sanctions, etc. (Thomas et al., 2004; Ezaki, 2021; Yoshida, 2020a). Thus, maintaining social stability and improving the economy of the nation should improve the financial condition of poor families and thus improve the enrolment status of children. Following the recent COVID-19 pandemic and the military coup, the national situation has been becoming more and more chaotic. How to manage such an emergency and whether or not it is possible to stabilise the social situation and develop the economy of the country will be important for the future educational development in Myanmar.

Our research has limitations. This case study examined the Yangon Region, an urban area within Myanmar; thus, the results are not representative of the whole country. Additionally, whether the results would be similar in regions that have many ethnic minority groups or in rural areas with different regional characteristics remains unclear. We suggest that further research attempt to assess how enrolment patterns of individual children in other regions differ from those in the analysis results of this study and whether the recent educational policies and reforms planned and implemented by the civilian administration are improving the enrolment status of children in other regions. To answer these questions and achieve universal primary education throughout Myanmar, further investigations of other aspects of education in other regions are necessary.

REFERENCES

Brophy, J. (2006). *Grade repetition*. The International Institute for Educational Planning (IIEP); The International Academy of Education (IAE).

Cameron, L., & Williams, J. (2009). Is the relationship between socioeconomic status and health stronger for older children in developing countries? *Demography, 46*(2), 303–324.

Department of Population, & Ministry of Immigration and Population. The Republic of the Union of Myanmar. (2015). *The 2014 Myanmar population and housing census, Yangon Region, census report volume 3-L, Department of Population, Nay Pyi Taw.*

Education Policy and Data Center. (2009). *Pupil performance and age: A study of promotion, repetition, and dropout rates among pupils in four age groups in 35 developing countries (Working Paper No. EPDC-09-02)*. Education Policy and Data Center.

Ezaki, N. (2019). Enrolment patterns of individual children left behind in the trend towards "quality education": A case study of primary education in Nepal. *Education 3-13, 47*(5), 520–533.

Ezaki, N. (2021). *Impact of the 2015 Nepal earthquakes on individual children's enrolment situation: Seeking "high-quality education"*. Union Press.

Ikeda, M., & García, E. (2014). Grade repetition: A comparative study of academic and non-academic consequences. *OECD Journal: Economic Studies, 2013*(1), 269–315.

International Labour Organization. (2015). *Rapid assessment on child labour in the Hlaing Thar Yar industrial zone in Yangon, Myanmar, 2015*. International Labour Organization.

Khaing, H. T., Nomura, S., Yoneoka, D., Ueda, P., & Shibuya, K. (2019). Risk factors and regional variations of malnutrition among children under 5 in Myanmar: Cross-sectional analyses at national and subnational levels. *BMJ Open, 9*(9), e030894.

Levy, M. B. (1971). Determinants of primary school dropouts in developing countries. *Comparative Education Review, 15*(1), 44–58.

Ministry of Education. The government of the Republic of the Union of Myanmar. (2012). *Education for all: Access to and quality of education in Myanmar, Ministry of Education, Nay Pyi Taw.*

Ministry of Education. The government of the Republic of the Union of Myanmar. (2016). *National education strategic plan 2016–21. Ministry of Education, Nay pyi thaw.*

Muta, H. (2020). Structural analysis of dropouts and repeaters in basic education schools in the Republic of the Union of Myanmar. *International Journal of Human Culture Studies, 2020*(30), 40–59.

Scott, J., & Marshall, G. (2009). *A dictionary of sociology* (3rd rev. ed.). Oxford University Press.

Sekiya, T. (2014). Individual patterns of enrolment in primary schools in the Republic of Honduras. *Education 3-13, 42*(5), 460–474.

Sekiya, T., & Ashida, A. (2017). An analysis of primary school dropout patterns in Honduras. *Journal of Latinos and Education, 16*(1), 65–73.

Spohr, C. (2015). *Republic of the Union of Myanmar: Support for postprimary education development (project number: 47177).* Asian Development Bank.

Sunny, B. S., Elze, M., Chihana, M., Gondwe, L., Crampin, A. C., Munkhondya, M., Kondowe, S., & Glynn, J. R. (2017). Failing to progress or progressing to fail? Age-for-grade heterogeneity and grade repetition in primary schools in Karonga District, northern Malawi. *International Journal of Educational Development, 52*(1), 68–80.

Thomas, D., Beegle, K., Frankenberg, E., Sikoki, B., Strauss, J., & Teruel, G. (2004). Education in a crisis. *Journal of Development Economics, 74*(1), 53–85.

UNESCO institute for statistics. (2022). *Myanmar.* Retrieved March 31, 2022, from http://uis.unesco.org/en/country/mm

Union of Myanmar. (1999). *Education for all (EFA): The year 2000 assessment, Union of Myanmar, Yangon.*

United Nations Educational, Scientific and Cultural Organization. (2011). *The hidden crisis: Armed conflict and education, Education for All Global Monitoring Report 2011.* UNESCO.

United Nations Educational, Scientific and Cultural Organization Institute for Statistics. (2020). *UIS. Stat.* Retrieved May 1, 2020, from http://data.uis.unesco.org/.

United Nations Educational, Scientific and Cultural Organization-IBE. (2012). (2010–2011), UNESCO-IBE. *World data on education* (7th ed.). Paris.

Wils, A. (2004). Late entrants leave school earlier: Evidence from Mozambique. *International Review of Education/Internationale Zeitschrift für Erziehungswissenschaft/Revue Internationale de l'Éducation, 50*(1), 17–37.

Yoshida, N. (2020a). Socio-economic status and the impact of the "continuous assessment and progression system" in primary education in Myanmar. *Education 3-13, 48*(6), 674–689.

Yoshida, N. (2020b). Enrolment status disparity: Evidence from secondary education in Myanmar. *International Journal of Comparative Education and Development, 22*(2), 101–114.

Yoshida, N. (2023). Column 4: Myanmar toshibu no OOSCY no tokucho [Column 4: Characteristics of OOSCY in urban Myanmar], In Inui, M. (Ed.), ASEAN shokoku no gakkou ni ikenai kodomotachi [Children out of school in ASEAN countries], pp. 68–72. Toshindo.

CHAPTER 9

Impact of 'Ethnic Affinity' Between Teachers and Children on Enrolment Status: Evidence from the Northern Lao PDR

Natsuho Yoshida

1   Introduction

Ethnic Minority Children Left Behind

Numerous times, the literature in the field of educational development has pointed out that the primary enrolment situation has significantly improved worldwide since the launch of Education for All (EFA) and the Millennium Development Goals (MDGs) in 1990 and 2000, respectively (UNESCO, 2015; United Nations, 2015a). Alternatively, the educational situation of vulnerable groups of children, such as the poor and ethnic minorities, is poor, such that they remain left behind. In response, the Sustainable Development Goals (SDGs), which were launched in 2015

N. Yoshida (✉)
Graduate School of Education, Hyogo University of Teacher Education, Kato, Japan
e-mail: nyoshida@hyogo-u.ac.jp

© The Author(s), under exclusive license to Springer Nature Switzerland AG 2024
T. Sekiya et al. (eds.), *Towards Ensuring Inclusive and Equitable Quality Education for All*, International and Development Education, https://doi.org/10.1007/978-3-031-70266-2_9

and the successor goals to the MDGs, established an education goal (SDG 4) to 'ensure inclusive and equitable quality education and promote life-long learning opportunities for all'. Target 4.5, which is subordinate to SDG 4, announced as follows: 'By 2030, eliminate gender disparities in education and ensure equal access to all levels of education and vocational training for the vulnerable, including persons with disabilities, indigenous peoples and children in vulnerable situations' (United Nations, 2015b).

A straightforward case of ethnic minority children being left behind in the education sector is Lao PDR (Hereafter "Laos"), a multi-ethnic country located in Southeast Asia. It has been indicated that the educational policy in the country lacks consideration of ethnic minority children. The reason is that only Lao, the language of the majority ethnic group, is prescribed as the medium of instruction at school, and teachers have less understanding of ethnic minority children. Moreover, teachers conduct classes based on the values of the majority ethnic group, which has contributed to the educational gap between ethnic majority and ethnic minority children (Chagnon & Rumpf, 1982; Thant & Vokes, 1997). In response, the government has gradually paid increased attention to minorities, including ethnic ones, and promoted bilingual education in the first year of primary education. These initiatives are intended to bridge the education gap for minorities and to introduce a one-year preparatory phase called the *grade zero system* in areas inhabited by ethnic minorities, among others (Inui, 2015, 2020).

However, despite the abovementioned approaches, the education gap between ethnic majority and ethnic minority groups remains unaddressed. For example, the never-school attendance rate for the majority ethnic group Lao is 5.7%, whereas minority ethnic groups Katang and Akha are extremely high at 40.9% and 49.7%, respectively (Lao Statistics Bureau, 2016). Perhaps, for this reason, the illiteracy rate in Lao is 6.7% compared with 49.0% and 63.8% for Katang and Akha, respectively, which, similar to the never-school attendance rate, is significantly higher (Lao Statistics Bureau, 2016). Furthermore, the Assessment of Student Learning Outcome in 2012 for third-grade primary school students reported significantly lower Lao language and mathematics scores for ethnic minority children compared with their majority ethnic counterparts (Inui, 2020). Against this background, addressing the educational disparity between the children of majority and minority ethnic groups in Laos is an urgent issue.

Prior Educational Research on Ethnic Minorities in Laos

Inui (2009), who conducted field research, such as participant observation in an area inhabited by a large number of ethnic minorities in Laos, stated that the consideration of teachers of ethnic minorities to match class progress to the relevant children and to teach in the ethnic language facilitates the understanding of the ethnic minority children about their learning. In response, Ban and Inui (2018), who also conducted a study on primary schools in a predominantly ethnic minority area of Laos, defined *ethnic affinity* as the level of understanding of ethnicity, such as culture, customs and language, by teachers of ethnic minority children. The authors then examined whether or not high levels of ethnic affinity between teachers and ethnic minority children contribute to the high levels of academic performance of ethnic minority children in the first year of each target primary school. The results demonstrated that schools with high levels of ethnic affinity between teachers and children tended to exhibit statistically significantly higher levels of academic performance. Moreover, schools with higher levels of teacher–child ethnic affinity tended to display less gap in academic performance among children and concentrated on average scores. In addition, building on the study of Ban and Inui (2018), Yoshida (2022) conducted a similar study on Grade 5 students in the partially same target primary school as that of Ban and Inui (2018). Yoshida (2022) then checked whether the effect of ethnic affinity between teachers and ethnic minority children is evident even among older children. The results demonstrate that the results of the analysis on fifth-grade primary school students depicted trends similar to those of Ban and Inui (2018). Therefore, the current study predicts that the understanding of teachers of the ethnicity, such as culture, customs and language, of ethnic minority children could lead to high levels of academic performance, which could contribute to the reduction of educational inequality between children of majority and minority ethnic groups.

Research Objective

As previously cited, the educational challenges for ethnic minority children in Laos include high rates of non-school enrolment, illiteracy and poor academic performance as well as grade repetition and school dropout. For example, in Vientiane, the capital city of Laos, the rate of grade repetition is 2.7%, while in Luang Namtha, where many ethnic minorities reside, this rate is 5.5%, which is more than twice the rate of the capital city (Lao Statistics Bureau, 2023). In previous studies conducted in developing countries, one of the main causes of grade repetition is poor academic performance (Liddell & Rae, 2001; Taniguchi, 2015; Zuilkowski et al., 2016). According to Ban and Inui (2018) and Yoshida (2022), previous scholars demonstrated that the understanding of teachers of the ethnicity of ethnic minority children in terms of culture, customs and language (i.e. ethnic affinity) contributes to improved academic performance of ethnic minority children. If so, then ethnic affinity between teachers and children may also contribute to the prevention of grade repetition among ethnic minority children. The current study longitudinally followed the enrolment trajectories of the first-year primary school children surveyed by Ban and Inui (2018) over a five-year period. It then intends to determine whether or not the teachers' understanding of the ethnicity, such as culture, customs and language (i.e. ethnic affinity), of ethnic minority children contributes to the prevention of grade repetition among them. The study also aims to aid in addressing the educational disparity between children of majority and minority ethnic groups.

2   Methodology

Target Area, Schools and Children

The study was conducted in District A, Luang Namtha Province in northwest Laos, which is considered a 'treasure trove of ethnic minorities'. The province is mainly composed of mountains (85%), and approximately 70% of the population is made up of ethnic minorities (Yamada, 2018). The researchers selected five primary schools from District A with large enrolment rates of children from ethnic minorities (i.e. S1, S2, S3, S4 and S5). The study obtained teachers' cooperation in the survey from these schools. The following text provides descriptions of the characteristics of each target school and its location.[1]

- Agriculture is the main industry in the village where S1 is located. Villagers mainly grow glutinous rice and vegetables, among others. According to preliminary interviews with teachers in S1, approximately 80%, 19% and 1% of the parents of the school children are

---

[1] Information of each target school and its location is partially based on Ban (2018).

farmers, civil servants (e.g. police, soldiers and teachers) and company employees, respectively. The school's headteacher strictly ensures that children are not absent from school.

- The main industry in the village in which S2 is located is agriculture with villagers growing glutinous rice and vegetables, among others. According to preliminary interviews with S2 teachers, approximately 60% of the parents of school children are farmers of glutinous rice, vegetables and fruits. The remaining 40% sell products at markets or on the streets.
- Rice cultivation is the main industry in the village in which S3 is located. Many villagers work in Chinese factories located in the village. Preliminary interviews with teachers in S3 indicated that the majority of the parents of school children are farmers of rice, vegetables and fruits.
- Rice farming is the main industry in the village in which S4 is located. Many of the parents work in factories in the village. Unfortunately, detailed information on the school and village of S4 could not be obtained due to the lack of prior interviews.
- The main industries in the village in which S5 is located are agriculture (e.g. rice and fruit farming) and factory labour (e.g. rubber factory). In preliminary interviews with the teachers in S5, nearly all parents of school children were engaged in one of these sectors.

A total of 78 children who were enrolled in Grade 1 as of academic year (AY) 2015 in each of the target schools were included. The children surveyed were partially consistent with those of Ban and Inui (2018).

Data Collection

First, to ascertain information on the ethnicity of teachers and children per target school, data books that contain this information were collected. Detailed information on the teachers' understanding of the ethnicity of ethnic minority children, which was not available from the data books, was collected through semi-structured interviews with the teachers in each target school. The study then collected data from academic enrolment registries, which record children's attendance and examination results, and compiled them into a database to determine the enrolment status of children in each target school, including grade repetition status. Based on the enrolment status of the children in the database, the researchers conducted semi-structured interviews with teachers from each target school. Data on the enrolment status of individual children, such as grade repetition, school dropout and transfer by academic year, were then collected.

Procedure for Analysis

To determine whether or not the teachers' understanding of ethnicity, such as culture, customs and language (i.e. ethnic affinity), contributes to the prevention of grade repetition among minority ethnic children, the study took the following steps. First, the study identified the level of ethnic affinity between teachers and children in each target school on the basis of the collected data. Using the information collected from academic enrolment registries and the results of the semi-structured interviews with the teachers, the enrolment status of individual children in each target school was traced longitudinally and depicted as patterns. The level of ethnic affinity between the teachers and children was then compared with the status of the grade repetition of the children to determine whether ethnic affinity between teachers and children contributed to its prevention.

3   RESULTS

Ethnic Affinity Between Teachers and Children at the Target Schools

As of the most recent census, the total number of official ethnic groups in Laos was 49 (Lao Statistics Bureau, 2016). The list of ethnic groups in Laos was similarly organised on the last page of the data book collected for the study (Table 9.1). Therefore, based on this classification, the study listed the ethnic groups of teachers and children per target school. Table 9.2 presents the ethnicity of teachers and children in each of the previous five years for each target school. The study determined the level of ethnic affinity between the teachers and children using the degree of agreement between their ethnicities as a guide and adding the results of semi-structured interviews with teachers to these data.

Regarding ethnic information for S1, the teachers were Khmou, Lue and Tai, and all the children were Lue. Regarding AY2015 in S1, the teacher in charge was Khmou. According to Ban and Inui (2018), however, this teacher has been living in this village for seven years after marrying into a Lue family. Therefore, she understands the Lue language and

Table 9.1 List of ethnic groups in Laos as listed in the data book

Family of languages	Name of ethnic groups
1. Lao–Tai (8)	Lao, Tai, Phouthay, Lue, Nhoaun, Yang, Xaek and Thaineua
2. Mon–Khmer (32)	Khmou, Pray, Xingmoun, Phong, Thaen, Oedou, Bid, Lamed, Samtao, Katang, Makong, Tri, Yrou, Trieng, Ta-oy, Yae, Brao, Katu, Harak, Oy, Kriang, Cheng Sadang, Xuay, Nhaheun, Lavy, Pacoh, Khmer, Toum, Ngouan, Moy and Kree
3. Hmong–Ewmien (2)	Hmong and Ewmien
4. Chinese–Tibet (7)	Akha, Pounoy, Lahou, Syla, Hayi, LoLo and Hor

Source: Prepared by the author based on the collected data

uses it on a daily basis. Furthermore, in terms of Lao culture, a tradition is that women adapt to the culture of the family (husbands) they marry into, such that this teacher is aware of Lue customs and culture and endeavours to adapt to it. Hence, for AY2015 in S1, the study concluded that ethnic affinity is very high, although no ethnic categorisation match exists between the teacher and children. Thus, the degrees of ethnic affinity for each year in S1 were AY2015 ≒100%, AY2016 = N/A, AY2017 = 100%, AY2018 = 100% and AY2019 = 85.7%. For ethnic information in S2, the teachers were Nhoaun, Khmou and Tai, while all children were Nhoaun. Thus, the levels of ethnic affinity for each year in S2 were AY2015 = 100%, AY2016 = N/A, AY2017 = 100%, AY2018 = 10.0% and AY2019 = 70.0%. Regarding ethnic information for S3, the teachers were Lao and Nhoaun, and the children were Lao, Tai, Lue, Nhoaun, Khmou and Pounoy. Information on the ethnicity of one child was unavailable. Thus, the degrees of ethnic affinity for each year in S3 were AY2015 = 7.1%, AY2016 = N/A, AY2017 = 7.1%, AY2018 = 7.7% and AY2019 = 30.8%. For ethnic information in S4, the teachers were Tai and Lue, and the children were Bid, Hmong and/or Lue. Therefore, the degrees of ethnic affinity for each year of S4 were AY2015 = 0%, AY2016 = N/A, AY2017 = 0%, AY2018 = 0–15.4% and AY2019 = 0%. The study was unable to identify the degree of ethnic affinity for AY2018, because the ethnicity of the two children in question was Hmong or Lue, which exceeded the abovementioned range. With regard to ethnic information in S5, the teachers were Pounoy, Tai, Nhoaun, Khmou and Lue, while all children were Hmong.

Table 9.2 Ethnic information of the target teachers and children and the degrees of ethnic affinity between them by academic year

Target schools	Academic year (AY)	Ethnic groups of teachers	Ethnic groups of children	民族親和性の度合い
S1	AY2015	[G1] Khmou	[G1] Lue (N = 15)	≒100%
	AY2016	[G2] N/A	[G2] Lue (N = 15)	N/A
	AY2017	[G3] Lue	[G3] Lue (N = 15)	100%
	AY2018	[G3 and G4] Lue	[G3] Lue (N = 2) / [G4] Lue (N = 13)	100%
	AY2019	[G4] Tai / [G5] Lue	[G4] Lue (N = 2) / [G5] Lue (N = 12)	85.7%
S2	AY2015	[G1] Nhoaun	[G1] Nhoaun (N = 14)	100%
	AY2016	[G2] N/A	[G2] Nhoaun (N = 14)	N/A
	AY2017	[G3] Nhoaun	[G3] Nhoaun (N = 13)	100%
	AY2018	[G3] Nhoaun / [G4] Khmou	[G3] Nhoaun (N = 1) / [G4] Nhoaun (N = 10)	10.0%
	AY2019	[G4] Tai / [G5] Nhoaun	[G4] Nhoaun (N = 2) / [G5] Nhoaun (N = 8)	70.0%

S3			
AY2015	[G1] Lao	[G1] Lao (N = 1), Tai (N = 2), Lue (N = 1), Nhoaun (N = 4), Khmou (N = 4), Pounoy (N = 1), N/A (N = 1)	7.1%
AY2016	[G2] N/A	[G1] Khmou (N = 1) [G2] Lao (N = 1), Tai (N = 2), Lue (N = 1), Nhoaun (N = 4), Khmou (N = 3), Pounoy (N = 1), N/A (N = 1)	N/A
AY2017	[G3] Lao	[G2] Khmou (N = 1) [G3] Lao (N = 1), Tai (N = 2), Lue (N = 1), Nhoaun (N = 4), Khmou (N = 3), Pounoy (N = 1), N/A (N = 1)	7.1%
AY2018	[G3] Lao [G4] Lao	[G3] Lao (N = 1), Nhoaun (N = 1), Khmou (N = 1) [G4] Tai (N = 2), Lue (N = 1), Nhoaun (N = 3), Khmou (N = 3), Pounoy (N = 1)	7.7%
AY2019	[G3] Lao [G4] Lao [G5] Nhoaun	[G3] Khmou (N = 1) [G4] Lao (N = 1), Nhoaun (N = 1) [G5] Tai (N = 2), Lue (N = 1), Nhoaun (N = 3), Khmou (N = 3), Pounoy (N = 1)	30.8%

(continued)

Table 9.2 (continued)

Target schools	Academic year (AY)	Ethnic groups of teachers	Ethnic groups of children	民族親和性の度合い
S4	AY2015	[G1] Tai	[G1] Bid (N = 2), Hmong (N = 9), Lue or Hmong (N = 4)	0%
	AY2016	[G2] N/A	[G1] Hmong (N = 4) [G2] Bid (N = 2), Hmong (N = 5), Lue or Hmong (N = 4)	N/A
	AY2017	[G2 and G3] Tai	[G2] Hmong (N = 4) [G3] Bid (N = 2), Hmong (N = 5), Lue or Hmong (N = 3)	0%
	AY2018	[G2 and G4] Lue [G3] Tai	[G2] Hmong (N = 2) [G3] Hmong (N = 3) [G4] Bid (N = 2), Hmong (N = 4), Lue or Hmong (N = 2)	0–15.4%
	AY2019	[G3 and G5] Tai [G4] Lue	[G3] Hmong (N = 3) [G4] Hmong (N = 2) [G5] Bid (N = 2), Hmong (N = 4)	0%

S5			
AY2015	[G1] Pounoy	[G1] Hmong (N = 20)	0%
AY2016	[G2] N/A	[G2] Hmong (N = 20)	0%
AY2017	[G2] Tai or Nhoaun	[G2] Hmong (N = 4)	0%
	[G3] Khmou	[G3] Hmong (N = 11)	
AY2018	[G2 and G3] Khmou	[G2] Hmong (N = 1)	0%
	[G4] Lue and Nhoaun	[G3] Hmong (N = 5)	
		[G4] Hmong (N = 4)	
AY2019	[G4] Lue or Nhoaun	[G2] Hmong (N = 1)	0%
	[G5] Tai	[G3] Hmong (N = 3)	
		[G4] Hmong (N = 2)	
		[G5] Hmong (N = 3)	

Note: For AY2015 in S1, the degree of ethnic affinity is also shown as ≒100%, because the teacher in charge was considered to have a very high level of understanding of the children's ethnicity, as previously mentioned. The ethnic information of the teachers and children in AY2016 for all schools is also shown as 'N/A', because several years had passed since the field survey was conducted, and the relevant data did not remain and could not be collected

Source: Prepared by the author based on the collected data

Therefore, the degrees of ethnic affinity for each year of S5 were 0% for all academic years.

In summary, the ethnic affinity between the teachers and children reveals that S1 and S2 are the groups with high levels of ethnic affinity, whereas S3, S4 and S5 are the groups with low levels of ethnic affinity. Notably, collecting ethnic information of teachers and children in AY2016 in the respective target schools was impossible, because keeping old documents for a long time is not customary in the target schools in Laos.

Ethnic Affinity and Repetition Status in Terms of Enrolment Patterns

To cross-check the degree of ethnic affinity between teachers and children with the grade repetition status of the children, Table 9.3 presents and tabulates the relevant data. The results demonstrated that 2 out of 15 (13.3%) and 2 out of 14 (14.3%) children in S1 and S2, respectively, with high levels of ethnic affinity repeated a grade. Those repeating a grade in S3, S4 and S5 with low levels of ethnic affinity were 3 out of 14 (21.4%), 5 out of 15 (33.3%) and 6 out of 20 (30.0%). According to the results of the cross-check analysis, schools with high degrees of ethnic affinity produced fewer students with grade repetition. Conversely, schools with low degrees of ethnic affinity produced more students with grade repetition. Analysis of the correlation between the mean value of the degree of ethnic

Table 9.3   Aggregate results of the degree of ethnic affinity and repetition status

Target schools	Degree of ethnic affinity between the teachers and children					No. of children in AY2015	Total no. of repeaters between AY2015 and AY2019	% of repeaters between AY2015 and AY2019
	AY 2015	*AY 2016*	*AY 2017*	*AY 2018*	*AY 2019*			
S1	≒100	N/A	100	100	85.7	15	2	13.3
S2	100	N/A	100	10.0	70.0	14	2	14.3
S3	7.1	N/A	7.1	7.7	30.8	14	3	21.4
S4	0	N/A	0	0–15.4	0	15	5	33.3
S5	0	N/A	0	0	0	20	6	30.0

Source: Prepared by the author based on the collected data

affinity and the percentage of students with grade repetition displayed a correlation coefficient of -0.90, which indicates that it is statistically significant at the 5% level and has a very strong negative correlation.

To analyse the relationship between ethnic affinity and the repetition status of the children in detail, the study longitudinally tracked the enrolment status of the children over the past five years and presented enrolment patterns by target school (Table 9.4). The numbers and symbols in the enrolment patterns refer to the following: numbers = academic grades, P = pass, F = fail, D = dropping out of school, T = transfer to another school, C = continue to attend target school even at the time of the survey, X = the child had passed away and - = N/A, and the repetition patterns are braided. The numbers in round brackets under the academic year for each school indicate the degree of ethnic affinity between teachers

Table 9.4 Level of ethnic affinity and enrolment patterns of the children, including repetition status

No.	Ethnic group	AY2015 (≒100)	AY2016 (N/A)	AY2017 (100)	AY2018 (100)	AY2019 (85.7)
S1						
1	Lue	1P	2P	3P	4T	—
2	Lue	1P	2P	3P	4P	5C
3	Lue	1P	2P	3P	4P	5C
4	Lue	1P	2P	3P	4P	5C
5	Lue	1P	2P	3P	4P	5C
6	Lue	1P	2P	**3F**	3P	4C
7	Lue	1P	2P	3P	4P	5C
8	Lue	1P	2P	3P	4P	5C
9	Lue	1P	2P	3P	4P	5C
10	Lue	1P	2P	3P	4P	5C
11	Lue	1P	2P	3P	4P	5C
12	Lue	1P	2P	3P	4P	5C
13	Lue	1P	2P	**3F**	3P	4C
14	Lue	1P	2P	3P	4P	5C
15	Lue	1P	2P	3P	4P	5C
No. of children in each academic year		15	15	15	15	14
No. of repeaters in each academic year		0	0	2	0	—
% of repeaters in each academic year		0	0	13.3	0	—

(*continued*)

Table 9.4   (continued)

No.	Ethnic group	AY2015 (100)	AY2016 (N/A)	AY2017 (100)	AY2018 (10.0)	AY2019 (70.0)
S2						
1	Nhoaun	1P	2P	3P	4P	5C
2	Nhoaun	1P	2P	3P	4P	5C
3	Nhoaun	1P	2P	3P	**4F**	4C
4	Nhoaun	1P	2P	3P	4P	5C
5	Nhoaun	1P	2P	3P	4P	5C
6	Nhoaun	1P	2P	3P	4P	5C
7	Nhoaun	1P	2P	3T	—	—
8	Nhoaun	1P	2P	3P	4T	—
9	Nhoaun	1P	2P	**3F**	3P	4C
10	Nhoaun	1P	2P	3P	4P	5C
11	Nhoaun	1P	2P	3P	4P	5T
12	Nhoaun	1P	2P	3T	—	—
13	Nhoaun	1P	2P	3P	4P	5C
14	Nhoaun	1P	2T	—	—	—
No. of children in each academic year		14	14	13	11	10
No. of repeaters in each academic year		0	0	1	1	—
% of repeaters in each academic year		0	0	7.7	9.1	—
No.	Ethnic group	AY2015 (7.1)	AY2016 (N/A)	AY2017 (7.1)	AY2018 (7.7)	AY2019 (30.8)
S3						
1	Nhoaun	1P	2P	3P	4P	5C
2	Khmou	**1F**	1P	2P	**3F**	3C
3	N/A	1P	2P	3T	—	—
4	Lao	1P	2P	**3F**	3P	4C
5	Tai	1P	2P	3P	4P	5C
6	Khmou	1P	2P	3P	4P	5C
7	Nhoaun	1P	2P	3P	4P	5C
8	Khmou	1P	2P	3P	4P	5C
9	Khmou	1P	2P	3P	4P	5C
10	Pounoy	1P	2P	3P	4P	5C
11	Tai	1P	2P	3P	4P	5C
12	Nhoaun	1P	2P	**3F**	3P	4C
13	Lue	1P	2P	3P	4P	5C
14	Nhoaun	1P	2P	3P	4P	5C
No. of children in each academic year		14	14	14	13	13
No. of repeaters in each academic year		1	0	2	1	—
% of repeaters in each academic year		7.1	0	14.3	7.7	—

(*continued*)

Table 9.4   (continued)

No.	Ethnic group	AY2015 (0)	AY2016 (N/A)	AY2017 (0)	AY2018 (0–15.4)	AY2019 (0)
S4						
1	Lue or Hmong	1P	2P	3T	—	—
2	Hmong	**1F**	1P	2P	**3F**	3D
3	Lue or Hmong	1P	2P	3P	4T	—
4	Lue or Hmong	1P	2T	—	—	—
5	Bid	1P	2P	3P	4P	5C
6	Lue or Hmong	1P	2P	3P	4T	—
7	Hmong	1P	2P	3P	4P	5C
8	Hmong	**1F**	1P	**2F**	2P	3C
9	Hmong	**1F**	1P	**2F**	2P	3C
10	Hmong	1P	2P	**3F**	3P	4C
11	Hmong	1P	2P	3P	4P	5C
12	Hmong	1P	2P	3P	4P	5C
13	Hmong	**1F**	1P	2P	3P	4C
14	Bid	1P	2P	3P	4P	5C
15	Hmong	1P	2P	3P	4P	5C
No. of children in each academic year		15	15	14	13	11
No. of repeaters in each academic year		4	0	3	1	—
% of repeaters in each academic year		26.7	0	21.4	7.7	—
No.	Ethnic group	AY2015 (0)	AY2016 (N/A)	AY2017 (0)	AY2018 (0)	AY2019 (0)
S5						
1	Hmong	1P	2P	3T	—	—
2	Hmong	1P	2P	3T	—	—
3	Hmong	1P	2P	3P	4P	5C
4	Hmong	1P	2D	—	—	—
5	Hmong	1P	2P	3P	4P	5C
6	Hmong	1P	2P	3P	4P	5C
7	Hmong	1P	2T	—	—	—
8	Hmong	1P	2P	3T	—	—
9	Hmong	1P	2X	—	—	—
10	Hmong	1P	2P	3T	—	—
11	Hmong	1P	2T	—	—	—
12	Hmong	1P	2P	3P	4—	—
13	Hmong	1P	2P	**3F**	3P	4C
14	Hmong	1P	**2F**	2P	3P	4C
15	Hmong	1P	**2F**	2P	**3F**	3C
16	Hmong	1P	**2F**	2P	**3F**	3-
17	Hmong	1P	2D	—	—	—
18	Hmong	1P	**2F**	**2F**	**2F**	2C

(*continued*)

Table 9.4   (continued)

19	Hmong	1P	2P	3D	—	—
20	Hmong	1P	2P	**3F**	**3F**	3C
No. of children in each academic year	20	20	15	10	9	
No. of repeaters in each academic year	0	4	3	4	—	
% of repeaters in each academic year	0	**20.0**	**20.0**	**40.0**	—	

Note: Numbers = academic grades, P = pass, F = fail, D = school dropout, T = transfer to other school, C = continue to attend target school even at the time of the survey, X = the child passed away and — = N/A. Numbers enclosed in parentheses under the academic year in each target school indicate the degree of ethnic affinity between teachers and children by academic year

Source: Prepared by the author based on the collected data

and children by academic year. Table 9.4 shows that in S1, two children were identified as repeaters of Grade 3 in AY2017, which represents 13.3% of the total number of repeaters in the same year. In S2, one child was identified as a repeater of Grade 3 in AY2017, and another one repeated Grade 4 in AY2018. The percentages of repeaters per year were 7.7% and 9.1%, respectively. In S3, the study identified one child as a repeater of Grade 1 in AY2015, two children repeated Grade 3 in AY2017 and one repeated Grade 3 in AY2018. The percentages of repeaters per year were 7.1%, 14.3% and 7.7%, respectively. In S4, four children repeated Grade 1 in AY2015, two repeated Grade 2 and one repeated Grade 3 in AY2017 and AY2018 each. The percentages of repeaters per year were 26.7%, 21.4% and 7.7%, respectively. In S5, four children repeated Grade 2 in AY2016, one repeated Grade 2 and two repeated Grade 3 in AY2017 and one repeated Grade 2 and three repeated Grade 3 in AY2018. The percentages of repeaters per year were 20.0%, 20.0% and 40.0%, respectively. When examining the grade levels in which the children repeated a grade (Table 9.4), the study found that children in S1 and S2 with high levels of ethnic affinity only repeated Grade 3 or above. Alternatively, in S3, S4 and S5 with low levels of ethnic affinity, a large number of children repeated the lower grades such as the first or second grade. Out of all repeaters in S3, S4 and S5, 64.3% repeated in the lower grades. Furthermore, exploring the frequency of repetition (Table 9.4), the study observed that the children who repeated a grade only once belonged to S1 and S2, both of which exhibited high levels of ethnic affinity. Conversely, in S3, S4 and S5, a large number of children repeated a grade more than once. Out of all repeaters in S3, S4 and S5, 57.1% repeated grades two or three times. These findings indicate that children in schools with low levels of ethnic affinity are more likely to stumble early on, such as in the first or second grade, and more likely to repeat grades frequently.[2]

4 Discussion: Does Ethnic Affinity Contribute to the Prevention of Grade Repetition Grade?

Analysis indicates that the higher the ethnic affinity between teachers and children, the less the grade repetition; conversely, the lower the ethnic affinity, the more the grade repetition. Can we conclude from the results that high levels of ethnic affinity contribute to the prevention of grade repetition among ethnic minority children? To further explore this point, Table 9.5 presents the reasons and background for repetition on the basis of information collected through the semi-structured interviews with teachers of the target schools. Table 9.5 presents that in S1, two students were identified as grade repeaters. The reasons for their repetition and the background were identified as 'because he could not pass the examination' and 'because he was affected by unfavourable family circumstances, such as the death of their father and the abandonment of their mother'. In S2, the study identified two students as grade repeaters, 'because his parents are often away from home on migrant work and there is no one at home to look after him well' and 'because her family is poor and her parents are busy with work, so they do not look after her well'. In S3, three students were identified as grade repeaters with the following reasons: 'his father was in custody and mother was taking him with her to various places, so he was also frequently absent from school', 'his father was in prison and his mother had a new baby to look after and was not taking enough care of him', and 'she came to school every day, but she was not very motivated and did not like studying much'. In S4, five students were identified as grade repeaters due to 'frequent absences due to eye disease', 'coming to school every day but not being able to pass the examinations because he/she did not fully understand Lao, the medium of instruction', and 'missing examination to help her parents with their work'. In S5, six students

---

[2] However, regardless of the degree of ethnic affinity, the results did not significantly differ between boys and girls in any of the target schools.

Table 9.5 Reasons and backgrounds underlying grade repetition for the target children

ID No.	Ethnic group	Sex	Repetition pattern	Reasons for grade repetition
S1 (repeaters = 2)				
6	Lue	M	1P2P3F3P4C	He basically attended school every day without missing a day but failed to get a passing mark in his examination and repeated a grade. Both his parents are alive and well, and he does not appear to have any major problems in his home environment
13	Lue	F	1P2P3F3P4C	She basically attended school every day without missing a day but was not able to get a passing mark in her examination and repeated a grade. In AY2017, when she repeated a grade, her father died. Her mother then left her and went away. She now lives with her grandparents, but as they are also very old, it is difficult for her to get support for her studies at home. The family is also very poor
S2 (repeaters = 2)				
3	Nhoaun	M	1P2P3P4F4C	His parents are often away from home on migrant work. As a result, he lives with grandparents or other relatives and there is no one to tell him to study at home
9	Nhoaun	F	1P2P3F3P4C	She basically came to school every day but was not able to study much. Her family was poor and her parents worked hard every day and did not have enough time to look after her. She has four older sisters, but they are also in school and are occupied with their own studies, so she does not get much help from them with her studies. She does not study much at home and her studies are basically done only at school
S3 (repeaters = 3)				
2	Khmou	M	1F1P2P3F3C	His father was in prison. His mother was also not always at home and frequently took him to different places, which meant that he was frequently absent from school. He is currently separated from his parents and lives with his grandmother. However, he is not well cared for in his study at home

(*continued*)

Table 9.5 (continued)

ID No.	Ethnic group	Sex	Repetition pattern	Reasons for grade repetition
4	Lao	M	1P2P3F3P4C	His father was arrested for drug offences and sent to prison. Meanwhile, his mother had a new baby and he was not well looked after. Support for his studies at home was also lacking and he failed to pass his examination and repeated a grade
12	Nhoaun	F	1P2P3F3P4C	Although she basically came to school every day, she did not seem to be highly motivated to study. She did not seem to like studying very much
S4 (repeaters = 5)				
2	Hmong	M	1F1P2P3F3D	He repeated grades because he missed a number of classes due to an eye disease; in AY2019 he dropped out of school because his eye condition became so severe that it was finally difficult for him to see
8	Hmong	M	1F1P2F2P3C	Although he basically came to school every day, he repeated grades because he could not understand Lao well enough due to his ethnicity and could not pass his examinations
9	Hmong	M	1F1P2F2P3C	Although he basically came to school every day, he repeated grades because he could not understand Lao well enough due to his ethnicity and could not pass his examinations
10	Hmong	F	1P2P3F3P4C	Although she basically came to school every day, she repeated grades because she could not understand Lao well enough due to her ethnicity and could not pass her examination
13	Hmong	F	1F1P2P3P4C	Her parents work in a banana plantation and she missed her examinations to help them with their work, so she repeated a grade
S5 (repeaters = 6)				
13	Hmong	M	1P2P3F3P4C	He was frequently absent from school. When he did come to school, he was often noisy in class and did not concentrate much on his studies. His parents live in the village where the target school is located and they take good care of him, but he does not seem to listen to his parents very much. He failed to pass his examination and repeated a grade

(continued)

Table 9.5 (continued)

ID No.	Ethnic group	Sex	Repetition pattern	Reasons for grade repetition
14	Hmong	M	1P2F2P3P4C	His family was poor and he was frequently absent from school, as the distance from home to school was long, requiring an hour's walk each way. Hence, he was unable to pass his examination and repeated a grade. As of December 2018, he has moved closer to the target school
15	Hmong	F	1P2F2P3F3C	Her parents work in their own rubber garden. In the meantime, she often missed school because she had to look after her younger brother. Hence, she was unable to pass her examinations and repeated grades
16	Hmong	F	1P2F2P3F4-	She was frequently absent from school as it was far from her home to school and required an hour's walk each way. Hence, she was unable to pass her examinations and repeated grades. Her parents work in a rubber garden they own
18	Hmong	M	1P2F2F2F2C	He has some brain defect. He does not usually play with his friends and is always alone. He cries when teachers get angry with him. His family lives in the village where the target school is located and takes good care of him
20	Hmong	F	1P2P3F3F3C	Her family is well-off and she basically comes to school every day. On the other hand, she did not study much and did not pass her examinations and repeated grades

Note: The ID No. in the table is signed with the number of children per target school in Table 9.4. The repetition pattern is greyed out

Source: Prepared by the author based on the collected data

were identified as grade repeaters for the following reasons: 'he was frequently absent or did not concentrate much on his studies at school and could not pass the examination', 'his/her family was poor and the school was far from his/her home and he/she was frequently absent from school and could not pass the examinations', 'her parents were at work and she had to look after her younger brother; so she was also frequently absent from school and could not pass the examinations', 'he has some brain damage', and 'she basically came to school every day but did not seem to study very much and could not pass the examinations'.

In summary, the reasons and backgrounds underlying grade repetition can be divided into four major categories, namely, (1) family circumstances, including poverty and parental problems (N = 9); (2) children's motivation to learn (N = 4); (3) problems in the medium of instruction, such as 'not understanding Lao' (N = 3); and (4) illness or disability (N = 2). According to these categories, less than half of all repeaters correspond to repetition due to problems with the children's motivation to learn or the medium of instruction, which may be particularly related to ethnic affinity. However, repetition due to family circumstances, such as poverty, parental problems and less care and support for children at home, is more common. Yoshida (2020), who examined the effects of the educational policy of revising the educational assessment system in the Republic of the Union of Myanmar, noted that although educational policies may improve repetition due to problems within the school, the effects of such educational policies may not reach those who repeat grades due to problems outside the school such as at home or in society. In view of Yoshida's (2020) findings, educational policies to increase ethnic affinity may be effective in preventing grade repetition due to problems in the medium of instruction and the low levels of motivation to learn. However, in the case of grade repetition due to problems outside school, such as unfavourable family circumstances, solving the problem using an ethnophilic education policy alone may be difficult. Therefore, although ethnic affinity between teachers and ethnic minority children may contribute to a certain extent to the prevention of grade repetition, it has its limitations. Therefore, implementing measures that can also address issues related to repetition due to problems outside of school, such as family circumstances, is necessary.

5   Conclusion

Given the educational development trends of the EFA and the MDGs from 1990 to the present, addressing the educational disparity of minority children, including ethnic minorities, who are still left behind, has become an urgent issue. This study focuses on Laos in Southeast Asia, which is considered a marginal case of ethnic minority children being left behind in the education sector. Building on previous studies (Ban & Inui, 2018; Yoshida, 2022) that found that ethnic affinity between teachers and children leads to high levels of academic performance among ethnic minority children, the current study examined whether or not ethnic affinity could also contribute to the prevention of grade repetition. Specifically, the study longitudinally tracked the enrolment trajectories of children over the past five years based on the academic enrolment registry of each target school. We then analysed whether or not ethnic affinity can effectively prevent grade repetition by examining the relationship between the enrolment status and degree of ethnic affinity of the school children.

The results demonstrate that target schools with high degrees of ethnic affinity produced fewer students who repeated grades, whereas target schools with low degrees of ethnic affinity had a large number of students who repeated grades. In target schools with high degrees of ethnic affinity, the children mostly repeated Grade 3 and above and no children repeated a grade more than once. Conversely, in target schools with low levels of ethnic affinity, a large number of children repeated lower grades, such as Grades 1 and 2, and a large number repeated grades more than once. This result indicates that children in schools with low levels of ethnic affinity are more likely to stumble in the early grades of schooling and experience increased difficulty, such as repeating a grade more than once. Furthermore, based on the results of the semi-structured interviews with the teachers, the study investigated the reasons and backgrounds underlying the repetition of the students. The result indicates that repetitions are mainly due to the family circumstances of the children, such as poverty and parental problems, in addition to repetition due to ethnic affinity such as problems with the medium of instruction. This finding highlights that educational policies to increase ethnic affinity may effectively prevent grade repetition due to problems inside but not outside the school, such as family circumstances. Therefore, to take a comprehensive approach to the problem of repetition among ethnic minority children and to reduce educational inequality, implementing educational policies, such as increasing ethnic affinity, is insufficient. However, implementing measures for tackling problems outside the school, such as those in the family and society, is necessary.

This study has its limitations. It examined the Luang Namtha Province, an area within Laos; thus, the results are not representative of the entire country. Additionally, whether or not the results would be similar in other provinces inside Laos and in other countries in which many ethnic minority groups reside remains unclear. Therefore, the need emerges to continue to examine whether or not results similar to those obtained from the current analysis can be achieved in other regions and countries. In addition, completing the full cohort was impossible, because tracking the enrolment trajectories of the children over the past five years was the only available option. Therefore, the study was unable to examine the effect of ethnic affinity in terms of repetition status instead of up to school completion and school dropout status. Therefore, the current study would like to continue the survey and complete the cohort to examine the relationship between ethnic affinity and school dropout, among others.

REFERENCES

Ban, H. (2018). *The relationship between teachers' and pupils' ethnic affinity and academic performance: The case of the Lao People's Democratic Republic* (in Japanese) [Master's thesis]. In the Graduate School of International Studies. Kwansei Gakuin University.

Ban, H., & Inui, M. (2018). Laos shotokyouiku niokeru minzoku chiiki kakusa: shogakkou niokeru Laos shousuu minzoku no kodomotachi [Ethnic and regional disparities in Lao primary education: Ethnic Lao minority children in primary schools]. In T. Sekiya (Ed.), *Kaihatsutojoukoku de manabu kodomotachi [Children learning in developing countries: A micro analysis of the actual enrolment status contributing to macro policy]* (pp. 159–182). Kwansei Gakuin University Press.

Chagnon, J., & Rumpf, R. (1982). Education: The prerequisite to change in Laos. In M. Stuart-Fox (Ed.), *Contemporary book company: Studies in the politics and society of the Lao People's Democratic Republic* (pp. 163–180). University of Queensland Press.

Inui, M. (2009). *Minority education and development in contemporary Laos.* Union Press.

Inui, M. (2015). Hmong women and education: Challenges for empowerment in the Lao PDR. *Hmong Studies Journal, 16*, 1–24.

Inui, M. (2020). Impact of the 'Grade Zero' system on minority children in Lao PDR – A qualitative study of pre-primary schools in a rural province. *Education 3-13, 48*(1), 118–130.

Lao Statistics Bureau. (2016). *Results of population and housing census 2015.* Ministry of Planning and Investment.

Lao Statistics Bureau. (2023). *Statistical yearbook 2022.* Ministry of Planning and Investment.

Liddell, C., & Rae, G. (2001). Predicting early grade retention: A longitudinal investigation of primary school progress in a sample of rural South African children. *The British Journal of Educational Psychology, 71*(3), 413–428.

Taniguchi, K. (2015). Determinants of grade repetition in primary school in sub-Saharan Africa: An event history analysis for rural Malawi. *International Journal of Educational Development, 45*, 98–111.

Thant, M., & Vokes, R. (1997). Education in Laos: Progress and challenges. In M. Than & J. L. H. Tan (Eds.), *Laos' dilemmas and options: The challenge of economic transition in the 1990s* (pp. 154–195). Institute of Southeast Asian Studies.

United Nations. (2015a). *The millennium development goals report 2015*. United Nations.

United Nations. (2015b). *Transforming our world: The 2030 agenda for sustainable development*. United Nations.

United Nations Educational, Scientific and Cultural Organization. (2015). *EFA Global Monitoring Report 2015: Education for all 2000–2015: Achievements and Challenges*. UNESCO.

Yamada, N. (2018). *Laos no kiso chishiki [Fundamental knowledge of Laos]*. Mekon.

Yoshida, N. (2020). Socio-economic status and the impact of the "continuous assessment and progression system" in primary education in Myanmar. *Education 3-13, 48*(6), 674–689.

Yoshida, N. (2022). *Impact of "ethnic affinity" between teachers and children on the ethnic minority's academic achievement in the northern Lao PDR*. Reporting at the conference of the Comparative Education Society of Hong Kong 2022.

Zuilkowski, S. S., Jukes, M. C. H., & Dubeck, M. M. (2016). 'I failed, no matter how hard I tried': A mixed-methods study of the role of achievement in primary school dropout in rural Kenya. *International Journal of Educational Development, 50*, 100–107.

CHAPTER 10

Examining Student Enrolment Patterns: Case of Lower Secondary School in Siem Reap, Cambodia

Akemi Ashida 🆔, *Chea Phal* 🆔, *and Yuto Kitamura*

1 INTRODUCTION

Education Expansion in Cambodia

In the late 1970s, the Cambodian education system was dismantled during the Pol Pot regime, resulting in a significant loss of educational infrastructure and human capital. In the aftermath, the Royal Government of Cambodia (RGC) prioritised education system reconstruction to rebuild human resources by expanding educational opportunities and enhancing educational quality. Since the 1980s, reconstruction has been a pivotal part of Cambodia's development agenda.

A. Ashida (✉)
Graduate School of International Development, Nagoya University, Nagoya, Japan
e-mail: ashida@gsid.nagoya-u.ac.jp

© The Author(s), under exclusive license to Springer Nature Switzerland AG 2024
T. Sekiya et al. (eds.), *Towards Ensuring Inclusive and Equitable Quality Education for All*, International and Development Education, https://doi.org/10.1007/978-3-031-70266-2_10

In the early 1990s, Cambodia committed to the World Declaration of Education for All, which reflected its commitment to universal access to education. This commitment was underscored when Phnom Penh hosted the National Conference on Education for All, where the major educational challenges were identified: 'quantity (access), quality, teacher training, preschool education, curriculum, assessment, adult literacy, girls' education, education for socially disadvantaged groups, dropouts, grade repetitions, education administration, statistics and planning' (State of Cambodia, 1991). Addressing these challenges, however, requires comprehensive strategies, such as building new rural schools, upgrading teacher qualifications, modernising curricula and transitioning from teacher-centred to student-centred pedagogical approaches.

Expanding educational access has been Cambodia's consistent priority in educational development. Initially centred on the expansion of access to primary education in the 1990s, the emphasis gradually expanded to include preschool and lower secondary education by the late 2000s. Influenced by organisations such as the World Bank and the Organisation for Economic Co-operation and Development (OECD), since the 2010s, the global education development movement has developed significant reforms to improve educational quality. Over the past three decades, Cambodia has received international assistance to support the implementation of many educational policies.

Cambodia has significantly expanded educational access, particularly in rural areas where access was previously limited. By 2019, the adjusted net primary school enrolment rate was 91% and the primary school completion rate was 74% (United Nations Educational, Scientific and Cultural Organization [UNESCO], 2023). Despite these achievements, challenges remain: the transition rate from primary to lower secondary education was only 62% in 2018, the net lower secondary enrolment rate was only 58% in 2019, and the lower secondary school completion rate was only 46% in 2019 (UNESCO, 2023). These statistics indicate that expanding educational access and improving lower secondary completion rates require further attention.

C. Phal
Cambodia Development Resource Institute (CDRI), Phnom Penh, Cambodia
e-mail: phalchea@cdri.org.kh

Y. Kitamura
Graduate School of Education, The University of Tokyo, Tokyo, Japan
e-mail: yuto@p.u-tokyo.ac.jp

The COVID-19 pandemic, which began in early 2020, caused widespread school closures and disrupted educational access across Cambodia (UNESCO, 2022). Therefore, the government introduced technology-based distance education; however, access to online learning was uneven, with studies indicating that only around 70% of children had access to distance education and only 30% were able to participate in online learning. The impact of the pandemic on education effectively reversed the educational progress made over the previous four years (Khoun, 2021). This setback highlights the need for more robust, resilient educational strategies that can withstand such disruptions and advance the goal of universal education for all.

Overview of the Kingdom of Cambodia

Cambodia is in the southern part of the Indochina Peninsula in Southeast Asia and borders Thailand, Vietnam and Laos. Cambodia faces the Gulf of Thailand, has an area of 181,035 km^2 and a population of 16.9 million, 90% of whom are Khmer. The capital city is Phnom Penh, Khmer is the official language and Buddhism is the national religion; however, Islam and Christianity are also freely practised. Cambodia's primary industries are agriculture (24.3% of GDP), industry (39.2% of GDP) and services (36.4% of GDP), with a GDP per capita of USD 1759 in 2022. Before the pandemic, Cambodia experienced rapid economic growth at around 7% per annum, and after contracting 3.1% in 2020, the economy bounced back with a growth rate of 5.2% in 2023 and an unemployment rate of 0.2% (Ministry of Foreign Affairs in Japan, 2024; World Bank, 2024). Cambodia's Human Development Index (HDI) is 0.6, ranking it 147th out of 193 countries, which is about medium (UNDP, 2024).

After gaining independence from France in 1953, Cambodia became destabilised in the late 1960s, which resulted in a civil war in the 1970s, which was followed by the Khmer Rouge's genocidal rule from 1975 to 1979. The subsequent liberation of Cambodia from the Khmer Rouge by Vietnamese troops in 1979 was seen by the West as a communist invasion supported by the Soviet Union, which resulted in a decade-long isolation from the international community (Kiernan, 1986). Following the signing of a peace agreement in 1991, the United Nations Transitional Authority in Cambodia (UNTAC) assumed control of Cambodia for two years to prepare for its first election in 1993. Consequently, the country was once again granted membership in international organisations such as the United Nations.

Subsequently, Cambodia experienced steady economic growth and significant poverty reduction. In July 2016, Cambodia was classified as a low-middle-income country. However, its economic structure remains fragile, particularly the disparity between urban and rural areas and the escalating urban problems in Phnom Penh (Ministry of Foreign Affairs of Japan, 2018). The education sector was significantly affected by the Khmer Rouge, who destroyed or closed many schools, which, in turn, resulted in the loss of teachers and other intellectuals and had a detrimental impact on the education system. The Khmer Rouge regime implemented a comprehensive programme of destruction and disruption to the education system, which saw a significant decline in the quality of education during the early 1980s. However, since 1993, with the support of developed countries and international organisations, there has been a notable shift towards positive educational developments (Chinnh & Dy, 2009). Although there have been continuous educational improvements, the system is still insufficient and further educational support is required. Therefore, international multilateral and bilateral aid agencies and international non-government organisations and companies are still providing aid and assistance.

Barriers to Lower Secondary Completion

There has been a significant expansion in Cambodia's primary education enrolments over the past three decades. By 2019, the net primary education enrolment rate had reached approximately 90% (UNESCO, 2023) and since the late 2000s, educational priorities have shifted towards improving primary education quality and expanding pre-primary and lower secondary education access. Issues with the transition from primary to lower secondary education, dropouts and grade repetition have hindered students from completing their lower secondary education.

Edwards et al. (2014) specifically focused on the transition from primary to lower secondary education in their extensive qualitative study on student continuation and dropout. As their results highlighted the weak relationships between school and home and the association with grade repetition, strengthening this relationship was identified as vital. Additional concerns were the need for subsidies to cover the cost of essentials, such as uniforms and school supplies, tuition fees for remedial work and the provision of safe routes to and from secondary schools. The study also emphasised the importance of parents' correct understanding of the necessary educational background with job requirements.

In more recent years, a reverse gender gap has been observed (Sivuthua et al., 2022). The expansion of educational access has particularly benefitted girls, which has resulted in a significant increase in the gender equality index. In 2013, the female lower secondary school enrolment rates exceeded males, and more recently, female academic performances have surpassed males (Chea et al., 2023). In 2019, the lower secondary education repetition rate was 2.7%: boys (3.9%) and girls (1.6%). More girls (46.5%) also completed lower secondary than boys (45.2%) (UNESCO, 2023). These figures indicate a growing gender disparity and highlight the need for targeted interventions to support boys in their educational journey.

Although Cambodia has made substantial progress in expanding access to primary education, the focus has now shifted to improving educational quality and expanding pre-primary and lower secondary levels. Addressing transition, dropout and grade repetition challenges and reversing the emerging gender gap are key areas for improvement to achieve SDG 4, aiming to ensure equitable and inclusive education for all.

Chapter Objective

Sekiya (2014) defines 'enrolment' as a student's year-by-year status in the school system, which includes the grade at which the student is registered, passing or failing a school year, grade repetition, dropping out, graduation and transfer to another school. 'Entrance' refers to a student's first entry into the education cycle; therefore, an 'enrolment pattern' describes a student's specific schooling situations and their progression, including passing and failing, from entrance to graduation or dropping out.

Sekiya (2014) and Ashida (2018) conducted school record studies to assess the actual enrolment status of children in the target schools in a regional city in Honduras. Their student enrolment pattern analyses, such as grade promotion, grade repetition and dropout, included an examination of the causes of these events. Similar student tracking studies using school records have been conducted in Latin America and South and Southeast Asia, including a study in a Nepali primary school (Ezaki, 2019) and a Myanmar lower secondary school (Yoshida, 2021). While Ezaki (2019) examined the differences between public and private schools and

Yoshida (2021) explored different socioeconomic patterns, neither applied a gender lens to analyse completion and dropout patterns.

This study employed a similar research methodology to examine lower secondary school completion in Cambodia, one of the least developed nations in Southeast Asia. As previously stated, Cambodia has faced significant basic education student transition and retention challenges. This study analysed school patterns to gain insights into Cambodia's education problems and understand the gender differences at an individual student level.

2   RESEARCH METHODS

The study compared the enrolment status of individual children and the grades they reached and represented this information as patterns describing student progression from enrolment in the first year of lower secondary school to the final years of their education. This was achieved using letters that indicated promotion, repetition and dropout for each grade. By using longitudinal data to track the learning trajectories of the target students, we revealed the processes that each student went through to reach each grade. This approach provided insights that could not be obtained from cross-sectional data (Sekiya, 2014). True cohort analysis, which utilises longitudinal data, requires comprehensive data collection and extensive school records to track student movements across school years (Gropello, 2003).

We selected one lower secondary school in a rural area of Siem Reap as the case study. Although the school is considered rural, it is relatively close to the national road and is a typical Cambodian lower secondary school. As seen in Fig. 10.1, there is only one lower secondary school in the commune that serves students from ten primary schools. The data analysis and interviews revealed that the greatest distance from student homes to the school is approximately 12 km.

After confirming that the school registration and evaluation records had been maintained relatively well for ten years, the team sought permission from the school director to copy the registration records and the year-end evaluation reports, which had information on each student's grade progression. The dropout information was also recorded in the transcripts, though there were some discrepancies by year and class. Most records and reports were handwritten in Khmer, with some typewritten hard copies.

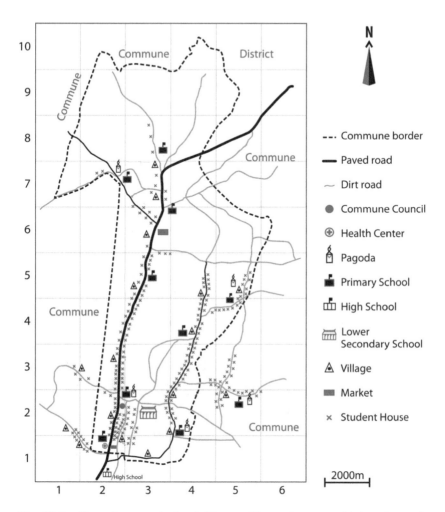

Fig. 10.1 Map of surveyed school. (Source: The author created it based on collected data)

The records and reports for 1855 grade 7, 8 and 9 students between 2005 and 2014 were copied and entered into Excel for cleaning and matching. However, for the analysis, we discarded three types of records: when we were unable to find matches using the student's name and date of birth; transfer-out students, as tracing these students was considered time-consuming; and students who transferred into the school in grades 8 or 9. The final analysis sample, therefore, was 1226 students who were enrolled in the school between 2005 and 2012, all of whom were considered as one cohort for the enrolment pattern analysis.

After obtaining the preliminary findings, the research team revisited the school to share the results with the school director and teachers. During this visit, the team conducted in-depth interviews to clarify unusual patterns and, more importantly, to understand the underlying reasons for the student dropouts. This qualitative data subsequently provided valuable insights for the study discussion.

3   Results

Enrolment and Student Characteristics

Figure 10.2 shows the enrolment figures for the target school disaggregated by year of entrance and gender. Despite some fluctuations, the overall new intake trends at the surveyed school had an upward trend. There were 93 new grade 7 students in 2005, which had more than doubled to 213 by 2012. These figures represent only the students being traced in the

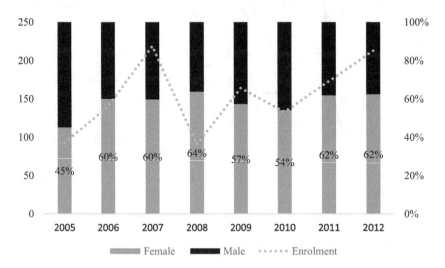

Fig. 10.2 Student enrolment by year and gender. (Source: Prepared by the authors based on the school registration records)

Table 10.1 Student ages in grade 7

Age	All		Female		Male	
	Number	%	Number	%	Number	%
10	4	0%	2	0%	2	0%
11	44	4%	27	4%	17	3%
12	117	10%	68	9%	49	10%
13	226	18%	141	20%	85	17%
14	286	23%	171	24%	115	23%
15	264	22%	148	21%	116	23%
16	142	12%	83	12%	59	12%
17	77	6%	41	6%	36	7%
18	34	3%	26	4%	8	2%
19	18	1%	7	1%	11	2%
20	4	0%	2	0%	2	0%
21	1	0%	1	0%	0	0%
22	1	0%	1	0%	0	0%
24	1	0%	1	0%	0	0%
Unknown	7	1%	2	0%	5	1%
	1226	100%	721	100%	505	100%

Source: School registration records

study; therefore, the actual new intake numbers could have been higher. From 2016 onwards, the female student proportion surpassed the male, and by 2012, female students comprised 62% of total new enrolments.

The official starting age for primary school is 6 years in Cambodia and that for typical lower secondary school grade 7 is 12 years. However, the data indicated that a small percentage (4%) of students began lower secondary school at a younger age, 10% started lower secondary school at the age of 12, and the majority started at 12 years or older. Notably, there were also a few students in their 20s. There were no noticeable gender differences in the lower secondary school starting ages (Table 10.1).

Enrolment Patterns

In total, we identified 29 distinct patterns: 7 full-cycle completion patterns, 17 dropout patterns and 5 incomplete or untraceable patterns for which we were unable to confirm if the students had completed lower secondary or dropped out, which may have been because of student transfers, incomplete records and unmatched names. In 2011, the share of

Table 10.2 Enrolment pattern frequencies

Year	Number of students	Complete LSS	Dropout	Unconfirmed
2005	93	32.26%	45.16%	22.58%
2006	140	40.71%	47.86%	11.43%
2007	219	35.16%	56.62%	8.22%
2008	91	36.26%	58.24%	5.49%
2009	164	51.83%	37.80%	10.37%
2010	133	48.12%	33.08%	18.80%
2011	173	1.73%	28.90%	69.36%
2012	213	39.44%	25.82%	34.74%
Total	1226	35.32%	40.54%	24.14%

Source: Based on the school registration records

unconfirmed patterns was noticeably higher than in the other years. The statistics in Table 10.2 suggest that less than half the students finished their lower secondary education.

Ordered by occurrence frequency, Table 10.3 summarises the most common grade progression patterns for the 2005–2012 cohort. Of these, only 6 patterns were common to 10 or more students and 17 were unique to only one student. The most frequent pattern was completing the course in three consecutive years without grade repetition (7P8P9P). The second most frequent pattern was passing grade 7, registering in grade 8, but becoming untraceable because of a lack of school records for the following year and no dropout confirmation (7P8U). The third most common pattern was dropping out in the first year of lower secondary school (7D). These top three patterns accounted for 71.2% of all patterns observed at the target school.

Grade repetition was much less common than dropping out, with grade repetition patterns only found from the seventh most frequent pattern onwards. No student repeated a grade more than twice. Patterns involving grade repetition were identified in 11 patterns for 24 students, which was less than 2% of all the student sample in this study.

Common Completion Patterns

Table 10.4 shows the lower secondary school completion patterns summarised in order of frequency. Only 433 students or 35.6% of the cohort completed lower secondary education. However, as approximately 25% of

Table 10.3 Frequency of enrolment patterns

Rank	Enrolment patterns	Number of students	%	Years registered	Last grade passed
1	7P8P9P	419	34.2%	3	9
2	7P8U	247	20.1%	2	7
3	7D	205	16.7%	1	-
4	7P8D	154	12.6%	1	7
5	7P8P9D	117	9.5%	3	8
6	7U	46	3.8%	1	-
7	7P8P**9R**9P	7	0.6%	4	9
8	**7R**7D	6	0.5%	2	-
9	7P8P**9R**9D	2	0.2%	4	8
9	7P8U9D	2	0.2%	3	8
9	7P8U9P	2	0.2%	3	9
9	**7R**7P8P9P	2	0.2%	4	9

Source: Based on school registration records

Notes:
- No. of patterns with 10 or more students: 6
- No. of patterns with only one student: 17
- No. of students with grade repetition: 24 with 11 patterns
- 'P' indicates the student passed the grade; 'R' indicates the student failed the grade (required to repeat it); 'D' stands for dropout; and 'U' refers to a lack of description in the school records

Table 10.4 Completion patterns

Rank	Enrolment patterns	All	Female	Male
1	7P8P9P	96.77%	98.02%	95.00%
2	7P8P**9R**9P	1.62%	0.79%	2.78%
3	**7R**7P8P9P	0.46%	0.00%	1.11%
3	7P8U9P	0.46%	0.40%	0.56%
5	7U8P9P	0.23%	0.40%	0.00%
5	7P**8R**8P9P	0.23%	0.40%	0.00%
5	7U9P	0.23%	0.00%	0.56%
Number of students		433	253	180

Source: School registration records

Notes:
- No. of completion patterns: 7
- No. of unique patterns with only one student: 3
- No. of grade repetition patterns: three for 10 students

the student statuses were unconfirmed, the actual completion rate may have been higher but was most likely below 50%. None of these students took more than four years to complete their studies, and nearly all (96.8%) completed their studies within three years without repeating a grade. Seven successful completion patterns were identified; however, the six less frequent patterns accounted for only 3.2% of the students, with the last three patterns being unique to individual students. The second most frequent successful completion pattern was grade repetition; however, this pattern was only observed in seven cases or 1.6% of the total students. Female students had a slightly higher completion rate, but the difference was minimal.

Common Dropout Patterns

Out of 1226 students, 497 or 40.54% of the cohort dropped out. The actual dropout rate was probably higher because of unconfirmed dropout cases. Seventeen distinct dropout patterns were identified, the three most common of which were dropping out in grade 7 (7D), dropping out in grade 8 (7P8D) and dropping out in grade 9 (7P8P9D), which accounted for 95% of all dropout cases. A few students who had dropped out later returned to school; however, none of these managed to complete lower secondary and eventually dropped out again.

Although females tended to stay in school longer, the dropout rates for the male (40.79%) and female (40.36%) students were similar. Dropping out in the first year of lower secondary was more frequent in the male students (50%) than the female students (35.05%). Grade repetition did not appear to be a significant factor in dropping out, as only 12 of the 497 dropouts had repeated a grade. None of the students in the three most common dropout patterns had experienced grade repetition (Table 10.5).

4   Discussion

Characteristics Observed in the Results

The observed enrolment surge aligned with the upward trends in global lower secondary enrolment rates (UNESCO, 2023; Chea et al., 2023). In Cambodia, females appear to have gained greater benefits from education expansion, resulting in a gender gap reversal (Bossavie & Kanninen, 2018). While current government policies in Cambodia seem to favour

Table 10.5 Dropout patterns

Rank	Enrolment patterns	All	Female	Male
1	7D	41.25%	35.05%	50.00%
2	7P8D	30.99%	30.58%	31.55%
3	7P8P9D	23.54%	29.21%	15.53%
4	7**R**7D	1.21%	1.37%	0.97%
5	7P8U9D	0.40%	0.69%	0.00%
5	7P8P9**R**9D	0.40%	0.69%	0.00%
Number of students		433	253	180

Source: School registration records

Notes:
- No. of dropout patterns: 17
- No. of unique patterns with only one student: 11
- No. of patterns with grade repetition: six for 12 students

females, recently, there has been a growing policy and academic focus on gender gap reversal (Chea et al., 2024).

The lower secondary school dropout rate in Cambodia was higher than that in primary schools in Honduras (Sekiya & Ashida, 2017) and lower secondary schools in Myanmar (Yoshida, 2021), whereas lower than that in primary schools in Nepal (Ezaki, 2019). Notably, in Myanmar, the grade repetition rates were higher than the dropout rates, and in Honduras, it was common for grade repeaters to complete their primary education. However, in Cambodia, grade repetition was very low, with none of the lower secondary completers in this study repeating a grade. Although Cambodia does not have an automatic promotion policy, it is more common to promote students even if they fail to acquire the knowledge and skills needed, which can lead to a lack of foundation skills and could be the reason for the high dropout rate and learning crisis in Cambodia (Chea et al., 2024; Marshall, 2022).

The analysis of the students' ages at the time of enrolment revealed that many entered grade 7 at an older age than the expected starting age of 12 years old. Studies have suggested that late enrolment is one of the factors that can lead to learning difficulties and eventual dropout (Wils, 2004). Our data also indicated that if students started lower secondary school after 14 years of age, the dropout likelihood was approximately twice as high as that of those who enrolled at the age of 13 years or younger.

Although the female and male dropout rates were roughly equal, they had different patterns, with males more often dropping out earlier and girls generally continuing until grade 9 before deciding to leave.

Barriers to Lower Secondary Completion

The predominant school dropout pattern in Cambodia occurred after the first year of lower secondary, particularly among male students. To investigate the underlying reasons for high male and female dropout rates, we presented the preliminary findings to the school director and teachers and conducted in-depth interviews to gain further insights.

The interview data revealed that one of the most prevalent reasons was economic family hardship. This finding aligned with the study by Sekiya and Ashida (2017), which examined similar cases in Honduras. Many students were compelled to contribute to their family's income, often by seeking employment. Migration to urban areas and neighbouring Thailand for work was a common trend for these dropouts. Previous studies in Cambodia (Benveniste et al., 2008; Bray & Bunly, 2005) have also highlighted this issue. Male students were more likely to leave school to seek employment than females.

While early marriage has become less common in Cambodia, particularly in urban areas, some rural female students still quit school when they get married. This is particularly true for those entering lower secondary at an older age. Most of the dropouts due to marriage were female students in this study. According to the teachers, these students often felt embarrassed attending school and studying with their younger peers after getting married.

Another factor identified in the interviews was the distance between the students' homes and the school. Edwards et al. (2014) found that the distance from home to school significantly impacted Cambodian lower secondary survival and completion rates. In rural Cambodia, the absence of public transportation, such as buses and trains, worsens this issue. Lower secondary school-aged children can be too young to ride motorbikes,[1] and many households cannot afford motorbikes for their children. However, many upper primary and lower secondary school children ride motorbikes on the street. On the basis of the school location map provided by the school director, there is only one lower secondary

---

[1] Legally, the driving license is applied to motorbikes of 150cc or above in Cambodia.

school in the commune, with students from nearby communes also commuting to this school. Therefore, the distance from home to school could be as far as 12 km one way, making it impractical or difficult for students to commute on foot or by bicycle. Our field visit observations noted that, except for a few main roads, most roads in the area were unpaved.

Through initiatives such as 'One Commune, One Lower Secondary School', the Cambodian government has made significant efforts to ensure schools are closer to students. The easier access to schools is intended to benefit disadvantaged students, particularly girls and those from poor families. As of 2021, there were 1409 communes in Cambodia and 1777 lower secondary schools (Chea et al., 2023). In the area covered by this study, students from ten primary schools are expected to transition to the lower secondary school examined in this study. However, despite the increase in lower secondary schools, commuting distances remain a challenge in some areas. As it is financially impractical to build more schools and deploy more teachers, individual support measures for disadvantaged students to encourage continued schooling should be considered to address this issue.

5   Conclusion

This chapter examined student enrolment and progression patterns at a lower secondary school in rural Cambodia. By examining individual student trajectories, this study provides significant insights into the complexities and challenges of completing lower secondary education in one of Southeast Asia's least developed countries, where primary to secondary transition rates are low and secondary dropout rates are high.

Nonetheless, the findings showed a positive lower secondary enrolment trend over the study period, with female students increasingly outnumbering male students. However, the age of entry for many students was older than the expected age of 12 years. This delay in starting lower secondary is indicative of the broader systemic issues affecting school readiness and access. The study identified 29 distinct enrolment patterns, with only 35.32% of students completing lower secondary and 40.54% dropping out. The most prevalent pattern for completers was advancing through the grades without repetition. However, the dropout patterns showed that students left school mainly in the first year and often without grade repetition. Gender differences in the dropout patterns were notable. Female students, although more likely to enrol, faced specific challenges, such as early marriage, which impacted their ability to complete education. Male students were more likely to drop out earlier because of economic pressures and the need to contribute to household income.

In conclusion, while significant progress has been made in increasing enrolment rates in Cambodia, the high dropout rates and gender-specific challenges identified in this study indicate that much work remains to be done. By addressing the economic and cultural barriers to education and by implementing targeted support strategies, Cambodia can improve the retention and completion rates of its lower secondary students, which would contribute to the broader goal of educational development and equity in the country and the region.

As this study focused exclusively on a single lower secondary school in the suburbs of Siem Reap, Cambodia, future studies should broaden the research scope to include a diverse range of schools to obtain a more comprehensive understanding of the current state of lower secondary education across Cambodia. Incorporating the geographic and socioeconomic backgrounds of the students would also enhance the ability to design interventions that can effectively support students prone to dropping out.

The school closures worldwide due to the COVID-19 pandemic had a substantial impact on schooling and learning outcomes. A 2021 survey conducted by the Cambodian Development Research Institute and the Ministry of Education, Youth and Sport (MoEYS) revealed that only about 50% of secondary school students were able to participate in real-time online classes (Chea et al., 2022). Although schools in Cambodia reopened in November 2021, the long-term effects of these closures on student learning remain uncertain. MoEYS statistics indicate a 2.4% increase in the lower secondary dropout rate during this period, rising from 15.8% in 2018/2019 to 18.2% in the academic year 2020/2021 (MoEYS, 2021). Given these findings, future research should explore the impact of the pandemic on enrolment patterns in Cambodia and globally. This exploration would provide valuable insights into the broader implications of the pandemic on education systems and help inform strategies for mitigating the adverse effects on student retention and progression.

REFERENCES

Ashida, A. (2018). *The actual effect on enrollment of "Education for All": Analysis using longitudinal individual data.* Union Press.

Benveniste, L., Marshall, J., & Araujo, M. (2008). *Teaching in Cambodia.* World Bank.

Bossavie, L., & Kanninen, O. (2018). *What explains the gender gap reversal in educational attainment?* World Bank Policy Research Working Paper.

Bray, M., & Bunly, S. (2005). *Balancing the books: Household financing of basic education in Cambodia.* University of Hong Kong.

Chea, P., Bo, C., & Minami, R. (2022). *Cambodia secondary school teachers' readiness for online teaching during the COVID 19 pandemic.* Working Paper Series 134. Phnom Penh: CDRI.

Chea, P., Nhem, D., Chea, S., & Bo, C. (2024). *The reversal of gender gap in learning: Why boys are falling behind in upper secondary schools.* Working Paper Series 145. Phnom Penh: CDRI.

Chea, P., Tek, M., & Nok, S. (2023). *Gender gap reversal in learning and gender-responsive teaching in Cambodia.* Working Paper Series 141. Phnom Penh: CDRI.

Chinnh, S., & Dy, S. (2009). Education reform context and process in Cambodia. In Y. Hirosato & Y. Kitamura (Eds.), *The political economy of educational reforms and capacity development in Southeast Asia: Cases of Cambodia, Laos, and Vietnam* (pp. 113–130). Springer.

Edwards, D. B., Zimmermann, T., Sitha, C., Williams, J. H., & Kitamura, Y. (2014). Student transition from primary to lower secondary school in Cambodia: Narrative insights into complex systems. *Prospects, 44*(3), 367–380.

Ezaki, N. (2019). Enrolment patterns of individual children left behind in the trend towards 'quality education': A case study of primary education in Nepal. *Education 3-13, 47*(5), 520–533. https://doi.org/10.1080/0300427 9.2018.1504100

Gropello, D. E. (2003). *Monitoring Educational Performance in the Caribbean,* World Bank Working Papers, No. 6, The International Bank for Reconstruction and Development/The World Bank, Washington, D.C.

Khoun, T. (2021). *Projected impacts of COVID-19 on the 2020 human development index in Cambodia and its neighbors.* Phnom Penh UNDP Cambodia.

Kiernan, B. (1986). William Shawcross, declining Cambodia. *Bulletin of Concerned Asian Scholars, 18*(1), 56–63.

Marshall, J. H. (2022). *Learning loss in the Covid-19 pandemic era: Evidence from the 2016–2021 grade six national learning assessment in Cambodia.* MoEYS and UNICEF.

Ministry of Education, Youth and Sport. (2021). *Education Congress: The education, youth and sports performance in the academic year 2019–2020 and goals for the academic year 2020–2021*. MoEYS.

Ministry of Foreign Affairs of Japan. (2018). Kunibetsu Kaihatsu Kyoryoku Houshin (country development cooperation policy). https://www.mofa.go.jp/mofaj/gaiko/oda/files/000072231.pdf.

Ministry of Foreign Affairs of Japan. (2024). Japan-Cambodia relations (basic data). https://www.mofa.go.jp/region/asia-paci/cambodia/data.html.

Sekiya, T. (2014). Individual patterns of enrolment in primary schools in the Republic of Honduras, Education 3–13. *International Journal of Primary, Elementary and Early Years Education, 42*(5), 460–474.

Sekiya, T., & Ashida, A. (2017). An analysis of primary school dropout patterns in Honduras. *Journal of Latinos and Education, 16*(1), 65–73.

Sivuthua, O., Vira, K., Sorphon, C., Sokhon, N., & Virak, S. (2022). *Analysis of gender parity in lower-secondary education using geospatial data: A case study of Cambodia*. The KIX EAP Hub. https://www.gpekix.org/sites/default/files/webform/submit_to_the_library/100/Analysis%20of%20gender%20parity%20in%20lower-secondary%20using%20geospatial%20data%20a%20case%20study%20of%20Cambodia.pdf

State of Cambodia. (1991). *National Conference on education for All Final Report* (pp. 2–6). SOC.

United Nations Development Program. (2024). *Human development report 2023–24: Breaking the gridlock: Reimagining cooperation in a polarised world*. New York.

United Nations Educational, Scientific and Cultural Organization. (2022). Global monitoring of school closures, COVID-19 impact on education. https://webarchive.unesco.org/web/20220629024039/https://en.unesco.org/covid19/educationresponse/.

United Nations Educational, Scientific and Cultural Organization. (2023). *Global education monitoring report 2023: Technology in education– A tool on whose terms?* UNESCO.

Wils, A. (2004). Late entrants leave school earlier: evidence from Mozambique. *International Review of Education, 50*(1), 17–37.

World Bank. (2024). Open data. World Bank. https://data.worldbank.org/country/cambodia?view=chart.

Yoshida, N. (2021). Socioeconomic status (SES) and the benefits of the 'continuous assessment and progression system (CAPS)' in lower secondary education in Myanmar. *International Journal of Comparative Education and Development, 23*(4), 335–352.

CHAPTER 11

Analysis of Student Retention in Primary Education Level Under Mongolia's Automatic Promotion Policy

Keiichi Ogawa ⓘ*, Khishigbuyan Dayan-Ochir,*
and Sheikh Rashid Bin Islam ⓘ

1   INTRODUCTION

Nestled between Russia and China, Mongolia stands as the world's second-largest landlocked country, strategically positioned across an expansive territory spanning approximately 1,564,000 square kilometres. Mongolia is administratively segmented into 21 provinces, commonly referred to as 'aimags', with its capital in Ulaanbaatar. As of the latest

K. Ogawa (✉)
Graduate School of International Cooperation Studies, Kobe University,
Kobe, Japan
e-mail: ogawa35@kobe-u.ac.jp

K. Dayan-Ochir
World Bank Mongolia Country Office, Ulaanbaatar, Mongolia
e-mail: khishid@gmail.com

available data in 2021, the nation's population is estimated at 3.3 million individuals, characterised by a notably youthful demographic, with 61% of its inhabitants under the age of 30. Statistics from the Mongolian Statistical Information Service (2021) reveal an average life expectancy of 70 years, with a demographic breakdown comprising 50.5% women, 49.5% men, and 38.0% children falling within the age bracket of 0–18 years (Heath-Brown, 2015; Javkhlan & Hyun, 2021).

Since 1990, Mongolia's education system has experienced substantial changes. Historically, the nation possessed a robust educational framework, which was significantly disrupted by the economic and financial crisis of the 1990s, consequent to Mongolia's transition from a socialist to a free-market economy. This economic transformation led to a marked decline in university enrolments and adversely affected multiple economic sectors. The adoption of the Mongolian constitution in 1992 mandated free basic education for all citizens, thus laying the foundation for a public education system predicated on equitable educational opportunities. Subsequent legislative enactments in 1998 included the Education Law and specific statutes governing preschool, primary and secondary, vocational, and higher education (Yembuu, 2010).

A pivotal educational reform occurred in 2008 when the government extended the school curriculum to a 12-year system, aligning Mongolia's educational framework with international standards. Mongolia's long-term development policy 'Vision 2050' outlines a strategic roadmap emphasising human development, secure living conditions, family well-being, and learning efficacy. The initial phase (2021–2030) aims to provide all citizens equitable access to quality education and establish a just education system. The objective is for primary and secondary school students to develop fundamental labour skills and engage in global collaboration. Schools are envisioned to become centres of human development, fostering children who are stable, positive, obedient, proud of their Mongolian heritage, noble, and patriotic while equipping them with essential knowledge and skills (Javkhlan & Hyun, 2021). Furthermore, introduced in January 2016, the Sustainable Development Vision 2030

S. R. B. Islam
Graduate School of International Cooperation Studies, Kobe University, Kobe, Japan
e-mail: 233i414i@stu.kobe-u.ac.jp

(SDV) spearheads Mongolia's commitment to realising the United Nations' Sustainable Development Goals (SDGs), enacted by the UN in 2015. Mongolia's SDV aims to eradicate poverty by fostering enduring economic progress and fostering a society that is both equitable and inclusive. Central to this vision is a robust emphasis on education, as encapsulated in SDG 4 (UNDP, 2021).

Central to achieving Mongolia's long-term goals is education, specifically primary education, with the highest rate of return. Educational statistics are often used to measure the effectiveness of these policies and the returns from education (Pastore, 2009). These educational statistics from international organisations, typically presented as cross-sectional data, offer valuable insights into the overall educational landscape of a country. However, because this data aggregates information into average values, it often fails to capture the unique educational conditions and challenges experienced by individuals. In Mongolia, this limitation means that cross-sectional data alone is insufficient to fully understand the educational difficulties children from lower socioeconomic backgrounds and rural areas face. Conversely, a longitudinal research method, which tracks individual students based on school records over time, can provide a clearer picture of educational trajectories. This approach can illuminate individual enrolment patterns, such as school entry, grade progression, repetition, and eventual school completion or dropout, as well as annual test scores across different grades. The effectiveness of this method is demonstrated in the study conducted by Sekiya (2014).

In line with this imperative, this chapter employs longitudinal data to meticulously monitor the enrolment patterns and annual test scores of children from diverse socioeconomic backgrounds, spanning rural and urban locales.[1] Through this approach, the aim is to gain nuanced insights into individuals' educational journeys. By scrutinising present enrolment statuses vis-à-vis socioeconomic context as well as the area of residence, the study endeavoured to unveil primary school pupils' retention rates and

---

[1] In this chapter, as outlined by the study conducted by Sekiya (2014), the term 'enrolment' denotes the status of an individual's involvement within the educational framework, encompassing factors such as registered grade, performance in end-of-year assessments, instances of grade repetition, successful completion, and instances of dropping out.

academic performance.[2] This analytical endeavour sought to assess learning outcomes through test score results and shed light on underlying factors, including the impact of teacher involvement, which may shape these educational outcomes.

2   BASIC EDUCATION IN MONGOLIA

Structure of the Mongolian Education System

In Mongolia, the school education framework comprises four distinct stages: pre-primary education, primary education, secondary education, and higher education, as delineated in Table 11.1. Pre-primary education or Early Childhood Education (ECE), though not obligatory, aims to establish universally accessible, standardised, and high-quality pre-primary education for all children. This objective emphasises the creation of a secure, healthful, and environmentally sustainable atmosphere that fosters parental involvement and facilitates children's transition to formal schooling. While government support is extended to public kindergartens, private counterparts operate independently of governmental assistance (Javkhlan & Hyun, 2021).

General education in Mongolia is structured into three levels: primary (six years), lower secondary (three years), and upper secondary (three years). Education is compulsory up to the lower secondary level, and public education is provided free of charge, although families may still incur some costs related to schooling. In 2020, Mongolia's general education system served a total of 680,800 students. Students are automatically promoted each year during the primary education phase, which includes grades 1 to 5. A school-based assessment system is in place to ensure continuous monitoring and evaluation of student progress. At the end of primary education, students must pass a standardised test to receive a certificate of completion, which is necessary for advancing to the next educational level (UNESCO IBE, 2011).

Since the 1990s, the landscape of public and private school education in Mongolia has undergone significant expansion, juxtaposed against the

---

[2] The 'retention rate' for schools is a measure of the percentage of students who continue their education at the same institution from one academic year to the next. It indicates how effectively a school can retain its students without them dropping out or transferring to another institution.

Table 11.1 Structure of the Mongolian education system

Official entrance age	Grade	Education level	Alternative route		
24+	-	Doctor of Philosophy (3-4 Years)	-	Higher Education	
22	2	Master's Degree (1-2 Years)	-		
	1				
18	4	Bachelor's degree (4-5 Years)	-		
	3				
	2				
	1				
15	3	Upper Secondary Education (3 Years)	Vocational Education (2 Years)		Free Education
	2				
	1				
12	3	Lower Secondary Education (3 Years)	-	Compulsory Education	
	2				
	1				
6	6	Primary Education (6 Years)	-		
	5				
	4				
	3				
	2				
	1				
3	3	Pre-Primary Education (3 Years)	-		
	2				
	1				

Note. For the case of grades 1–5, an automatic grade promotion policy is in effect for the primary education level of Mongolia, which is indicated graphically in the table through an arrow '⟹'

Source: Created by the authors

nascent development of the higher education system. The inaugural establishment of the National University of Mongolia in 1942 marked the inception of higher education in the country. Subsequently, a proliferation of both national and private universities ensued. Until 1993, higher education in Mongolia was publicly funded, with full-time students receiving stipends to defray living expenses. Post-1993, the transition to a tuition-based model ensued, with student tuition fees constituting the primary revenue stream for higher education institutions. Presently, private expenditure, predominantly through tuition fees, forms the principal source of financing for Mongolia's higher education sector, accounting for 70.0–85.0% of the aggregate funds (UNESCO IBE, 2011).

Teachers' Salary and Performance in Mongolia

In the past, educators who themselves or whose students succeeded in academic competitions were regarded as exemplary teachers. Both school and teacher evaluations incorporated benchmarks such as the facilitation of students' readiness for national or international academic contests like the 'International Mathematical Olympiad', as well as their participation and performance. Notably, competition outcomes were closely associated with teacher effectiveness and the compensation structure. The remuneration system for teachers comprised a base salary, supplementary allowances, and bonuses. Base salaries were determined primarily by a teacher's tenure and experience. Supplementary allowances, introduced in Mongolia in 1995, were allocated based on various factors, including serving as a homeroom teacher, undertaking additional responsibilities beyond regular hours, possessing advanced professional qualifications, overseeing specific administrative tasks such as managing a classroom or laboratory, leading subject-specific teaching departments, demonstrating specialised skills, or teaching in rural areas (Adiyasuren & Galindev, 2023; Steiner-Khamsi, 2012).

The introduction of 'outcomes-based education' in Mongolia in 2003 ushered in a shift towards performance-linked compensation for educators. Under this system, teacher salaries became contingent upon fulfilling predetermined performance criteria outlined in individualised 'outcome contracts' or scorecards. These criteria encompassed ten distinct indicators, with only two directly related to student outcomes: effective classroom management and student development. Additionally, bonuses were disbursed annually, four times a year, predicated upon evaluations conducted by school administrators to assess teacher performance. Under the current educational framework, the 2012 education reform placed a renewed emphasis on the holistic development of each student, thereby reshaping the perception of what constitutes a proficient or commendable educator. Criticisms highlighting the tendency of teachers to prioritise high-achieving students bound for national competitions at the expense of others prompted a reevaluation of teacher criteria. The teacher evaluation system evaluates educators' effectiveness across five key dimensions: students' academic performance, character cultivation, talent nurturing, health promotion, and parental satisfaction. Quarterly incentive supplements are contingent upon the outcomes of both teacher self-assessments and evaluations conducted by school principals or instructional managers, which appraise performance against these criteria (Adiyasuren & Galindev, 2023).

According to a recent study on school management (Khurelbaatar, 2020), over 70.0% of teachers perceive the evaluations conducted by school management as instrumental in enhancing their instructional practices. However, a prevailing practice is the equitable distribution of a school's total incentive supplement budget among all teachers, irrespective of individual performance. This practice is particularly pertinent given that salary supplements constitute approximately 41.0% of a teacher's total income (UNESCO, 2019), rendering it significant. Furthermore, it merits acknowledgement that the salary supplement received for additional teaching hours represents the most considerable portion of a teacher's monthly earnings, excluding the base salary. In an effort to acknowledge and incentivise effective teaching, the government is poised to introduce a performance-based salary system for educators in the near future. Preceding this initiative, the government ratified a new regulation in 2019 aimed at school self-monitoring and evaluation. This regulation delineates evaluation rubrics comprising five domains to assess school performance, one of which explicitly addresses lesson management and quality directly correlated with teachers' instructional practices. Within this domain, school principals or education managers are tasked with monitoring 17 specific criteria to evaluate teachers' pedagogical approaches through classroom observations.

These observations are anticipated to serve as invaluable resources for teacher professional development and the enhancement of classroom instruction. Notably, several criteria outlined in the regulation bear striking resemblance to items within the 'International Comparative Analysis of Teaching and Learning' (ICALT). Specifically, these include elements such as fostering a safe and stimulating educational environment, delivering clear and structured instruction, implementing effective teaching-learning strategies, and employing differentiated instruction. Insights into the job satisfaction of Mongolian educators are gleaned from the 'Teaching and Learning International Survey' (TALIS) 2013 questionnaire. With a 4-point rating scale, teachers reported an average job satisfaction rating of 3.4, with satisfaction regarding the work environment rated at 3.3. Interestingly, analysis by years of teaching experience reveals that teachers with up to 5 years and those with over 21 years exhibit the highest levels of job satisfaction, mirroring findings from the TALIS-2013 survey. Moreover, the study underscores that factors contributing to job satisfaction predominantly revolve around teacher-student relationships and collaborative interactions among educators rather than school-specific variables (Adiyasuren & Galindev, 2023).

Contemporary Context of Basic Education in Mongolia

In Mongolia, enrolment in basic education experienced a significant decline in the 1990s. For instance, in 1987, the net enrolment ratio (NER) for primary education was 95.0%, but by 1995, it had fallen to 81.0%.[3] However, the government has substantially boosted enrolment rates, resulting in notable improvements in recent years. By 2015, the NER for primary education had increased to 96.0%, with 94.0% of graduates advancing to lower secondary education. This upward trend continued, with the primary NER reaching 98.0% by 2018. Similarly, the NER for secondary education rose from 59% in 1995 to 82.0% in 2006. The NER is illustrated in Fig. 11.1. Despite these advancements, children from low-income Mongolian families in rural and urban settings continue to face significant barriers to accessing elementary and secondary education. Additionally, considerable disparities in access remain for traditionally disadvantaged groups across all educational levels (Loo et al., 2022).

Despite recent advancements and high enrolment rates, previous reports indicate that educational development in Mongolia still lags behind the Education for All (EFA) goals in several key areas. In 2006, the

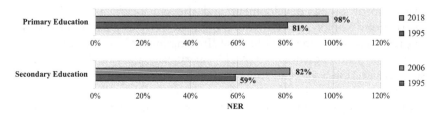

Fig. 11.1 NER for primary (1995 and 2018) and secondary education (1995 and 2006) in Mongolia. (Source: Created by authors based on Loo et al. (2022))

[3] The 'net enrolment rate' (NER) for schools is the percentage of children of official school age who are enrolled in school, regardless of level, as a ratio to the total population of the official school-age group.

gross enrolment ratio (GER) in kindergartens (ages 3–5) was approximately 50.0%.[4] The survival rate from grade 1 to grade 4 (primary school) was 88.3%, and from grade 1 to grade 8 (basic education) it was 83.0%.[5] The gender parity indices for all levels of education, from preschool to higher education, consistently exceed 1, indicating a disparity in favour of females. The annual number of instructional hours falls short of the benchmark of 850–1000 hours per year proposed in the EFA Fast-Track Initiative (FTI) Indicative Framework. In Mongolia, the annual duration of contact hours was 720 hours for primary school students (grades 1–5), increasing to 782 hours when extra-curricular activities are included. Both adult and youth literacy rates are reported to be approximately 98.0%, but these figures may be overestimated due to potential reporting loopholes (Steiner-Khamsi & Gerelmaa, 2008). One area where Mongolia has addressed previously reported issues and demonstrated further progress, as recently reported, is in maintaining relatively low dropout rates. These rates stand at 2.0% for primary education, 4.3% for lower secondary education, and 4.5% for upper secondary education (UNESCO, 2021). These findings are depicted in Fig. 11.2.

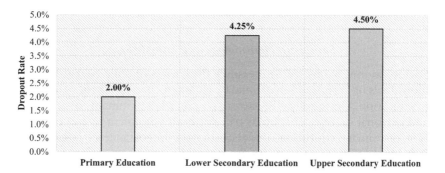

Fig. 11.2 Dropout rate for basic education in Mongolia (2020). (Source: Created by authors based on UNESCO, 2021)

[4] The 'gross enrolment ratio' or 'gross enrolment rate' (GER) is a statistical measure used in the education sector to indicate the total enrolment within a specific level of education, regardless of age, expressed as a percentage of the eligible official school-age population corresponding to that level of education.

[5] The terms 'survival rate' and 'retention rate' in education are often used interchangeably, as they share the same definition and calculation method.

3   METHODOLOGY

Database

The study relied on academic enrolment registries to gather essential information about children's enrolment and academic progress. These registries were instrumental in developing a detailed database that monitored students' enrolment paths at specific schools, covering their journey from initial entry to eventual outcomes such as completing primary education, dropping out, or transferring to other institutions. Based on their entry year, each new cohort of students was analysed separately to provide insights into annual patterns of student admissions and departures. This cohort-based approach showed how many students completed their education, dropped out, or transferred each year. Students who transferred at the beginning of the school year were tracked separately to identify trends in school transfers. In addition to enrolment data, the study also utilised registries containing annual test scores to build a database that tracked students' academic performance over time. This enabled a comprehensive longitudinal analysis of academic outcomes, offering valuable insights into students' educational trajectories and performance throughout their primary education at the target schools.

Sampling Methodology and Sample Size

Socioeconomic status (SES) measures the socioeconomic background of individuals or groups, often defined by factors such as occupation, income, or education. Universally, SES factors are crucial determinants of academic and personal success. This holds true for both enrolment in and completion of primary education, underscoring the importance of considering individuals' SES (Hartas, 2011). Another influential factor affecting retention rates and enrolment patterns is the student's area of residence or the school's geographic location (Pal, 2010). Therefore, for this study, five schools in Mongolia were purposefully selected to represent three different SES (high, medium, and low) and were categorised utilising their geographic location (urban or rural), enabling a comprehensive analysis of how SES factors and geographic location influence retention rates. SES group identification was made with assistance from school registries and staff. From these five selected target schools, a sample of 840 students was chosen for the study outlined in this chapter. The focus was on primary

Table 11.2   Characteristics of targeted schools and sample

SES group	Targeted school	Location	Number of students (%)
High	S1	Urban	168 (20.0)
	S2	Urban	34 (4.0)
Medium	S3	Urban	49 (5.8)
Low	S4	Rural	345 (41.1)
	S5	Rural	244 (29.1)
Total	**5**		**840 (100)**

Source: Created by the authors

education, specifically from grade 1 to grade 5. This range was chosen to observe retention rates under the automatic promotion policy, which is in effect from grade 1 to grade 5, and to compare it with the transition rate to grade 6 from grade 5, where the policy no longer applies. Additionally, the study aimed to evaluate students' academic performance across these grades. Detailed information about the targeted schools and the sample characteristics can be found in Table 11.2.

Data Analysis

The data analysis in this study employs a blend of univariate and trace techniques to investigate the educational landscape thoroughly. Univariate analysis plays a pivotal role in generating frequencies and percentages, providing valuable insights into students' distribution as well as socioeconomic and geographical characteristics. This approach facilitates a detailed understanding of student demographics, particularly regarding SES and the geographical location of selected schools. The study unveils nuanced patterns and disparities by dissecting the data along these dimensions. SES and geographical location factors significantly influence educational outcomes, revealing distinct trends among students from various socioeconomic backgrounds and geographical areas.

Moreover, the tracing technique provided a comprehensive longitudinal perspective by monitoring students from grade 1 through grade 5. This analysis proved vital for understanding students' educational trajectories over time, facilitating the identification of critical intervention points, and evaluating the effectiveness of educational policies and programmes. Additionally, through this tracing technique, this chapter investigated student retention rates by documenting instances of passing, dropout, and transfer cases, capturing transitions between schools or exits from the educational system. Furthermore, it included annual test scores for students from grade 1 to grade 5, offering valuable insights into their academic performance over the years. The data analysis techniques employed in this study are based on the study conducted on similar topics by Sekiya (2014).

4   RESULTS

Retention Rate and Inward Transfer Rate by SES Group

Table 11.3 shows the student retention rate for grades 1 to 6, categorised using the SES group. The table shows that the transition from grade 1 to grade 2 sees a retention rate of 100% for high and medium and 96.3% for low SES groups, with an overall rate of 97.4%. However, after this peak, the retention rates for all groups decrease during the transition from grade 2 to grade 3 and from grade 3 to grade 4 before rising again.

For the high SES group, the lowest retention rates occur during the transitions from grade 2 to grade 3 and from grade 3 to grade 4, at 88.1% and 88.9%, respectively. The medium SES group experiences its lowest retention rate of 89.8% during the transition from grade 2 to grade 3. The low SES group sees its lowest rates of 85.1% and 85.3% during the transitions from grade 3 to grade 4 and from grade 4 to grade 5, respectively.

Table 11.3 The student retention rate for grades 1–6 categorised using SES group

SES group	G1–G2 (n = 840)	G2–G3 (n = 830)	G3–G4 (n = 740)	G4–G5 (n = 655)	G5–G6 (n = 591)	Total
High (n = 202)	202 (100%)	180 (88.1%)	160 (88.9%)	147 (91.9%)	139 (94.6%)	68.8%
Medium (n = 49)	49 (100%)	44 (89.8%)	40 (90.9%)	38 (95.0%)	37 (97.4%)	75.5%
Low (n = 589)	567 (96.3%)	504 (88.9%)	429 (85.1%)	366 (85.3%)	352 (96.2%)	62.1%
Total	818 (97.4%)	728 (87.7%)	629 (85.0%)	551 (84.1%)	528 (89.3%)	62.9%

Note. G = Grade

Source: Created by the authors

Overall, the highest retention rate across all SES groups is 97.4% during the transition from grade 1 to grade 2, and the lowest is 84.1% during the transition from grade 4 to grade 5. The medium SES group has the highest overall retention rate at 75.5%, followed by the high SES group at 68.8% and the low SES group at 62.1%.

Students' overall survival or retention rate from grades 1 to 6 is staggeringly low at 62.9%. This figure is a surprise, especially considering the government of Mongolia's implementation of automatic promotion policies and free education for compulsory education levels. This low survival rate suggests low internal efficiencies in the context of schools as well as other external factors, which may be attributed to various underlying and unaddressed factors.

Table 11.4 illustrates the influx of students transferring into the school at the beginning of each academic year.[6] Interestingly, during grade 2, transfer rates are at their lowest: 0% for the high SES group, 2.0% for the medium SES group, and 3.7% for the low SES group. However, these rates increase from grade 3 onwards for all SES groups. The peak transfer rate for the high SES group occurs during grade 6 at 16.5%, for the medium SES group during grade 3 at 11.4%, and for the low SES group

Table 11.4 Student inward transfer rate from grades 2 to 6 categorised using SES group

SES group	G2 (n = 840)	G3 (n = 830)	G4 (n = 740)	G5 (n = 655)	G6 (n = 591)	Total
High (n = 202)	0 (0.0%)	25 (13.9%)	18 (11.3%)	12 (8.2%)	23 (16.5%)	78 (38.6%)
Medium (n = 49)	1 (2.0%)	5 (11.4%)	3 (7.5%)	1 (2.6%)	1 (2.7%)	11 (22.4%)
Low (n = 589)	21 (3.7%)	37 (7.3%)	48 (11.2%)	54 (14.8%)	13 (3.7%)	173 (29.4%)
Total	22 (2.6%)	67 (8.1%)	69 (9.3%)	67 (10.2%)	37 (6.3%)	262 (31.2%)

Note. G = Grade

Source: Created by the authors

[6] Throughout the chapter and study, the inward transfer rate for students is not factored into the retention rate analysis. The inward transfer rate represents the number of students, in addition to the existing students at that grade, who enrolled for the following grade.

during grade 5 at 14.8%. Subsequently, transfer rates for all SES groups begin to decline after reaching their respective peaks. Overall, the highest transfer rate across all SES groups is observed during grade 5 at 10.2%, while the lowest is during grade 2 at 2.6%. High SES groups experience the highest total transfers at 38.6%, followed by low SES groups at 29.4% and medium SES groups at 22.4%. The overall inward transfer of students at the primary education level for Mongolia stands at 31.2%.

Retention Rate and Inward Transfer Rate by Geographical Location

Table 11.5 displays the student retention rates from grades 1 through 6, segmented by the geographical location of the schools, which in turn reflects the areas where students reside. Analysis of the table reveals that the transition from grade 1 to grade 2 exhibits a retention rate of 100% for urban areas and 96.3% for rural areas, resulting in an overall rate of 97.4%. Similarly, akin to the analysis based on SES groups, the retention rate shows a declining trend from grade 1 to grade 2 promotion, continuing until the transition from grade 5 to grade 6, where the retention rate stands at 95.1% for urban areas and 96.2% for rural areas, with an overall rate of 89.3%.

Upon analysis, it becomes apparent that the most significant drop in retention rates occurs during the transition from grade 4 to grade 5, reaching 84.1%. Notably, schools and students in urban areas exhibit their

Table 11.5 The student retention rate for grades 1–6 categorised using geographical location

Geographical location	G1–G2	G2–G3	G3–G4	G4–G5	G5–G6	Total
	(n = 840)	(n = 830)	(n = 740)	(n = 655)	(n = 591)	
Urban	251	224	200	185	176	70.1%
(n = 251)	(100.0%)	(89.2%)	(89.3%)	(92.5%)	(95.1%)	
Rural	567	504	429	366	352	59.8%
(n = 589)	(96.3%)	(88.9%)	(85.1%)	(85.3%)	(96.2%)	
Total	818	728	629	551	528	62.9%
	(97.4%)	(87.7%)	(85.0%)	(84.1%)	(89.3%)	

Note. G = Grade

Source: Created by the authors

lowest retention rates during the promotion from grade 2 to grade 3 and from grade 3 to grade 4, both standing at 89.2% and 89.3%, respectively. Similarly, for schools and students in rural areas, the lowest retention rates are observed during the transitions from grade 3 to grade 4 and from grade 4 to grade 5, hovering around 85.1% and 85.3%. Strikingly, urban and rural areas experience their lowest retention rates during the grade 3 to grade 4 transition, hinting at underlying concerns that warrant attention.

The retention or survival rate for students at the primary education level is notably higher for schools and students located in urban areas, reaching 70.1%. In contrast, schools and students in rural areas exhibit a considerably lower retention or survival rate of 59.8%. The overall retention or survival rate is 62.9% when considering urban and rural areas, aligning closely with previous SES group analyses.

The disparity in retention rates between schools and students in urban versus rural areas can be attributed to various factors and differing levels of facilities available in each setting. This contrast becomes particularly evident from the results observed.

Table 11.6 shows the influx of students transferring into schools at the beginning of each academic year, categorised by the geolocation of the schools, which reflects the areas where the students reside. The lowest inward transfer rate for urban schools and students occurs in grade 2, at 0.4%. In contrast, rural schools experience the lowest inward transfer rates in grades 2 and 6, both at 3.7%. These rates increase from grade 3 onwards for both urban and rural schools, with peaks at different levels.

Table 11.6 Student inward transfer rate from grades 2 to 6 categorised using geographical location

Geographical location	G2	G3	G4	G5	G6	Total
	(n = 840)	(n = 830)	(n = 740)	(n = 655)	(n = 591)	
Urban	1	30	21	13	24	89
(n = 251)	(0.4%)	(13.4%)	(10.5%)	(7.0%)	(13.6%)	(35.5%)
Rural	21	37	48	54	13	173
(n = 589)	(3.7%)	(7.3%)	(11.2%)	(14.8%)	(3.7%)	(29.4%)
Total	22	67	69	67	37	262
	(2.6%)	(8.1%)	(9.3%)	(10.2%)	(6.3%)	(31.2%)

Note. G = Grade

Source: Created by the authors

In urban areas, the highest inward transfer rates are observed in grades 3 and 6, at 13.4% and 13.6% respectively. The highest inward transfer rate for rural areas occurs in grade 5, at 14.8%. Overall, the highest inward transfer rate is seen in grade 5, with a rate of 10.2%, while the lowest occurs in grade 2, at 2.6%. The average inward transfer rate is 31.2% throughout the primary education period.

An intriguing observation is the notable influx of inward transfers observed in grade 4, which stands out as the second-highest across both urban and rural areas. Specifically, grade 4 marks the third-highest inward transfer rate for urban schools, reaching 10.5%, and the second-highest for rural schools, at 11.2%. This observation is particularly intriguing given that the analysis of retention rates based on geographical location indicated the lowest retention rate during the promotion from grade 3 to grade 4. It's plausible that the higher inward transfer rates in grade 4 could be a contributing factor to the observed decrease in retention rates during this transition period. This correlation suggests a potential explanation for the retention rate trend observed during this specific promotion phase.

Annual Academic Test Scores

From grade 1 to grade 5, the analysis utilises annual test scores for four specific subjects: national language, mathematics, natural sciences, and social sciences; each scored on a scale of 100. This analysis aims to observe student performance throughout primary education, particularly in the context of the automatic promotion policy and its conclusion. By examining these scores, the analysis provides insights into not only the academic performance of students but also the influence of teachers in both teaching and scoring these annual tests.

The average test scores are obtained by dividing the total scores obtained by all the students for each subject by the number of students. This process is repeated for each grade across all cohorts. These average annual scores are then categorised by SES groups and the geographical location of the schools, allowing for a detailed comparison of student performance across different demographics and regions.

Table 11.7 displays the average test scores for students across three different SES groups for each grade, covering four subjects: national language, mathematics, natural sciences, and social sciences. The data reveals a consistent trend among students from high and medium SES groups,

Table 11.7 Average test scores for students across different SES groups from grades 1 to 5

SES group	Subject	G1	G2	G3	G4	G5
		(n = 840)	(n = 830)	(n = 740)	(n = 655)	(n = 591)
High	National Language	78.0	76.0	75.0	87.0	87.0
(n = 202)	Mathematics	79.0	76.0	74.0	84.0	86.0
	Natural Sciences	85.0	80.0	81.0	88.0	87.0
	Social Sciences	85.0	81.0	85.0	90.0	88.0
Medium	National Language	76.0	75.0	73.0	87.0	86.0
(n = 49)	Mathematics	78.0	76.0	70.0	85.0	83.0
	Natural Sciences	84.0	77.0	80.0	87.0	85.0
	Social Sciences	85.0	78.0	82.0	87.0	87.0
Low	National Language	94.0	77.0	89.0	87.0	83.0
(n = 589)	Mathematics	90.0	84.0	89.0	90.0	85.0
	Natural Sciences	91.0	90.0	93.0	90.0	87.0
	Social Sciences	90.0	91.0	93.0	91.0	88.0

Note. G = Grade

Source: Created by the authors

wherein their average scores tend to increase as they progress from grades 1 to 5 across all subjects.

However, a notable contrast is observed for students from low SES backgrounds. Here, it becomes evident that their test scores gradually decline as they transition from grades 1 to 5. This pattern suggests that students from low SES groups may face challenges in maintaining academic performance over time, likely influenced by the socioeconomic disparities they encounter.

An interesting observation emerges when comparing subject-specific performance among different SES groups. Both high and medium SES groups tend to exhibit lower performance in natural language and mathematics while demonstrating stronger performance in natural sciences and social sciences. In contrast, the low SES group consistently performs relatively well across all subjects.

Upon further analysis, it becomes apparent that, overall, the low SES group outperforms their high and medium SES counterparts. Throughout primary education, the low SES group frequently achieves average marks in the 90th and 80th percentile, whereas the high and medium SES groups

Table 11.8 Average test scores for students across different geographical location from grades 1 to 5

Geographical location	Subject	G1 (n = 840)	G2 (n = 830)	G3 (n = 740)	G4 (n = 655)	G5 (n = 591)
Urban (n = 251)	National Language	77.0	75.5	74.0	87.0	86.5
	Mathematics	78.5	76.0	72.0	84.5	84.5
	Natural Sciences	84.5	78.5	80.5	87.5	86.0
	Social Sciences	85.0	79.5	83.5	88.5	87.5
Rural (n = 589)	National Language	94.0	77.0	89.0	87.0	83.0
	Mathematics	90.0	84.0	89.0	90.0	85.0
	Natural Sciences	91.0	90.0	93.0	90.0	87.0
	Social Sciences	90.0	91.0	93.0	91.0	88.0

Note. G = Grade

Source: Created by the authors

typically attain average marks in the 70th and 80th percentile, with occurrences in the 90th percentile being rare.

Table 11.8 presents the average test scores for students categorised by two different geographical locations—urban and rural—for each grade, spanning four subjects: national language, mathematics, natural sciences, and social sciences. Upon examination, a notable trend becomes evident. For schools and students located in urban areas, there is a consistent increase in average test scores for each subject as they progress from grades 1 to 5. In contrast, schools and students in rural areas experience a reverse trend, wherein the average test scores tend to decrease as they advance from grades 1 to 5.

Additionally, a compelling pattern emerges when comparing subject-specific performance between schools and students in urban and rural areas. Urban schools and students tend to demonstrate lower performance in natural language and mathematics while excelling in natural sciences and social sciences. Conversely, rural schools and students consistently perform relatively well across all subjects.

Upon deeper analysis, it becomes evident that, overall, rural schools and students outperform their urban counterparts. Throughout primary education, rural schools and students frequently achieve average marks in the 90th and 80th percentile, whereas urban schools and students typically attain average marks in the 70th and 80th percentile, never reaching the 90th quantile. These findings align closely with the results observed in Table 11.7, reinforcing the notion of notable academic achievements among rural schools and students despite potential challenges.

5   Discussion

Low Overall Retention Rate in Primary Education

The remarkably low retention rate or survival rate of 62.9% for grades 1 to 5 of primary education in Mongolia, despite the implementation of free education at the compulsory level and the automatic promotion policy, is indeed surprising. This finding resonates with earlier studies (Steiner-Khamsi, 2012; Steiner-Khamsi & Gerelmaa, 2008). However, it's important to note that these studies reported retention rates using macro-level data, providing an overall average. In contrast, the present analysis offers insights at a more granular, micro-level, shedding light on the specific retention status within Mongolia's primary education system.

Previous studies by Alcocer Escalante and Aguilar Riveroll (2021) as well as Mathu (2016) have highlighted the positive impact of policies such as free education and the automatic promotion of NER. Free education policies remove financial barriers, ensuring all children have access to education regardless of socioeconomic background. Similarly, automatic promotion policies reduce the stigma associated with grade repetition, fostering a more inclusive learning environment. While these studies showcase the positive aspects of these policies and their impact on NER, they fall short of explaining why retention rates remain low despite the implementation of these policies. The discrepancy between the intended positive outcomes of these policies and the persistently low retention rates suggests that there may be underlying factors or challenges within the education system that these policies alone cannot address.

One significant factor that likely plays a role in the low retention rate is the overall internal efficiency of the school or educational system. This encompasses various elements such as school management, the dynamics between teachers and students, instructional methods, classroom organisation, teacher-parent communication, support systems for struggling students, curriculum relevance, and the quality of facilities, among other factors (Alam et al., 2022; Ibrahim, 2018; Idenyenmhin, 2024). Another significant factor could be the indirect costs associated with primary education, which may not be covered by the government's free education policy in Mongolia. This includes expenses such as school uniforms, supplies, and the opportunity cost of attending school, which families must bear (Wambua, 2009).

Moreover, a low retention rate implies a higher likelihood of students repeating their grades or dropping out altogether. This not only inflates the administrative expenses associated with grade repetition but also undermines the effectiveness of initiatives and endeavours pursued by the government of Mongolia to attain its national objectives and align with the SDGs, particularly Goal 4, aiming for inclusive and quality education, set to be achieved by 2030. Therefore, addressing these challenges is paramount for the educational system's efficiency and the broader socioeconomic development aspirations of Mongolia (Van Der Berg et al., 2019).

An intriguing discovery emerges when examining retention rates across the three SES groups within schools. Surprisingly, the middle SES category boasts the highest retention rates, surpassing both the high and low SES groups. This suggests a noteworthy efficacy in retaining students within schools classified under the middle SES bracket. Delving deeper into transfer patterns, an exciting trend surfaces: students from low SES backgrounds and those attending schools in rural areas tend to switch schools during the middle grades of their primary education journey. Several factors may underlie this phenomenon. One plausible explanation is that families actively pursue enhanced educational opportunities, relocating their children to schools that offer superior resources or academic performance. Moreover, the nomadic lifestyle prevalent among many Mongolian families might significantly contribute to this mobility and frequent school transfers. As families traverse different regions in pursuit of livelihood opportunities or traditional practices, such mobility naturally influences educational pathways, prompting students to switch schools along with their families (Steiner-Khamsi & Stolpe, 2005).

Likewise, the high SES and middle SES segments, along with schools and students in urban locales, also witness student transfers, potentially influenced by akin motivations. However, a striking contrast emerges in retention rates between students from high SES backgrounds compared to their middle SES counterparts, as well as between urban and rural school settings. This intriguing variance demands a closer examination of underlying dynamics. One plausible explanation for this discrepancy lies in the diverse factors influencing educational choices. For instance, families with higher SES and schools in urban areas might have access to a broader range of educational options, including private institutions or specialised programmes. Consequently, they may opt to transfer their children to schools that offer specific curricula or are perceived as providing superior academic standards.

Additionally, the frequent relocations of affluent families, driven by career or personal reasons, likely contribute to the lower retention rates observed in high SES schools and among urban students. Intertwined with pursuing educational excellence or specialised programmes, this mobility factor underscores the complexity of educational dynamics within different socioeconomic strata and geographical settings. Further exploration is necessary to unravel the nuanced interplay of these multifaceted influences on student retention patterns.

In contrast, the middle SES group appears to strike a balance, maintaining higher retention rates possibly due to a combination of stability and satisfactory educational quality that meets their students' needs without requiring frequent transfers. Understanding why middle SES schools are more successful in retaining students compared to high SES schools could provide valuable insights into improving retention strategies across all SES groups. Further research could explore the specific factors contributing to the high retention rates in middle SES schools and the reasons behind the comparatively lower retention in high SES schools.

High Academic Performance of Disadvantaged Group

Another intriguing observation is the high average test scores across all three SES groups and two geographical locations of schools and students in Mongolia. This could suggest two possibilities: Either the quality of education and educational delivery is uniformly high across all SES groups or other factors influence these scores. Previous studies indicate that low SES groups tend to have lower academic performance due to various socioeconomic challenges; one study that supported this was done by Cosgrove and Castelli (2018). However, this trend is not observed in Mongolia, where low SES groups also achieve high average test scores. This anomaly can potentially be explained by the student performance-based pay incentives provided to teachers in Mongolia.

These incentives are designed to reward teachers based on their student's performance, which might encourage teachers to promote students to the next grade level and potentially provide more straightforward test questions or award higher scores to boost overall performance metrics. While this system aims to improve educational outcomes by incentivising teachers, it may inadvertently lead to inflated test scores that do not accurately reflect students' actual learning and understanding. Such a system, characterised by poor teacher salaries supplemented by performance-based bonuses, might have unintended consequences. While it could temporarily boost retention and apparent academic performance, it may undermine the proper educational development of students. Over time, this could lead to a lack of critical skills and knowledge necessary for students' long-term success and well-being (Schriewer, 2016).

Therefore, while the high test scores across all SES groups and geographical locations might initially seem like a positive outcome, they may mask underlying issues related to the effectiveness of the incentive structures. This calls for a careful review and potential restructuring of incentive policies to ensure that they genuinely enhance educational quality without compromising the integrity of student assessments and learning outcomes.

6   CONCLUSION

Despite Mongolia's sustained efforts to provide quality and equitable education for its citizens through initiatives such as free compulsory education and automatic promotion policies, the effectiveness of these measures has been limited, resulting in a notably low retention rate across primary education levels. Furthermore, a critical issue persists in low teacher salaries, exacerbated by performance-based bonuses linked to students' academic achievements.

This compensation system, though well-intentioned, inadvertently fosters practices that prioritise superficial metrics over genuine learning outcomes. For instance, educators may feel pressured to advance students regardless of their readiness or resort to simplifying test content to inflate scores. Such actions compromise the integrity of the educational process and may hinder students' long-term academic and personal growth.

Addressing the challenges of low retention rates and unethical practices, such as inflating test scores, requires the government to adopt proactive measures that encompass both the enhancement of teacher and student welfare, as well as a holistic approach to educational reform. Firstly, the government must consider demand- and supply-side factors when addressing low retention rates. This entails a focus on improving internal efficiencies within schools and the education system as a whole. The government can create an environment that fosters better student engagement and retention by identifying and addressing inefficiencies in school management, teacher-student dynamics, teaching methodologies, and curriculum relevance.

Furthermore, the government must acknowledge and address the indirect costs of education, which often serve as barriers to retention. This includes school uniforms, supplies, and opportunity costs associated with attending school. Implementing measures to alleviate these financial burdens for families can significantly impact retention rates by ensuring that education remains accessible to all.

In tandem with these efforts, elevating teacher salaries to competitive levels is crucial. By offering attractive compensation packages, the government can reduce reliance on performance-based bonuses and attract highly skilled educators. This not only ensures a stable income for teachers but also safeguards academic standards by mitigating the temptation to compromise educational integrity for financial gain. Additionally, restructuring incentive systems to encompass a broader range of evaluation criteria is essential. A more comprehensive and equitable assessment can be achieved by evaluating teacher performance based on factors such as dedication, student engagement, and longitudinal learning progress rather than solely focusing on test scores. This encourages educators to prioritise holistic student development and fosters a supportive learning environment conducive to long-term retention and success.

By adopting these multifaceted approaches, the government can effectively tackle the root causes of low retention rates and inflated test scores, ensuring a more inclusive, equitable, and high-quality education system for all students and teachers.

REFERENCES

Adiyasuren, A., & Galindev, U. (2023). Effective teaching in Mongolia: Policies, practices and challenges. In R. Maulana, M. Helms-Lorenz, & R. M. Klassen (Eds.), *Effective teaching around the world: Theoretical, empirical, methodological and practical insights* (pp. 245–255). Springer International Publishing. https://doi.org/10.1007/978-3-031-31678-4_11

Alam, M. J., Islam, S. R. B., & Ogawa, K. (2022). Discrete primary education curriculum in Bangladesh: implications of gamification for quality education. In C.-A. Lane (Ed.), *Advances in game-based learning (pp. 716–730).* IGI Global. https://doi.org/10.4018/978-1-7998-7271-9.ch036

Alcocer Escalante, L. M., & Aguilar Riveroll, Á. M. (2021). Approach to the international scene of automatic promotion and school retention at the basic educational level. A systematic review. *Revista Innovaciones Educativas, 23*(35), 175–192.

Cosgrove, J. M., & Castelli, D. M. (2018). Physical activity and academic performance among adolescents in low-SES schools. *American Journal of Health Education, 49*(6), 354–360. https://doi.org/10.1080/19325037.2018.1516167

Hartas, D. (2011). Families' social backgrounds matter: Socioeconomic factors, home learning and young children's language, literacy and social outcomes. *British Educational Research Journal, 37*(6), 893–914. https://doi.org/10.1080/01411926.2010.506945

Heath-Brown, N. (2015). Mongolia. In N. Heath-Brown (Ed.), *The statesman's yearbook 2016: The politics, cultures and economies of the world* (pp. 845–848). Palgrave Macmillan UK. https://doi.org/10.1007/978-1-349-57823-8_281

Ibrahim, K. (2018). Influence of school based policies on internal efficiency in public day secondary schools in Nyatike Sub County. *Kenya. American Journal of Educational Research, 6*(3), 161–169. https://doi.org/10.12691/education-6-3-1

Idenyenmhin, D. O. (2024). *Management of internal efficiency for improved educational outcome in rural public basic schools in Ikwerre local government area, rivers state.* https://doi.org/10.5281/ZENODO.11038777

Javkhlan, B., & Hyun, Y. (2021). Overview of the education system in Mongolia. *Asia Pacific Journal of Educational Research, 4*(2), 33–49. https://doi.org/10.30777/APJER.2021.4.2.02

Khurelbaatar, S. (2020). Experience of the Mongolian education reform and main issues. *Review of Socioeconomic Perspectives, 5*(4), 121–140. https://doi.org/10.19275/RSEP100

Loo, B., Narantuya, D., & Enkhtuya, G. (2022, August 8). *Education in Mongolia.* WENR. https://wenr.wes.org/2022/08/education-in-mongolia

Mathu, W. N. (2016). *The influence of free primary education on the pupils retention rate: The case of Gatanga district, Muranga county, Kenya* [PhD Thesis, University of Nairobi]. http://erepository.uonbi.ac.ke/bitstream/handle/11295/100981/WINFRED%20MATHU-%20PROJECT%20REPORT.pdf?sequence=1

Pal, S. (2010). Public infrastructure, location of private schools and primary school attainment in an emerging economy. *Economics of Education Review, 29*(5), 783–794. https://doi.org/10.1016/j.econedurev.2010.02.002

Pastore, F. (2009). School-to-work transitions in Mongolia. *The European Journal of Comparative Economics, 6*(2), 245.

Schriewer, J. (2016). The case: The triple bonus system in Mongolia. In *World culture re-contextualised: Meaning constellations and path-dependencies in com-*

parative and international education research. Routledge. https://doi.org/10.4324/9781315667614

Sekiya, T. (2014). Individual patterns of enrolment in primary schools in the Republic of Honduras. *Education 3-13 - International Journal of Primary, Elementary and Early Years Education, 42*(5), 460–474. https://doi.org/10.1080/03004279.2012.715665

Steiner-Khamsi, G. (2012). The global/local nexus in comparative policy studies: Analysing the triple bonus system in Mongolia over time. *Comparative Education, 48*(4), 455–471. https://doi.org/10.1080/03050068.2012.681120

Steiner-Khamsi, G., & Gerelmaa, A. (2008). Quality and equity in the Mongolian education sector. *Prospects, 38*(3), 409–414. https://doi.org/10.1007/s11125-008-9079-5

Steiner-Khamsi, G., & Stolpe, I. (2005). Non-traveling 'best practices' for a traveling population: The case of Nomadic education in Mongolia. *European Educational Research Journal, 4*(1), 22–35. https://doi.org/10.2304/eerj.2005.4.1.2

UNDP. (2021). *Mapping the SDGs against Mongolia's national development plans and policies.* https://www.undp.org/publications/mapping-sdgs-against-mongolias-national-development-plans-and-policies

UNESCO. (2019). *Education in Mongolia: A country report.*

UNESCO. (2021). *Mongolia education fact sheets 2020.* United Nations Educational, Scientific and Cultural Organization. https://data.unicef.org/wp-content/uploads/2021/11/MICS-EAGLE_Education_Fact-sheets_2020_Mongolia.pdf

UNESCO IBE. (2011). *World data on education—Mongolia.* International Bureau of Education - UNESCO. https://daneshnamehicsa.ir/userfiles/file/Resources/18-1)%20Asia/Mongolia.pdf

Van Der Berg, S., Wills, G., Selkirk, R., Adams, C., & Van Wyk, C. (2019). *The cost of repetition in South Africa.* https://papers.ssrn.com/sol3/papers.cfm?abstract_id=3505854

Wambua, J. M. (2009). *A case of the indirect costs of free primary education and its impact to the achievement of universal free primary education in Matungulu division, Machakos district* [Doctoral dissertation, University of Nairobi]. http://erepository.uonbi.ac.ke/handle/11295/17673

Yembuu, B. (2010). Mongolia (Current situation of Education, Mongolia). In *International encyclopedia of education* (pp. 681–686). Elsevier.

CHAPTER 12

Educational Strategies of Children Living in a Developing Country: A Longitudinal School Record Study of Malawi Secondary Schools

Jun Kawaguchi

1 INTRODUCTION

The Republic of Malawi, located in central South East Africa, is considered to be one of the poorest countries in the world and is consequently a recipient of international aid to support projects of various kinds, including those implemented in the educational field. Annually, over 80% of the government budget for education is spent on recurrent expenses such as teacher salaries, utilities, and facility maintenance. Funding for educational development and research is mostly from external sources (Malawi MoE, 2023).

J. Kawaguchi (✉)
Department of Education, Faculty of Letters, Keio University, Tokyo, Japan
e-mail: kawaguchi.jun@keio.jp

© The Author(s), under exclusive license to Springer Nature
Switzerland AG 2024
T. Sekiya et al. (eds.), *Towards Ensuring Inclusive and Equitable
Quality Education for All*, International and Development
Education, https://doi.org/10.1007/978-3-031-70266-2_12

247

Recent research studies related to education in Malawi highlight problems such as the low quality of education, low teacher motivation, and inadequate school facilities. Particularly in secondary education, low enrollment and high dropout rates have been identified as serious challenges (Aiden, 2010). Girls are perceived as being more vulnerable to these challenges than boys, and more generally, any quantitative or qualitative educational benefits for girls are lower than for boys. Furthermore, macro data indicate that the vulnerability of girls to identified educational challenges increases as they progress through primary, secondary, and tertiary levels of schooling (UNESCO, 2020; Malawi MoE, 2023).

Malawi families, like African families and communities in general, tend to give priority in schooling to boys over girls, but there are also large regional disparities in educational opportunities as shown through the analysis of data comparing boys in urban areas with girls in rural areas where the disparity is considerable (Malawi MoE, 2023). The research of Kunje (2007) shows that marriage and childbearing take priority over the completion of secondary school for girls, and especially early marriages impact school attendance in late primary and secondary education. A study by Kadzamira and Rose (2003) also found that in addition to the economic factor of nonpayment of school fees, female students more easily drop out of school than male students due to marriage and pregnancy.

It is of significance to note that students do not make decisions about schooling or further education based solely on their personal problems, but rather within a context of what is strategically best for the family as a whole. For instance, abandoning schooling midway through a course of study, even though the student may wish to continue, is common practice if it means moving so another family member can obtain a better job (Kawaguchi, 2011). The children are not just sent to the best or nearest school, but rather each family will have an educational plan with strategies for a schooling that is appropriate in cost and quality for each child. Shimizu et al. (2013) have identified the concept of "educational strategy" as part of the reproducible function of each social group, pointing out that it is a broad concept including not only intentional but also unintentional attitudes and actions. According to Shimizu (2013), not only the wealthy but also the poor and minority families are constantly searching for reproducible strategies that most favor capital formation (Shimizu et al., 2013).

In what has been so far described, it is difficult to accurately understand the complexity of factors impacting individual situations by simply analyzing broad trends captured with macro data. Therefore, rather than reading overall trends, this longitudinal study traces individual school records and examines the separate factors resulting in school transfers, advancement to higher education, school withdrawals, and other outcomes. The analysis of the results will be used to support suggestions for educational development that cannot be derived from the cross-sectional data.

2   OVERVIEW OF SECONDARY EDUCATION IN MALAWI

Malawi gained independence from the United Kingdom in 1964 and has followed the British educational system since independence, adopting the 8-4-4 system. The local language is the language of instruction in primary school until grade 4, but all classes in secondary school are taught in English. Although passing the Primary School Leaving Certificate Examination (PSLCE) is a requirement for admission to secondary school, there have been cases of students entering secondary school without it (Kawaguchi, 2011).

Secondary schools are divided into two types, namely, large schools known as Secondary Schools (SS) and small schools known as Community Day Secondary Schools (CDSS). Compared to SS, which are located in urban areas and considered to be elite, CDSS are numerous, relatively small, and are scattered throughout rural areas, often utilizing the facilities of distance learning centers originally built by the community when distance secondary education was offered as part of adult education. The government selects students for the type of school according to their PSLCE scores and allocates enrollment in SS to the best students. After two years of secondary school, students are awarded the JCE (Junior Certificate of Education), and in the fourth year they can take the MSCE (Malawi Secondary School Certificate of Education), a secondary school graduation examination. The MSCE is not only required for university entrance examinations but is also an important qualification for teacher training programs and for employment in Malawi.

The pass rates for the MSCE in 2014 were 49% (Female) and 59% (Male), respectively (Malawi MoE, 2015). Passing the MSCE with a high score enables students to enter higher education. However, student enrollment in university is limited by the small number of these institutions, there being only around ten national and ten private universities throughout the country. Furthermore, the number of students who are able to enter universities and other institutions of higher education in Malawi is small, due to limiting family economic situations (World Bank, 2010).

Enrollment in secondary education, on the other hand, is on the rise, partly due to the impact of the increase in primary education completions since 1994. In 1998, there were approximately 60,000, in 2004 approximately 180,000, and in 2014 approximately 360,000 (Malawi MoE, 2015). As of 2014, the total enrollment rate in secondary education was around 47.3% (World Bank, 2014) and the net enrollment rate was 33% (World Bank, 2014). The net enrollment rate by gender was slightly higher for boys, at 33.3% compared to 32.6% for girls (World Bank, 2014). The dropout rate was higher for girls than for boys, and the average years of schooling for boys was shown to be longer than for girls, although the average years of schooling for students in general continues to increase over the years. In 2008 it was approximately 1.7 years for girls and 2.1 years for boys, in 2011 it was approximately 2.0 years for girls and 2.2 years for boys, and in 2014 it was approximately 3 years for boys and about 2.6 years for girls (World Bank, 2014).

Secondary school tuition varies from school to school due to the cost of maintaining school facilities, which ranges from around US$ 170 to US$ 300 per year for public schools with dormitories, US$ 20 to US$ 60 for commuter public schools, and US$ 15 to US$ 40 for CDSS. Government spending on secondary education accounts for about 5% of all spending and about 24% of educational spending (World Bank, 2014). SS is the government's priority in financing expenditures for school activities other than teacher salaries, but as mentioned earlier, much of the education development budget is dependent on external funding.

3   SURVEY METHODS FOR LONGITUDINAL SCHOOL ATTENDANCE RECORDS

The survey can be divided into three main parts which consider school attendance records, family environment, and reasons for leaving school. In preparing the survey a database of student profiles was constructed. The school attendance record books kept by each secondary school for the past five years were utilized to longitudinally trace the school attendance of each student. Following this, based on interviews with the target students regarding their family environment, such as the family structure and parents' occupation, a database was created for each individual. Finally, the reasons for students having dropped out of school were investigated through interviews with their teachers, the students themselves, and their parents. Teachers were a main focus of the survey in investigating the reasons and background of why the students in question had stopped attending school. It was possible to target five schools and 200 students despite it being rare to find schools that keep complete school attendance records for more than five years. A summary of the five targeted schools is presented in Table 12.1.

In selecting the target schools, constraints were kept to a minimum due to the scarce availability of schools with record books. The three points that were considered in the selection process, however, were region, ethnic group, and school type. The target regions were selected to best represent the situation in Malawi, with three schools selected from rural areas as well as those from urban areas. Although selection from all regions was difficult due to data limitations, schools included those from the Central, Southeast, and South regions. Regarding ethnic groups, three schools were selected with a predominantly Chewa population, which is the majority group in Malawi. The remaining two schools were of mixed ethnicity although with a predominance of Chilomwe, which is a minority ethnic

Table 12.1 Overview of the surveyed schools

School (regions)	Number of students (male/female)	Urban/ rural	Ethnic group	Other features
A Lilongwe Girl's (Capital)	41(0/41)	Urban	Chewa	One of the best quality girls' schools in Malawi, SS
B Mitundu (Capital)	40(21/19)	Rural	Chewa	CDSS
C Murunguti (Southeastern Zomba)	39(21/18)	Urban	Mixed	Best quality school in the area, with dormitory, SS
D Grundi (Southern Chiradzulu)	40(24/16)	Rural	Chilomwe	Inclusive school with general quality, SS
E Modosa (Southern)	40(22/18)	Rural	Chewa	CDSS
Total	200(88/112)			

Source: Prepared by the author

group. Three schools were classified as SS and two as CDSS. Due to the higher percentage of SS, it was assumed that the academic performance and quality of education of the target students would be classified as high among secondary schools in Malawi. All five target schools were public schools; private schools were not included in this survey. One of the target schools was a girls' high school, so the total number of girls was 112 and of boys was 88.

4   Survey Results

Gender Disparities in Timing of Student Enrollment

The survey results regarding the timing of student enrollment showed that less than half (46%) of the students entered school at the appropriate age as defined by the Malawi government, of 14 or 15 years old. The timing of enrollment and subsequent progression and completion rates showed that the group of students who enrolled at the appropriate age did better than the group of students who enrolled outside of the appropriate age group. The youngest student was a boy who had entered secondary school at age 11. He had entered primary school at the age of 4, completed primary school and then entered secondary school. In contrast, the student who entered the school at the latest age was a female student who did so at the age of 21. She entered primary school at the age of 7 and completed primary school at 16. After that, she did not enter secondary school immediately, but worked as a domestic helper at home before entering secondary school at the age of 21 with the aim of becoming a teacher. Students who entered school earlier than the recommended entry age were mostly boys, while those who entered later were mostly women. One teacher explained the reasons for this as follows;

Teacher M.V. (School E, 40s, female)

The age at which children enter the school varies widely; it is not unusual for students to enter in their late twenties. However, most of the students who enter the school as "adults" are female. Boys, on the contrary, often enter school too early. This is probably because parents often send boys to higher education immediately, while women get married, save up money, and enter higher education of their own volition.

According to this teacher, because of family preferences, boys are still given priority over girls to have the opportunity to go to secondary school. As already pointed out, existing studies suggest girls may not be sent to secondary school immediately after completing primary education but may instead first help with family work or engage in marriage and child rearing. Interestingly however, women are more likely to go on to post-secondary education even after they have passed the appropriate age to enter school, such as in their late twenties. It is general opinion that women's desire to go on to higher education is high.

Individual interviews revealed that the understanding of the idea of "enrolling in school" was ambiguous. For example, some students who were supposedly enrolled in one of the five schools surveyed had previously dropped out of another school and re-enrolled from the first grade. In addition, seven students enrolled in one school were found to have registered but not attended during the first year, instead starting the following year. These seven students had not taken any leave of absence from school. In Malawi, the school administrative system, in both secondary and primary schools, seems to be implemented in a liberal manner without being bound by strict regulations. These flexible responses to the needs of students and families at the local level are despite there being educational regulations at the national level.

Trajectory of Students Who Have Dropped Out of School

Of the 200 students included in this survey, 33 students were identified as having "dropped out" from school. The school records of these students can be roughly classified into four patterns, depending on the time of withdrawal. An "'A" in the table indicates that the student went on to higher education, and a "D" indicates that the student withdrew from school. The number represents the school year.

As can be seen from Table 12.2, there were a certain number of students who attended secondary school for only two years and then dropped out in the third year after obtaining JCE. There were no particularly significant differences between male and female students, but according to teachers, this can be identified more often in Malawi's secondary schools than in other schools. There is a strong perception among parents, teachers, and students themselves that obtaining JCE is a fixed goal.

The analysis of the factors around expulsion explained in individual interviews and other sources confirmed that there were a certain number

Table 12.2   Order of frequency of dropout students and percentage of total

Order by frequency	Track record of school progression (esp. that of students going on to higher education)	Number of students (% of total) (male/female)
1	1A2A3D	16 (8%, 8/8)
2	1A2D	8 (4%, 3/5)
3	1A2A3A4D	7 (4%, 3/4)
4	1D	2 (1%, 2/0)

Source: Provided by the author

Table 12.3   Subsequent career paths for students who have been expelled from school

School	Student (sex/ age of entrance)	Track record of school progression (esp. that of students going on to higher education)	Reasons for withdrawal
	D.I (female, 14)	1A2A3D..T3A4C	Pregnancy
A	J.V (female, 16)	1A2A3A4D.4C	Failure to pay tuition fees
	L.N (female, 17)	1A2D..T1A2A3A4C	Unknown
B	E.H (male, 12)	1A2A3D.3A4C	Finding employment
C	N/A		
D	A.Y (male, 13)	1D.2A3D.3A4D	First year: poor gradesOthers: unknown
	O.T (female, 15)	1A2A3D.3A4C	Pregnancy, marriage
E	R.K (female, 19)	1D...2A3A4C	Failure to pay tuition fees

Source: Provided by the author

of misleading cases recorded as expulsions when in fact students had attended other schools or returned to school after dropping out for some time. Table 12.3 shows the trajectories of students who had not completely quit school after dropping out, but rather started a new course of study. As in Table 12.2, the numbers indicate the school year, An 'A' indicates the school year of advancement, a 'D' indicates the school year of withdrawal, and a 'T' indicates the school year of transfer. The number of '·' indicates the number of years. For example, '…' indicates that the student has not attended school for three years. All initials in the names are pseudonyms.

In the previous section, attention was drawn to the ambiguity of the understanding of the notion of enrollment, and the situation with regard to the understanding of the notion of withdrawal is similar. For example, a student in School D withdrew from school six months after admission, but six months after his withdrawal, he reentered in the second grade. This is an unusual advancement as normally he would have had to start the first grade again. Another student, who belongs to School E, withdrew from school in the first grade, but returned to school four years later in the second grade. When investigating the reasons for these unusual schooling trajectories teachers could not give clear explanations for their occurrences.

Although some cases were listed as dropouts on the record, the boundary between the term dropout and leave of absence is vague. In the case of secondary education in Malawi, students who have not paid school fees are suspended by the school after a certain period of nonpayment, and expelled if they remain unpaid for two or three years. However, even after being expelled, students can easily be reinstated to the same grade if they pay their school fees. According to teachers and principals, it is rare in Malawi for a student to be re-admitted into the first grade even after being expelled for nonpayment of school fees.

Results of Interviews Regarding Reasons for Withdrawal

The following results of interviews regard students who have dropped out of school. Since the definition of dropouts is ambiguous, the term "students who have withdrawn" has been used instead. The results are from interviews with the students, their teachers, and their guardians regarding the reasons for their withdrawal.

Withdrawn student R.A. (withdrew after attending school B for one year, age 19, female)

I withdrew from secondary school not because of poor grades, but because my sister and two younger brothers were also in secondary school and the tuition fees were so high that I needed to shift my timing. I would also start attending at a time when my family could afford it.

The above is the opinion of a student who was currently withdrawing from school. As can be inferred from the interview results, the student does not feel that he/she has dropped out of school, but rather is taking a leave of absence. In this survey, many of the students who had dropped out of school felt that they would start their studies again at some other time. However, although others, like this student, said, "I will resume attending school when my family can afford it," it seems according to the results of the teacher interviews that the situations when Malawi families "can afford it" are not common.

Teacher P.K. (School B, 47, male)

Few students return to school after the economic situation of the families of those who have not paid their tuition fees improves. In fact, they resume attending school once they are selected for scholarships from NGOs or international organizations. The waiting list for scholarships is long at all schools. Later, it is not only the economic situation, but also the family situation that is relevant. For example, when a family member becomes ill, it is often the case that a female student will not be able to attend school in order to take care of her family member.

The students themselves believe that their ability to study is due to their family's financial situation, but actually they rely heavily on the support of others, including scholarships. Another teacher noted the following differences between men and women with regard to returning to school.

Teacher B.H. (School D, age 51, female)

Female students can easily return to school even after dropping out, but it is difficult for male students to return to school once they have dropped out. Once they leave school, it is unlikely that they will return. In Malawi, once they get a job, it may be difficult for them to quit, and they may feel embarrassed to go to school with younger students.

According to this teacher, once a man has a cash income job in Malawi, it is risky to give it up to go back to school. It was also pointed out that for men to return to school in their mid-twenties would be embarrassing, since it would be equated with announcing to the school and community that they were unemployed. On the other hand, several interviewees said that women are not so reluctant to return to school.

Family Educational Strategies and the Use of Absence

This section analyzes the survey results and examines the factors behind them. First, an analysis of individual schooling trajectories and enrollment ages suggests that in Malawi's secondary schools, the sense of horizontal alignment is not strong because there is a relatively flexible custom and mindset pertaining to attendance depending on individual circumstances. In particular, women were found to be more influenced by family educational strategies that benefit from this flexibility than men. It was apparent that they make decisions about their schooling through considering not only the family situation into which they were born but also their family situation after marriage.

While studying at secondary school leads to employment, families bear both direct and opportunity costs. In Malawi as one of the poorest countries in the world, not many families can economically afford both the costs. It is important therefore for poor families with multiple children to have an "education strategy" such as staggering the timing of when several children attend school for instance or selecting only children with good academic performance to attend school.

In addition, as mentioned, many international organizations and NGOs are active in Malawi, to the extent that the country is often derided as an "aid testing ground," and many parents have the perception that direct costs are not something they can raise on their own, but rather something for which they can receive assistance. There is a wide variety of scholarships available. Most scholarships are awarded to students with outstanding grades, but some scholarships are limited to other groups such as women only, families in remote areas, families with disabled persons, and those with various other specific socioeconomic factors. As is the case in many developing countries, many of Malawi's scholarship programs are limited in number and time. Therefore, although many students and families plan to have children return to school after obtaining a scholarship, as explained in the interviews, whether or not they can actually obtain a scholarship depends on a variety of factors.

An examination of the aspect of opportunity cost shows that it is not constant, but varies depending on the relationship with siblings, family health status, and new family members. In addition, the students' own socioeconomic characteristics may also affect the amount of money they spend. For example, while girls may be more valuable as domestic helpers in the home than boys when they are in their teens, the opportunity cost for men in their twenties will be higher if they obtain wage jobs. Although the amount of opportunity cost may fluctuate in any country, especially in Malawi where there are many poor people, the results suggest that the amount of fluctuation is highly influenced by the decision to study. In other words, the frequent suggestion in existing studies that the decision to return to school depends on the "family's economic situation" is only one aspect of what is a comprehensive decision based on a combination of factors such as socioeconomic characteristics, employment status, and the family situation of the student in question. An additional social situation that has influence on decisions about school attendance is that primary education is free in Malawi, and there is a shortage of primary teachers. Therefore, it is relatively easy for those who have completed secondary education to become primary teachers. Primary teaching is one of the best jobs for women in their 20s to earn cash income while raising children, and completing secondary education for this purpose is consequently in high demand.

Female Students Taking Advantage of "Leave of School"

In this section, the discussion will focus on the reasons why students withdraw from school. This study confirmed the reality that women, viewed as vulnerable in existing studies, utilize "leave of absence" and "late enrollment" to secure scholarships and tuition fees. The study confirms that girls are taking advantage of schooling in a flexible and resilient manner. The ways in which they are seeking opportune times for schooling over the long term, taking into account factors unique to their family situation and the availability of scholarships, present a picture of strong and resilient African women that could not be seen in the cross-sectional data.

Researchers and aid staff from developed countries analyzing the schooling situation might be misled by the stereotype that suggests girls do not attend school, while in reality, the study confirmed that they are instead flexibly planning their schooling. It is important however to distinguish between active and passive leaves of absence. The line between choosing not to go to school and not being able to go to school is blurred, and it is necessary to look at the effects of leave of absence rather than simply interpreting it all through a negative lens. Similarly, it is necessary to examine the effects of scholarships from different angles as well.

Although boys may be seen as privileged over girls with macro-level figures in terms of dropout, they are shown to be vulnerable in this other aspect where it is difficult for them to return to school later after dropping out in a microanalysis. In addition to examining viewpoints about preventing students from dropping out of school, this study showed the necessity of also recognizing the need to support males more than females for returning to school.

This factor suggests the need for further research on educational development. Research and practice around gender issues in education in places like Malawi tend to focus on girls' education and women's situations and very often on gender disparities. But this microanalysis has shown that while girls' education is in need of improvement, on the other hand, however there is also a need to focus on the issue of men returning to school as one of the gender issues in education.

5   CONCLUSION

This chapter has examined the individual schooling conditions that can be read from the longitudinal schooling records of secondary schools in Malawi, with a focus on factors around the idea of dropout. Some aspects of individual circumstances and educational strategies that cannot be read from cross-sectional data have therefore been clarified. The results of this survey provide glimpses of the educational strategies of individuals in their various family circumstances and reveal life plans which would otherwise be hidden if only macro data were analyzed. For example, the resilience of women who take a long-term view of their lives and make strong investments in their future was made clear as was the vulnerability of men in returning to school.

It should be noted that, from the standpoint of data management, the target schools for this study are among the highest quality schools in Malawi. Many of the students attending the target schools were also children from relatively well-off families, leaving the study limited and problematic in terms of representativeness in Malawi. However, even in such target schools, many students experienced school dropout while planning their future and educational strategies. For children from lower quality schools and families with lower socioeconomic characteristics, one might speculate that they would be forced to develop more demanding strategies.

Acknowledgments Mr. Chikoza Piri of the Ministry of Education kindly contributed his great help to conduct the survey in Malawi. The research was financed by a Grant-in-Aid for Scientific Research (2010–2012, Grant-in-Aid for Scientific

Research (B), "Longitudinal Study of School Enrollment and Surrounding Environment of Children in Developing Countries after Primary Education," PI: Prof. Takeshi Sekiya, Kwansei Gakuin University). We would like to express our sincere gratitude to all those involved.

REFERENCES

Aiden. (2010). *Teacher training issue in anglophone Africa*. World Bank.

Kadzamira, E., & Rose, P. (2003). Can free primary education meet the needs of the poor?: Evidence from Malawi. *International Journal of Educational Development, 23*, 501–516.

Kawaguchi, J. (2011). The function and value of primary school from parents' perspectives: A case study of public schools in Malawi. *Africa Education Research Journal*, Africa Education Research Forum, *2*, 65–77.

Kunje, D. (2007). *Teacher issues in Malawi*. Malawi University.

Malawi MoE. (2015). *Basic education statistic Malawi 2014/2015: Ministry of Education in Malawi*. Lilongwe.

Malawi MoE (Ministry of Education). (2023). *Basic Education Statistic Malawi: MOE Lilongwe Malawi*.

Shimizu, K., Yamamoto, A. B., Kaji, I., & Hayashizaki, K. (2013). *Oukansuru hitobitono Kyoiku sennryaku*. Akashi Shoten.

UNESCO. (2020). *Malawi: Education Country Brief*.

World Bank. (2010). The Education System in Malawi. World Bank Working Paper No. 182.

World Bank. (2014). *Education Statistics: Core Indicator 2014*. Washington, D.C.

CHAPTER 13

Analysis of Students' Flow Patterns from Primary Through Lower Secondary Cycle Under Automatic Promotion Policy in Uganda

James Wokadala and Keiichi Ogawa ⓘ

1   Background

Formal education in Uganda is regarded as a fundamental human right for all its citizens and is aligned with the goals of achieving the Education for All (EFA), Millennium Development Goals (MDGs), and Sustainable Development Goals (SDGs). The education system in Uganda consists of a four-tiered structure of formal training. At the basic level, there are seven

J. Wokadala
School of Statistics and Planning, Makerere University, Kampala, Uganda
e-mail: james.wokadala@mak.ac.ug

K. Ogawa (✉)
Graduate School of International Cooperation Studies, Kobe University, Kobe, Japan
e-mail: ogawa35@kobe-u.ac.jp

© The Author(s), under exclusive license to Springer Nature Switzerland AG 2024
T. Sekiya et al. (eds.), *Towards Ensuring Inclusive and Equitable Quality Education for All*, International and Development Education, https://doi.org/10.1007/978-3-031-70266-2_13

Table 13.1 Structure of Uganda basic education system

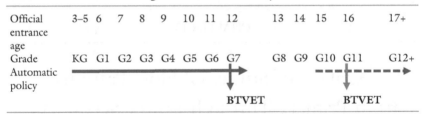

Official entrance age	3–5	6	7	8	9	10	11	12		13	14	15	16		17+
Grade	KG	G1	G2	G3	G4	G5	G6	G7		G8	G9	G10	G11		G12+

Automatic policy

BTVET   BTVET

Source: Developed by the authors based on Nakabugo et al. (2008)

Note: Compulsory automatic promotion is applied from KG to Grade 7, while automatic promotion practice is encouraged from Grade 7 to Grade 11; BTVET stands for Business, Technical, Vocational Education and Training

years of compulsory primary education (Table 13.1). At the end of the first cycle, a pupil sits for the Primary Leaving Examination (PLE) before moving on to the second cycle. The second cycle comprises secondary education, which is a two-tier structure consisting of four years of lower secondary, which is the focus of this study, and two years of upper secondary. Upon successful completion of the lower secondary level, students receive a Uganda Certificate in Education (UCE) and a Uganda Advanced Certificate in Education (UACE) at the upper level, respectively (MoES, 2004). After implementing the Universal Secondary Education (USE) policy at the lower secondary level in 2007, students' performance in basic core and compulsory subjects has been monitored, mainly after nine years of child schooling. This measure has been one way of monitoring the quality of education in a growing student population environment (Syngellakis & Arudo, 2006).

The lower secondary education cycle provides a broad-based curriculum, with students delving into relevant subjects and themes. Nevertheless, it is recognized that one of the purposes of end-of-cycle attainment tests is to assess students' proficiency levels and identify meritorious students for higher education, primarily at tertiary levels. It is important to note that upon leaving lower secondary education (i.e., at the end of Senior 4 or S4 level), students have the option to enter the job market directly, pursue further studies in upper secondary education, or enroll in vocational training institutions. Specifically, some S4 graduates may choose to attend institutions such as primary or basic teacher education colleges for a two- or three-year program leading to a teaching qualification. Additionally, the cycle opens up the system to learners with a wider range of interests and abilities, often matching the Senior 6 (S6) graduate profile to the needs of formal or informal sectors.

In Uganda, after S4, learners are placed in either the regular academic track or vocational track for apprenticeship training, after which the graduates can seek formal employment. Uganda was one of the first African countries to adopt the Universal Primary Education (UPE) policy in 1997. According to the National Development Plan (NDP) II, the UPE program since 1997 attracted an increase in enrollment and access from 2.5 million pupils in 2013 (National Planning Authority, 2019). Free secondary education was included in the election manifesto of President Museveni in November 2005, and secondary education gradually became free through the implementation of the Universal Secondary Education (USE) Initiative and Universal Post Primary Education and Training (UPPET) program since 2007 (UNESCO, 2010).

The introduction of free education resulted in the implementation of an automatic promotion policy in 2005 as an interventionist strategy aimed at enhancing the internal efficiency and quality of primary education (Ozturk, 2001, & MoES, 2005). The policy is implemented only in government primary schools because of internal inefficiencies such as a high repetition rate, high dropout rate, low survival rate, and low completion rate, which were, on average, higher among these schools. Moreover, government schools form the bulk of primary schools in the country (12,203 out of 18,079) that implemented UPE and continue to display significant inefficiencies. This results in wasted resources for both the government and households, as well as lost time for students. This highlights that the UPE policy is still trying to address issues such as grade repetition, school dropout rates, and the effectiveness and duration of teaching, with the ultimate goal of improving learning outcomes (Ndaruhutse, 2008).

Under the UPE program, the government pays tuition for all students enrolled in UPE-implementing schools, and parents cover costs related to scholastic materials such as school uniforms, pens, pencils, exercise books, school meals, and so forth. The adoption and subsequent implementation of automatic promotion came as a response to the high internal inefficiency prevailing within the primary education sub-sector, along with the low quality of education (Albrigh, 2015; Ojuji, 2015; Nannyonjo, 2014). Inefficiency was evident through high repetition and dropout rates, which by 2004 were recorded at approximately 35.0% and 21.0%, respectively. The low quality of education was reflected by low academic achievements at all primary grades and characterized by disparities along gender and rural-urban dimensions. For instance, according to the National Assessment of Progress in Education (NAPE) 2004, pass rates for English and Mathematics at primary three (P3) were 37.0% and 44.0%, respectively, and even lower for primary six (P6), 25.0% and 27.0% respectively. By 2010, these rates had improved, albeit still below regional and international averages. Literacy and numeracy at P3 improved to 57.0% and 72.0%, respectively, whereas at P6, they improved to 50.0% and 54.0%, respectively.

Uganda's learning outcomes regarding gender and rural-urban dimensions are lower among female students by approximately 5.0 percentage points and in rural areas by approximately 15.0 percentage points. P3 pupils in urban private schools perform relatively better than their counterparts studying in government primary schools. By 2010, the proportion of pupils rated proficient in literacy had improved to 57.0% (i.e., 64.0% for private schools and 50.0% for government schools). In 2010, the proportion of students rated proficient improved to 72.0%, with those in urban schools accounting for 80% and those in rural schools accounting for 64.0%. In the context of Sub-Saharan Africa, Ndaruhutse (2008) acknowledges the existence and persistence of these disparities in schooling. Other scholars, for instance, Nannyonjo (2014), asserted that enrolling children in primary education at the appropriate age and promoting them each year is a good policy measure for Uganda. However, in tandem with the enforcement of automatic promotion, it may be necessary to understand the students' flow patterns at various grades at the primary and lower secondary levels, respectively. However, it is also important to demonstrate that in the face of an automatic promotion policy, there are possible learning bottlenecks along the path that could result in repetitions and dropouts. Thus, the objectives of the study are to evaluate enrollment patterns in Grade 1 at the primary level by socioeconomic status (SES), gender, and school location; to trace learner completion rates at various grades by SES, gender, and school location; and to assess the dropout rates of learners at different education levels by SES, gender, and school location.

2   Methodology

Sample

This study employed a non-probability sampling technique to determine the subjects included in the sample (Battaglia, 2008). In this technique, the tracked sample was based solely on the availability of complete information on the learners to be tracked, which was available in official school records. This analysis employed a tracer study approach on longitudinal data on 300 pupils who enrolled in Grade 1 and studied all through up to Grade 11 (lower secondary cycle). The tracer[1] approach involves tracing the movement of an individual or unit along the time path. Tracer studies have been proven effective in evaluating over 100 educational loan projects in developing nations (Schiefelbein & Farrell, 1987). Therefore, the learners were tracked from the time they enrolled in Grade 1 until they completed Grade 11 or dropped out before completing the primary or secondary cycle. The focus was on completion and dropout rates within the framework of the automatic promotion policy. The survey was conducted between July and September 2022 with funding from Makerere University, Uganda, and technical support from the Uganda's Ministry of Education and Sports (MoES) officials as co-researchers. This commissioned action research aimed to inform policy and planning in primary education.

A random sample was selected from seven districts: Masaka in the Central region; Apac, Kitgum, Lira, and Pader in the Northern region; Mbale in the Eastern region; and Arua in the West Nile region. The selection was based on school enrollment, in-school survival, and completion rates at the district and school levels. The districts were chosen to represent different regions of the country, and approximately half of the selected schools had good progress records in terms of completion and academic achievement. While the remaining half of the schools (in refugee hosting districts of Arua, Kitgum, and Pader) faced challenges in retaining learners until completion. For data collection, level one information was obtained from schools' records, covering the period from Grade 1 to Grade 7, and level two data was gathered from both the school administrators and the parents. Efforts were made to reach out to the learners and dropouts themselves to elicit qualitative information, particularly regarding the reasons for dropout or delayed school completion. This approach helped the research team to determine the learners' placements after the end of the primary cycle.

---

[1] A tracer study refers to investigations in which a sample of individuals is studied at a given time, and then located and studied again at one or more successive stages of their lives. The essential feature of such studies is that the characteristics of the same subjects are observed at two or more points in time (Schiefelbein & Farrell, 1987).

Table 13.2   Distribution of learners by gender, SES, and location

District	Rural (%)	Urban (%)	Female (%)	Male (%)	Primary schools visited
APAC (n = 30)	0.0	100.0	60.0	40.0	1) Arocha
Arua (n = 58)	100.0	0.0	44.8	55.2	1) Arua Hill 2) Jako
KITGUM (n = 38)	36.8	63.2	42.1	57.9	1) Akworo 2) Kitgum Public
LIRA (n = 42)	0.0	100.0	57.1	42.9	1) Abutoadi 2) Otara
Masaka (n = 38)	42.1	57.9	52.6	47.4	1) St. Bruno Sserunkuuma 2) St. Gregory Butende
Mbale (n = 56)	0.0	100.0	35.7	64.3	1) St. Jude Namanyonyi 2) Nabuyonga
Pader (n = 38)	36.8	63.2	26.3	73.7	1) Opolacen 2) Pader Kilak
Total (n = 300)	34.0	66.0	44.7	55.3	13 districts

Source: Created by the authors based on survey data

In terms of sample distribution, 300 learners were selected as follows: Apac (30), Arua (54), Kitgum (38), Lira (42), Masaka (38), Mbale (56), and Pader (38). Except for Apac, where one primary school was chosen, two schools were selected from each of the remaining six districts, resulting in a total of 13 schools. The selected schools were conventional government-aided and owned schools with significant enrollment numbers for both genders. Of these learners, 69.0% came from the north and northwest of Uganda, 66.0% lived in urban areas, and 55.3% were males. All learners from Apac, Lira, and Mbale were based in urban areas, while all learners from Arua were in rural areas. Table 13.2 provides details of the distribution of learners by gender, SES, and location.

The Socioeconomic Status (SES) and Calculation

The SES is a measure of welfare within the home environment where the learners stay. According to Uganda Bureau of Statistics framework measure of SES is a composite index of household conventional items, the economic well-being of the family as well as education level of the household heads. In the study case, it was a weighted index comprising of the education level of the household head (tertiary weighted – 3; secondary – 2; primary – 1; and no complete primary – 0); the nature of the floor of the household dwelling (cement – 3; soil – 1; and nothing – 0); source of light at home (electricity – 2; and otherwise – 0); nature of the house wall (cement – 3; adobe – 2; and any other materials – 1); availability of clean water supply (yes – 1; and otherwise – 0); roofing materials of the house (iron sheets – 3; grass – 1; and otherwise – 0); and sanitation situation at home (available flush toilets – 2; and pit toilet – 1). The scores were categorized as low (0–6), average (7–12), and high (13+). From the analysis, the average SES score was (10.4) with a standard deviation of 3.79 and a range of 4–17, respectively.

Data Analysis

For data analysis, univariate, bivariate, and tracer techniques were used. The univariate analysis generated frequencies and percentages to indicate the individual distribution as well as socioeconomic characteristics of the learners by gender, SES, rural-urban, and district, respectively. The bivariate analysis provided an understanding of the association between completion at Grade 7 (G7) and S4 with conventional household socioeconomic characteristics such as the education level of the parents, Grade 1 entrance age groups, average travel time (in minutes) to access the school, the type of floor of home shelter, availability of electricity at home, availability of clean water at home, house roofing material as well as type of toilet used in the household. The tracing technique helped to track the learners to and at the various grades up to Grade 11. A detailed analysis is presented, tracing and examining data by SES, learner gender, and rural-urban location. Additionally, the study outlines cases of repetitions, dropouts, and the various reasons why learners left school at different grades. The class patterns were labeled as follows: P = Pass, F = Fail, and D = Dropped Out.

3   ANALYSIS AND DISCUSSION OF THE RESULTS

The majority (58.0%) of the students came from families with an average SES. Only 13.0% of learners were from poor families; on the other hand, 29.0% of the learners came from households with high SES. Therefore, the sample distribution had a socioeconomic diversity; most respondents were from families with average SES. About 66.0% of the families with average SES were located in the urban area.

Table 13.3 Socioeconomic characteristics of pupils, parents, and home-learning environment

Aspect	Rural (%)	Urban (%)
Socioeconomic status (SES)		
Low (*n* = 38)	31.6	68.4
Average (*n* = 174)	34.5	65.5
High (*n* = 88)	34.1	65.9
Total (*n* = 300)	34.0	66.0
% of female learners (*n* = 134)	29.8	70.2
Education level of the parents		
No education attained (*n* = 12)	16.7	83.3
Completed primary (*n* = 54)	48.2	51.8
Completed secondary (*n* = 66)	33.3	66.7
Completed tertiary (*n* = 168)	30.9	69.1
Living with a parent, Yes = 1, (*n* = 198)	27.3	72.7
Entrance age group (years)		
4–6 (*n* = 123)	36.6	63.4
7–9 (*n* = 135)	27.4	72.6
10+ (*n* = 42)	47.6	52.4
Average distance of travel to school daily (min)	28.3	22.5

Source: Created by the authors based on survey data

Table 13.3 shows the socioeconomic characteristics of pupils, their parents, and the home-learning environment. The parents' education is regarded as a prerequisite for their children's effective learning. The results reveal that about 83.0% of the learners have parents with no education level attained, and 72.7% live with parents from urban areas. Rural learners often travel an average of 28.3 minutes to reach their schools daily. This finding is consistent with the results that learners' commute times tend to be negatively associated with their learning and academic achievements, and this correlation varies across rural and urban areas (Ding & Feng, 2022).

Moreover, most of the learners (56.0%) had parents who attained tertiary education, with 69.0% of these families living in urban areas. Conversely, the majority of learners (66.0%) were still living with their parents, predominantly in urban areas (72.7%). The starting school age of the learner often determines the actual classroom attendance as well as the progression at various grades (Wils, 2004). In Uganda, age for Grade 1 entrance varies significantly between rural and urban areas of residence. By the age of nine, 86.0% of learners had started their education. In rural areas, 47.6% of learners began their education at age ten or older (Table 13.3). There is evidence of significant associations between completion at Grade 7 and S4 with conventional household socioeconomic characteristics in developing countries.

The results presented in Table 13.4 reveal a statistically significant relationship ($p < 0.01$) between parents' education and the completion of

Table 13.4 Associations of completion at G7 and S4 with conventional household socioeconomic characteristics

Aspect/variable	Category	% completed G7 (n = 218)	% completed S4 (n = 89)
The education level of the parents	No education	2.5	0.0
	Primary	19.3	0.0
	Secondary	13.5	12.0
	Tertiary	64.7	88.0
	Chi (p-value)	61.3 (0.00)	123.2 (0.00)
G1 entrance age	4–6	44.1	44.7
	7–9	47.5	42.0
	10+	8.4	13.3
	Chi (p-value)	30.0 (0.00)	14.3 (0.001)
Average travel time (min.)		24.5	21.5
		p-value (0.334)	p-value (0.001)
Floor of the HH shelter	Soil	59.7	46.7
	Cement	40.3	53.3
	Chi (p-value)	2.55 (0.110)	28.4 (0.000)
Electricity as a source of light (yes = 1)	Yes	33.6	42.7
	Chi (p-value)	4.70 (0.030)	14.9 (0.000)
Wall of the HH shelter	Adobe	7.6	4.0
	Bricks	59.7	65.3
	Other	32.3	30.7
	Chi (p-value)	0.108(0.947)	9.54 (0.008)
Availability of clean water at home	Yes	22.7	30.7
	Chi (p-value)	16.11 (0.000)	14.7 (0.000)
House roofing material	Grass	54.6	44.0
	Iron sheets	42.9	54.7
	Other	1.7	0.0
	Chi (p-value)	38.6 (0.000)	29.5 (0.000)
Used type of toilet	Pit toilet	91.6	88.0
	Flush toilet	8.4	12.0
	Chi (p-value)	1.91 (0.384)	14.5 (0.001)

Source: Created by the authors based on survey data

Grade 7 and S4. This is an anticipated phenomenon because educated parents value and appreciate education, which they pass on to their children. They are also more likely to provide material and moral support to help their children succeed. Therefore, parents' education levels correlate with the successful completion of Grade 7 or S4 classes. Specifically, this implies that variables are not independent but connected in that parents' education levels affect their children's academic performance at these specific grades (Haris & Goodall, 2008). Moreover, the entrance age significantly correlates ($p < 0.001$) with the successful completion of Grade 7 or S4 study levels, respectively. The entrance age and education completion are not independent; instead, they are associated with each other in a way that entrance age affects children's academic performance.

The learners' commute time from home to school and back home influences the level of classroom attendance as well as active class participation. In Uganda, there is evidence that learners, especially those from rural areas, have to walk long distances and arrive late at school (MoES, 2004). Results show that the travel time of learners to schools is not significantly associated with their academic completion in Grade 7 ($p > 0.05$). However, a significant ($p < 0.001$) connection exists between completion at S4 and the learner's travel time to school and back home. Some of the features, such as the nature of the household dwelling floor, the shelter wall, and the type of toilet, are not significantly associated with academic completion in Grade 7. On the other hand, electricity as a source of light ($p < 0.05$), availability of clean water at home ($p < 0.001$), and house roofing material ($p < 0.001$) are said to be correlated with the completion of Grade 7 and Grade 11, respectively. The household environment often plays a critical role in child learning both at school and at home, and these findings are consistent with the results that family SES triggers learning and, ultimately, completion (Shah et al., 2012). Table 13.5 illustrates enrollment patterns at Grade 1 in primary schools, categorized by SES, gender, and school location.

For Grade 1 learners, the majority (58.0%) come from families with an average SES, compared to 12.7% from low economic status, respectively. For senior students, the majority (59.1%) come from average SES families, with only 7.9% from low-SES and 33.9% from high-SES families. The percentage of female students reduces from 44.7% in Grade 1 to 42.0% in Senior 1 (S1) due to dropout incidents. About 34.0% of schools serving Grade 1 students are located in rural areas, compared to only 28.4% of schools for senior students. Conclusively, the results show that students

Table 13.5 Enrolment patterns at Grade 1 at the primary level by SES, gender, and school location

	SES			Gender		School location	
	Low	Average	High	Female	Male	Rural	Urban
Grade 1							
No.	38	174	88	134	166	102	198
%	12.7	58.0	29.3	44.7	55.3	34.0	66.0
Senior 1							
No.	14	104	58	74	102	50	126
%	7.9	59.1	32.9	42.0	58.0	28.4	71.6

Source: Created by the authors based on survey data

Table 13.6 Trace of the learners and their completion at various grades in primary education by SES, gender, and school location

		Rank	G1→G7 (n = 218)	G1→G6 (n = 242)	G1→G5 (n = 245)	G1→G4 (n = 252)	G1→G2 (n = 262)
SES	Low	3	34 (15.6)	36 (14.9)	36 (14.7)	36 (14.3)	36 (13.7)
	Average	1	118 (54.1)	137 (56.6)	139 (56.7)	145 (57.5)	154 (58.8)
	High	2	66 (30.3)	69 (28.5)	70 (28.6)	71 (28.2)	72 (27.5)
Gender	Female	2	100 (45.9)	112 (46.3)	114 (46.5)	116 (46.0)	120 (45.8)
	Male	1	118 (54.1)	130 (53.7)	131 (53.5)	136 (54.0)	142 (54.2)
Location	Rural	2	60 (27.5)	70 (28.9)	72 (29.4)	73 (29.0)	74 (28.2)
	Urban	1	158 (72.5)	172 (71.1)	173 (70.6)	179 (71.0)	188 (71.8)

Source: Created by the authors

Note: Figures in brackets are percentages (%); '→' implies promoted from grade to grade

from average socioeconomic backgrounds make up the most significant portion at both grade levels. The percentage of female students declines slightly from primary to secondary school. A higher percentage of primary schools compared to secondary schools are located in rural areas and vice versa for urban settings. These patterns broadly reveal that gender issues are still a challenge in progression, predominantly from primary to lower secondary in Uganda. Table 13.6 presents the trace of learners and their completion at various grades in primary education, categorized by SES, gender, and school location.

A key automatic policy outcome was the completion of grades 7 and 11 for all learners, regardless of SES, gender, and rural-urban differences (MoES, 2005). However, the results reveal different outcomes. For instance, out of the 300 children who enrolled in Grade 1, 12.6% (=38/300) dropped out after just one year of study without repeating the grade. The number of learners who completed Grade 2 was 36 (13.7%) in low SES, 154 (58.8%) in middle SES, and 72 (27.5%) in high SES. In Grade 4 (G4), the number of learners who completed their education dropped by 3.8% to 252. While the completion rate in Grade 4 increased from 13.7% to 14.3% for low-SES learners and from 27.5% to 28.2% for high-SES learners, the completion rate for those in the middle-SES reduced from 58.8% to 57.5%. The patterns reveal that high dropouts were observed among children with average SES, female learners, and those from rural areas of residence. The results reveal that student self-concept and socioeconomic eco-system are essential to learning and completion (Chohan & Khan, 2010).

In Grade 7, the number of learners who completed their education dropped significantly from 262 to 218, hence representing a drop rate of 16.8%. The completion rate generally decreased from Grade 2 to Grade 7, with the steepest drop occurring between Grade 6 and Grade 7. The completion rate was highest for middle-SES students in Grade 2, which declined over time, whereas the rates for low-SES and high-SES learners increased. The urban completion rate was much higher than the rural rate throughout, despite the gap narrowing by Grade 7. Table 13.7 shows the trace and completion of learners at various grades in lower secondary education, classified by SES, gender, and school location.

At S4, the number of learners who completed the education level reduced from 150 in S2 to 89 in S4, with a lower percentage of girls (48.3%) than boys (51.7%). The reduction in the completion rate accounted for over 40.0% of the dropout rate among learners in the study. The percentage of learners from schools located in rural areas reduced from 26.7% in S2 to 24.7% in S4, while in urban areas, it increased from 73.3% to 75.3%. Furthermore, the completion rate was lowest at 3.4% for learners from low-SES backgrounds, while learners from high-SES backgrounds saw an increase from 34.7% to 49.4%, and those from middle-SES backgrounds decreased from 58.7% to 47.2%. The total number of learners completing secondary school experienced a significant decline,

Table 13.7 Learners trace and their completion at various grades in lower secondary education by SES, gender, and school location

Aspect	Category	Rank	S1→S2→S3→S4 (n = 89)	S1→S2→S3 (n = 108)	S1→S2 (n = 150)
SES	Low	3	3 (3.4)	4 (3.7)	10 (6.7)
	Average	1	42 (47.2)	52 (48.2)	88 (58.7)
	High	2	44 (49.4)	52 (48.2)	52 (34.7)
Gender	Female	2	43 (48.3)	54 (50.0)	64 (42.7)
	Male	1	46 (51.7)	54 (50.0)	86 (57.3)
Location	Rural	2	22 (24.7)	24 (22.2)	40 (26.7)
	Urban	1	67 (75.3)	84 (77.8)	110 (73.3)

Source: Created by the authors

Note: Figures in brackets are percentages (%); '→' implies promoted from grade to grade

dropping from 1500 to only 89 in S4, resulting in a dropout rate of over 40.0%. Notably, the percentage of girls completing school also dwindled each year. The lower the SES of the child's family, the more likely they are to drop out of school (Sekiya & Ashida, 2017). While the completion rate peaked for middle-SES learners in S2, it gradually diminished in subsequent years. Conversely, the rate for high-SES learners consistently increased yearly, eventually surpassing that of middle-SES learners by S4. On the other hand, low-SES learners consistently exhibited low completion rates, which gradually declined throughout the course. Table 13.8 presents the dropout trends of learners at various primary education levels, categorized by SES, gender, and school location.

The number of learners who dropped out of school gradually increased from 38 in Grade 2 to 82 in Grade 7. Most of the learners who dropped out fell under the average SES class, with 20 (52.6%) in Grade 2 and 56 (68.3%) in Grade 7. Under low SES, the number of learners dropping out of school was minimal compared to learners in high SES and middle SES. As the dropout rate increased under middle SES, the rate of dropouts in high SES gradually reduced as learning transitioned from Grade 1 to Grade 7. Each year, more girls than boys dropped out of school, though the dropout rates for girls reduced, and that of the boys increased as learning transitioned from Grade 1 to Grade 7. These results strengthen the argument that in developing countries, dropouts have been directly correlated with SES (Levy, 1971). The dropout rates for learners in the schools in the rural areas kept on improving from 73.6% in Grade 2 to

Table 13.8 Dropout trends of learners at various education levels in primary education by SES, gender, and school location

Aspect	Category	Rank	Dropped out at G7 (n = 82)	Dropped out at G6 (n = 58)	Dropped out at G5 (n = 55)	Dropped out at G4 (n = 48)	Dropped out at G2 (n = 38)
SES	Low	1	4 (4.9)	2 (3.4)	2 (3.6)	2 (4.2)	2 (5.3)
	Average	3	56 (68.3)	37 (63.8)	35 (63.6)	29 (60.4)	20 (52.6)
	High	2	22 (26.8)	19 (32.7)	18 (32.7)	17 (35.4)	16 (42.1)
Gender	Female	1	34 (41.5)	22 (37.9)	20 (36.4)	18 (37.5)	14 (36.8)
	Male	2	48 (58.5)	36 (62.1)	35 (63.6)	30 (62.5)	24 (63.2)
Location	Rural	2	42 (51.2)	32 (55.2)	30 (54.5)	29 (60.4)	28 (73.6)
	Urban	1	40 (48.8)	26 (44.8)	25 (45.5)	19 (39.6)	10 (26.3)

Source: Created by the authors

Note: Figures in brackets are percentages (%)

51.2%, while the urban rates worsened from 26.3% in Grade 2 to 48.8% in Grade 7. The common reasons for dropping out of high school included financial difficulties, family issues, lack of motivation to continue schooling, and health problems. Learners often cited insufficient funds to pay school fees, particularly in cases where they came from large families facing financial strain. Within the realm of family issues, some learners reported a lack of parental care, while others highlighted instances of domestic violence between their parents, negatively impacting their education. Additionally, the challenges of adolescence crisis led some learners to prioritize other concerns over their studies.

Table 13.9 illustrates the dropout trends of learners at various education levels in lower secondary education, categorized by SES, gender, and school location. The dropout rates in Uganda exhibit a discernible pattern, with the number of students leaving school increasing from 124 in the first year to nearly doubling at 211 in the fourth year. Interestingly, there was an overall decrease in dropout rates as students progressed from the first to the fourth year, with one exception noted among those in the middle-SES group. Additionally, each year recorded a percentage of boys dropping out compared to girls, suggesting a gender-based disparity in dropout rates, with boys being more likely to leave school prematurely. This suggests that rural schools may be more effective at retaining students compared to schools in urban areas facing challenges with student retention. The notable dropout rates, particularly in specific areas and

Table 13.9 Dropout trends of learners at various education levels in lower secondary education by SES, gender, and school location

Aspect	Category	Rank	Dropped at S4 (n = 211)	Dropped at S3 (n = 192)	Dropped at S2 (n = 150)	Dropped at S1 (n = 124)
SES	Low	1	35 (16.5)	34 (17.7)	28 (18.7)	24 (19.3)
	Average	2	132 (62.6)	122 (63.5)	86 (57.3)	70 (56.4)
	High	2	44 (20.8)	36 (18.7)	36 (24.0)	30 (24.2)
Gender	Female	1	91 (43.1)	80 (41.6)	70 (46.6)	60 (48.4)
	Male	2	120 (56.9)	112 (58.3)	80 (53.3)	64 (51.6)
Location	Rural	1	80 (37.9)	78 (40.6)	62 (41.3)	52 (41.9)
	Urban	2	131 (62.1)	114 (59.4)	88 (58.7)	72 (58.1)

Source: Created by the authors

Note: Figures in brackets are percentages (%)

among boys, underscore the necessity for targeted interventions addressing the root causes of school dropout in Uganda. It is crucial for stakeholders to collaborate and address the challenges faced by urban schools and boys and girls to ensure all students have equal opportunities to complete their education. Table 13.10 illustrates the class patterns, the extent of dropout, and the reasons why a child did not continue to attend school.

It is clear that dropout cases exhibit different patterns. The typical patterns include successfully progressing from Grade 1 to Grade 6 and finally dropping out in Grade 7 (1-6P7D), successfully progressing from G1 through G4, and dropping out in G5. There are also occasional cases of repetitions and, finally, dropouts attributed to various factors. One case involved a pattern of passing in Grade 1 and failing in Grade 2 (i.e. 1P2F2P3P4P5D), which was attributed to the sudden disappearance of the student's father, affecting their education and leading to them dropping out in Grade 5. Another case in a rural area involved a student whose father had many children and inadequate resources to support their education, resulting in below-average performance and the decision to give up education (1P1D). Several reasons were identified to explain the dropout cases, including the influence of the adolescence stage on learners, poor parental care, sickness or death of parents, children's choice to join the priesthood, general family conflict between parents, and parents' separation due to wars, among others.

Table 13.10 The extent of dropout and factors affecting school discontinuation

HH No.	SES level	Year of entrance	Sex	Rural/ urban	Patterns of grades attended	Class patterns	Reason for dropping out
183	1	2002	M	Urban	G1→G7	1-6P7D	Because their family did not have money
256	1	2002	F	Rural	G1→G6	1P2P3P4P5F5P	Adolescence stage, the influence of boys, and poor parental care
251	1	2001	M	Rural	G1	1F1P	Lacked money to pay school fees
159	1	2001	F	Urban	G1→G7	1-6P7D	Because their family did not have money
165	1	2000	F	Urban	G1→G7	1-6P7D	Because their family did not have money
26	2	2003	F	Urban	G1→G5	1P2P3P4P5D	Because their family did not have money
108	2	2003	F	Rural	G1	1P1D	Lack of money
246	2	2005	M	Rural	G1	1P1D	The family did not have enough money and were many children
261	2	2007	F	Rural	G1→G6	1-4P5F5P6D	The mother was sick, so they attended to her in the hospital. They broke down because of a heart problem/stress
95	2	2004	M	Rural	G1	1P1D	The child wanted to join the priesthood but could not when his parents died in a motor accident
5	2	2003	M	Urban	G1→G7	1-5P6F6P7D	Because they did not like to go to school
155	2	2003	M	Urban	G1→G7	1-6P7D	Because they did not like to go to school
142	2	1991	M	Urban	G1→G7	1-6P7D	Parents never cared about educating their children
280	2	1998	F	Urban	G1→G4	1P2P3F3P4F	Lack of money, boy-girl relationships

(*continued*)

Table 13.10 (continued)

HH No.	SES level	Year of entrance	Sex	Rural/ urban	Patterns of grades attended	Class patterns	Reason for dropping out
135	2	1999	M	Urban	G1→G4	1P2P3P4F	The family conflict between the mother and father
292	2	1991	M	Urban	G1→G6	1-4P5P6D	Parents never cared about educating their children
285	2	1999	M	Urban	G1→G3	1P2P3F3D	Family conflict between the mother and father
144	2	1999	F	Urban	G1→G4	1P2P3P4D	Death of the father
286	2	1999	F	Urban	G1→G6	1-5P6D	The father wanted her to get married, and the mother struggled to educate her
247	3	2002	M	Rural	G1	1P1D	Father had many children, and money was not enough; his performance was below average, so he decided to give up
118	3	2005	M	Rural	G1	1P1D	Separation due to wars
263	3	2002	M	Rural	G1→G4	1P2P3P4F4D	Lack of money. Sickness like malaria
97	3	2002	M	Rural	G1	1P1D	Father had many children and inadequate resources
113	3	2002	M	Rural	G1→G6	1-5P6D	Lack of money. Sickness like malaria
259	3	2006	F	Rural	G1	1P1D	The school was costly
188	3	2005	F	Rural	G1→G7	1-6P7D	Stopped in G7, and there was no money for further education
296	3	2000	F	Urban	G1→G5	1P2F2P3P4P5D	The sudden disappearance of their father affected her education

Source: Created by the authors

4   Conclusion

The study revealed that completion rates at G7 and S4 were 72.7% and 29.7%, respectively, indicating low internal efficiency in schooling. Additionally, significant associations were found between learner completion at G7 and G11 and various household characteristics, including the education level of the household head, Grade 1 entrance age, availability of electricity as the primary source of lighting at home, availability of clean water at home, and house roofing material, all at the 1.0% level of significance. Approximately 54.1% of learners who completed G7 were from average SES, while 72.5% resided in urban areas. Moreover, 75.3% of those who completed S4 were urban dwellers, with nearly half (49.4%) coming from high-SES backgrounds. Conversely, 27.3% (82 out of 300) of learners dropped out before reaching Grade 7, while 70.3% (211 out of 300) dropped out by Grade 11. Reasons for dropout included lack of funds to pay school fees, sickness or death of parents, and a general lack of concern or care from parents, particularly toward girls. Thus, there is a clear need for mitigation measures to improve survival and completion rates in education, extending beyond mere access.

References

Albrigh, A. (2015). *Global partnership for education, 7th Education World Congress.* https://www.globalpartnership.org/sites/default/files/2015-07-alice-albright-remarks-_ei-world-congress.pdf

Battaglia, M. P. (2008). Nonprobability sampling. *Encyclopedia of Survey Research Methods, 1*, 523–526.

Chohan, B. I., & Khan, R. M. (2010). Impact of parental support on the academic performance and self-concept of the student. *Journal of Research and Reflections in Education, 4*(1), 14–26.

Ding, P., & Feng, S. (2022). How school travel affects children's psychological well-being and academic achievement in China. *International Journal of Environmental Research and Public Health, 19*, 13881. https://doi.org/10.3390/ijerph192113881

Haris, A., & Goodall, J. (2008). Do parents know they matter? Engaging all parents in learning. London centre for leadership in learning institute of education, UK. *Educational Research, Routledge, 3*, 277–289. https://doi.org/10.1080/00131880802309424

Levy, M. B. (1971). Determinants of primary school dropouts in developing countries. *Comparative Education Review, 15*(1), 44–58. https://doi.org/10.1086/445512

MoES. (2004). Education Sector Strategic Plan- 2004–2015.

MoES. (2005). Annual Sector Performance Report- 2004/05–2005/16.

Nakabugo, M. G., Byamugisha, A., & Bithaghalire, J. (2008). Future schooling in Uganda. *Journal of International Cooperation in Education, 11*(1), 55–69.

Nannyonjo. (2014). *Automatic promotion policy and academic performance in selected primary schools in Kabale Municipality.* https://idr.kab.ac.ug/bitstreams/405e0d1f-8d84-48a7-8102-9bfd9d8b0c67/download

National Planning Authority of Uganda. (2015/16–2019/20). *National Development Plan II.* https://www.ugandainvest.go.ug/wp-content/uploads/2016/03/National-Development-Plan-2015-16-to-2019-20.pdf

Ndaruhutse, S. (2008). *Grade repetition in primary schools in Sub-Saharan Africa: An evidence base for change.* CfBT Education Trust.

Ojuji, P. (2015). *Review of the education policy in Uganda* [Working paper]. National Curriculum Development Centre.

Ozturk, L. (2001). The role of education in Economic development. *A theoretical perspective Journal of Human Resources, 33*(1), 39–47. https://doi.org/10.2139/ssrn.1137541

Schiefelbein, E., & Farrell, J. P. (1987). *Trace studies* (pp. 382–385). *Economics of Education.* https://doi.org/10.1016/B978-0-08-033379-3.50084-X

Sekiya, T., & Ashida, A. (2017). An analysis of primary school dropout patterns in Honduras. *Journal of Latinos and Education, 16*(1), 65–73. https://doi.org/10.1080/15348431.2016.1179185

Shah, M., Atta, A., Qureshi, M. I., & Shah, H. (2012). Impact of Socioeconomic Status (SES) of family on the academic achievement of student. *Gomal University Journal of Research, 28*(1), 12–17.

Syngellakis, K., & Arudo, E. (2006). *Uganda: Education Sector policy overview paper.* UK ENABLE- Energy for Water.

UNESCO. (2010). *Education for all global monitoring report: Reaching the marginalized.* https://unesdoc.unesco.org/ark:/48223/pf0000187279

Wils, A. (2004). Late entrants leave school earlier: Evidence from Mozambique. *International Review of Education, 50*(1), 17–37. https://doi.org/10.1023/B:REVI.0000018201.53675.4b

CHAPTER 14

Individual Learners' Enrolment Status in Primary and Secondary Education: A Case Study of a Rural City in Zambia

Naruho Ezaki 🆔

1   ENVIRONMENTS OF PRIMARY AND SECONDARY EDUCATION IN ZAMBIA

Current Trends in Educational Development from 1990 to the Present

Education for All (EFA) was adopted at the World Conference on Education for All in 1990, and the Millennium Development Goals (MDGs) were formulated via consensus at the United Nations General Assembly in 2000. Since then, various efforts have been made to improve and promote primary education as an issue for the international community. As a result, school enrolment rates markedly improved, particularly in

N. Ezaki (✉)
Faculty of Global Culture and Communication, Aichi Shukutoku University, Nagoya, Japan
e-mail: nezaki@asu.aasa.ac.jp

© The Author(s), under exclusive license to Springer Nature   281
Switzerland AG 2024
T. Sekiya et al. (eds.), *Towards Ensuring Inclusive and Equitable Quality Education for All*, International and Development Education, https://doi.org/10.1007/978-3-031-70266-2_14

developing countries, and significant improvements were also witnessed in sub-Saharan Africa, where school enrolment had been poor. According to the EFA Global Monitoring Report, the net enrolment rate for primary education in the region increased from 59% in 1999 to 79% in 2012 (United Nations Educational, Scientific and Cultural Organization [UNESCO], 2015) and has maintained a similar net enrolment rate since then (UNESCO, 2020).

Among them, the Republic of Zambia (hereafter, Zambia), the country covered in this chapter, is considered an honour student because of its high enrolment and completion rates compared to other countries in Sub-Saharan Africa in terms of access to primary education. As of 2014, which is a year before the deadline for achieving the MDGs, the net enrolment and completion rates for primary education in the country reached 94.3% and 86.2%, respectively[1] (Directorate of Planning and Information, 2016), which indicates that quantitative diffusion is nearly achieved. Therefore, the Zambian government shifted its focus from primary to secondary education (UNESCO, 2016). Meanwhile, a number of challenges are observed in secondary education in terms of access to and quality of education, including the shortage of classrooms, qualified teachers, teaching materials and equipment, low student achievement (Ministry of Education, Science, Vocational Training and Early Education [MESVTEE], 2015) and internal efficiency issues such as grade repetition and temporary dropout (Ezaki & Nakamura, 2018). Thus, it is desired that the schooling situation will be improved such that more children can gain access to secondary education and graduate from the final grade without undergoing grade repetition or temporary dropout.

Basic Information on and the School System in Zambia

Zambia, the country featured in this chapter, is a landlocked country located in sub-Saharan Africa. It covers an area of approximately 752,610 km^2, with a population of approximately 19.61 million (Zambia Statistics Agency, 2022), which comprises 73 tribes. The official language is English, but seven other local languages, including Bemba, Nyandjia

---

[1] Since then, the net enrolment rate has remained above 80% and the completion rate has remained above 85%, although there have been increases and decreases (Directorate of Planning and Information, 2022).

and Tongan, are used for local state-run news broadcasts and as the medium of instruction from Grades 1 to 4 at the primary education level. The main industries are mining, agriculture and tourism, while the economy is a monoculture economy dependent on copper production.

Zambia has not experienced conflict since gaining independence from the United Kingdom in 1964, and it is known as one of the most peaceful countries in Africa. Zambia has also actively contributed to peace and stability in the region by accepting and sheltering refugees from neighbouring countries, such that it is highly regarded in the international community due to its peaceful diplomatic stance. In 2006, the country launched its long-term national strategy called Vision 2030 (Republic of Zambia, 2006), which aims to become a middle-income country by 2030. According to the classification of member countries by income level of the World Bank (2024), the country could move from a low-income to a lower–middle income country classification in 2023. However, it ranks only 154th out of 191 countries in the ranking of the Human Development Index, which is a comprehensive index that assesses long-term progress in the three basic dimensions of human development, namely, healthy longevity, access to knowledge and a humane standard of living (United Nations Development Programme, 2022). To overcome this situation, efforts are being focused on social development, including education and health, in addition to economic development through the diversification of the domestic industry.

The education system in Zambia is composed of seven years of primary education (Grades 1–7) and five years of secondary education (two years of lower secondary education [Grades 8–9] and three years of upper secondary education [Grades 10–12]). Pre-primary education has been provided mainly in private schools; however, it has also been provided in public schools in recent years. An automatic promotion system is basically adopted within the same educational level, but in the case where the academic performance of a child is poor, teachers may opt to retain the child after consulting with the parents of the child.[2] At the end of the final year of each educational level (Grades 7, 9 and 12), a nationwide standardised examination is administered and only those who pass the subjects and number of subjects specified by the Ministry of Education (MOE) can

---

[2] This information was collected from a person related to the Ministry of Education (MOE) during field research.

obtain a full certificate for each level. Consequently, according to their performance, they can advance to the next educational level based on the results of the examination.

History of Educational Development in Zambia and its Current Challenges

In 1996, the Government of Zambia announced 'Educating Our Future' as the national policy for the education sector, which states that access to quality education is a fundamental human right and that the government is obligated to promote the highest standard of education and learning for all (MOE, 1996). Subsequently, the government mainly focused on basic education and concentrated on improving its quantitative and qualitative aspects. In terms of quantitative expansion, the Program for the Advancement of Girls' Education was implemented to promote the enrolment of girls in school, while the Re-entry Policy was introduced to enable pregnant girls to return to school after childbirth. These efforts were integrated with other measures in the Basic Education Subsector Investment Program (BESSIP), which was launched in 1999 with the objective of comprehensively developing the entire basic education sector. In addition, the Free Basic Education Policy was introduced for Grades 1–7 in 2002. Moreover, the following year, a School Feeding Programme was implemented with the aim of improving the attendance of socially vulnerable groups in collaboration with the World Food Programme. In the mid-2000s, the implementation of foreign debt relief measures by donor countries by the achievement of structural adjustment targets imposed on heavily indebted poor countries and higher copper prices due to the increased international demand drove the upturn in the economy of Zambia. Therefore, the allocation for education in the national budget has also increased. As a result, the enrolment status, especially in primary education, has significantly improved with the net enrolment rate reaching 94.3% in 2014 (Directorate of Planning and Information, 2016).

Although the quantitative expansion of primary education is, thus, close to being achieved, the quality of education has become an issue in recent years. Notably, the quality of education in public schools has declined as various initiatives have allowed more children to access schools and the number of children per class has increased. Therefore, the idea that private schools are better than public schools is widespread, especially in urban areas. This trend has also been observed even at the preschool level. For example, in urban informal settlements, a strong demand for low-fee private preschools has been observed, and parents of the urban poor have increasingly viewed investment in these preschools as an important household strategy for the transformation of their children into modern citizens and out of stigmatised lifestyles and marginalised social status (Okitsu et al., 2023). Therefore, qualitative improvement in primary education is also an important issue as emphasised in SDG4, which is the education sector goal of Sustainable Development Goals (SDGs).

As previously mentioned, a number of challenges have been observed in secondary education. In terms of internal efficiency, the repetition rates in 2019 were 2.5%, 6.1%, 1.0% and 1.2% for Grades 8–11, respectively (Directorate of Planning and Information, 2019), which indicates that students are facing challenges in the lower secondary education. Moreover, according to the local teachers, students temporarily drop out of school due to pregnancy, illness, financial difficulties, family circumstances and other reasons. The dropout rates were 2.3%, 2.9%, 1.0% and 1.5% for Grades 8–11, respectively (Directorate of Planning and Information, 2019). The dropout rate in lower secondary education is higher than that in upper secondary education and relatively few students drop out of school when they advance to upper secondary education. Then, what measures are needed to improve the enrolment situation, such that more students can access secondary education and graduate straight from the final grade without undergoing grade repetition or temporary dropout?

Providing an overview of schooling status using a cross-sectional data approach is common. However, cross-sectional data are an amalgamation of various individual cases and are only a picture that appears in the aggregate. Therefore, retrospectively understanding enrolment status based on cross-sectional data is impossible. To achieve the SDGs with the slogan 'No one will be left behind', focusing on enrolment patterns and examining when and what challenges students are facing are important. In recent years, studies have been conducted using longitudinal data focusing on individuals, but the number of such studies remains few.

Based on this awareness of the problem, the author has conducted a research on primary and secondary education in Zambia by tracing the longitudinal trajectories of enrolment using the records of target schools and the results of interviews with subjects and related persons. This study analysed each of the phenomena related to schooling, such as promotion, repetition and dropout, by viewing school enrolment as a pattern and examined the real status and background of these phenomena. In this chapter, the study attempts to present concrete measures that could lead to improvement in primary and secondary education based on cases identified through analysis of longitudinal data thus far and recent trends.

Target Area, School and Data of Study

The target area was selected to be Chipata, the capital of the Eastern Province, which tends to exhibit a lower completion rate in primary education compared with those of other provinces (Directorate of Planning and Information, 2016). The Eastern Province is located at an altitude of 1100 m above sea level and borders Malawi. It has a population of approximately 2.45 million, which makes it the third most populous of the 10 provinces (Zambia Statistics Agency, 2022). Agriculture is flourishing in the area with tobacco, maize, cotton, wheat and other crops being grown.

The target schools for primary education were those that met two criteria, namely, (1) schools with records that could be used to track enrolment patterns and (2) schools where teachers and children were cooperative, because conducting interviews regarding enrolment patterns based on school records was necessary. Given these criteria, the study selected School A, one of the large public schools in Chipata. Classes range from preschool to secondary education. The target schools for the secondary education were limited to schools that were willing to cooperate with the survey. To eliminate bias, four schools were selected: two coed schools, including School A, one boys' school and one girls' school. The three schools apart from School A (Schools B–D) are public schools with only secondary education classes.

The subjects for primary education are children who entered in the target school between 2004 and 2005 and graduated or dropped out from the school by 2014. The secondary education subjects were 12th grade students at the target schools. The longitudinal data were constructed from school records of the target schools, the results of interviews and a questionnaire survey. For recent trends, the study used statistical materials and articles published by the Zambian government and various related literature.

2   ACTUAL ENROLMENT STATUS OF CHILDREN IN PRIMARY EDUCATION

Frequent Enrolment Patterns

As previously mentioned, the net enrolment and completion rates in primary education reached 94.3% and 86.2%, respectively, in 2014 (Directorate of Planning and Information, 2016). However, to the best of our knowledge, studies that elucidated the educational trajectories of children before graduating or dropping out of school are lacking. Therefore, Ezaki and Sekiya (2017) used longitudinal data to identify the enrolment patterns of 204 children. Table 14.1 lists the individual enrolment patterns in descending order of frequency with patterns applicable to two or more persons. Numbers represent grades, while letters represent end-of-year evaluations: *P* stands for pass, *F* for fail, *T* for transfer and *D* for dropout. Those who fail the national standardised examination for Grade 7 and cannot advance to secondary education are denoted as *FL* (L = leave).

The most frequent pattern was '1P2P3P4P5P6P7... P' (i.e. the pattern in which children advance to Grade 7 without grade repetition from the time of admission to the final year of school), which accounts for approximately half of the subjects (90 children; 44.1%). Such a pattern is called *straight progression*. The end-of-year evaluation for Grade 7 was denoted as '7...P' instead of 7P. The reason is that although the study confirmed through the interviews that children who fall under this pattern have

Table 14.1   Ranking of enrolment patterns in primary education

Rank	Enrolment pattern	No. of children	Ratio
1	1P2P3P4P5P6P7...P	90	44.1
2	1P2T	24	11.8
3	1P2P3P4T	22	10.8
4	1P2P3T	17	8.3
5	1P2P3P4P5T	13	6.4
6	1P2P3P4P5P6P7FL	11	5.4
7	1T	9	4.4
8	1P2P3P4P5P6T	6	2.9
9	1P2P3P4P5P6P7D	2	1.0
9	1P2P3P4P5P6D	2	1.0
	Total	204	

Source: Reproduced by the author based on Ezaki and Sekiya (2017)

passed Grade 7, the results of the national standardised examination are outdated and indecipherable, such that the study could not obtain detailed information[3] (Ezaki & Sekiya, 2017). The second frequent pattern was '1P2T' (24 children; 11.8%), while the third was 1P2P3P4T (22 children; 10.8%), which are patterns of school transfers. This pattern of school transfers continues until the fifth place of the ranking of enrolment patterns. In terms of school transfers, 91 out of 204 children transferred, which indicated that a similar number of children as those in the most frequent pattern moved out of the target school during primary education (Ezaki & Sekiya, 2017). Such high number of school transfers is also evident in other surveys conducted by the author. Finally, a pattern of failure to advance to secondary education emerged in the sixth place and a pattern of leaving school with a *D* was first identified in the ninth place.

Enrolment Pattern of Failure to Advance to Secondary Education

Out of the previous 204 children, 19 failed to progress to secondary education (Ezaki & Sekiya, 2017). In this section, the study focuses on enrolment patterns and examines the characteristics of the patterns of failure to progress to secondary education.

Table 14.2 displays only patterns that fail to progress to secondary education (Ezaki & Sekiya, 2017). The most frequent pattern was

Table 14.2   Enrolment patterns of children who were unable to progress to secondary education

No.	Enrolment pattern	No. of children	Ratio
1	1P2P3P4P5P6P7FL	11	5.4
2	1P2P3P4P5P6P7D	2	1.0
3	1P2P3P4P5P6D	2	1.0
4	1P2P//4P5P6P7D	1	0.5
5	1P2P3P4P5P6F6P//7FL	1	0.5
6	1P2P3P4P5D	1	0.5
7	1P2P3P4P5F5P6D	1	0.5
	Total	19	

Source: Reproduced by the author based on Ezaki and Sekiya (2017)

[3] This pattern can be a pattern of passing the examination at first take (7P), failing the examination once and passing it the next time (7F7P), among others.

1P2P3P4P5P6P7FL (i.e. children with straight progression towards Grade 7 without grade repetition but left school after failing the national standardised examination for Grade 7). This proportion is composed of the majority of students who cannot progress to secondary education (11 children). The next most common patterns were 1P2P3P4P5P6P7D and 1P2P3P4P5P6D, which indicates advancement to the next grade but dropping out of school in Grade 7 or 6, respectively. Thus, 16 out of the 19 children fit the pattern of moving straight to the next grade and then suddenly dropping out of school. In other words, the percentage of non-straight progression (an enrolment pattern that includes F for failing or a '//'for temporary dropout) in primary education is extremely low.

In addition, all of the children, even those who eventually left school, were promoted to higher grades. Simply put, while many developing countries tend to exhibit high dropout rates in the early grades, dropouts in the target schools in Zambia have been in school longer than those who dropped out. In addition, in countries such as Zambia, which conduct nationally standardised examinations in the final year of primary education, children tend to drop out of school in the upper grades (UNESCO, 2011).

3   ACTUAL ENROLMENT STATUS OF STUDENTS IN SECONDARY EDUCATION

The previous section discussed that many children advanced straight through primary education and the percentage of non-straight progression was extremely low even when focusing on the pattern of failure to advance to secondary education. What, then, is the ratio of straight and non-straight progression in secondary education, which faces challenges in internal efficiency? In addition, in the case of non-straight progression, when and what challenges do students face? In this section, the study focuses on these points and elucidates the actual enrolment status in secondary education.

Straight and Non-straight Progression

Ezaki and Nakamura (2018) analysed the percentage of straight and non-straight progression by gender using data from 100 students (Fig. 14.1). The results demonstrated that straight progression was the highest for

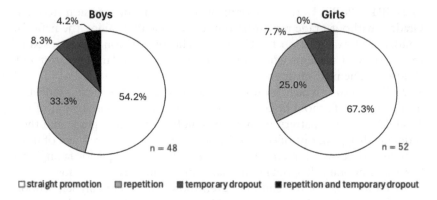

Fig. 14.1 Percentage of straight and non-straight progression by gender. (Source: Reproduced by the author based on Ezaki and Nakamura [2018])

boys and girls, which accounts for more than half of the total for each. The percentage was higher for girls than for boys (boys: 54.2%, girls: 67.3%), although the study identified no statistically significant difference. One of the reasons for this result is that girls are more likely to drop out than repeating a grade if they receive negative academic results (IOB, 2008; Ministry of Education, Science, Vocational Training and Early Education & UNICEF, 2014). In other words, a possibility exists that a proportion of girls whose performance was less favourable dropped out of school, which results in a lower proportion of non-straight progression and that, as a result, the proportion of boys with non-straight progression was higher.

Non-straight progression, including repetition (boys: 33.3%, girls: 25.0%), followed by non-straight progression, including temporary dropout (boys: 8.3%, girls: 7.7%), follows the percentage after straight promotion. The pattern of experiencing repetition and temporary dropout was observed only among boys (4.2%).

When and What Challenges Do Students Face?

Ezaki and Nakamura (2018) focused on 39 students who did not achieve straight progression and analysed their enrolment patterns in detail. First, examining the pattern of those who failed at the end-of-year evaluation (Table 14.3), the highest number of students failed at lower secondary education (18 students), out of whom one failed in Grade 8, while the

Table 14.3 Enrolment patterns of students who failed the end-of-year evaluation

No.	Enrolment pattern	No. of children	Years of schooling	No. of repetitions
1	1-1P2P3P4P5P6P7P8P9P10P11P12	1	13	1
2	1F1F1P2P3P4P5P6P7P8P9P10P11P12	1	14	2
3	1P2P3F3P4P5P6P7P8P9P10P11P12	1	13	1
4	1P2P3P3P4P5P6P7P8P9P10P11P12	1	13	1
5	1P2P3P4F4P5P6P7P8P9P10P11P12	1	13	1
6	1P2P3P4F3P4P5P6P7P8P9P10P11P12	1	14	1
7	1P2P3P4P5F5P6P7P8P9P10P11P12	1	13	1
8	1P2P3P4P5P6F6P7P8P9P10P11P12	2	13	1
9	1P2P3P4P5P6P7F7P8P9P10P11P12	2	13	1
10	1P2P3P4P5P6P7P8F8P9P10P11P12	1	13	1
11	1P2P3P4P5P6P7P8P9F//9P10P11P12	2	14	1
12	1P2P3P5P6P7P8P9P9P10P11P12	1	12	1
13	1P2P3P4P5P6P7P8P9F9P10P11P12	10	13	1
14	1P2P3P4P5P6P7P8P9F8P9P10P11P12	2	14	1
15	1P2P3P4P5P6P7P8P9F9F9P10P11P12	1	14	2
16	1P2P3P4P5P6P7P8P9-9-9P10P11P12	1	14	2
17	1P2P3P4P5P6P7P8P9P10P11F11P12	2	13	1
	Total	31		

Source: Reproduced by the author based on Ezaki and Nakamura (2018)

others failed in Grade 9. The finding of many repetitions in Grade 9 among students in secondary education is consistent with the national data (Directorate of Planning and Information, 2022). Regarding the number of times that a student failed in the evaluation, 28 failed once, while 3 students failed twice, which indicates that the number of students who failed two or more times tends to be extremely small.

Moreover, focusing on individual patterns, the study identified two extraordinary patterns (Ezaki & Nakamura, 2018). The first is a pattern in which a student fails the end-of-year evaluation in one grade and then starts over one grade lower instead of repeating the same grade in the following year (Nos. 6 and 14). For example, student No. 14 failed the end-of-year evaluation in Grade 9; however, instead of re-registering in Grade 9 the following year, he registered in Grade 8, which is one grade lower and remediated two years of lower secondary education

(1P2P3P4P5P6P7P8P**9F8P**9P10P11P12).[4] The second is a pattern in which a student passes in the end-of-year evaluation for one grade but repeats the same grade the following year (Nos. 4 and 12). For instance, student No. 12 is still registered in Grade 9 in the following year despite previously passing the end-of-year evaluation in Grade 9 (1P2P3P4P5P6P 7P8P**9P9P**10P11P12).

Next, Table 14.4 depicts the enrolment patterns of those who temporarily dropped out of school. In terms of timing, two students dropped out during primary education, seven during secondary education and one between primary and secondary education. The result indicated that, similar to the repetition pattern, temporary dropout is relatively common in secondary education (Ezaki & Nakamura, 2018). Moreover, eight out of ten students have suddenly and temporarily left school without grade repetition. Regarding duration, six and four students dropped out for one and two years, respectively. Although the target area covered by Ezaki

Table 14.4 Enrolment patterns of students who experienced temporary dropout

No.	Enrolment pattern	No. of children	Years of schooling	No. of repetitions
1	1-////4P5P6P7P8P9P10P11P12	1	12	2
2	1P2P3P4P//5P6P7P8P9P10P11P12	1	13	1
3	1P2P3P4P5P6P7P//8P9P10P11P12	1	13	1
4	1P2P3P4P5P6P7P8P//9P10P//11P12	1	14	2
5	1P2P3P4P5P6P7P8P9F//9P10P11P12	2	14	1
6	1P2P3P4P5P6P7P8P9P//10P11P12	1	13	1
7	1P2P3P4P5P6P7P8P9P////10P11P12	1	14	2
8	1P2P3P4P5P6P7P8P9P10-//11P12	1	13	1
9	1P2P3P4P5P6P7P8P9P10P////11P12	1	14	2
	Total	10		

Source: Reproduced by the author based on Ezaki and Nakamura (2018)

[4] Contrary to the period covered by the data in the study (Ezaki & Nakamura, 2018), nowadays, if a student fails a national standardized examination for Grade 9, he or she can choose to repeat either Grade 8 or 9. Therefore, it is conceivable that the number of students with such a pattern, like No. 14, has increased.

(2019) was different, the number of years of temporary dropout was also one or two, which analysed temporary dropout patterns. This finding implies that the likelihood of returning to school decreases after three or more years out of school.

4 Factors That Inhibit the Progression and Continuation of Schooling

Barrier of the National Standardised Examination

In Sect. 2, the study analysed the actual enrolment status in primary education, while in Sect. 3, the study analysed the actual enrolment status in secondary education. A national standardised examination is administered at the end of the final year of each level of education and the study found that the examination was a barrier for children in both levels of education (Ezaki & Sekiya, 2017; Ezaki & Nakamura, 2018).

The national standardised examination for Grade 7 effectively functioned as a ranking that sifts children into secondary education, because an insufficient capacity (number of acceptable students) was previously noted in secondary education. Education officials determined the passing line for the national standardised examination on the basis of available school space in each state. Therefore, an urgent need emerged to improve the environment, such as expanding the number of classrooms and teachers in lower secondary education. The efforts of the Zambian government have been successful, such that the pass rate for the national standardised examination for Grade 7 in 2018 was 100%, which enabled all children who took the examination to advance to Grade 8 (Kachabe, 2018). This phenomenon continued through 2019 (Directorate of Planning and Information, 2019) and 2020 (Directorate of Planning and Information, 2022). However, a few stakeholders in education have emerged to oppose this move (Lusaka Times, 2022), because a number of children are insufficiently proficient in learning and this topic has been highly controversial. In 2023, the automatic promotion from Grades 7 to 8 was abolished with a pass rate of only 69.72% for the current year (Ministry of Education, 2023). Therefore, the future challenge is to improve the quality of education and level of proficiency.

For the national standardised examination for Grade 9, the pass rates in 2019 and 2020 were 46.14% (Directorate of Planning and Information,

2019) and 53.07% (Directorate of Planning and Information, 2022), respectively, which indicates the extent of the hurdle. According to the Directorate of Planning and Information (2022), the pass rates of Grade 9 are not based on available spaces in Grade 10. Therefore, the proficiency of students in the content they are learning is important. Alternatively, analysis of enrolment patterns in the previous section identified a pattern of students failing the national standardised examination for Grade 9 and registering in Grade 8, which is one grade below, instead of registering in Grade 9 in the following year (Ezaki & Nakamura, 2018). According to the teachers at the target schools, if a classroom of Grade 9 is already full, students may be placed one grade level below where space is available (Ezaki & Nakamura, 2018). In other words, in addition to their lack of academic ability, students may face challenges beyond their personal scope, such as inadequate school facilities, which leads to less favourable patterns of conditions compared with typical repetition.[5]

Impact of Economic Situation and Birth Order on Progression

Various factors have been cited as disincentives for progression and continued schooling. For example, the Ministry of Education, Science, Vocational Training and Early Education and the United Nations Children's Fund (MESVTEE & UNICEF, 2014) cite demand side economics, such as household poverty, child labour and rural/urban residence, and sociocultural factors, including early marriage, teenage pregnancies and gendered roles and responsibilities, as barriers and bottlenecks to education.[6] Previous studies have reported economic reasons as the most significant of these factors (e.g. Central Statistical Office, 2011; Central Statistical Office & ORC Macro, 2003; USAID, 2014). In the study by Ezaki and Nakamura (2018), the reasons for non-straight progression included 'my family was financially weak and I had to work to help with the family farming business', 'I was working while also attending school and did not have enough time to study' and 'I could not afford to pay the examination fee for the national standardized examinations'. Therefore, Ezaki and Nakamura

[5] However, as previously mentioned, unlike the period covered by this research data (Ezaki & Nakamura, 2018), presently, if a student fails a national standardised examination for Grade 9, he or she can choose to repeat either Grade 8 or 9.
[6] It also cited supply side including education facilities and services, school health and nutritional interventions, and capacities of education institutions (schools) (MESVTEE & UNICEF, 2014).

(2018) categorised the subjects into straight and non-straight progression groups and compared the composition of economic levels in both groups and focused on the number of possessions for each household. The results revealed that straight progression exhibited the highest percentage of families with more possessions, while non-straight progression displayed the highest percentage of families with fewer possessions (Fig. 14.2). This scenario indicates that students from families with fewer possessions (i.e. those considered belonging to low economic levels) are more likely to become non-straight progression[7] (Ezaki & Nakamura, 2018).

Moreover, in Zambia and many other developing countries, as previously noted, children typically help households by joining the labour force during economic hardship. In such cases, older siblings are considered more likely to participate in such labour[8] (Dammert, 2010; Seid & Gurmu, 2015). Meanwhile, younger siblings are more likely to go to school and achieve higher educational attainment than siblings who came in earlier in

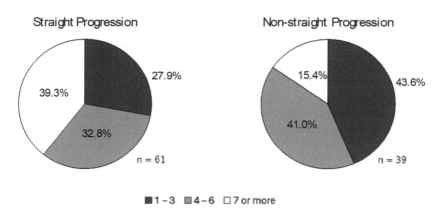

Fig. 14.2 Percentage of the number of possessions in straight and non-straight progression. (Source: Reproduced by the author based on Ezaki and Nakamura [2018])

---

[7] When the same analysis was conducted by gender, it became clear that girls had a higher percentage of households with more possessions, whereas boys had by far the highest percentage of households with fewer possessions (Ezaki & Nakamura, 2018). Therefore, one of the reasons for the higher percentage of straight progression for girls (Fig. 14.1) is also their economic level.

[8] The reason is that parents tend to engage these children in more labour believing that the older ones have more physical power and are mentally mature and, therefore, can earn more.

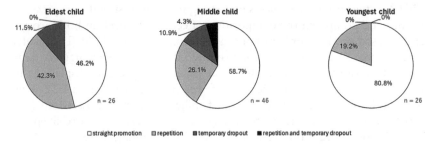

Fig. 14.3 Percentage of straight and non-straight progression by birth order. (Source: Reproduced by the author based on Ezaki and Nakamura [2018])

the birth order (Ejrnæs & Pörtner, 2004; Kumar, 2016). Therefore, the study analysed birth order in terms of straight and non-straight progression and found that the proportion of the youngest child was higher than the eldest child in straight progression, whereas that of the eldest child was higher than the youngest child in non-straight progression (Ezaki & Nakamura, 2018). Moreover, a comparison of enrolment status by birth order reveals that none of the youngest students experienced temporary dropout (Fig. 14.3). In other words, the youngest children do not experience engaging in labour and not going to school due to their difficult economic situation.

Based on the two abovementioned points, the study infers that students who are in a difficult economic situation and eldest children tend to exhibit low rates of straight progression due to the burden of labour and other commitments.

5   Towards Improvement of the Enrolment Status

This chapter examined the actual enrolment status and the challenges faced by learners in primary and secondary education through cases that have been revealed by the analysis of longitudinal data thus far and recent trends. Results showed that in primary education (Ezaki & Sekiya, 2017), the most common pattern was to progress straight from Grade 1 to Grade 7 without grade repetition or temporarily dropout. Moreover, dropout patterns revealed that straight progression was more common. In other words, internal efficiency is in a favourable condition. However, there is a great deal of controversy surrounding the national standardised examinations for Grade 7 children. Since a number of children lack sufficient proficiency in learning, future challenges include improving quality and proficiency.

In secondary education (Ezaki & Nakamura, 2018), students with non-straight progression represent approximately 40% of the total, which reveals very diverse enrolment patterns. Among them, the study noted patterns in which students failed the end-of-year evaluation but were not registered in the same grade in the following year. Instead, they were registered one grade below, which is a worse case than normal repetition. Moreover, another scenario in which students temporarily dropped out from school and then returned after two years was found. Furthermore, there are a number of different challenges like lack of classrooms, grade repetition, temporary dropout and national standardised examinations in Zambia, but the study found that students who were in economic hardship and the eldest students were more likely to face these challenges.

To enable more students to access to secondary education, progress straight through and continue their studies, regular attention and care to these students and support in school life is essential. Moreover, urgently resolving issues that extend beyond the scope of individuals, such as the lack of school facilities and classrooms, the shortage of qualified teachers and the reduction of the burden of school fees and other educational expenses through free secondary education, will also be important.

This study is a case study that analysed the actual enrolment status in target schools located in the Eastern Province. Therefore, the results cannot be applied to Zambia as a whole. As such, conducting similar surveys in capital cities and other states with different regional environments and comparing their respective trends in the future are desirable avenues for further research.

REFERENCES

Central Statistical Office. (2011). *Living conditions monitoring survey report 2006 and 2010*. Central Statistical Office.

Central Statistical Office, ORC Macro. (2003). *Zambia DHS EdData survey 2002: Education data for decision-making*. Central Statistical Office, ORC Macro.

Dammert, C. A. (2010). Siblings, child labor, and schooling in Nicaragua and Guatemala. *Journal of Population Economics, 23*(1), 199–224.

Directorate of Planning and Information, Ministry of Education, Republic of Zambia. (2019). *Educational statistical bulletin 2019*. Ministry of Education.

Directorate of Planning and Information, Ministry of Education, Republic of Zambia. (2022). *Educational statistical bulletin 2020*. Ministry of Education.

Directorate of Planning and Information, Ministry of General Education, Republic of Zambia. (2016). *2015 Educational statistical bulletin*. Ministry of General Education.

Ejrnæs, M., & Pörtner, C. C. (2004). Birth order and the intrahousehold allocation of time and education. *The Review of Economics and Statistics, 86*(4), 1008–1019.

Ezaki, N. (2019). Enrolment patterns of individual children left behind in the trend towards 'quality education': A case study of primary education in Nepal. *Education 3–13, International Journal of Primary, Elementary and Early Years Education, 47*(5), 52–533.

Ezaki, N., & Nakamura, S. (2018). Sutorēto ni shinkyū dekinai Zambia chūtō kyōiku no seitotachi [Secondary education students who cannot advance to the next grade smoothly in Zambia]. In T. Sekiya (Ed.), *Kaihatsu tojōkoku de manabu kodomotachi: Makuroseisaku ni shisuru mikurona shūgakujittaibunseki [Children who are learning in developing countries: Micro analysis of state of enrolment that contributes to macro policies]* (pp. 119–138). Kwansei Gakuin University Press.

Ezaki, N., & Sekiya, T. (2017). Study on individual children's enrollment patterns in the Republic of Zambia: Focusing on children who cannot move on to secondary education. *Kwansei Gakuin University Social Science Review, 22*, 19–31.

IOB (Policy and Operations Evaluation Department). (2008). *Primary education in Zambia*. IOB Impact Evaluation. No. 312. IOB.

Kachabe, H. (2018, December 24). ECZ records 100% pass rate on Grade 7 results. *Lusaka Star*. https://lusakastar.com/news/ecz-records-100-pass-rate-on-grade-7-results

Kumar, S. (2016). The effect of birth order on schooling in India. *Applied Economics Letters, 23*(18), 1325–1328.

Lusaka Times. (2022, January 3). Some stakeholders in the education opposed to Decision to allow all grade 7 pupils progress to Grade 8. *Lusaka Times*. https://www.lusakatimes.com/2022/01/03/some-stakeholders-in-the-education-opposed-to-decision-to-allow-all-grade-7-pupils-progress-to-grade-8/

Ministry of Education, Republic of Zambia. (1996). *Educating our future: National policy on education*. Ministry of Education.

Ministry of Education, Republic of Zambia. (2023, December 26). 2023 Grade 7 & 9 examinations released. *Ministry of Education*. https://www.edu.gov.zm/?p=5389

Ministry of Education, Science, Vocational Training and Early Education & United Nations Children's Fund (MESVTEE & UNICEF). (2014). *Global initiative on out-of-school children*. MESVTEE & UNICEF.

Ministry of Education, Science, Vocational Training and Early Education (MESVTEE). (2015). *Education for all 2015 National review: Zambia.* MESVTEE.

Okitsu, T., Edwards, B. D., Mwanza, P., & Miller, S. (2023). Low-fee private preschools as the symbol of imagined 'modernity'?—Parental perspectives on early childhood care and education (ECCE) in an urban informal settlement in Zambia. *International Journal of Educational Development, 97,* 1–18.

Republic of Zambia. (2006). *Vision 2023: A prosperous middle-income nation by 2030.* Republic of Zambia.

Seid, Y., & Gurmu, S. (2015). The role of birth order in child labour and schooling. *Applied Economics, 47*(49), 5262–5281.

United Nations Development Programme (UNDP). (2022). *Human development report 2021/2022: Uncertain times, unsettled lives: Shaping our future in a transforming world.* UNDP.

United Nations Educational, Scientific and Cultural Organization (UNESCO). (2011). *EFA global monitoring report 2011—The hidden crisis: Armed conflict and education.* UNESCO.

United Nations Educational, Scientific and Cultural Organization (UNESCO). (2015). *EFA global monitoring report 2015: Education for all 2000–2015: Achievements and challenges.* UNESCO.

United Nations Educational, Scientific and Cultural Organization (UNESCO). (2016). *Zambia education policy review: Paving the way for SDG 4—Education 2030.* UNESCO.

United Nations Educational, Scientific and Cultural Organization (UNESCO). (2020). *Global education monitoring report 2020—Inclusion and education: All means all.* UNESCO.

United States Agency for International Development (USAID). (2014). *Baseline Survey: School WASH Facility Assessment.*

World Bank. (2024). World Bank Country and Lending Groups. *World Bank.* https://datahelpdesk.worldbank.org/knowledgebase/articles/906519-world-bank-country-and-lending-groups

Zambia Statistics Agency. (2022). *2022 Census of population and housing: Preliminary report.* Zambia Statistics Agency.

PART III

International Comparative Analysis: Factors Preventing Children from Enrolment

Common Enrolment Patterns, Grade Repetition and Unique Cases: International Comparative Analysis on Enrolment Status

Naruho Ezaki 🆔

1 INTRODUCTION

In Part 2, we used longitudinal data to analyse the enrolment status in target countries in Latin America, Africa and Asia and captured them as patterns. What are the similarities and differences seen in the results and trends? In Part 3, we examine the factors that hinder schooling by conducting an international comparison of the actual enrolment status that has been revealed thus far.

This chapter focuses on three countries, namely, Honduras in Central America, Nepal in South Asia and Myanmar in Southeast Asia. The study compares the actual enrolment status in primary education and analyses the similarities and differences among them. It also examines the factors

N. Ezaki (✉)
Faculty of Global Culture and Communication, Aichi Shukutoku University, Nagoya, Japan
e-mail: nezaki@asu.aasa.ac.jp

© The Author(s), under exclusive license to Springer Nature Switzerland AG 2024
T. Sekiya et al. (eds.), *Towards Ensuring Inclusive and Equitable Quality Education for All*, International and Development Education, https://doi.org/10.1007/978-3-031-70266-2_15

that hinder children from continuing their studies by addressing the factors frequently mentioned by previous studies such as the reality of grade repetition and temporary dropout; the relationship between grade repetition, dropout and age at school entry.

2   EDUCATION SYSTEM AND EDUCATIONAL STATUS IN TARGET COUNTRIES

To compare the actual enrolment status in the three countries, this section briefly summarises the education system and scenario in each country.[1] Honduras, Nepal and Myanmar features the 9–3 (i.e. 9 years of basic education and 3 years of secondary education), 8–4 (8 years of basic education and 4 years of secondary education) and 5–4–2 (5 years of primary education, 4 years of lower secondary education and 2 years of upper secondary education) system, respectively. With regard to primary education (lower basic education) covered in this chapter, Honduras has 6 years, while Nepal and Myanmar have 5 years.

Although much discussion has been held about an automatic promotion system in recent years (e.g. United Nations Educational, Scientific and Cultural Organization [UNESCO], 2020), Honduras has not permanently adopted an automatic promotion system, which was only implemented when Hurricane Mitch and a military coup had occurred in 1998 and 2009, respectively. In Nepal, a similar system called continuous assessment system (CAS) was introduced since the ninth plan (1997–2002) by the Ministry of Education of Nepal. CAS was originally initiated for lower grades; however, it has been available for Grades 1–7 since 2009. In Myanmar, the continuous assessment and progression system (CAPS) was introduced in 1998 to eliminate the high rate of grade repetition and dropout. Since the introduction of CAPS, the educational assessment system in Myanmar at the primary education stage has effectively become automatic promotion. The official age at school entrance is 6 years old in Honduras, while in Nepal and Myanmar, it is 5 years old.

Against this background, using data from the Global Education Monitoring Report[2] (UNESCO, 2015, 2017, 2020) published by the

---

[1] For more information, see the chapters for each country (Honduras: Chap. 5; Nepal: Chap. 7; Myanmar: Chap. 8).

[2] The 2015 report is called the 'EFA Global Monitoring Report'. Since 2016, the name of the report has been changed to the 'Global Education Monitoring Report'.

Table 15.1   Net enrolment and completion rates in the target countries

	Net enrolment rate				Completion rate	
	1999	*2012*	*2015*	*2018*	*2010–2015*	*2018*
Honduras	88	94	94	80	83	87
Nepal	69	99	97	96	75	73
Myanmar	–	–	95	98	81	83

Source: Prepared by the author based on the data from UNESCO (2015, 2017, 2020)

UNESCO, this section reviews trends in net enrolment and completion rates in primary education for each target country (Table 15.1). The net enrolment rates since 1999 for Honduras were 88% in 1999 and reached 94% in 2012. However, by 2018, the rate had dropped to 80%. As for Nepal, this rate reached 69% as of 1999, which is approximately 20% lower than that of Honduras. However, subsequent efforts by the government and international aid agencies have been successful, which reached 99% in 2012. Since then, the rate has remained at more than 95%. For Myanmar, the data for 1999 and 2012 were unavailable, but the quantitative expansion of education is close to being achieved, as they reached 95% and 98% as of 2015 and 2018, respectively. For completion rates, the study obtained data for 2010–2015 (UNESCO, 2017) and 2018 (UNESCO, 2020). The completion rate in Honduras was 83% in 2010–2015, which increased to 87% in 2018. For Nepal, the rate has slightly decreased from 75% in 2010–2015 to 73% in 2018. For Myanmar, the rate slightly increased from 81% in 2010–2015 to 83% in 2018. These statistics show that the completion rate of Nepal is lower than that of the other two countries. Finally, the study notes the percentage of overaged learners as of 2018 (UNESCO, 2020). Honduras has only 12%, while Nepal has three times as many at 36%. Although the study was unable to identify the data for Myanmar, Yoshida (2018) noted overage issues in the country.

3   RESEARCH METHODS

This chapter compares the enrolment status in primary education in Honduras, Nepal and Myanmar to elucidate the similarities and differences among the three countries. The study also examines the factors that hinder children from continuing their studies. Table 15.2 provides

Table 15.2 Characteristics of target data

	Honduras	*Nepal*	*Myanmar*
Target country	Suburban area	Suburban area	Urban area
No. of target schools	6 schools	5 schools	5 schools
No. of subjects	1210	84	4509
Entrance years of subjects	1986–1994	2003–2007	2008–2012

Source: Prepared by the author for this chapter based on the respective cited papers (Sekiya, 2014; Ezaki, 2019; Yoshida, 2024)

information[3] on target areas, schools and subjects[4] for each target country. The target schools in Honduras are composed of 6 schools located in rural cities, which covers 1210 children entered school between 1986 and 1994. The target schools in Nepal are 5 schools located in a suburban area in which 84 children entered school between 2003 and 2007. The target schools in Myanmar are 5 schools located in urban areas, which covers 4509 children entered school between 2008 and 2012.

The data sources are composed of school records such as school registers and mark ledgers. The study longitudinally tracked the information from these school records on registration, dropouts and transfers to target schools, as well as end-of-year evaluation by teachers, to construct a database. The study also conducted semi-structured interviews with principals and teachers as well as home visit surveys to confirm the consistency of the data.

As mentioned in Part 2, this study captures enrolment status as patterns, which are represented by a string of letters as an accumulation of grade promotion, repetition and dropout. The study then compares the results of the three countries with a focus on two aspects: (1) ranking of enrolment patterns in terms of frequency of occurrence and (2) enrolment patterns leading to graduation or dropout.

Table 15.2 demonstrates how the data for the target countries differ in terms of year, region and number of subjects, among others. Therefore, the similarities and differences among the three countries, which will

---

[3] For details, see the respective papers (Honduras: Sekiya (2014), Nepal: Ezaki (2019), Myanmar: Yoshida (2024)).

[4] In this study, in principle, the children who were included in the analysis were those who were confirmed to have graduated from or dropped out of the target schools, died or left the target schools due to a transfer.

emerge after the analysis of enrolment patterns and factors that have been frequently mentioned in previous studies, are discussed and examined instead of the positive and negative points of the enrolment status.

4 RESULTS

Ranking of Enrolment Patterns

Table 15.3 lists the enrolment patterns of children in the target schools in the three countries in descending order of frequency, from first to tenth place or to the rank of two or more applicable children.[5] The numbers in the pattern refer to grades, while the letters refer to end-of-year evaluations in which *P*, *F* and *D* denote pass, fail and dropout, respectively. '//' indicates that the children have not attended school for 1 year (i.e. a temporary dropout).

For the target schools in Honduras, the study identified 291 enrolment patterns for 1210 subjects (Sekiya, 2014). The most common pattern was straight graduation (1P2P3P4P5P6P), in which children registered in Grade 1 and graduated without grade repetition or temporary dropout until Grade 6, which is the final year in primary education. The second most common pattern was for children to drop out of school less than 1 year after registering for the first year (1D). The third most common pattern was for children to fail in their first year but to advance steadily thereafter and graduate (1F1P2P3P4P5P6P). The fourth most common pattern was that of children who passed the first grade and advanced to the second grade but dropped out (1P2D). Furthermore, the fifth most common pattern was that of children who failed in the first year and re-registered in the first grade in the second year but dropped out in the middle of the year (1F1D). Patterns including grade repetitions were identified from the third place of the ranking of enrolment patterns.

For the target schools in Nepal, the study identified 38 enrolment patterns for 84 subjects (Ezaki, 2019). The most frequent pattern was straight graduation (1P2P3P4P5P), as target schools in Honduras. The next two patterns followed in a tie for second place; the first one was '1D', in which the children dropped out of school within less than 1 year after registering

---

[5] Regarding the enrolment pattern ranking for Nepal, up to seventh place is a pattern with two or more applicable persons and eighth place is a pattern with only one applicable person. Therefore, the patterns of the eighth place are not shown in Table 15.3.

Table 15.3 Ranking of enrolment patterns in target schools in each target country

Rank	Enrolment pattern	No. of students	Ratio
Honduras			
1	1P2P3P4P5P6P	352	29.1
2	1D	110	9.1
3	1F1P2P3P4P5P6P	79	6.5
4	1P2D	47	3.9
5	1F1D	42	3.5
6	1P2F2P3P4P5P6P	27	2.2
7	1P2P3D	24	2.0
8	1P2P3F3P4P5P6P	23	1.9
9	1P2P3P4F4P5P6P	20	1.7
10	1P2P3P4D	16	1.3
Total	291 patterns	1210	
Nepal			
1	1P2P3P4P5P	26	31.0
2	1D	6	7.1
2	1P//2P3P4P5P	6	7.1
4	1F1P2P3P4P5P	4	4.8
4	1F1F1P2P3P4P5P	4	4.8
6	1P2P3P4P5D	3	3.6
7	1P2P3P4D	2	2.4
7	1P2F2D	2	2.4
7	1P2D	2	2.4
Total	38 patterns	84	
Myanmar			
1	1P2P3P4P5P	4341	96.3
2	1P	30	0.7
3	1F1P2P3P4P5P	26	0.6
4	1P2F2P3P4P5P	25	0.6
5	1P2P3P	15	0.3
5	1P2P	15	0.3
7	1P2P3P4P	9	0.2
8	1P2P3F3P4P5P	8	0.2
9	1F1P2P3P4P5C	5	0.1
10	1P2P3P4F4P5P	4	0.1
Total	34 patterns	4509	

Source: Prepared by the author for this chapter based on the respective cited papers (Sekiya, 2014; Ezaki, 2019; Yoshida, 2024)

for the first year; the second one was 1P//2P3P4P5P: after passing the first grade, the children took a year off (temporary dropout) in the second year, returned to Grade 2 in the third year and then progressed smoothly to graduation. Moreover, the next two patterns tie in the fourth place: a pattern of failure in the first year but straight progress in the second and subsequent years (1F1P2P3P4P5P) and a pattern in which the children repeated a grade for two consecutive years in the first grade, then progressed smoothly to the next grade and graduated (1F1F1P2P3P4P5P). Patterns including grade repetitions were identified from the fourth position, while those including temporary dropout from school were identified from the second position of the ranking of enrolment patterns.

For the target schools in Myanmar, the study noted 34 enrolment patterns for 4509 subjects (Yoshida, 2024). The most common pattern was straight graduation pattern (1P2P3P4P5P), as target schools in Honduras and Nepal. The second most common pattern was leaving the target school after passing the first year (1P). The third most common pattern was for children to fail in their first year and then smoothly advance and graduate (1F1P2P3P4P5P). The fourth most common pattern was for children to fail in the second grade in the second year and then progress steadily and graduate (1P2F2P3P4P5P). Next, the next two patterns are in a tie for the fifth place. The first is a pattern of children who advanced from Grade 1 to 3 without grade repetition but left the target school after passing Grade 3 (1P2P3P). The second refers to a pattern of leaving the target school after passing Grade 2 in the second year without grade repetition (1P2P). Patterns including grade repetition were confirmed from the third place of the ranking.

Graduation and Dropout Patterns

The study compared previous enrolment patterns by dividing them into frequent graduation patterns among graduates and frequent dropout patterns among dropouts. First, in terms of graduation pattern (Table 15.4), the study observed the most frequent pattern of straight graduation (1P2P3P4P5P or 1P2P3P4P5P6P) without grade repetition or temporary dropout in all target schools in Honduras, Nepal and Myanmar. For the second most frequent patterns, the study observed a pattern of children who repeated the first grade in the first year of registration and then smoothly progressed to graduation (1F1P2P3P4P5P or 1F1P2P3P4P5P6P) in the target schools in Honduras and Myanmar. In contrast, in the target schools

Table 15.4 Ranking of graduation patterns in target schools in each target country

Rank	Enrolment pattern	No. of students	Ratio
Honduras			
1	1P2P3P4P5P6P	352	29.1
2	<u>1F</u>1P2P3P4P5P6P	79	6.5
3	1P<u>2F</u>2P3P4P5P6P	27	2.2
4	1P2P<u>3F</u>3P4P5P6P	23	1.9
5	1P2P3P<u>4F</u>4P5P6P	20	1.7
Nepal			
1	1P2P3P4P5P	26	31.0
2	1P<u>//</u>2P3P4P5P	6	7.1
3	<u>1F</u>1P2P3P4P5P	4	4.8
3	<u>1F1F</u>1P2P3P4P5P	4	4.8
Myanmar			
1	1P2P3P4P5P	4341	96.3
2	<u>1F</u>1P2P3P4P5P	26	0.6
3	1P<u>2F</u>2P3P4P5P	25	0.6
4	1P2P<u>3F</u>3P4P5P	8	0.2
5	1P2P3P<u>4F</u>4P5P	4	0.1

Source: Prepared by the author for this chapter based on the respective cited papers (Sekiya, 2014; Ezaki, 2019; Yoshida, 2024)

in Nepal, the study noted a pattern of children who passed the first grade that underwent a 1-year leave of absence (temporary dropout) in the second year, returned to Grade 2 in the third year and then smoothly advanced and graduated (1P//2P3P4P5P). The third through fifth places in the target schools in Honduras and Myanmar displayed similar enrolment patterns in which children repeat the same grade once in Grades 2–4, in descending order, but otherwise advance through the grades and graduate without grade repetition. Alternatively, for the target schools in Nepal, the third place was occupied by two patterns: in the first, children repeated Grade 1 in their first year of registration and then smoothly progressed to graduation (1F1P2P3P4P5P) and in the second, children repeated the first grade twice, but after that progressed smoothly and graduated (1F1F1P2P3P4P5P).

Next, in terms of patterns leading to drop out from the target schools in Honduras and Nepal (Table 15.5), the pattern of dropping out of school after less than 1 year of registration (1D) ranked first. In Myanmar, the pattern of leaving the target school without registering for the next

Table 15.5 Ranking of dropout patterns in target schools in each target country

Rank	Enrolment pattern	No. of students	Ratio
Honduras			
1	1D	110	9.1
2	1P2D	47	3.9
3	**1F**1D	42	3.5
4	1P2P3D	24	2.0
5	1P2P3P4D	16	1.3
Nepal			
1	1D	6	7.1
2	1P2P3P4P5D	3	3.6
3	1P2P3P4D	2	2.4
3	1P**2F**2D	2	2.4
3	1P2D	2	2.4
Myanmar			
1	1P	30	0.7
2	1P2P3P	15	0.3
3	1P2P	15	0.3
4	1P2P3P4P	9	0.2

Source: Prepared by the author for this chapter based on the respective cited papers (Sekiya, 2014; Ezaki, 2019; Yoshida, 2024)

year after passing the first grade (1P) was the most frequent pattern in the target schools. Therefore, early dropout from school after registration was the most frequent pattern in all target countries. Moreover, in the target schools in Honduras and Nepal, the pattern of dropout, including grade repetition, was excluded from the first and second places but included in the third place. The study identified no patterns of dropout, including grade repetition, in the target schools in Myanmar.

5   DISCUSSION

Similarities and Differences in the Rankings of Enrolment Patterns

The most frequent pattern in the target schools in Honduras, Nepal and Myanmar (Table 15.3) was straight graduation, in which children graduated without grade repetition or temporarily dropout. This pattern is the most ideal among the enrolment patterns. Next was the pattern of early dropout from school after registration, such as dropout in the middle of

Grade 1 or after passing it. This pattern is the least desirable, which is contrary to the pattern of straight graduation. In terms of subsequent rankings, children from the target schools in Honduras were divided into two patterns: those that took the second shortest 7 years to graduate and those that failed to complete 1 year or passed Grades 1–3 and then dropped out. This trend was also observed in target schools in Myanmar. This situation is called the *enrolment divide*, that is, a polarisation of enrolment status (Sekiya, 2014). With the population in such a state of near polarisation, believing that the repetition rate, dropout rate and years of completion, which are viewed simply as averages, accurately represent the group is difficult. In other words, the averages calculated from them are less valid and using them as a basis for policy decisions is difficult. When formulating macro educational policies, elucidating such micro educational realities is important (Sekiya, 2018), especially now that the SDGs advocate for the motto 'No one will be left behind'. As such, focusing on each and every child is critical.

Regarding the number of enrolment patterns, the study identified 291 patterns for 1210 children in the target schools in Honduras, 38 patterns for 84 children in the target schools in Nepal and 34 patterns for 4509 children in the target schools in Myanmar (Table 15.3). Based on these figures, the ratio of the number of subjects to the number of enrolment patterns was calculated to be 1:0.240 for Honduras, 1:0.452 for Nepal and 1:0.008 for Myanmar. What do these numbers mean? The enrolment pattern consists of a combination of registered grades, end-of-year evaluations, such as pass or fail, and the timing of temporary dropout or dropout. In other words, an enrolment pattern differs by the frequency and timing of failure (grade repetition) or temporary dropout from school, such that the more often children experience them, the more complex the enrolment pattern becomes. Moreover, the more such children, the more diverse their enrolment patterns, and therefore the greater their number. Conversely, where an automatic promotion system is adopted, such as primary education in Japan, nearly all children graduate without grade repetition or temporary dropout, such that the enrolment pattern is as close to 1 as possible. In terms of the abovementioned ratio of the number of subjects to the number of enrolment patterns, that number becomes lower.

Based on this assumption, re-examining the ratio of the number of subjects to the number of enrolment patterns in the three countries, the figure for Myanmar tends to be extremely low, while that of Nepal tends to be high. In other words, variation within a single population in Myanmar tends to be small, while that of Nepal tends to be large. Why do these differences occur? Examining whether or not an automatic advancement system exists, Myanmar uses a similar system called CAPS, while Nepal uses CAS. Myanmar has long been governed as a nation by a military junta, such that school governance by the government is very strict and institutional operations at the school level are thorough. For example, school records indicated that they were strictly documented. If an error occurs, it was then crossed out from the top with a double line and the correct one was written. It was also always signed over by the principal as proof of approval. This scenario suggests that CAPS has also been rigorously implemented in the target schools in the country. Conversely, in Nepal, the complexity of CAS (Poyck et al., 2016) and difficulties in its operation (Dahal et al., 2019; British Council, 2020) have been notable. Moreover, in the target schools (Ezaki, 2019), the reality of school management, which was by no means rigorous, was evident; for instance, the same person was registered in more than one school (double registration), and community members pointed out that teachers were late and that classes were not being held. Based on the abovementioned discussion, regarding the target schools in Myanmar and Nepal, differences in the rigour of the state system and the operation of the system at the school level may be considered as one of the factors that affected the number (variation) of enrolment patterns.

Extraordinary Enrolment Patterns

This section provides details on the extraordinary patterns identified in the target schools in Honduras and Nepal, which were nearly non-existent in the target schools in Myanmar in which the variation in enrolment patterns is extremely small (Table 15.6).

An extraordinary pattern identified in the target schools in Honduras (Sekiya, 2014) were patterns of multiple repetitions and temporary dropouts with six as the highest number of repetitions. All patterns revealed the surprising reality that although the children have been registered for more than 7 years, they have completed only Grade 1 or 2. For example, No. 1 boy left the target school during his first year of school. The following year, he re-registered in the first grade and attended school until the end of the school year; he missed only 13 days but failed his end-of-year evaluation. After repeating the same experience, he was finally able to pass the

Table 15.6   Extraordinary patterns identified in target schools in Honduras and Nepal

No.	Enrolment pattern	No. of repetition	No. of temporary dropout	Years registered
Honduras				
1	1D1F1F1F1P2F2P3F3D	5	1	9
2	1F1F1D1F1P2P3F3D	4	1	8
3	1F1F1D1P2D2F2F2D	4	2	8
4	1D1F1P2D2F2P3F3D	3	2	8
5	1F1F1P2F2F2F2D	5	0	7
6	1D1F1F1P2F2F2D	4	1	7
7	1F1F1F1F1P2F2F2D	6	0	8
Nepal				
1	1-////1D	0	2	2
2	1F1F//1F1D	3	1	4
3	1F1-////1P2D	1	2	4
4	1F1P//2F2F2D	3	1	5
5	1P2P3P̱Ṯ1P2P3P4P5P	0	0	8
6	1F1F1Ṯ3P4P5P	2	0	5
7	1Ṯ01P02P03P̱Ṯ3P4P5P	0	0	6

Source: Prepared by the author for this chapter based on the respective cited papers (Sekiya, 2014; Ezaki, 2019)

first grade in his fifth year. The following year, he was promoted to second grade but missed 95 days of school and failed his end-of-year evaluation. In the seventh year, he re-registered for the second grade; this time, he was able to pass. In the eighth year, he registered for the third year, but was again unsuccessful. Then, in the ninth year, he re-registered in the third grade but dropped out of school in the middle of the school year. Afterwards, his data in school records could not be verified (Sekiya, 2014).

In the target schools in Nepal, the study identified patterns of children experiencing multiple repetitions and temporary dropouts, as well as placement in grades of questionable legitimacy due to transfers (Ezaki, 2019). For example, No. 4 child failed Grade 1 in the first year of registration but re-registered and passed the following year. However, in the third year, he did not register in the target school and temporarily dropped out of school. In the fourth year, he registered for Grade 2 but failed in the end-of-year evaluation. In the fifth year, he failed in the second grade again. He re-registered in the second grade in his sixth year but dropped out of school in the middle of the school year. The study has been unable to verify his data in school records since then (Ezaki, 2019). Although the child had been registered in the target school for a total of 5 years, excluding 1 year in which he temporarily dropped out of school, he was only able to complete the first grade. As for Nos. 5–7, the patterns demonstrate placement in a grade level of questionable legitimacy due to school transfers. No. 5 is a pattern in which the child's grade goes down from Grade 3 to Grade 1 at the time of transfer and No. 6 exhibits the opposite pattern, in which the grade of the child goes up from Grade 1 to Grade 3 at the time of transfer. No. 7 is a pattern in which the child's grade goes down and up at the time of transfer.[6] This change in two or more grades, up or down, at the time of transfer is likely to result in the loss of continuity in learning (Ezaki, 2019).

The study observed these extraordinary enrolment patterns not only in the target schools in Honduras and Nepal but also in target schools in African countries such as Malawi (Kawaguchi, 2018) and Zambia (Ezaki & Nakamura, 2018). Although the backgrounds of the countries differ, the number of children who fall under this peculiar pattern is not small. The enrolment status of these children is likely to be overlooked in cross-sectional data. However, now that the SDGs explicitly state that 'No one will be left behind', these children are the ones who truly need support.

Relationship Between Grade Repetition and Dropout

A number of previous studies (Agarwal, 2020; Brophy, 2006; Jimerson et al., 2002; Rose & AI-Samarrai, 2001) have pointed to a strong association between grade repetition and dropout, such that if repetition rates are high, then dropout rates tend to be high. Alternatively, in recent years, a few reports (e.g. Kabay, 2016) have failed to find that repeating a grade increases the likelihood of dropping out, while others consider repeating a grade and dropping out as two separate constructs (Eisemon, 1997; Sekiya & Ashida, 2017).

What trends can be observed in this three-country comparison? Examining the frequency ranking of dropout patterns (Table 15.5), the study noted that the most frequent pattern was leaving school after less than 1 year of registration or after completing the first year in the target schools in the three countries (Honduras, Nepal and Myanmar). The

---

[6] The patterns of placement in grades of questionable legitimacy associated with school transfers are discussed in detail in Chap. 7 of this book and should be referred to there.

pattern of dropout, including grade repetitions, was excluded from the first and second places for the target schools in Honduras and Nepal, but included from the third place. No patterns of dropout, including grade repetitions, were identified in the target schools in Myanmar. Based on this perspective, the study can predict the magnitude of children who suddenly drop out of school without grade repetition (i.e. those who drop out for reasons unrelated to grade repetition). The ranking of the frequency of graduation patterns (Table 15.4) also revealed that although straight graduation was the most common pattern in the three countries, the number of children who eventually graduated despite experiencing several grade repetitions was large. Based on these results, the study cannot infer that grade repetition was the primary cause of school dropout.

In addition, analysis of enrolment patterns revealed that many children in all target schools repeated a grade or dropped out of school in their first year or lower grades (Tables 15.3, 15.4, and 15.5). To improve internal efficiency in education, caring for these younger children, especially first graders, is important.

Enrolment Patterns by Age at School Entry

Why do children drop out of school if they are not repeating a grade? Reporting that grade repetition did not increase the likelihood of dropping out of school, Kabay (2016) found that rather the age at school entry was important. Moreover, in previous studies on various countries (Branson et al., 2014; UIS/UNICEF, 2005; UNESCO, 2009; Wils, 2004), the issue of overage has been pointed out. Therefore, the study compared the enrolment patterns of the target schools by classifying them into three groups according to age at school entry (Table 15.7), namely, (1) underage and official entrance age, (2) overage: 1 or 2 years older than the official entrance age and (3) overage: 3 years and older than the official entrance age.

In the target schools in Honduras (Sekiya, 2014), the most frequent pattern for Group 1 is straight graduation (1P2P3P4P5P6P) followed by a pattern in which children repeated the first grade and then progressed smoothly to graduation (1F1P2P3P4P5P6P). The third place was occupied by dropping out of school after less than 1 year (1D). For Group 2, the most frequent occurrence was straight graduation (1P2P3P4P5P6P), similar to Group 1, but the second most frequent was leaving school after less than 1 year (1D). Group 3, alternatively, has dropout patterns from

Table 15.7 Enrolment patterns by age at school entry in target schools in each target country

Rank	Enrolment pattern	No. of students	Ratio
Honduras			
Group 1: 5–6 years old			
1	1P2P3P4P5P6P	190	37.6
2	1F1P2P3P4P5P6P	41	8.1
3	1D	21	4.2
4	1P2P3F3P4P5P6P	15	3.0
5	1P2F2P3P4P5P6P	11	2.2
Group 2: 7–8 years old			
1	1P2P3P4P5P6P	156	26.9
2	1D	61	10.5
3	1F1P2P3P4P5P6P	36	6.2
4	1F1D	22	3.8
5	1P2D	17	2.9
Group 3: 9 years old and older			
1	1D	28	22.6
2	1P2D	20	16.1
3	1F1D	10	8.1
4	1P2P3D	7	5.6
5	1P2P3P4P5P6P	6	4.8
Nepal			
Group 1: 4–5 years old			
1	1P2P3P4P5P	4	14.3
1	1P//2P3P4P5P	4	14.3
3	1F1P2P3P4P5P	3	10.7
3	1F1F1P2P3P4P5P	3	10.7
5	1F1P2P3P4F4P5P	2	7.1
5	1D	2	7.1
7	1P2P3P4P5F5P	1	3.6
7	1P2P3P4P5D	1	3.6
7	1P2P3P2P3P4P5P	1	3.6
7	1P2P3P1P2P3P4P5P	1	3.6
7	1P//2P3P4P5D	1	3.6
7	1P//2P//3P4P5-03P1P3P7P	1	3.6
7	1F1F1P2P3P4P3P4P6	1	3.6
7	1F1F1P2P3P42P3P4P5P	1	3.6
7	1F1F1F1P2P3P4P5P	1	3.6
7	1F1F13P4P5P	1	3.6
Group 2: 6–7 years old			

(*continued*)

Table 15.7 (continued)

Rank	Enrolment pattern	No. of students	Ratio
1	1P2P3P4P5P	11	55.0
2	1P2P3-3P4P5P	1	5.0
2	1P2F2P3P4D	1	5.0
2	1F1P2P3P4P5P	1	5.0
2	1F1P2P3P4P5F5P	1	5.0
2	1F1P2P3F3P4P5P	1	5.0
2	1F1F1P2P3P4P5D	1	5.0
2	1F//1P//2P3P4P5P	1	5.0
2	1D	1	5.0
2	101P02P03P3P4P5P	1	5.0
Group 3: 8 years old and older			
1	1P2P3P4P5P	10	31.3
2	1D	3	9.4
3	1P2P3P4P5D	2	6.3
3	1P2P3P4D	2	6.3
3	1P2F2D	2	6.3
3	1P//2P3P4P5P	2	6.3
7	1P2P3F3P4F4D	1	3.1
7	1P2P3D	1	3.1
7	1P2D	1	3.1
7	1F1P2P3D	1	3.1
7	1F1P2-2F2D	1	3.1
7	1F1P//2F2F2D	1	3.1
7	1F1F//1F1D	1	3.1
7	1F1-////1P2D	1	3.1
7	1-1F1F1D	1	3.1
7	1-1D	1	3.1
7	1-////1D	1	3.1
Myanmar			
Group 1: 4–5 years old			
1	1P2P3P4P5P	4244	96.8
2	1P2F2P3P4P5P	19	0.4
3	1F1P2P3P4P5P	18	0.4
4	1P	14	0.3
5	1P2P3P	3	0.1
Group 2: 6–7 years old			
1	1P2P3P4P5P	92	82.9
2	1P	4	3.6
3	1P2P3P	3	2.7
3	1P2F2P3P4P5P	3	2.7
5	1P2P	2	1.8

(*continued*)

Table 15.7 (continued)

Rank	Enrolment pattern	No. of students	Ratio
5	1F1P2P3P4P5P	2	1.8
7	1P2P3F3P4P5P	1	0.9
7	1P2F2P3P4P5P5F5P	1	0.9
7	1P2F2P3P	1	0.9
7	1F1P2P3P	1	0.9
7	1F1P2P	1	0.9
Group 3: 8 years old and older			
1	1P2P3P4P5P	5	38.5
2	1P2P	2	15.4
2	1P	2	15.4
4	1P2P3F3P4P5P	1	7.7
4	1P2P3P	1	7.7
4	1P2P3P4P	1	7.7
4	1P2P3P4P5F5C	1	7.7

Source: Prepared by the author for this chapter based on the respective cited papers (Sekiya, 2014; Ezaki, 2019; Yoshida, 2024)

first to fourth places with a graduation pattern finally emerging from the fifth place. The percentage of straight progress graduates decreased from Groups 1 to 3: 37.6%, 26.9% and 4.8%.

In the target schools in Nepal (Ezaki, 2019), the most frequent patterns for Group 1 were straight graduation (1P2P3P4P5P) and taking 1 year off (temporarily dropout) after passing the first grade, then advancing smoothly to the next grade and graduating (1P//2P3P4P5P). The top three places were under the graduation pattern. In Group 2, similar to Group 1, straight progress graduation (1P2P3P4P5P) was the most frequent followed by various patterns of one applicable person. In Group 3, similar to Groups 1 and 2, straight graduation (1P2P3P4P5P) was the most frequent pattern; however, those that follow were frequently dropout patterns. Examining the percentage of straight progress graduates, the highest to lowest were Groups 2 (55.0%), 3 (31.3%) and 1 (14.3%). However, Groups 1 and 2 displayed similar percentages of graduates (Group 1: 85.7%, Group 2: 85.0%), while Group 3 has less than half the numbers of Groups 1 and 2 (37.5%). One of the reasons for the low percentage of straight progress graduated in Group 1 is that preschool classes were not widespread in the target area at the time and that the readiness of children was insufficient, which resulted in a high rate of grade repetition in Grade 1.

In the target schools in Myanmar (Yoshida, 2024), the most frequent pattern was straight progress graduation in Group 1 (1P2P3P4P5P6P), which accounts for the majority of the total. The second and third places also depicted a graduation pattern. In Group 2, similar to Group 1, the most frequent pattern was straight progress graduation (1P2P3P4P5P6P), while the second most frequent pattern was leaving the target school without registering the following year after passing the first year (1P). In Group 3, similar to Groups 1 and 2, straight progress graduation (1P2P3P4P5P) was the most frequent pattern followed by patterns of leaving the target schools before reaching the final grade. The percentage of straight progress graduates decreased from Groups 1 to 3: 96.8%, 77.2% and 40.0%.

These results indicated that enrolment status of the underage and official school entrance age groups was preferable and that the older a child at school entry, the worse the enrolment status and the more likely the children will drop out, particularly in target schools in Honduras and Myanmar. For the target schools in Nepal, the study found that enrolment status extremely deteriorated when the age at school entry was more than 3 years past the official school entrance age. This aspect shows the importance of registering children at the official school entrance age.[7]

6   Conclusion

This chapter compared the enrolment status in primary education in Honduras, Nepal and Myanmar and analysed the similarities and differences among the three countries. The study also examined the factors that hinder children from continuing their studies by addressing the factors frequently mentioned by previous studies, such as the reality of grade repetition and temporary dropout and the relationship between grade repetition and dropout and age at school entry.

The results revealed similarities in the polarisation of the enrolment divide among the target schools. Specifically, the most frequent enrolment pattern in the target schools was the most ideal pattern that is, straight graduation, in which children advance to graduation without grade

---

[7] Note that in the study by Ezaki (2019), the underage and official school entrance age groups were categorized into separate groups for a total of four groups for analysis. As a result, the study recommended a review of age at school entrance, because the situation was more favourable for the 6–7-year-old group than for the official school entrance age group. For more information, see Ezaki (2019).

repetition or temporary dropout. However, the next most common pattern was that of early school dropout after registration such as dropping out in the middle of the first year or after passing the first year, which is the worst enrolment pattern. With the population in such a state of near polarisation, believing that the repetition rate, dropout rate and years of completion, which are viewed simply as averages, accurately represent the group is difficult. Extraordinary enrolment patterns, which are likely to be overlooked by such figures, were also revealed in the target schools in Honduras and Nepal. Therefore, focusing on each child and shedding light on the micro educational status and then formulating macro educational policies based on this elucidation are desirable initiatives.

With regard to the relationship between grade repetition and dropout, the target schools shared the same large number of children who suddenly dropped out without grade repetition, such as those who dropped out for certain reasons unrelated to grade repetition. Conversely, it was also evident that not a small number of children experienced grade repetition but eventually graduated. These results suggest that grade repetition cannot be pinned as the primary cause of dropout.

Regarding grade repetition and dropout, many children repeated a grade or dropped out of school in their first year or lower grades in the target schools in all three countries. This scenario demonstrates that caring for the younger children, especially those in Grade 1, is important for improving internal efficiency in education.

Regarding age at school entry, the study found that the higher the age at school entry, the worse the enrolment status and the more likely the children will drop out, especially in the target schools in Honduras and Myanmar. For the target schools in Nepal, the study found that the enrolment status extremely deteriorated when age at school entry was more than 3 years older than the official school entrance age. This result indicates the importance of registering children at the official school entrance age.

This study conducted an international comparative analysis based on the actual enrolment status of the target schools located in one region of each target country, such that the results are not applicable to the entire target country. In the future, analysing the results of surveys on the actual state of enrolment in regions with different characteristics and comparing their respective trends are desirable initiatives.

REFERENCES

Agarwal, M. (2020). *Retain, promote or support: How to reduce inequality in elementary education.* Global Education Monitoring Report Fellowship Paper. Paris: UNESCO.

Branson, N., Hofmeyr, C., & Lam, D. (2014). Progress through school and the determinants of school dropout in South Africa. *Development Southern Africa, 31*(1), 106–126.

British Council. (2020). *Nepal's school sector development plan: TA facility.* Capacity and institutional assessment (CIA) for implementation of the SSDP, Final report. Kathmandu: British Council.

Brophy, J. (2006). *Grade repetition.* The International Institute for Educational Planning & The International Academy of Education.

Dahal, T., Topping, K., & Levy, S. (2019). Educational factors influencing female students' dropout from high schools in Nepal. *International Journal of Educational Research, 98,* 67–76.

Eisemon, T. O. (1997). *Reducing repetition: Issues and strategies.* UNESCO.

Ezaki, N. (2019). Enrolment patterns of individual children left behind in the trend towards 'quality education': A case study of primary education in Nepal. *Education 3-13, International Journal of Primary, Elementary and Early Years Education, 47*(5), 520–533.

Ezaki, N., & Nakamura, S. (2018). Sutorēto ni shinkyū dekinai Zambia chūtō kyōiku no seitotachi [Secondary education students who cannot advance to the next grade smoothly in Zambia]. In T. Sekiya (Ed.), *Kaihatsu tojōkoku de manabu kodomotachi: Makuroseisaku ni shisuru mikurona shūgakujittaibunseki [Children who are Learning in Developing Countries: Micro analysis of state of enrolment that contributes to macro policies]* (pp. 119–138). Kwansei Gakuin University Press.

Jimerson, R. S., Anderson, E. G., & Whipple, D. N. (2002). Winning the battle and losing the war: Examining the relation between grade retention and dropping out of high school. *Psychology in the Schools, 39*(4), 441–457.

Kabay, S. (2016). Grade repetition and primary school dropout in Uganda. *Harvard Education Review, 86*(4), 580–606.

Kawaguchi, J. (2018). 'Kyūgaku' wo katsuyou suru Malawi no zyoshi seitotachi: Malawi no chūtō gakkou no zyūdanteki shūgaku kiroku kara [Female students who take advantage of leave on absence in Malawi: From the longitudinal enrolment record of secondary education school in Malawi]. In T. Sekiya (Ed.), *Kaihatsu tojōkoku de manabu kodomotachi: Makuroseisaku ni shisuru mikurona shūgakujittaibunseki [Children who are Learning in Developing Countries: Micro analysis of state of enrolment that contributes to macro policies]* (pp. 119–138). Kwansei Gakuin University Press.

Poyck, C. M., Koirala, N. B., Aryal, N. P., & Sharma, K. N. (2016). *Joint evaluation of Nepal's school sector reform plan programme 2009–16.* GFA Consulting Group GmbH.

Rose, P., & Al Samarrai, S. (2001). Household constraints on schooling by gender: Empirical evidence from Ethiopia. *Comparative Education Review, 45*(1), 36–63.

Sekiya, T. (2014). Individual patterns of enrolment in primary schools in the Republic of Honduras. *Education 3–31: International Journal of Primary, Elementary and Early Years Education, 42*(5), 460–474.

Sekiya, T. (Ed.). (2018). *Kaihatsu tojōkoku de manabu kodomotachi: Makuroseisaku ni shisuru mikurona shūgakujittaibunseki [Children who are Learning in Developing Countries: Micro analysis of state of enrolment that contributes to macro policies].* Kwansei Gakuin University Press.

Sekiya, T., & Ashida, A. (2017). An analysis of primary school dropout patterns in Honduras. *Journal of Latinos and Education, 16*(1), 65–73.

UNESCO Institute for Statistics (UIS)/UNICEF. (2005). *Children Out of School: Measuring Exclusion from Primary Education.* UNESCO UIS.

United Nations Educational, Scientific and Cultural Organization (UNESCO). (2009). *EFA Monitoring Report 2009: Overcoming inequality: Why governance matters. Regional overview: Latin America and the Caribbean.* UNESCO.

United Nations Educational, Scientific and Cultural Organization (UNESCO). (2015). *EFA global monitoring report 2015 –Education for all 2000–2015: Achievements and challenges.* UNESCO.

United Nations Educational, Scientific and Cultural Organization (UNESCO). (2017). *Global education monitoring report 2017 – Accountability in education: Meeting our commitments.* UNESCO.

United Nations Educational, Scientific and Cultural Organization (UNESCO). (2020). *Global education monitoring report 2020 –Inclusion and education: All means all.* UNESCO.

Wils, A. (2004). Late entrants leave school earlier: evidence from Mozambique. *International Review of Education, 50*(4), 7–37.

Yoshida, N. (2024). Analysis of enrolment patterns in Myanmar's primary education by socioeconomic status. In T. Sekiya, K. Ogawa, Y. Kitamura, & A. Ashida (Eds.), *Towards ensuring inclusive and equitable quality education for all: Implications from a longitudinal analysis of school enrolment patterns.* Palgrave Macmillan.

Yoshida, N. (2018). Myanmar shotō kyōiku ni okeru kodomotachi no shūgakukiseki [Enrolment patterns of primary education children in Myanmar]. In Sekiya, T. (Ed.), *Kaihatsu tojōkoku de manabu kodomotachi: Makuroseisaku ni shisuru mikurona shūgakujittaibunseki [Children who are Learning in Developing Countries: Micro analysis of state of enrolment that contributes to macro policies].* Kwansei Gakuin University Press, 239–265.

CHAPTER 16

Lessons from Japanese Educational Development Experiences: Comparison of Enrolment Status Between Developing Countries and the Meiji of Japan

Natsuho Yoshida

1 Introduction

The Japanese educational experience is often referenced in evaluations of national educational challenges. Japan, which was on par with developing countries only 150 years ago, achieved universal basic education relatively quickly because of proactive educational reforms. Japan achieved its current inclusive education system, which has attracted global attention, through two historical events: (1) the introduction of the modern education system at the end of the nineteenth century and (2) during the

N. Yoshida (✉)
Graduate School of Education, Hyogo University of Teacher Education,
Kato, Japan
e-mail: nyoshida@hyogo-u.ac.jp

© The Author(s), under exclusive license to Springer Nature
Switzerland AG 2024
T. Sekiya et al. (eds.), *Towards Ensuring Inclusive and Equitable
Quality Education for All*, International and Development
Education, https://doi.org/10.1007/978-3-031-70266-2_16

country's occupation by the US after losing World War II. Against this backdrop, in this chapter, it first reviews Japan's educational development from the early Meiji era, when modern schooling was introduced, to the post-World War II period, particularly with regard to changes in school enrolment. JICA (2004) and various historical documents are reviewed, providing a detailed picture of the actual enrolment status of children at the time. The study will focus on repetition, school dropout, the child labour and gender gap to capture the actual enrolment status at the time. Based on these discussions, common issues in educational development between Japan and developing countries and Japan-specific educational experiences are summarised. Finally, the chapter will examine how Japan's educational experiences can be utilised by developing countries to achieve SDG4.

2   EDUCATIONAL REFORMS AND CHANGES IN SCHOOL ENROLMENT IN JAPAN: BEGINNINGS OF MODERN SCHOOLING

In 1868, the government headed by the Shogun (Tokugawa family), the top samurai who had long governed Japan, collapsed. The political change, known as the 'Meiji Restoration (Meiji Ishin)', resulted in a new government (the Meiji Government) headed by the Emperor. This new government aimed to modernise Japan, modelled on Western countries, under the slogans of 'Civilization and Enlightenment' and 'Enrich the Country, Strengthen the Military' (Ministry of Education, 1992a). Education reform and modernisation were positioned at the heart of this modernisation policy. During the former Tokugawa regime (Edo era), schools for children of the samurai warrior class (Shoheizaka academies and fief schools), private academies and schools for the common children (tera-koya) were widespread throughout Japan (Ito, 2011). Japan's educational culture during this period was not low. However, these traditional educational institutions had the following characteristics and lacked the features of modern school systems: a 'liberal arts bias with an emphasis on the classics', 'educational differences and discrimination according to social class', 'inconsistent duration of study and learning content' and 'individualized teaching methods, inadequate examination and promotion systems and course recognition' (Saito, 2004a). As soon as the Meiji Restoration began, the new government gathered information and researched school systems in the West.

In 1871, the Ministry of Education (Monbu-sho) was established as the central government ministry in the field of education. In 1872, an education ordinance (Gakusei) was promulgated as Japan's first systematic education law (Ministry of Education, 1992b). Japan followed the US school system model at the time, consisting of three levels: elementary, middle and university. However, Japan adopted a centralised educational administration system with school districts based on the French system (Ogasawara, 1980; Ministry of Education, 1981a; Saito, 2004a). The Meiji Government planned to establish more than 50,000 elementary schools nationwide (Saito, 2004a). The education ordinance allowed establishing elementary schools in a form appropriate to the particular situation of the public (Table 16.1). It stipulated that all participation in

Table 16.1 Overview of elementary schools specified in the education ordinance (Gakusei)

Kinds of elementary school	Targeted children	Characteristics
Ordinary schools	Boys and girls 6–9 (lower division); boys and girls 10–13 (upper division)	Elementary schools consisted of an upper and a lower division, and both boys and girls within the specified age range were expected to attend without fail until graduation. The curriculum consisted of 14 subjects in the lower division, and 18 in the upper division, with additional subjects added as necessary. Each school had rules
Girls' schools	Girls	In addition to the standard school curriculum, handicrafts were added
Village schools	Children of farmers who lived in distant villages or people outside the standard age range	Much more relaxed rules than in the standard schools. Evening classes which harmonised with working patterns were also permitted
Schools for the poor	Children from poor families	Institutions supported by donations from rich families. Also known as 'charity schools'
Elementary private academies	Unclear	Lessons given in private houses by teachers who held a teacher's licence
Infant schools	Infant boys and girls below the age of 6	Pre-school education

Source: Table prepared by Kobayashi and Murata (2004) based on chapters 21–27 of 'The Education Ordinance', cited by the author

these schools was to be regarded as 'schooling' (National Institute for Educational Policy Research, 1974a). These elementary schools provided a total of eight years of schooling, four years each for the upper and lower divisions (Ministry of Education, 1992b). Furthermore, in principle, all children were required to attend school, regardless of gender, parental occupation or social status. Furthermore, as teacher training was not fully developed then, many elementary schools were taught by teratoma masters, samurai warriors who had lost their jobs during the Meiji Restoration and priests and priestesses who could read and write (Saito, 2014).

Educational reform in Japan since the Meiji Restoration has focused on developing higher education and spreading elementary education (Ministry of Education, 1992b). Regarding higher education, the Meiji Government hired foreign experts at exceptionally high salaries to introduce advanced Western learning, technology and systems quickly (Nakamura, 1964). The Meiji Government also implemented a policy of sending many talented young Japanese abroad to study so that they could apply their learning in Japan on their return (Tsuji, 2008). As the Meiji Government spent much of its education budget on these higher education initiatives, the elementary education sector was stretched thin. Hence, establishing and operating elementary schools depended on local contributions, levies on school district residents and tuition fees paid by each family. In the early Meiji era, the education budget burden was borne overwhelmingly by municipalities rather than the national government (Yamaguchi, 2004; Nakamura & Higuchi, 2013).

Disconnect Between the Ideals of Education Reform and Social Reality

As mentioned above, in principle, the public was to bear the cost associated with elementary education, such as establishing and operating elementary schools. However, as people at that time were not affluent, raising these expenses was a great burden for each family. In addition, most of the population at the time was small farmers dependent on family labour. Therefore, sending children to school was synonymous with the loss of labour, amplifying the family burden (Kobayashi & Murata, 2004). Nevertheless, Japanese elementary school education at the time was modelled on the US system, with each subject taught in US elementary schools adopted directly in Japan. Textbooks were also used as they were either translated or copied from Western textbooks. As a result, the educational content diverged from the actual conditions and needs of daily life in Japan. Hence, both teachers and parents questioned the elementary school education at the time (Kishimoto, 1952; Saito, 2004a). Furthermore, the eight-year schooling period established by the education ordinance was much longer than the traditional one- to two-year schooling of terakoya, which was far removed from the social practices of Japan at the time. In addition, some elementary school children failed to pass their progression exams due to poor academic performance and were forced to repeat grades, further extending the school year and increasing the burden on families. Indeed, it was common for students to drop out of school after repeating grades because of family circumstances (Saito, 2003). In this situation, elementary education as promoted through the education ordinance resulted in popular discontent. Schools became the target of attacks as symbols of the modernisation policy, resulting in 'school revolts' and 'school burning incidents' (Kurasawa, 1963).

The Meiji Government encouraged elementary school enrolment by promulgating the education ordinance; nevertheless, by 1883, 10 years after the education ordinance took effect, the enrolment rate for elementary education was only 47% (Fig. 16.1). Elementary school attendance rates were even lower (Table 16.2). Therefore, it can be assumed that even fewer children attended school and studied daily than the school

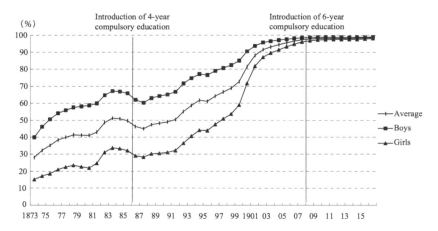

Fig. 16.1 Trends in elementary school enrolment rates in Japan between 1873 and 1915. (Source: Figure prepared by Kobayashi and Murata (2004) based on data from the Ministry of Education (1962), cited by the author)

Table 16.2 Trends in the number and percentage of children enrolled in and attending elementary schools in 1873–1886, 1890, 1895 and 1899

Year	Enrolment rate (M/F) %	Children of an age eligible to attend school (A) persons	Number of children (B) persons	Average number of children regularly attending school (C) persons	Percentage of children regularly attending school (C/B×100)%	Children of elementary school age (D) persons	Average number of elementary school age children regularly attending school (E) persons	Percentage of school attendance (E/A×100) %
1873	39.9/15.1	4,205,341	1,145,802	742,530	64.80	1,037,501	672,361	15.99
1874	46.17/17.22	4,923,272	1,590,561	1,165,922	73.30	1,464,450	1,073,464	23.18
1875	50.80/18.72	5,168,660	1,928,152	1,428,619	74.09	1,815,803	1,345,331	26.03
1876	54.16/21.03	5,160,618	2,067,801	1,547,881	74.86	1,966,288	1,471,880	28.52
1877	55.97/22.48	5,251,807	2,162,962	1,530,164	70.74	2,073,284	1,466,662	27.93
1878	57.59/23.51	5,281,727	2,273,224	1,596,976	70.25	2,169,979	1,524,473	28.86
1879	58.21/22.59	5,371,383	2,315,070	1,607,979	69.46	2,186,860	1,518,897	28.28
1880	58.72/21.91	5,533,196	2,348,859	1,655,598	70.49	2,218,834	1,563,878	28.26
1881	59.95/24.67	5,615,007	2,607,177	1,686,391	64.68	2,456,238	1,588,749	28.29
1882	64.65/30.98	5,750,946	3,004,137	1,948,362	64.86	2,838,092	1,840,618	32.01
1883	67.16/33.64	5,952,000	3,237,507	2,104,839	65.01	3,059,719	1,989,283	33.42
1884	66.95/33.29	6,164,190	3,233,226	2,126,687	65.78	3,163,080	2,080,538	33.75
1885	65.80/32.07	6,413,684	3,097,235	1,957,392	63.20	3,097,235	1,957,392	30.52
1886	61.99/29.01	6,611,461	2,802,639	1,827,123	65.19	–	–	27.64
1890	65.14/31.13	7,195,412	3,096,400	2,248,030	72.60	–	–	31.24
1895	76.65/43.87	7,083,148	3,670,345	2,829,570	80.32	–	–	39.95
1899	85.06/59.04	7,097,430	4,302,623	3,461,383	83.16	–	–	48.77

Source: Table prepared by Kobayashi and Murata (2004) based on National Institute for Educational Policy Research (1974a, 1974b), partly modified to fit this chapter and cited by the author

enrolment rates at the time would suggest. In 1879, in response to this difficult situation, the Meiji Government abolished the education ordinance and promulgated a new education order (Kyoiku-rei), which adopted the US democratic education system. The school district system was abolished, and schools were to be governed by boards of education publicly elected by local residents. The eight-year schooling period for elementary education was also drastically shortened to suit the social realities: 'at least 16 months during the school age period'. The obligatory nature of school enrolments was also eased. However, under these relaxed education decrees, many regions moved to stop construction of new school buildings or close current schools to reduce costs at the discretion of local authorities (Kurasawa 1963). As a result, enrolment in elementary education also temporarily declined around 1880 (Fig. 16.1), resulting in an amendment of the education order only a year later, in 1880. The revised education order once again strengthened the centralised educational administration system by strictly regulating three years of elementary schooling (at least 16 weeks each year) (Ministry of Education, 1981b). Thus, the Meiji Government's educational reforms were restarted.

Steps Taken to Achieve Universal Education

In 1885, the Meiji Government introduced a cabinet system. The country's first Minister of Education, Mr. Arinori MORI, had served as a diplomat in Western countries. In 1886, he promulgated separate decrees for each school level encompassing the entire education system and replacing the education order. For the elementary education level, the Elementary School Order was issued. Elementary schools were divided into two levels, the ordinary and the higher division, with four years of compulsory education in the former (Ministry of Education, 1981c, 1981d).[1]

By the 1890s, elementary school enrolments had steadily increased, reaching 69% by 1898 (Fig. 16.1). Furthermore, in 1890, it was decided to make elementary school free and to abolish the promotion system by examination, which was replaced by an automatic promotion system (Saito, 2003). In 1907, the period of compulsory education was extended

---

[1] However, in some local circumstances, compulsory education was replaced by a three-year simplified elementary course. However, this system was abolished in 1900, when elementary education became widespread, and compulsory education was standardised at four years.

from 4 to 6 years, as the elementary school enrolment rate neared 100% (Ministry of Education, 1981e). This practically eliminated adult illiteracy by the early 2000s. It is also assumed that this increase in elementary school enrolment rate was partly due to the economic development resulting from the victory in the Sino-Japanese War between 1894 and 1895 (Ministry of Education, 1981e; Miwa, 2013). Thus, just over 30 years after promulgating the education ordinance, the elementary education enrolment rate surpassed 95% (Fig. 16.1), largely solving the problem of the enrolment of children in school. However, as can be seen from the attendance and commuting rates shown in Table 16.2, we can read at the same time that not all children for whom the school enrolment rate was calculated attended school every day, even during this period. It is assumed that it took some more time for this problem to be fully resolved.

Educational Reforms and School Enrolment in the Pre- and Postwar Periods

In the 1910s and 1920s, John Dewey's ideas were introduced to Japan. The ideas of the global New Education Movement began to influence Japanese education, including a move towards practices such as child-centred education in some elementary schools affiliated with teacher training colleges and private elementary schools. These trends in the field of education were collectively known as 'The Progressive Education Movement of the Taisho era' (Nakano, 1968; Wakai, 2014). In contrast, in the 1930s, Japanese education policy rapidly became increasingly characterised by ultranationalism. In 1941, following Japan's entry into World War II, traditional elementary schools were renamed 'national schools'. Nationalist education was strengthened starting from elementary school. Towards the end of World War II, children were evacuated to rural areas to avoid air raids (Ministry of Education, 1992c). By the end of the war, in 1945, Japan's schooling system was almost completely paralysed.

Japan was occupied by the Allied Forces following its defeat in 1945. From this time until the end of the occupation by the San Francisco Peace Treaty in 1951, the General Headquarters of the Allied Forces administered Japan (hereafter GHQ). The GHQ requested the dispatch of a 'US Education Mission to Japan'[2] to implement the overall concept of postwar Japanese educational reform (Sakamoto, 2017). The group came to Japan

---

[2] It is a group of more than 20 US education experts (Murai, 1979).

in March 1946 and, in collaboration with a group of Japanese educators, vigorously analysed and investigated Japanese education. A month later, they submitted the 'Report of the United States Education Mission to Japan', containing a series of recommendations for Japanese education (Sakamoto, 2017). Subsequent major reforms of the postwar Japanese education system, with a focus on democratising education and providing equal opportunities, were essentially based on these recommendations.[3]

Subsequently, new education-related laws and regulations were enacted one after another, including the 1947 Fundamental Law of Education. The new education system based on these included: (1) converting the prewar dual school system to a single-track system, known as the 6–3–3–4 system; (2) extending compulsory education to nine years in elementary and middle schools; (3) establishing coeducation in principle; (4) establishing boards of education at the prefectural and municipal levels; and (5) abolishing teacher training schools and establishing a university-based pre-service training system (Saito, 2004a). Furthermore, in the 1950s, legislation was enacted to improve the schooling environment. For example, in 1954, the School Lunch Law was enacted, and in 1956, the school lunch programme was extended to middle schools (Tsuchiya & Sato, 2012). In 1963, the Law concerning the Free Provision of Textbooks in Compulsory Education Schools was enacted, introducing a system of free textbooks. The scope of the free distribution of textbooks was progressively expanded in annual plans, and by 1969, this system at the compulsory education stage in elementary and middle schools was completed (Elementary and Secondary Education Bureau, 2021). Due to these postwar educational reforms, high school and university enrolment rates increased significantly in addition to compulsory elementary and middle school enrolment (Fig. 16.2). The elementary and middle school enrolment rates were almost 100% as of 1955, and the high school enrolment rate has been above 90% since 1975 (Fig. 16.2). It should also be noted that underlying this increase in school enrolment is the dramatic recovery of Japan's economy from the devastation of World War II. Rapid economic growth was triggered by demand from the Korean War, etc., contributing to increased demand for education.

---

[3] The report praises the group's achievements. However, it is also indicated that it is impossible to comprehensively and accurately grasp the educational situation in Japan, a country with a history of approximately 2700 years, considering historical, social and cultural backgrounds, in just one month of research by foreigners.

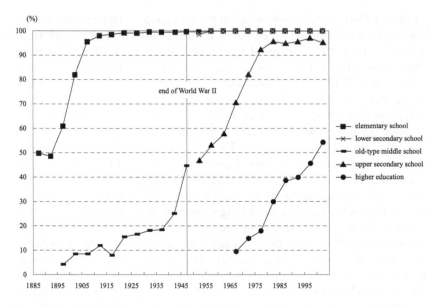

Fig. 16.2 Trends in enrolment rates by stage of education between 1885 and 2005. (Source: Figure prepared by Yamaguchi (2004) based on data from the Ministry of Education, cited by the author)

Educational Achievements and Challenges in Postwar Japan

Japan's postwar educational reforms were also aided by the meshing of education and the economy, with steadily increasing enrolment rates at all levels (see Fig. 16.2). The achievements of Japanese school education were also evidenced in international educational attainment surveys. The first International Association for the Evaluation of Educational Achievement (IEA) was held between 1964 and 1967 with the participation of 12 countries, including Japan, European countries, the US and Israel. The results of Japanese 13-year-old children in mathematics were extremely good, ranking in the top alongside those of Israel (Saito, 2004a). Furthermore, in a later survey on science education between 1970 and 1973, Japanese children in the fifth and third grades of elementary and middle schools ranked first among all 19 participating countries (Saito, 2004a). However, according to the OECD (1971), severe competition for university entrance examinations, described as 'exam hell', was causing 'distortion' in elementary and secondary education and cramming education with rote memorisation deprived children of developing an inquisitive and creative mind. However, once students pass the rigorous university entrance examinations, Japanese universities do not demand rigorous study from them, leading to the comment that 'universities are like a leisureland' (OECD, 1971). This situation has hardly improved in over 50 years since the OECD's criticism. Since the Meiji Restoration, Japanese education has indeed made remarkable progress in a short time. However, this does not mean the education system is perfect, and more efforts are required to improve educational issues further.

3   Actual Enrolment Status Regarding Repetition

Situation of Children's Repetition in the Early Meiji Era

The 1872 education ordinance included adopting a promotion system by examination. According to Saito (1995) and Saito (2003), elementary schooling at that time lasted for a total of eight years, four years each for the lower and upper divisions. In addition, in each of the lower and upper divisions, each grade was divided into two stages, from the lowest stage eight to the highest stage one. Children had to sit for a progression examination every six months and could progress to the next stage if they passed. Children who failed to pass examinations due to poor academic performance had to repeat the same stage. On completion of the final stage of the lower division, children had to sit for a graduation examination covering the entire lower-division curriculum and were allowed to move on to the upper division only once passing the exam. The same promotion system by examinations was used in the upper and lower divisions. These promotion and graduation examinations were fairly rigorous.[4] Although there were regional differences between the prefectures, the passing score for each exam was approximately 60–70% of the total score. In addition, children with excellent academic performance could skip a stage to advance to a higher stage, shortening their schooling period.

---

[4] For example, to ensure the fairness and rigor of the examinations, the examination system gradually became standardised at the prefecture level. In addition, the following initiatives were implemented: exam questions were prepared by teachers other than the students' class teachers, exam questions were approved by local officials and local officials were present at the exam sites.

According to the National Institute for Educational Policy Research (1974a), this grading system was introduced due to the demands of 'Civilization and Enlightenment', which required rapid and mass learning of Western technology and culture. Because this grading system was based entirely on the principle of meritocracy, great emphasis was placed on the examinations, which were the only means of determining advancement. However, the examination promotion system has resulted in many students repeating stages.

Educational statistics in Japan were incomplete at the time, and national figures on repetition and other factors are uncertain. However, according to the fragmentary statistical data, on average, 20–30% of candidates failed these promotion exams (Saito, 2004b). Furthermore, many students did not take the promotion examinations in anticipation of failing, which is not represented in the statistics. In some prefectures, the number of children who failed examinations due to nonattempts is 15–20% of the total number of children (Saito, 2004b). The high number of students who repeated (failed) can be seen partly from the number and percentage of students enrolled by grade at the time. For example, Table 16.3 shows the percentage of children enrolled in the first grade (i.e. Stages 8 and 7 in the lower division) of elementary school as of 1876 was between late 70% and

Table 16.3 Percentage of students in Grade 1 (Stages 8 and 7 of lower division) out of all students in the lower division of elementary schools in Aomori, Aichi, Mie, Shiga, Kyoto and Oita Prefectures between 1876 and 1880

Academic year	Prefectures					
	Aomori	*Aichi*	*Mie*	*Shiga*	*Kyoto*	*Oita*
1876	80.2	77.2	84.9	87.6	79.4	76.6
1877	80.5	72.4	68.9	66.5	68.6	76.5
1878	61.3	60.3	63.5	62.9	68.8	70.7
1879	55.4	52.3	58.5	63.5	70.0	66.5
1880	53.2	45.6	53.6	64.3	N/A	60.7

Note: Aomori Prefecture adopted a Stage 10 system with no divisions from 1879; therefore, the numbers of children in Stages 10 and 9 were used. Shiga Prefecture also adopted a second division system (upper and ordinary divisions) with six stages for each division starting in 1879, so the numbers of children in the sixth and fifth stages of its ordinary division were used

Source: Table prepared by the National Institute for Educational Policy Research (1974a, p. 538) based on data from the annual report of the Ministry of Education for each year, partially modified and translated into English and cited by the author

late 80% of all children in each prefecture of Aomori, Aichi, Mie, Shiga, Kyoto and Oita. This means that most children enrolled in elementary school at that time could not progress and remained in the first grade (i.e. Stages 8 and 7 of the lower division). Next, the number of children enrolled by stage and their proportion of the total number of children in each prefecture in 1979 (Table 16.4) shows that in all prefectures, approximately 80% all children remained in Grade 2 (Stages 8–5 of lower division) alone. Furthermore, the overall proportion of children enrolled in the lower division of elementary schools in each prefecture was approximately 98%, while that of the upper division was only around 2%, which shows how unrealistic the higher division of elementary schools was. Thus,

Table 16.4 Number of students enrolled by stage in Aichi, Mie and Oita Prefectures and their percentage of the total number of students in 1879

Prefectures		Aichi	Mie	Oita
	Stages	No. of students (%)	No. of students (%)	No. of students (%)
Upper division	1	2 (0.00)	34 (0.07)	12 (0.02)
	2	17 (0.02)	10 (0.02)	6 (0.01)
	3	30 (0.04)	23 (0.04)	20 (0.04)
	4	65 (0.09)	58 (0.11)	23 (0.05)
	5	107 (0.14)	74 (0.14)	95 (0.20)
	6	201 (0.27)	133 (0.26)	163 (0.34)
	7	280 (0.38)	22 (0.04)	212 (0.44)
	8	756 (1.02)	619 (1.19)	460 (0.95)
	Subtotal	1458 (1.98)	973 (1.88)	991 (2.04)
Lower division	1	1732 (2.35)	868 (1.68)	754 (1.55)
	2	2334 (3.16)	1508 (2.91)	1214 (2.50)
	3	4050 (5.49)	2834 (5.47)	1694 (3.49)
	4	5504 (7.46)	3501 (6.76)	2376 (4.89)
	5	8450 (11.45)	5218 (10.07)	3833 (7.89)
	6	11,689 (15.84)	6582 (12.70)	5429 (11.17)
	7	16,473 (22.32)	9971 (19.24)	8162 (16.80)
	8	22,106 (29.96)	20,356 (39.29)	24,129 (49.67)
	Subtotal	72,338 (98.02)	50,838 (98.12)	47,591 (97.96)
Total		73,796 (100)	51,811 (100)	48,582 (100)

Source: Table prepared by the National Institute for Educational Policy Research (1974a, pp. 539–541) based on data for each prefecture in the annual report of the Ministry of Education, partially modified and translated into English and cited by the author

the promotion system by examinations at the time may have kept most children in the lower stages of the lower division, preventing them from advancing to the higher stages.

Age Range and Enrolment Status

Under the grading system based on the promotion by examinations, discrepancies between grade/stage and standard age were unavoidable. For example, according to the number and percentage of elementary school children enrolled by age and stage in Aomori Prefecture (Table 16.5), although 99.5% of all children in the upper and lower divisions of elementary schools were enrolled in the lower division, only about 50% of children were below the school age of the lower division of elementary schools. This means that approximately 50% of the remaining children were studying in the lower division, even though they were above the school age of the upper division in elementary schools. In the case of Kyoto Prefecture, where more detailed information is available (Table 16.6), 98.2% of children aged 10 and above were enrolled in the lower division of elementary schools, suggesting that many older children who should have been studying in the upper-division stages were stuck in the lower-division stages due to failing examinations and not being able to advance.

However, the opposite was observed in some cases, where some children of lower-division age were promoted to a higher stage, far beyond the standard age, by early schooling or skipping stages (e.g. cases where children were promoted to lower-division Stage 6 at the age of 5 or younger [standard age was 7] [N = 1], to lower-division Stage 3 at the age of 7 [standard age was 8] [N = 10] or to upper-division Stage 8 at the age of 8 [standard age was 10] [N = 4]). Also, for example, Table 16.6 shows that some children were enrolled in the lower-division Stages 8–6 from younger than age 5 to over 15 years of age. It must have been difficult for teachers to teach such a group with such a wide age gap in simultaneous classes, which may have led to a decline in the quality of education and affected the students' examination results. This analysis of the age of children provides some insight into the schooling environment of children at the beginning of the Meiji era.

Table 16.5 Number and percentage of elementary school children enrolled by age and grade in Aomori Prefecture in 1877

Age		Under school age (under 5 years)	Lower-division age (6–9 years)	Upper-division age (10–13 years)	School age and above (14 years and above)	Total (%)
Division	Stage					
Upper division	1	N/A	N/A	N/A	N/A	N/A
	2	N/A	N/A	N/A	N/A	N/A
	3	N/A	N/A	N/A	3	3 (0.02)
	4	N/A	N/A	N/A	9	9 (0.05)
	5	N/A	N/A	N/A	N/A	N/A
	6	N/A	N/A	6	14	20 (0.11)
	7	N/A	N/A	7	26	33 (0.18)
	8	N/A	N/A	11	17	28 (0.15)
	Subtotal	N/A	N/A	24	69	93 (0.49)
Lower division	1	N/A	20	31	16	67 (0.36)
	2	N/A	26	62	20	108 (0.57)
	3	N/A	26	147	45	218 (1.16)
	4	N/A	119	362	52	533 (2.83)
	5	N/A	394	539	87	1020 (5.42)
	6	N/A	658	852	124	1634 (8.69)
	7	2	1692	1816	290	3800 (20.20)
	8	166	6475	4320	374	11,335 (60.27)
	Subtotal	168	9410	8129	1008	18,715 (99.51)
Total (%)		168 (0.89)	9410 (50.03)	8153 (43.35)	1077 (5.73)	18,808 (100)

Source: Table prepared by the National Institute for Educational Policy Research (1974a, p. 544), partly processed and translated into English and cited by the author

Table 16.6 Number and percentage of elementary school children enrolled by age and stage in Kyoto Prefecture in 1877

Division	Stage	Under 5 years old	6 years old	7 years old	8 years old	9 years old	10 years old
Upper division	1	N/A	N/A	N/A	N/A	N/A	N/A
	2	N/A	N/A	N/A	N/A	N/A	N/A
	3	N/A	N/A	N/A	N/A	N/A	N/A
	4	N/A	N/A	N/A	N/A	N/A	1
	5	N/A	N/A	N/A	N/A	N/A	1
	6	N/A	N/A	N/A	N/A	4	8
	7	N/A	N/A	N/A	N/A	N/A	2
	8	N/A	N/A	N/A	4	3	13
	Stage	11 years old	12 years	13 years old	14 years old	15 years and over	Subtotal of enrolments in each grade of the upper division (%)
	1	N/A	N/A	N/A	N/A	N/A	N/A
	2	N/A	N/A	N/A	N/A	N/A	N/A
	3	1	1	1	N/A	N/A	3 (0.00)
	4	1	1	N/A	N/A	N/A	3 (0.00)
	5	2	3	5	1	N/A	12 (0.02)
	6	7	4	10	5	4	42 (0.08)
	7	16	27	18	6	3	72 (0.14)
	8	45	74	96	23	26	284 (0.54)

(*continued*)

Table 16.6 (continued)

Lower division	Stage	Under 5 years old	6 years old	7 years old	8 years old	9 years old	10 years old
	1	N/A	N/A	N/A	1	10	41
	2	N/A	N/A	N/A	1	20	138
	3	N/A	N/A	10	11	123	309
	4	N/A	N/A	14	90	428	745
	5	N/A	6	43	266	774	1082
	6	1	17	180	698	1550	1460
	7	10	217	1133	2558	3003	2258
	8	1287	4256	5480	5162	3646	2181
	Stage	11 years old	12 years	13 years old	14 years old	15 years and over	Subtotal of enrolments in each lower division (%)
	1	78	130	108	40	16	424 (0.80)
	2	180	230	203	57	39	868 (1.64)
	3	488	426	299	69	53	1788 (3.37)
	4	756	636	304	82	55	3110 (5.87)
	5	908	647	270	57	51	4104 (7.75)
	6	1026	608	247	74	45	5906 (11.15)
	7	1421	672	247	67	120	11,706 (22.09)
	8	1164	674	333	118	357	24,663 (46.55)
Total enrolments by age group (%)		Under 5 years old	6 years old	7 years old	8 years old	9 years old	10 years old
		1298 (2.45)	4496 (8.49)	6860 (12.95)	8791 (16.59)	9561 (18.04)	8239 (15.56)
		11 years old	12 years old	13 years old	14 years old	15 years and over	Total
		6093 (11.50)	4133 (7.80)	2141 (4.04)	559 (1.13)	769 (1.45)	52,985 (100)

Source: Table prepared by the National Institute for Educational Policy Research (1974a, p. 545), partly processed and translated into English and cited by the author

Necessary Conditions for Conversion to an Automatic Promotion System

As mentioned above, the promotion system by examination would have resulted in a lot of students repeating grades (stage). At the beginning of school education in Meiji era, however, if an automatic promotion system had been introduced under the educational circumstances with challenges (e.g. unfamiliar educational content modelled on Western primary schools, lack of teachers trained in modern pedagogy, low school attendance rates, large disparities in educational conditions among schools/regions and teachers' dependence on examinations), it might have created a significant achievement gap between children, and some children might not have been able to read or write despite having graduated from elementary school (Saito, 2003). Therefore, it can be inferred that the government had to resort to quality (academic achievements) control through the examination system.

By 1900, however, the promotion system by examinations had been abolished in Japan, and a shift was made to an automatic promotion system. The Elementary School Order called for the evaluation of children's learning attainment based on daily and continuous observation by teachers. Since then, Japan's problem of student repetition has been eliminated. What educational conditions made this change possible? Saito (2003, 2004b) summarised the conditions and background to Japan's successful conversion to an automatic promotion system as follows:

(1) In early Meiji Japan, Japanese elementary schools attempted to imitate Western countries and teach several subjects (more than 20 subjects). These were gradually integrated and consolidated into basic subjects. Consistent with this, the education content was also refined and adapted to the actual situation in Japan.

(2) Through the Normal School Order of 1886 and the Normal Education Order of 1897, the teacher training system was expanded and the teacher licensing system was developed. Students were required to graduate from a teacher's normal school or to have their academic qualifications recognised by a teacher certification examination to obtain a formal teaching licence. As a result, the proportion of qualified teachers was less than 30% in 1880, exceeded 50% in 1900 and reached more than 80% in 1925. Furthermore, these developments were accompanied by changes in teacher attitudes and behaviours. Teaching methods that forced

mechanical memorisation and cramming of knowledge with only exam preparation in mind were criticised, and teachers challenged the new teaching methods, such as developmental teaching. Thus, the quality of teachers improved as a new professional image of teachers began to be constructed.

(3) From the 1890s onwards, compulsory education enrolment and attendance rates gradually improved. The enrolment rate had already exceeded 80% by 1900, when the automatic promotion system was introduced, and has continued to increase steadily (see Fig. 16.1). In 1907, Japan's compulsory education enrolment rate reached almost 100%. The attendance rate (see Table 16.2) has also exceeded 80% since 1895, suggesting that children who were only registered but had no actual status were disappearing. These developments indicate that children's school attendance was steadily taking root in Japan.

(4) The revision of the Elementary School Order in 1900 standardised compulsory education through four-year ordinary elementary schools. In addition, the local education administrative structure was developed, and the basic education administration system ('Minister of Education–Prefectural Governor–District Mayor–Municipality') was implemented. As a result, disparities in educational conditions between regions and between schools were corrected, standardising educational conditions nationwide.

Thus, in Japan at that time, the key educational conditions for the conversion to the automatic promotion system were in place, including fruitful educational content, the quality of teachers, children's improved enrolment and attendance, and standardised education throughout the country. Hence, it can be assumed that Japan's automatic promotion system worked and the repetition problem was successfully eliminated.

4   Enrolment Status Regarding Dropping Out of School

Dropping Out of School (Not Graduating) and the Gender Gap

The aforementioned promotion system by examination produced many school dropouts and repetitions. Dropping out of school has not been eliminated in many developing countries, despite the introduction of automatic promotion systems (Yoshida, 2020a, 2021). Japan introduced its automatic promotion system in 1900, but has the number of school dropouts declined steadily since then? Or was there a period when the problem of school dropouts was unresolved in Japan, as is the case in developing countries today?

By 1900, when the automatic promotion system was introduced, Japan's elementary education enrolment rate had already exceeded 80% (see Fig. 16.1), reaching nearly 100% approximately 10 years later. However, a higher enrolment rate did not immediately eliminate the school dropout problem. Comparing 'the number of children enrolled in school' in each year with 'the number of children who graduated' in the year in which they should have graduated, Hijikata (2002) depicts in Fig. 16.3 the percentage of children who did not graduate (i.e. dropped out of school) of all children enrolled in school. Nearly 30% of boys were nongraduates (dropouts) in 1895–1898. In the early years of introducing automatic promotion, 1903–1906, the proportion of nongraduates (dropouts) temporarily fell below 10%. However, following the extension

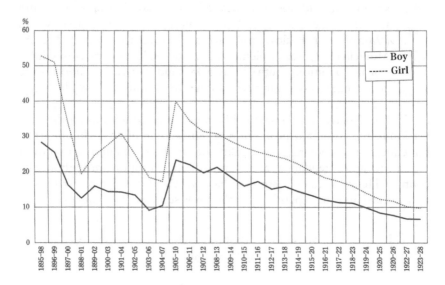

Fig. 16.3 Percentage of nongraduates (dropouts) in elementary schools in Japan. (Source: Figure prepared and processed by Hijikata (2002, p. 27) based on Amano (1997), translated into English and cited by the author)

of compulsory education in 1907, the proportion of nongraduates (dropouts) rose again to over 20%, after which the number of nongraduates (dropouts) continued to decline steadily, with the proportion falling to approximately 7% in 1923–1928. In the case of girls, more than 50% had not graduated (dropped out) as of 1895–1898, indicating that more than half of the girls who enrolled in elementary school during this period left without graduating. Around 1900, when the automatic promotion system was introduced, the number of nongraduates (dropouts) temporarily began to decline, with the proportion falling to less than 20%. However, following the extension of compulsory education in 1907, the proportion of nongraduates (dropouts) rose again to around 40%. From then on, the number of nongraduates (dropouts) steadily declined, 10% in 1923–1928. Thus, there was a nearly twofold difference between boys and girls in the proportion of nongraduates (dropouts), suggesting that girls were overwhelmingly at a disadvantage. Conversely, from 1905 to 1910, the gender gap steadily narrowed, reaching a difference of only a few per cent by 1923–1928. This trend of a narrowing gender gap for nongraduates (dropouts) is also very similar to the trend in enrolment rates (Fig. 16.1 in the previous tilt).

The Child Labour Situation

Several cases of school dropouts due to child labour have been reported in developing countries (Huisman & Smits, 2015; Thi et al., 2023; Xayavong & Pholphirul, 2018). As mentioned above, there was also a period in Japanese elementary education when there were many dropouts. What was the actual situation of child labour in Japan at that time? For example, Tanaka (1976) and Hijikata (2002) show that many school-aged children were employed in 1919 and in what occupations (Table 16.7). In 1919, the number of working children under age 12 in Japan was approximately 70,000. The occupation that accounted for the largest number of these was babysitting (32.7%), with the next most common being factory hand (16.2%). However, the Minimum Age for Factory Workers Act was enacted in 1923, prohibiting school-aged children under age of 12 from working in factories. As a result, the number of school-aged children working in factories gradually decreased in Japan, as shown in Table 16.8.

Table 16.7 Number of school-aged working children by occupation in Japan in 1919

The type of occupation	9 years old and under		10–11 years		Total
	Boy	Girl	Boy	Girl	
Commercial apprenticeship	1273	651	4338	980	7242
(Factory) hand	1018	1185	3729	5325	11,257
Apprentice	746	175	2861	596	4378
Male and female servants	354	334	1396	1515	3599
Street vendor	127	46	396	82	651
Government server, etc.	87	40	324	79	530
Labourers (e.g. construction, haver, etc.)	685	415	1167	645	2912
Geisha	N/A	53	N/A	200	253
Apprentice geisha	N/A	145	N/A	568	713
Barmaid	N/A	2	N/A	78	80
Performer of the art of amusement	19	53	49	140	261
Babysitting	1244	4358	3313	13,786	22,701
Other	3176	3176	4454	3994	14,800
Total	8829	10,633	22,027	27,988	69,372

Note: Based on a survey by the Ministry of Agriculture and Commerce in March 1919, this table shows the number of working children under the age of 12 according to the type of work in which they were employed. Although other forms of juvenile labour may include housework, we have restricted ourselves here to children working for hire to give an overview of the numbers

Source: Table prepared by Tanaka (1976, p. 153) and partly revised by Hijikata (2002, p. 181), translated into English and cited by the author

A survey of some 1800 students at an ordinary night school in Tokyo also shows the children's first job and their age of employment (Table 16.9), confirming the results as those shown in Table 16.7, with the most children working as 'babysitters'. One child was employed as a babysitter at the age of only six, illustrating the harsh conditions of child labour in Japan. Table 16.9 shows that the lower the age, the less variation in jobs available, and conversely, the higher the age, the greater the variation in jobs available. This may explain why more older children were employed. In developing countries, older children are more likely to find work and, therefore, are more likely to drop out of school (Yoshida, 2020b). It is likely that such a situation also existed in Japan at that time.

Table 16.8 Information on school-aged children working in factories

Year	Total number of school-aged children	Number of school-aged children as percentage of number of factory workers (%)	Daytime				At night			
			School	Factory	Other	Total	School	Factory	Other	Total
1918	23,308	1.6	4438	3342	182	7962	4417	8993	147	13,557
1919	22,170	1.4	3665	5233	149	8898*	2443	10,102	75	12,620
1920	21,332	1.5	3778	4652	174	8704	2895	7899	1481	13,275*
1921	19,435	1.3	3092	5058	121	8271	2498	8272	394	11,164
1922	17,179	1.0	2185	4548	45	6778	1890	8329	182	10,401
1923	12,049	0.8	1807	3850	55	5712	1211	4918	208	6337
1924	8427	0.5	1296	2718	41	4055	944	3161	262	4371
1925	6709	0.4	1444	2018	5	3467	668	2386	188	3242
1926	4134	0.2	579	1501	10	2090	518	1491	35	2044

Note: For the years 1918–1925 the figures are based on surveys at the end of the year, but only for 1926 the figures are based on surveys as of 1 October. The '*' indicates that the totals do not add up but are shown in their original data

Source: Table prepared by Hijikata (2002, p. 180) based on the Social Affairs Bureau (1928), p. 27), translated into English and cited by the author

Table 16.9   Children's first job and age of employment

First position (in a business, etc.)	Chronological age of employment								Unknown	Total
	6 years old	7 years old	8 years old	9 years old	10 years old	11 years old	12 years	12 years and over		
Babysitting	1	5	9	24	36	49	50	27	1	202
Apprentice geisha	0	1	1	5	11	35	48	20	1	122
Apprentice glassworker	0	0	2	1	4	3	4	72	0	86
Maid of honour	0	0	3	4	11	21	19	24	0	82
Candy store boy	0	0	1	5	7	9	8	29	0	59
Metalworking apprentice	0	0	1	1	0	4	8	25	0	39
Apprenticeship in western sewing	0	0	0	2	4	5	7	19	0	37
Canning help	0	0	0	1	5	3	9	18	0	36
Apprenticeship in blacksmithing	0	1	0	3	2	4	8	16	0	34
Apprentice bookbinder	0	1	0	3	4	6	7	10	0	31
Fishmonger	0	0	0	5	5	4	7	8	0	29
Greengrocer	0	0	0	11	2	3	6	6	0	28
Furniture making apprenticeship	0	0	0	3	5	6	6	7	0	27
Other	0	5	12	50	102	186	247	418	2	1,022
Total	1	13	29	118	198	338	434	699	4	1,834

Source: Table prepared by Hijikata (2002, p. 182) based on Tokyo Prefecture (1931, p. 58), translated into English and cited by the author

5   CONCLUSION: JAPAN'S EDUCATIONAL EXPERIENCE AND POTENTIAL APPLICATION IN DEVELOPING COUNTRIES

In conclusion, Japan's educational problems, which used to be similar to those in developing countries, included underdeveloped education infra-structure, discrepancies between educational content and real life, parents' lack of understanding of their children's education and a lack of qualified teachers. It is also likely that these issues related to the content and quality of education affected children's enrolment status, such as low enrolment and attendance rates, problems with repetition and school dropouts, and gender gap in children's enrolment. Japan's challenges with basic education were similar to those of many developing countries. On the other hand, the unique features of Japanese educational development have been noted as follows (Murata, 2004):

(1) There were initial conditions conducive to educational development. During the Edo era, which enjoyed approximately 260 years of stability and peace, society's cultural maturity was greatly enhanced. In addition, the literacy rate of the population at the time was very high by world standards, as fief schools, private academies and teratoma were widespread throughout Japan. In addition, the relatively homogeneous cultural and linguistic traditions facilitated using Japanese as the single language of instruction from when school education was introduced. Additionally, the foundations for a system of personnel promotion based on academic qualifications were already in place in the early Meiji era. These initial conditions facilitated educational development in Japan at a faster-than-normal rate.

(2) The Government attached extreme importance to education policy in the country's development policies (the modernisation policy of the Meiji era and the democratisation policy after World War II). Japan actively learned from other countries and incorporated this into its educational development. It also made repeated attempts to improve its education system over a short time. Japan particularly excelled in this self-help effort and its ability to accept and apply the educational experiences of other countries. Thus, Japan achieved quantitative expansion and qualitative improvement in its education system in only approximately 30 years in both the Meiji era and the post-World War II period, which were very different situations.

(3) Japan's educational administration system was centralised except for the period after World War II. In developing educational reforms and improvements homogeneously nationwide, the centralised educational administration, which relied on the Japanese bureaucracy, was extremely effective. In contrast, developing countries' current education development trend is towards decentralising education administration. Hence, centralised educational

administration is often viewed negatively. In addition, countries that receive aid from several donors may find it difficult to decide how to use their own education budgets, as seen in cases such as the Poverty Reduction Paper. Hence, in such developing countries, 'selection and concentration' of educational development cannot be achieved, and promoting educational development in a single stroke is challenging.

(4) Teachers' ingenuity and self-improvement are highlighted. The Government of Japan has implemented various initiatives to improve the quality of teachers, such as expanding teacher training programmes, developing the teacher licence system and improving teachers' working conditions. Teachers have responded by working hard to improve themselves to acquire the knowledge and skills appropriate for education professionals. It was common for some teachers to try to improve their expertise by participating in training and study groups and conducting class research independently. Japan is considered to have excelled in this type of teacher awareness.

However, at the same time, it is difficult to transfer Japan's educational experiences to developing countries with different historical, social and cultural backgrounds (Kubota et al., 2020). Therefore, when applying Japan's educational experience to developing countries, it should only be regarded as a case study for reference to be applied based on the circumstances in the target country.

REFERENCES

Amano, I. (1997). *Kyoiku to kindaika: nihon no keiken [Education and modernisation: The Japanese experience]*. Tamagawa University Press.

Elementary and Secondary Education Breau. (2021). *Kyokasho seido no gaiyou [Overview of the textbook system]*. Ministry of Education, Culture, Sports, Science and Technology.

Hijikata, S. (2002). *Tokyo no kindai shogakkou: kokumin kyoiku seido no seiritsu katei [Modern elementary schools in Tokyo: The process of establishing a "national" education system]*. University of Tokyo Press.

Huisman, J., & Smits, J. (2015). Keeping children in school: Effects of household and context characteristics on school dropout in 363 districts of 30 developing countries. *Sage Open, 5*(4). https://doi.org/10.1177/2158244015609666

Institute for International Cooperation Japan International Cooperation Agency (JICA). (2004). *The History of Japan's educational development: What implications can be drawn for developing countries today*. Research Group Institute for International Cooperation (IFIC) and Japan International Cooperation Agency (JICA).

Ito, H. (2011). Kyoikushi kara mita bakumatsu kara Meiji shoki no kyoiku [Japanese Education from Late edo to Early Meiji]. *Otemae journal, 12*, 17–32.

Kishimoto, Y. (1952). Meiji no kyoiku: obei kyouiku no moho to kokuminkosei no hakken [Education in the Meiji era: imitating Western education and discovering national individuality]. *The Journal of Kokugakuin University, 53*(3), 76–85.

Kobayashi, K., & Murata, T. (2004). Encouraging school enrollment and attendance in the Meiji era: Tackling local problems. In JICA (Ed.), *The History of Japan's educational development: What implications can be drawn for developing countries today*. Research Group Institute for International Cooperation (IFIC) and Japan International Cooperation Agency (JICA).

Kubota, K., Kishi, M., Tokito, J., Konno, T., Yamamoto, R., Wai, T., Pitagan, F. B., & Saroeun, N. (2020). Nihon no kyouiku keiken wo katsuyou shita tojokoku e no kyouiku shien ni hitsuyouna kanten no kouchiku: Myanmar, Philippine, Cambodia no jireibunseki wo toshite [Applying Japanese educational experiences to the construction of essential perspectives for educational development in developing countries: Case studies of Myanmar, the Philippines, and Cambodia]. *Journal of informatics, 50*, 11–31.

Kurasawa, T. (1963). *Shogakkou no rekishi I: gakuseiki shogakkou no hossoku katei [History of elementary school I: Inauguration process of elementary schools during Gakusei]*. Japan Library Bureau.

Ministry of Education. (1962). *Nihon no seichou to kyoiku: kyoiku no tenkai to keizai no hattatsu [Growth and education in Japan: Educational expansion and economic development]*. Gyosei.

Ministry of Education. (1981a). Kindai kyoiku seido no soshi to kakuju, Kindai kyoiku seido no soshi (Meiji gonen - Meiji juhachinen, Gaisetsu, Gakusei no seitei [Founding and expansion of modern education, Founding of the modern education system (1872–1885), Outline, Establishment of the student]. In Ministry of Education (Ed.), *Gakusei hyakunenshi [100-year history of the school system]*. Gyosei, online.

Ministry of Education. (1981b). Kindai kyoiku seido no soshi to kakuju, Kindai kyoiku seido no soshi (Meiji gonen - Meiji juhachinen), Shoto kyouiku, Kyouikurei, kaisei kyoikurei to shogakkou no seido [Founding and expansion of modern education, Founding of the modern education system (1872–1885), primary education, Education decree, revised education decree and the elementary school system]. In Ministry of Education (Ed.), *Gakusei hyakunenshi [100-year history of the school system]*. Gyosei, online.

Ministry of Education. (1981c). Kindai kyoiku seido no soshi to kakuju, Kindai kyoiku seido no kakuritsu to seibi (Meiji jukyunen – Taisho gonen), Gaisetsu, Mori bunsho to shogakkourei no kofu [Founding and expansion of modern education, Establishment and development of the modern education system (1890–1916), Outline, Minister of Education Mr. Mori and promulgation of the School Ordinance]. In Ministry of Education (Ed.), *Gakusei hyakunenshi [100-year history of the school system]*. Gyosei, online.

Ministry of Education. (1981d). Kindai kyoiku seido no soshi to kakuju, Kindai kyoiku seido no kakuritsu to seibi (Meiji jukyunen – Taisho gonen), Shoto kyouiku, Shogakkourei no seitei [Founding and expansion of modern education, Establishment and development of the modern education system (1890–1916), Primary education, Enactment of the elementary school ordinance]. In Ministry of Education (Ed.), *Gakusei hyakunenshi [100-year history of the school system]*. Gyosei, online.

Ministry of Education. (1981e). Kindai kyoiku seido no soshi to kakuju, Kindai kyoiku seido no kakuritsu to seibi (Meiji jukyunen – Taisho gonen), Shoto kyouiku, Gimukyouiku nengen no encho [Founding and expansion of modern education, Establishment and development of the modern education system (1890–1916), Primary education, Extension of compulsory education years]. In Ministry of Education (Ed.), *Gakusei hyakunenshi [100-year history of the school system]*. Gyosei, online.

Ministry of Education. (1992a). Kindai kyoiku seido no hossoku to kakuju, Bakumatsuishinki no Kyoiku, Bakumatsuki no kyoiku [Inception and expansion of the modern education system, Education at the end of the Edo era and during the Restoration, Education at the end of the Edo era]. In Ministry of Education (Ed.), *Gakusei hyakunijunenshi [120-year history of the school system]*. Gyosei, online.

Ministry of Education. (1992b). Kindai kyoiku seido no hossoku to kakuju, Kindai kyoiku seido no soshi to seibi, Kindai kyoiku seido no soshi [Inception and expansion of the modern education system, Founding and development of the modern education system, Founding of the modern education system]. In Ministry of Education (Ed.), *Gakusei hyakunijunenshi [120-year history of the school system]*. Gyosei, online.

Ministry of Education. (1992c). Kindai kyoiku seido no hossoku to kakuju, Kyouiku seido no kakuju, Gaisetsu, Dainiji sekaitaisenka no kyouiku [Inception and expansion of the modern education system, Expansion of the education system, Outline, Education during World War II]. In Ministry of Education (Ed.), *Gakusei hyakunijunenshi [120-year history of the school system]*. Gyosei, online.

Miwa, Y. (2013). Senzen, sengo ni okeru shoto, chuto kyouiku seido no henyo katei [Transformation process of the Elementary education and secondary education system after the war, before the war]. *Journal of Teaching Course, Aichi Shukutoku University, 9*, 51–61.

Murai, M. (1979). *Report of the United States education mission to Japan*. Kodansha Gakujutsu bunko.

Murata, T. (2004). Chapter 14. Toward the application of Japan's educational experience to developing countries. In JICA (Ed.), *The History of Japan's educational development: What implications can be drawn for developing countries today*. Research Group Institute for International Cooperation (IFIC) and Japan International Cooperation Agency (JICA).

Nakamura, F., & Higuchi, N. (2013). Gakuseiki wo chushin to shita kyoiku zaisei no seidoshi [A historical analysis of the educational finance during the period of the establishment of the modern school system]. *Meisei university, school of education, 3*, 17–30.

Nakamura, T. (1964). Oyatoi gaikokujin no kenkyu: tokuni kazu no kosatsu [About the foreigners employed by The Japanese Government: With special reference to the number]. *Journal of Hōsei Historical Society, 16*, 65–75.

Nakano, A. (1968). *Taisho jiyu kyouiku no kenkyu [Research on Taisho liberal education]*. ReimeiShobo.

National Institute for Educational Policy Research. (1974a). *Nihon kindai kyoiku hyakunenshi 3 gakkou kyoiku I [A century of modern Japanese: Vol.3 school education I]*. National Institute for Educational Policy Research.

National Institute for Educational Policy Research. (1974b). *Nihon kindai kyoiku hyakunenshi 3 gakkou kyoiku II [A century of modern Japanese: Vol.3 school education II]*. Institute for Educational Policy Research.

Ogasawara, M. (1980). Senzen Nihon no kyoikuhosei no rekishiteki kento (I) [Historical study on education laws in pre-war Japan (I)]. *Hirosaki gakuin university & Hirosaki gakuin junior college, 16*, 49–63.

Organization for Economic Co-operation and Development. (1971). *Reviews of national policies for education (Japan)*. OECD.

Saito, T. (1995). *Shiken to kyoso no gakkoushi [School history of examinations and competitions]*. Heibonsha.

Saito, Y. (2003). Ryunen, chutotaigaku mondai e no torikumi: Nihon no rekishiteki keiken [Approaches to the problem of repetition and drop-out: Japan's historical experience]. *Journal of International Cooperation in Education, 6*(1), 43–53.

Saito, Y. (2004a). Chapter 1. The Modernization and Development of Education in Japan. In JICA (ed.), *The History of Japan's educational development: What implications can be drawn for developing countries today*. Research Group Institute for International Cooperation (IFIC) and Japan International Cooperation Agency (JICA).

Saito, Y. (2004b). Chapter 9. Tackling the Problem of "Repeaters" and "Dropouts". In JICA (ed.), *The History of Japan's educational development:*

What implications can be drawn for developing countries today. Research Group Institute for International Cooperation (IFIC) and Japan International Cooperation Agency (JICA).

Saito, Y. (2014). Kindaiteki kyoshokuzo no kakuritsu to hensen: Nihon no keiken [Japanese Teaching Profession in Historical Perspective]. *Journal of international cooperation in education, 17*(1), 17–29.

Sakamoto, Y. (2017). GHQ senryoka ni okeru kyouikuseidokaikaku no gendai-tekiigi: "Beikoku kyouiku shisetsudan houkokusyo" no kyouikuseidoshi-tekikenkyu [The contemporary significance of educational system reform under the GHQ occupation: a historical study of the educational system in the Report of the American Educational Mission to Japan]. *Kyoshokukenkyu: Heisei International University Kyoshoku shien center, 2*, 79–120.

Tanaka, K. (1976). Jido roudou to kyoiku: tokuni 1911nen koujouhou no shikou o megutte [Child labor and education: In relation to enforcement of the factory act of 1911]. *Journal of Educational Sociology, 22*(0), 148–161.

The Social Affairs Bureau in the Home Office. (1928). *Taisho 15nen (Showa gan-nen) koujou kantoku nempou [Annual report of the supervision of factories in 15 year of the Taisyo era (first year of the Showa era)]*.

Thi, A. M., Zimmerman, C., & Ranganathan, M. (2023). Hazardous child labour, psychosocial functioning, and school dropouts among children in Bangladesh: A cross-sectional analysis of UNICEF's multiple indicator cluster surveys (MICS). *Children, 10*(6), 1021.

Tokyo Prefecture. (1931). *Roudou jidou chousa [Labour child survey]*.

Tsuchiya, K., & Sato, O. (2012). Gakkou kyushoku no hajimari ni kansuru rekishi-tekikosatsu [Historical Consideration about Beginning of the school meal]. *Fukushima University sogo kyouiku kenkyu center kiyou, 13*, 25–28.

Tsuji, N. (2008). Nijuseikishoto ni okeru monbusho ryugakusei no haken jittai to sono henka ni tsuite no ichi kosatsu [The functional conversion of sending students abroad system by the ministry of education in Japan in the early 20th century]. *Journal of the history of Tokyo University, 26*, 21–38.

Wakai, S. (2014). Jido rikai wo fukameru kyoushitachi: Nara joshi daigaku fuzoku shogakkou no jidorikai ni manabu [Teachers deepening their understanding of children: learning to understand children at Nara Women's University Elementary School]. *Sodai Education Study, 23*, 1–13.

Xayavong, T., & Pholphirul, P. (2018). Child labour and school dropout in least-developed countries: Empirical evidence from Lao PDR. *International Journal of Education Economics and Development, 9*(1), 1–23.

Yamaguchi. (2004). Appendix: Educational Statistics. In JICA, *The History of Japan's educational development: What implications can be drawn for developing countries today*. Research Group Institute for International Cooperation (IFIC) and Japan International Cooperation Agency (JICA).

Yoshida, N. (2020a). Socio-economic status and the impact of the "continuous assessment and progression system" in primary education in Myanmar. *Education 3-13, 48*(6), 674–689.

Yoshida, N. (2020b). Enrolment status disparity: Evidence from secondary education in Myanmar. *International Journal of Comparative Education and Development, 22*(2), 101–114.

Yoshida, N. (2021). Socioeconomic status (SES) and the benefits of the "continuous assessment and progression system (CAPS)" in lower secondary education in Myanmar. *International Journal of Comparative Education and Development, 23*(4), 335–352.

CHAPTER 17

Conclusion: Prospects and Implications from Individual Children's School Enrolment Analysis

Takeshi Sekiya, Keiichi Ogawa ⓘ*, Yuto Kitamura, and Akemi Ashida* ⓘ

1 FINDINGS AND OBSERVATIONS

This book is composed of three parts. With reference to international initiatives on global educational development, the studies in Part 1 (Chaps. 2, 3, and 4) employed cross-sectional data to examine macro-level regional student enrolment changes. The findings suggest that macro

T. Sekiya
School of International Studies, Kwansei Gakuin University,
Nishinomiya, Japan
e-mail: tsekiya@kwansei.ac.jp

K. Ogawa
Graduate School of International Cooperation Studies, Kobe University,
Kobe, Japan
e-mail: ogawa35@kobe-u.ac.jp

© The Author(s), under exclusive license to Springer Nature
Switzerland AG 2024
T. Sekiya et al. (eds.), *Towards Ensuring Inclusive and Equitable
Quality Education for All*, International and Development
Education, https://doi.org/10.1007/978-3-031-70266-2_17

cross-sectional data alone does not provide a complete understanding of student grade repetition and dropouts. The studies in Part 2 (Chaps. 5, 6, 7, 8, 9, 10, 11, 12, 13 and 14) used longitudinal data to highlight the significance of examining the micro-level specifics of individual child enrolment to identify the underlying factors. The studies in Part 3 (Chaps. 15 and 16) present an international comparison between the three countries discussed in Part 2: Honduras, Nepal and Myanmar. It also includes an analysis of the Japanese experience of educational development, which the authors have referred to in examining the challenges faced by each country.

Chapter 2 reviewed Latin American and Caribbean education trends from the 1980s to the present. Specifically, to determine education access in these regions, this chapter investigated gross and net enrolment rates, determining that the percentage of over-aged children, which was previously believed to be the result of high gross enrolment rates, has improved in recent years, with the gross enrolment rate of 104.6% in 2022 close to the appropriate value. Although it is still difficult to say that suitable age groups are being enrolled, compared to primary education, a significant improvement has been observed in secondary education enrolments in the past 40 years. Moreover, gender inequality improvements were noted, with the gap between girls and boys nearly equal in both regions from the 1980s. Furthermore, grade repetition and dropouts, reflecting internal education efficiency, were examined, from which it was found that the primary education repetition rate decreased from 14.1% in 1980 to 4.3% in 2015. In addition, primary education and lower secondary education completion rates reached 94.9% and 74.1%, respectively.

However, when population and economic growth are compared, the educational outcomes in these regions still lag behind other regions. Therefore, to achieve Sustainable Development Goal 4, which is targeted to be achieved by 2030, the Latin American and Caribbean regions should

Y. Kitamura
Graduate School of Education, The University of Tokyo, Tokyo, Japan
e-mail: yuto@p.u-tokyo.ac.jp

A. Ashida (✉)
Graduate School of International Development, Nagoya University, Nagoya, Japan
e-mail: ashida@gsid.nagoya-u.ac.jp

address certain educational challenges, namely out-of-school children, dropouts, low academic achievements and educational disparities. The learning opportunities lost due to the COVID-19 pandemic are expected to continue to exacerbate educational inequalities, with children from lower socio-economic status (SES) groups, younger age groups and rural and country areas being particularly vulnerable. Moreover, this chapter called for long-term observations of the impacts of these lost learning opportunities, rather than temporary observations based on macro cross-sectional data.

With a focus on historical, political, economic and cultural diversity, Chapter 3 focused on the Southeast and South Asian regions' education dissemination trends from the 1990s to the present. Education access and gender equality issues in these regions have mostly been resolved. However, when country-level data were more closely examined, there were marked differences in the educational opportunities. The analysis of the grade repetition trends in each country identified regional differences when there were automatic promotion policies. It was also found that the macro cross-sectional data were not able to accurately grasp the real grade repetition and dropout situations. The authors found that because of regional ethnic and linguistic diversity, it was necessary to more closely examine the educational disparities for ethnic minorities, medium of instruction, socio-economic backgrounds and the challenges faced when seeking to progress to secondary education.

Chapter 4 examined the African countries' educational development history since many countries gained independence in the 1960s and summarised the remaining and emerging challenges in meeting the Sustainable Development Goals. The gross primary education enrolment ratio in the 1970s was slightly higher than 60% and nearly 40% for girls; however, the secondary education enrolment ratio was below 20% for both boys and girls. There have been significant achievements in recent years, with around 100% of boys and girls enrolled in primary education and between 40% and 50% enrolled in lower secondary. The remaining challenges are that there are still many out-of-school children, and the primary education completion rate remains less than ideal. For example, while the completion rate in most of Africa is close to 90%, it is only 64% in sub-Saharan Africa, which highlights the regional and socio-economic disparities between the African regions. This chapter also addresses education quality and the need to address issues such as diverse tribal groups, a medium of instruction unduly influenced by colonial history, over-aged students and low academic achievements with a quantitative expansion of educational opportunities. This chapter also examines the recent rise of low-fee private schools and the negative impact of the COVID-19 pandemic on the African region but also highlights the strong positive economic growth and job creation potential because of Africa's median age of around 20 years, making it the youngest population in the world. The authors then stressed the importance of expanding access to and improving education quality across the region.

The country case studies in Part 2 report on the enrolment findings and patterns found in longitudinal data. The Honduran case study in Chap. 5 followed 4,390 primary school children in three regions, namely the capital, a regional city and an insular zone. The results revealed that the proportion of pupils graduating without repeating a grade increased in the capital and regional cities but not in the insular zone. In all three regions, most children register for primary education at the official school entry age; however, grade repetitions and dropouts were noted. In the capital and insular zone, the students dropped out at a relatively low age (6–8 years), but in the regional city, dropouts were observed across all age groups, suggesting a variation in the age at which students dropped out by region. These findings underscored the importance of implementing measures based on regional characteristics such as socio-economic conditions. Furthermore, the introduction of an automatic promotion system could reduce grade repetitions and dropouts. However, the study summarised that providing timely and individually focused remedial measures for children with low academic performance that may occur due to the implementation of an automatic promotion system is crucial.

Chapter 6 focused on female enrolment in primary and lower secondary during and immediately after the El Salvadoran civil war (1979-1992). The study focused on 1758 girls, who were divided into three cohorts: the early 1980s, the late 1980s and the 1990s. The results showed that as in Honduras, there was a polarisation between girls who dropped out in the first few years and those who continued until graduation. The dropout analysis revealed that grade repetition was not the main reason for dropping out. After the severe disruptions of the civil war, the educational situation in El Salvador has improved significantly in recent years. The close observation and examination of the El Salvadoran case provide valuable insights for countries that have experienced similar educational interruptions due to conflicts.

Chapter 7 examined basic Nepalese education from Grades 1 to 5. While there have been stagnant completion rates, the quantitative expansion of basic education is close to being achieved; therefore, the focus must be on developing concrete measures to increase the basic education completion rates. The analysis of the enrolment patterns found that issues beyond the children's control, such as family finances, parental illness or death, health concerns, disabilities and marriage, were obstacles to completing basic education. Other problems identified were a lack of parental understanding, no educational incentives and students over the appropriate school age. Several recommendations are given, namely support for disadvantaged children, promotion of preschool education and a reconsideration of the rules regarding school transfers. The study also identified a mismatch between educational attainment and future employment and recommended that each child's circumstances be considered, attractive jobs be created and education incentives be provided.

Chapter 8 analysed the individual primary education enrolment patterns for children from varied socio-economic statuses (SES) in Myanmar. The results revealed that the lower the SES, the more complex the enrolment pattern, and the more frequent the grade repetitions and dropouts. Furthermore, it determined that the grade repetition rate was higher and grade repetition more frequent. Due to family economic deprivation, groups with lower SES were found to be less likely to continue their studies after leaving the target school. However, the higher SES group was more likely to continue their studies at an international or overseas school after leaving the target school, leading to higher educational attainment. Thus, poor readiness for school, particularly for the lower SES group, is expected to benefit from the new curriculum, which was revised in 2016. This new curriculum emphasises the practice of learning through play—a preparatory period for school learning before moving to academic teaching. It is hoped to decrease grade repetitions in the early school years. Further, due to the issue of malnutrition in some children, a school lunch programme will be introduced, with the hope that it can eliminate chronic ill health. To address the family economic deprivation, the author recommends that these families be given some financial support to continue their children's schooling, thereby reducing the school dropouts.

Chapter 9 focused on ethnic minority children in primary education in Lao PDR and examined whether an ethnic affinity between the teachers and children is contributing to a decrease of grade repletion in these ethnic minority children. The results reveal that there was less grade repetition in target schools that have high ethnic affinity than those with low ethnic affinity. The semi-structured interviews with teachers identified the reasons for grade repetition, with the main reasons being family environment, such as poor economic status due to parental occupations, parental absence due to migration or death and child abandonment. Moreover, grade repetitions due to ethnic affinity and medium of instruction problems were observed. Considering these findings, the study recommended that educational policies be implemented to increase ethnic affinity, and measures be taken to tackle outside-school family and social problems.

Chapter 10 examined lower secondary education in Cambodia, focusing on girls, whose enrolment has improved markedly in recent years. The results demonstrated that a remarkable increase was observed in enrolment rates, particularly for females, and a trend towards greater educational opportunities throughout Cambodia. These results confirmed the remarkable progress made in narrowing and then reversing the gender gap. While the most common enrolment pattern was completion without grade repetition, this only accounted for approximately a third of the students, with many dropping out in Grades 7 and 8 and others failing to complete the final year of secondary school. Several reasons were identified, such as leaving school to find a job, marriage of female students, difficulties in continuing school due to the long distance from home to school and lack of transportation. Therefore, various challenges exist for students from disadvantaged backgrounds in completing basic education or continuing their studies. As it is financially impractical to increase the number of schools and the associated teaching staff, individual support for students who have difficulties continuing their studies is required.

Chapter 11 examined enrolment in Mongolia, which has free compulsory primary education and an automatic promotion system. In the study, 5 schools and 840 pupils were surveyed using a longitudinal approach and follow-up univariate analysis to examine these dynamics over time. It was found that the automatic promotion system and the free compulsory education policy had little effect, as the primary level retention rate was only 62.9%. However, academic performances were high in all SES strata, which was different from global trends that show that schools in low SES and rural areas often have lower academic performances. The study also pointed to the undesirable effects of low teacher salaries and performance-based bonuses linked to academic performance as this had led to teachers simplifying test content to help students achieve higher scores. To address the low retention rate and unethical academic practice challenges, it is recommended that the government implement measures that consider the psychological stability of both students and teachers and educational reform. The authors also pointed to the importance of raising teacher salaries to a competitive level to prevent them from being overly dependent on bonuses.

Chapter 12 analysed the enrolment situation in Malawi's secondary schools, particularly the individual attitudes to dropping out. It was found that educational strategies and individual family life plans led to many students strategically dropping out of school. However, in contrast to the stereotypical attitude of girls attending school, flexible plans for school attendance were observed. The study also suggests that it is important to distinguish between active and passive school absences because the line between the choice not be able to attend school and the choice not to go to school is blurred. Therefore, it is recommended that the effects of school absences be examined rather than simply interpreting everything in a negative light. It is also necessary to recognise the need to support males more than females to return to school, not only to prevent them from dropping out but also to support them in returning to school.

Chapter 13 investigated a sample of 300 students from 13 schools in 7 districts in Uganda to determine the Grade 7 and Grade 11 continuations. It was found that 72.7% continued their studies to Grade 7, but only 29.7% completed lower secondary education. About half (54.1%) who completed G7 were from average SES and 72.5% lived in urban areas. Of those who completed lower secondary, 75.3% were from urban areas and 49.4% had high SES. Most dropouts progressed well from Grades 1 to 6 and dropped out in Grade 7 or progressed well to Grade 4 and then dropped out. The reasons for dropping out varied, such as parental illness or death, separation from parents due to conflict, financial issues at home and lack of parental interest or care in female education. Therefore, rather than simply providing access to education, mitigation measures are needed to improve completion rates.

Chapter 14 examined Zambian primary and secondary enrolment and the educational challenges. It was found that the most common enrolment pattern in primary education level was for students to complete the final grade without grade repetition or temporarily dropping out. Failure to progress to secondary education was one of the top five most frequent patterns. When the reasons for the failure to progress to secondary education were examined, it was found that the children either left in the upper grade or progressed without repeating a grade but failed the national standardised Grade 7 examinations. The enrolment pattern analysis in secondary education level found that about 40% of students were classified as non-straight progression. This unusual enrolment pattern was more prevalent in students who had difficult economic situations or were the eldest child. As many students were found to have inadequate learning proficiencies, the future challenges are improving the education quality and student learning proficiencies. To improve secondary education school attendance, it is important to focus daily on the at-risk students and support them based on their individual circumstances. It is also vital to address other administrative issues, such as inadequate school facilities and classrooms and the lack of qualified teachers.

Chapter 15 of Part 3, which is an international comparison, compared the Honduran longitudinal study with Nepal and Myanmar. The analysis revealed a bipolar pattern in the three target countries, namely 'straight graduation' in which students advance to the next grade without grade repetition or temporarily dropping out and 'early dropout' in which students leave school early after registering for the school year. Grade repetition may not be the main reason for dropping out, as some children suddenly dropped out of school without repeating a grade and some graduated despite repeating a grade. Furthermore, the negative effect of overaged students was noted, confirming the importance of age at school entry. A notable difference was that specific enrolment patterns were observed in Honduras and Nepal, whereas none were observed in Myanmar. This is due to the automatic promotion system in Myanmar and because school records, including revised records, are highly accurate due to the strict school governance by the military junta government and operations system rigour, affecting the variations in the number of schooling enrolment patterns.

Chapter 16 discussed the Japanese educational experience, which is often referenced when assessing its educational challenges. This is because Japan achieved universal basic education relatively quickly through positive educational reforms, although it was on a par with developing countries 150 years ago. This chapter provided an overview of Japan's educational development from the early Meiji period, when the modern schooling system was introduced, to the post-World War II period. Furthermore, it clarified children's schooling at these times, especially school enrolment changes. The study focused on grade repetitions, dropouts, child labour, gender disparity and regional education differences, as well as identified common educational development issues in Japan and developing countries and educational experiences specific to Japan.

The challenges that are also common to developing countries were identified, such as underdeveloped educational infrastructure, discrepancies between educational content and life, lack of parental understanding of education, low enrolment and attendance rates, grade repetition and dropouts and gender disparities between regions and schools. The experiences unique to Japan include a high level of cultural maturity in promoting education due to Japan's relatively stable, conflict-free and homogeneous cultural and linguistic environment. The emphasis on education in Japanese development policies, such as the modernisation policies in the Meiji era, democratisation policies post-World War II and centralised educational administration system in place, with the exception of a period after World War II, has been effective in developing homogeneous education throughout the country. Notably, aligning the Japanese experience with developing countries is challenging due to different historical, social and cultural backgrounds. Therefore, when examining Japanese educational experiences and educational developments in developing countries, examining the case studies based on the circumstances in each of the target countries is imperative.

2   Significance of Micro-educational Research

Education policies and their implementation can be studied in developing countries from both macro and micro perspectives. The macro perspective examines the degree to which education policies and plans are reflected at the school level, and the micro-perspective analyses data at the school and household levels to identify problems on the ground. As national or central policymakers often have little understanding of what is happening on the ground, micro-perspective analyses can identify school and household-level problems and clarify the gaps between policy at the macro level and the current situation on the micro-school frontline. The ten country case studies reveal individual circumstances only because of the focus on every student, which highlights the importance of micro-perspective studies.

However, quantitative and qualitative research from this micro perspective is not a perfect tool. While international organisations, such as the World Bank, can objectively analyse a large sample size of data from an entire country, the results tend to be superficial and are often far removed from reality. However, although qualitative studies with smaller sample sizes than quantitative studies provide increasingly specific analyses, making policy recommendations from small samples may not address all areas. In other words, easy generalisations are risky. Therefore, combining macro and micro analyses is more appropriate to ascertain the actual situation.

Another recent trend in research methods is the use of mixed-methods research, which uses both qualitative and quantitative methods (Tashakkori et al., 2020; Johnson, et al., 2007). This specific procedure involves conducting a quantitative analysis using micro-individual data, such as household surveys, and then narrowing down the sample to conduct a qualitative analysis. Alternatively, in certain cases, a qualitative analysis is conducted followed by a quantitative analysis; that is, the situation is analysed for quality and subsequently analysed and examined using quantitative methods. The opposite approach is to first use quantitative analysis and subsequently examine the situation from a qualitative perspective. As each view has its advantages and limitations, conducting research using both methods, even if the analysis takes a micro perspective, is crucial. The use of macro and micro perspectives may be necessary to achieve SDG 4, as this approach would place greater emphasis on improving education quality as well as expanding education provision.

The strength of this approach is its micro-level focus on the actual state of enrolment, offering a flexible examination of quantitative expansion as well as information on qualitative issues. For example, when there are major changes in education policy, various enrolment patterns and students who transfer schools several times can be identified. Transferring schools is more than a change in the schools; it is also an event that requires attention due to the possible loss of learning continuity. Therefore, by examining quantitative data, we can focus on the qualitative aspects associated with learning content continuity.

In addition, as phenomena beyond the imagination of people in developed countries may occur in developing countries, research projects targeting developing countries must account for micro realities. Researchers conducting research in the field of education in developing countries must consider a perspective that can reveal what is happening on the ground and how this connects with policy decisions. If we are to call ourselves educational development researchers, we need to be conscious of our role in connecting policy and practice; otherwise we would be unable to find meaning in our research. This is not an argument that both should be balanced as we can focus more on policy or closely examine on-the-ground practices. When taking a micro perspective and observing, we need to stay aware that the macro perspective makes the most of micro-perspective findings, allowing the macro perspective to become visible.

Thus, when analysing enrolment patterns, particular attention needs to be paid to macro- and micro-data interpretations. In other words, flexibly analysing the events from both macro and micro perspectives revealed in the data is essential. We were reminded of the need for researchers to be more conscious of moving between these two perspectives when analysing data.

Finally, understanding development policy formulation and implementation in schools and other settings can only be possible through research. It is not realistic for international donors or the Ministry of Education officials to frequently visit actual school sites. Therefore, research expertise and funding are critical to ensure increasingly accurate results, which hopefully generate more effective macro policies. Here, if we say that researchers 'should' do this, we will get all sorts of misrepresentations and objections, but we believe that this is not the case and that this is one of the jobs that can only be done by researchers. It is also necessary to obtain the cooperation of the Ministry of Education of the country under study, as this will facilitate the efficient execution of the research. In order to fully utilise the results of the research, it will be necessary to maintain cooperative assistance with the Ministry of Education and other donors in a coordinated manner.

REFERENCES

Johnson, R. B., Onwuegbuzie, A. J., & Turner, L. A. (2007). Towards a definition of mixed methods research. *Journal of Mixed Methods Research, 1*(2), 112–133.
Tashakkori, A. M., Johnson, R. B., & Teddlie, C. B. (2020). *Foundations of mixed methods research: Integrating quantitative and qualitative approaches in the social and behavioral sciences* (2nd ed.). SAGE Publishing.

Index[1]

[1] Note: Page numbers followed by 'n' refer to notes.